D0859359

Geomorphology and Land Management in a Changing Environment

British Geomorphological Research Group Symposia Series

Geomorphology and Land Management in a Changing Environment

Edited by

Duncan F. M. McGregor

and

Donald A. Thompson

Centre for Environmental Analysis and Management
Department of Geography, Royal Holloway, University of London, UK

JOHN WILEY & SONS
Chichester · New York · Brisbane · Toronto · Singapore

Copyright ©1995 by John Wiley & Sons Ltd,
Baffins Lane, Chichester,
West Sussex PO19 1UD, England

Telephone   National   01243 779777
International (+44) 1243 779777

Other Wiley Editorial Offices

John Wiley & Sons, Inc., 605 Third Avenue,
New York, NY 10158-0012, USA

Jacaranda Wiley Ltd, 33 Park Road, Milton,
Queensland 4064, Australia

John Wiley & Sons (Canada) Ltd, 22 Worcester Road,
Rexdale, Ontario M9W 1L1, Canada

John Wiley & Sons (SEA) Pte Ltd, 37 Jalan Pemimpin #05-04,
Block B, Union Industrial Building, Singapore 2057

Library of Congress Cataloging-in-Publication Data

Geomorphology and land management in a changing environment/edited
by Duncan F. M. McGregor and Donald A. Thompson.
p.   cm.—(British Geomorphological Research Group symposia series)
Includes bibliographical references and index.
ISBN 0-471-95511-6
1. Geomorphology—Congresses.   2. Land use—Management—Congresses.
I. McGregor, Duncan F. M.   II. Thompson, Donald A.   III Series.
GB400.2.G439   1995   94–24604
333.73′15—dc20   CIP

British Library Cataloguing in Publication Data

A catalogue record for this book is available from the British Library

ISBN 0-471-95511-6

Typeset in 10/12 pt Times by Dobbie Typesetting Limited, Tavistock, Devon
Printed and bound in Great Britain by Bookcraft (Bath) Ltd

Contents

List of Contributors

Stephen Anderton Department of Civil Engineering, University of Newcastle upon Tyne, Newcastle upon Tyne NE1 7RU, UK

Adrian C. Armstrong ADAS Soil and Water Research Centre, Anstey Hall, Maris Lane, Trumpington, Cambridgeshire CB2 2LF, UK

P. S. Basigos Forestry Directorate, Nomarchia Messinias, GR-24100 Kalamata, Greece

Kawi Bidin Department of Geography, University of Manchester, Manchester M13 9PL, UK

Richard Bigwood Department of Geology, Royal Holloway, University of London, Egham, Surrey TW20 0EX, UK

D. J. Boakes Department of Geography, University of Wales Swansea, Singleton Park, Swansea, West Glamorgan SA2 8PP, UK

D. A. Castle ADAS Soil and Water Research Centre, Anstey Hall, Maris Lane, Trumpington, Cambridgeshire CB2 2LF, UK

Antonio Cendrero Graduate Center for Public Policy and Administration, California State University, Long Beach, CA 90840-4602, USA

C. de O. A. Coelho Departamento de Ambiente e Ordenamento, Universidade de Aveiro, Aveiro, Portugal

M. De Dapper Department of Geography, Universiteit Gent, Krijgslaan 281 (S8), B-9000 Gent, Belgium

B. M. De Vliegher Department of Geography, Universiteit Gent, Krijgslaan 281 (S8), B-9000 Gent, Belgium

Edward Derbyshire Department of Geography, Royal Holloway, University of London, Egham, Surrey TW20 0EX, UK and Geological Hazards Research Institute, Gansu Academy of Sciences, Lanzhou, People's Republic of China

J. R. Díaz de Terán Facultad de Ciencias, Universidad de Cantabria, Avda. de los Castros, s/n, 39005 Santander, Spain

Richard Dikau Geographisches Institut, University of Heidelberg, 69120 Heidelberg 1m Neuenheimer Feld 348, Germany

John C. Doornkamp Department of Geography, University of Nottingham, University Park, Nottingham NG7 2RD, UK

Peter W. Downs   Department of Geography, University of Nottingham, University Park, Nottingham NG7 2RD, UK

Ian Douglas   Department of Geography, University of Manchester, Manchester M13 9PL, UK

David Favis-Mortlock   Environmental Change Unit, University of Oxford, 1a Mansfield Road, Oxford OX1 3TB, UK

A. J. Ferreira   Departamento de Ambiente e Ordenamento, Universidade de Aveiro, Aveiro, Portugal

Enrique Francés   Facultad de Ciencias, Universidad de Cantabria, Avda. de los Castros, s/n, 39005 Santander, Spain

A. González   Facultad de Ciencias, Universidad de Cantabria, Avda. de los Castros, s/n, 39005 Santander, Spain

Tony Greer   Department of Geography, National University of Singapore, 10 Kent Ridge Crescent, Singapore 0511

John Gunn   Limestone Research Group, Department of Geographical and Environmental Sciences, The University of Huddersfield, Queensgate, Huddersfield HD1 3DH, UK

Jonathan M. Harbor   Department of Geology and Water Resources Research Institute, Kent State University, Ohio 44242-0001, USA

Stefan Jäger   Geographisches Institut, University of Heidelberg, 69120 Heidelberg 1m Neuenheimer Feld 348, Germany

David K. C. Jones   Department of Geography, London School of Economics, Houghton St, London WC2A 2AE, UK

Stephen P. Leatherman   Laboratory for Coastal Research, Department of Geography, 1113 LeFrak, University of Maryland, College Park, MD 20742, USA

Keith A. McClintock   West Chester County Department of Planning, 414 Michaelian Office Building, White Plains, NY 10601, USA

Duncan F. M. McGregor   Centre for Environmental Analysis and Management, Department of Geography, Royal Holloway, University of London, Egham, Surrey TW20 0EX, UK

Xingmin Meng   Geological Hazards Research Institute, Gansu Academy of Sciences, Lanzhou, People's Republic of China and Department of Geography, Royal Holloway, University of London, Egham, Surrey TW20 0EX, UK

Robert J. Nicholls   School of Geography and Environmental Management, University of Middlesex, Queensway, Enfield, Middlesex EN3 4SF, UK

Lewis A. Owen   Centre for Environmental Analysis and Management, Department of Geography, Royal Holloway, University of London, Egham, Surrey TW20 0EX, UK

Brian Reynolds   Institute of Terrestrial Ecology, Bangor Research Unit, University College of North Wales, Deinol Road, Bangor, Gwynedd LL57 2UD, UK

Helen M. Scoging   Department of Geography, London School of Economics, Houghton St, London WC2A 2AE, UK

Rick A. Shakesby   Department of Geography, University of Wales Swansea, Singleton Park, Swansea, West Glamorgan SA2 8PP, UK

Milap C. Sharma   Department of Geography, Royal Holloway, University of London, Egham, Surrey TW20 0EX, UK

Waidi Sinun   Department of Geography, University of Manchester, Manchester M13 9PL, UK

Christopher Soulsby   Department of Geography, University of Aberdeen, St Mary's, High Street, Aberdeen AB9 2UP, UK

Mike Spilsbury   Fountain Forestry, Banbury, Oxfordshire, UK

Jadda Suhaimi   Department of Geography, University of Manchester, Manchester M13 9PL, UK

Azman bin Sulaiman   Department of Geography, University of Manchester, Manchester M13 9PL, UK

A. D. Thomas   Department of Geography, University of Wales Swansea, Singleton Park, Swansea, West Glamorgan SA2 8PP, UK

Donald A. Thompson   Centre for Environmental Analysis and Management, Department of Geography, Royal Holloway, University of London, Egham, Surrey TW20 0EX, UK

Rory P. D. Walsh   Department of Geography, University of Wales Swansea, Singleton Park, Swansea, West Glamorgan SA2 8PP, UK

Timothy P. Wilson   Department of Geology and Water Resources Research Institute, Kent State University, Ohio 44242-0001, USA

Series Preface

The British Geomorphological Research Group (BGRG) is a national multidisciplinary Society whose object is "the advancement of research and education in geomorphology". Today, the BGRG enjoys an international reputation and has a strong membership from both Britain and overseas. Indeed, the Group has been actively involved in stimulating the development of geomorphology and geomorphological societies in several countries. The BGRG was constituted in 1961 but its beginnings lie in a meeting held in Sheffield under the chairmanship of Professor D. L. Linton in 1958. Throughout its development the Group has sustained important links with both the Institute of British Geographers and the Geological Society of London.

Over the past three decades the BGRG has been highly successful and productive. This is reflected not least by BGRG publications. Following its launch in 1976 the Group's journal, *Earth Surface Processes* (since 1981 *Earth Surface Processes and Landforms*) has become acclaimed internationally as a leader in its field, and to a large extent the journal has been responsible for advancing the reputation of the BGRG. In addition to an impressive list of other publications on technical and educational issues, including 30 *Technical Bulletins* and the influential *Geomorphological Techniques*, edited by A. Goudie, BGRG symposia have led to the production of a number of important works. These have included *Nearshore Sediment Dynamics and Sedimentation*, edited by J. R. Hails and A. P. Carr; *Geomorphology and Climate*, edited by E. Derbyshire; *Geomorphology, Present Problems and Future Prospects*, edited by C. Embleton, D. Brunsden and D. K. C. Jones; *Mega-geomorphology*, edited by R. Gardner and H. Scoging; *River Channel Changes*, edited by K. J. Gregory; and *Timescales in Geomorphology*, edited by R. Cullingford, D. Davidson and J. Lewin. This sequence of books culminated in 1987 with a publication, in two volumes, of the *Proceedings of the First International Geomorphology Conference*, edited by Vince Gardiner. This international meeting, arguably the most important in the history of geomorphology, provided the foundation for the development of geomorphology into the next century.

This current BGRG Symposia Series has been founded and is now being fostered to help maintain the research momentum generated during the past three decades, as well as to further the widening of knowledge in component fields of geomorphological endeavour. The series consists of authoritative volumes based on the themes of BGRG meetings, incorporating, where appropriate, invited contributions to complement chapters selected from presentations at these meetings under the guidance and editorship of one or more suitable specialists. Although maintaining a strong emphasis on pure geomorphological research, BGRG meetings are diversifying, in a very positive way, to consider links between geomorphology *per se* and other disciplines such as ecology, agriculture, engineering and planning.

The first volume in the series was published in 1988. *Geomorphology in Environmental Planning*, edited by Janet Hooke, reflected the trend towards applied studies. The second volume, edited by Keith Beven and Paul Carling, *Floods— Hydrological, Sedimentological and Geomorphological Implications*, focused on a traditional research theme. *Soil Erosion on Agricultural Land* reflected the international importance of the topic for researchers during the 1980s. This volume, edited by John Boardman, John Dearing and Ian Foster, formed the third in the series. The role of vegetation in geomorphology is a traditional research theme, recently revitalized with the move towards interdisciplinary studies. The fourth in the series, *Vegetation and Erosion—Processes and Environments*, edited by John Thornes, reflected this development in geomorphological endeavour, and raised several research issues for the next decade. The fifth volume, *Lowland Floodplain Rivers— Geomorphological Perspectives*, edited by Paul Carling and Geoff Petts, reflects recent research into river channel adjustments, especially those consequent to engineering works and land use change. The sixth volume *Landscape Sensitivity*, edited by David Thomas and Robert Allison, addresses a vital geomorphological topic. This concerns the way in which landscape and landforms respond to external changes; important concepts for understanding landform development and crucial to an appreciation of human-induced response in the landscape. The seventh in the series, *Geomorphology and Sedimentology of Lakes and Reservoirs*, edited by John McManus and Robert Duck, provided a stimulating mixture of pure and applied research which appealed to a wide audience, and the eighth in the series, *Process Models and Theoretical Geomorphology* edited by Mike Kirkby, reported some important new numerical and field results from a variety of environments. The ninth in the series, *Environmental Change in Drylands*, edited by Andrew Millington and Ken Pye, continues the current trend of analysing recent palaeoenvironmental change in order to understand and to control present day systems and includes examples from Europe, Africa, North America and Australia. The tenth, *Rock Weathering and Landform Evolution*, edited by D. A. Robinson and R. B. G. Williams, presents an extensive review of rock weathering processes through geochronology and the application of the results to landforms in tropical, temperate and high latitudes.

The present volume (the eleventh in the series), *Geomorphology and Land Management in a Changing Environment*, edited by Duncan McGregor and Donald Thompson, accurately reflects a wide diversity of approaches to the broad theme. This timely and important new book focuses on the practical application of geomorphology to the problems of environmental change.

Jack Hardisty
BGRG Publications Committee

Preface

This volume represents a selection of papers delivered as the British Geomorphological Research Group's contribution to the Institute of British Geographers' Annual Conference in January 1993, held at Royal Holloway, University of London. In keeping with one of the conference themes of *environmental change*, the British Geomorphological Research Group session focused on the practical application of geomorphology to land management in a changing environment. Reflecting the diversity of approach and opinion engendered by this all embracing theme, the papers presented range widely across geomorphology and geomorphological hydrology. The contributions also reflect a wide diversity of methodologies from field process monitoring using erosion plots to hypothetical computer modelling.

Fifteen of the eighteen chapters are results of oral presentations given over the one and a half days of the symposium while three were submitted subsequently. The diversity of contributions contributed to an interesting editorial task; but four major themes emerged around the general idea of human/natural process interaction: ground instability and land management; the effects of land use on hydrological response of geomorphological systems; geomorphological aspects of the management of environmental impact and risk; and aspects of modelling and management of geomorphological systems. The contributions reflect an international perspective, and include contributions from researchers in Belgium, China, Germany, Greece, India, Malaysia, Portugal, Spain, USA as well as the UK.

All contributions have been refereed and we extend thanks to all those who helped us so efficiently and constructively in this capacity.

We also thank Helen Bailey, Abi Hudlass and Claire Walker at John Wiley, the local organising committee of the IBG conference at Royal Holloway and the committee of the BGRG for their support.

Duncan McGregor
Donald Thompson

Part 1

INTRODUCTION

1 Geomorphology and Land Management in a Changing Environment

DUNCAN F. M. McGREGOR and DONALD A. THOMPSON
Department of Geography, Royal Holloway, University of London, UK

ABSTRACT

This introduction highlights the practical application of geomorphology and geomorphological hydrology to environmental management through four major themes: ground instability and land management, the effect of land use on the hydrological response of geomorphological systems, geomorphological aspects of environmental impact and risk, and aspects of the modelling and management of geomorphological systems undergoing environmental change. The chapter sets the volume of contributions in the context of changing environments and human impact, and brings attention to the scale problem in geomorphological research. It outlines issues and strategies of land management, and comments briefly on the prospects for "environmental geomorphology".

INTRODUCTION

This volume represents a selection of papers delivered as the British Geomorphological Research Group's contribution to the Institute of British Geographers' Annual Conference in January 1993, together with a number of invited contributions. In keeping with one of the conference themes of *environmental change*, the British Geomorphological Research Group session focused on the practical application of geomorphology to land management in a changing environment. It is perhaps not surprising that this all-embracing theme produced a diversity of approach and opinion during the one and a half days of presentations! Reflecting this, the papers presented here range widely across geomorphology and into hydrology, and reflect both the diversity of geomorphology itself and the differing interpretations of the theme by individual authors. This has presented the editors with a demanding editorial task, and the groupings of papers is regarded as less important than the ethos that they put forward, of the importance and applicability of geomorphology to land management. If this engenders debate and reflection within the subject and its practitioners, we will consider ourselves to have achieved some success. If the debate and reflection extends outside the subject, a major aim of the book has been achieved.

As Hooke (1988:4) notes, ". . . the rate of [environmental] change and the ability of humans to alter the landscape is increasing. Also, as population increases and resources diminish the pressure on the remaining resources grows." Hooke (1988) illustrates this with reference to the field of public policy, largely in the UK. In a wider context, Thomas and Allison (1993) consider the sensitivity of landscapes to environmental change, and underline that this sensitivity is a key concern to scientists and policy makers alike. The driving force of climate and the modifying influence of human activity are pervasive themes of much of their text. A knowledge of landscape sensitivity is particularly critical in circumstances where the geomorphological system is close to a threshold of change, and where even minor changes in land management may promote threshold exceedance. The issue of geomorphological sensitivity is also critical in locating areas which require careful management, and also those where the optimum style of management may differ over differing time periods.

Geomorphology and Land Management in a Changing Environment takes these concerns further, and highlights the practical application of geomorphology and geomorphological hydrology to environmental management, through examination of the ways in which geomorphology is relevant to, and contributes to, proper management of land resources. Effective land use should be seen as dependent on the integration of geomorphological principle and practice within the decision-making process. Successful forecasting of the effects of land use change requires both a secure geomorphological data base and a reliable working model—however defined—of the process–response system within which land use change is taking place. Identifying and targeting appropriate management strategies is therefore critical under conditions of environmental change, and the effective utilization of economic resources associated with the land is of national and international governmental significance.

The book first critically reviews the progress of "applied geomorphology" in addressing the issues of practical applicability of geomorphology. In the Conference keynote address, David Jones (Chapter 2) asks if the "product" offered to managers by geomorphologists is correct and indeed raises the question of whether most geomorphologists understand the term "management" itself. Jones notes that while much process work has been applied in the context of site evaluations, too little attention is paid to the possibility of larger scale "landform" based approaches which could forge links with the fields of landscape architecture and landscape aesthetics.

This volume then focuses on four major themes within this human/natural process interaction: ground instability and land management; the effect of land use on the hydrological response of geomorphological systems; geomorphological aspects of the management of environmental impact and risk; and aspects of modelling and management of geomorphological systems undergoing environmental change. The individual chapters examine scenarios of environmental change in the context of how these would alter the geomorphological and hydrological parameters for land management. By integrating a wide range of case studies from the developed and the developing world, the book offers a distinctive insight into the range and utility of geomorphological research, and signposts for environmental planners and decision makers at all levels the necessity of geomorphological input to environmental management.

Whilst many recent books and collections of essays on geomorphology have focused on a relatively narrow theme within geomorphology, the present volume sets out to illustrate the wider range of geomorphological contributions to practical land management problems. It takes a broad approach to environmental change, ranging from the effects of human-induced environmental change through population increase and economic growth, to aspects of the projected consequences of global warming. It also takes an international perspective, and encompasses a wide range of geographical and geomorphological environments. Further, it illustrates the wide methodological diversity of geomorphology, encapsulated in range from the field monitoring approach to problem-oriented computer modelling strategies.

CHANGING ENVIRONMENTS AND HUMAN IMPACT

Environmental change is of course nothing new. It is as old as the planet itself. Climate change has had a radical effect on the nature and rates of geomorphological processes through time, at all spatial scales. Nor is human influence on environmental change the exclusive province of the post-Industrial Revolution society. For example, temperate latitude deforestation has been ongoing for at least 5000 years (Mannion, 1991), while Flenley (1988) suggests that extensive removal of forests for agricultural purposes may have been in train for perhaps 9000 years in parts of south and south-east Asia.

With environmental change, the changing balance of factors, natural or human, on geomorphological processes has often been difficult to determine, especially since relatively few geomorphological processes have remained unaffected by human activity. Indeed, it has often been argued in the literature that there is no such thing as a "natural hazard", and that natural events are only of actual or potential hazard if human activity is taking place in the area affected by the natural event. Perhaps the only province of geomorphological enquiry where it can be argued that there is no two-way interaction between humans and the process–response system is that of regional-scale tectonic activity. Otherwise, there is now continuous feedback between human land use and geomorphological process, extending to cases of changing process rates constraining economic activity, such as that of soil erosion.

As human activity has intensified over the millennia, particularly since the Industrial Revolution, so environmental hazards have increased in relation (Alexander, 1993:1–3; Smith, 1992:34–40). Further, Wijkman and Timberlake (1984) argue cogently that, increasingly, the burden of disaster falls on those least able to cope with it. A geomorphological hazard event in a developing area may well have more radical effects on the social system it affects than a similar event in a developed area. Extensive construction in earthquake-prone zones (Owen *et al.*, Chapter 5) and slope loading and drainage on loessic soils (Derbyshire and Meng, Chapter 6) illustrate this point, with respect to densely-populated developing areas; while Nicholls and Leatherman (Chapter 14) indicate how the potential losses of land and property due to projected sea-level rise are loaded differentially against a selection of developing areas.

The nature of environmental change may be viewed in terms of *scales of change*. These have been, and continue to be, critical variables in the geomorphological system, as introduced below and exemplified by the chapters of this volume and elsewhere (e.g. Thornes, 1990).

SCALES OF CHANGE

The nature and spatial scale of geomorphological change can vary through both time and space, from gradual to catastrophic, from micro-scale to macro-scale (Thornes and Brunsden, 1977). For example, the longer the time-scale under consideration, the more likely it becomes that a more rare event of greater magnitude will be experienced. Further, a geomorphological system which appears to be in equilibrium over a short time span may, when considered over a longer time period, be in a state of actual or potential disequilibrium. This has implications for the linkages between geomorphological forecasting and management; not least because, as Favis-Mortlock (Chapter 16) points out, modelling strategies often underestimate the extreme event.

As Goudie (1990) notes, the scale of environmental change may be transformed in coming decades as a result of the nature of climate changes that may be in the process of induction through human activity. Although as yet shrouded in uncertainty, it seems likely that global warming will contribute to changing environments worldwide, with significant knock-on effects on rates of operation of geomorphological processes at regional levels. For example, the projected effects of Amazonian rainforest clearance include short-term soil compaction and increased runoff and erosion; but include in the longer term, despite regional reduction in precipitation, accelerated runoff (due to reduction of interception), increased fluvial discharge and sediment load, and increased peak flood levels (Eden and McGregor, 1994). There is therefore a need for regional-scale approaches to assessment of geomorphological hazard data suitable as input into land management strategies, as illustrated here by Dikau and Jäger (Chapter 4) and González et al. (Chapter 11).

That regional-level change will lead to differing process–response interactions at local levels seems inevitable (see, for example, Armstrong and Castle (Chapter 9) and Favis-Mortlock (Chapter 16)); while the problem of stability—whether change is self-limiting (negative feedback) or self-reinforcing (positive feedback)—is illustrated here at the local scale by the case of source area liming and upland hydrology (self-limiting: Soulsby and Reynolds, Chapter 8) and by agricultural terrace degradation in southeast Spain (self-reinforcing: Thompson and Scoging, Chapter 10). Critical in this context is the question of whether changes in land management are designed to be short-term, and more likely to be governed by self-regulation; or long-term and more likely to promote self-reinforcement. Thus, there is a need to distinguish between management strategies which cope with short-term pulsed events and those which are appropriate to deal with progressive "ramped" changes. Sensitivity is again a critical consideration, as exemplified by Downs' discussion of the implications for management of river channel adjustment sensitivity (Chapter 15); while at the microscale, Armstrong and Castle (Chapter 9) demonstrate the predictive potential of modelling the hydrological consequences of environmental change in highly sensitive pasture land.

LAND MANAGEMENT: ISSUES AND STRATEGIES

Issues

As Jones (Chapter 2) notes, geomorphologists have been criticized as having an unclear idea of what is implied by the term "management". The complex socio-political framework within which land management takes place explains this to an extent. As Blaikie and Brookfield (1987) point out, chains of explanation in land degradation are often complex, and positive intervention is often difficult to implement effectively. Jones argues that the geomorphologist's tendency to simplify the institutional process into structural form (see Figure 2.1) gives further weight to this criticism.

Jones regards land management as involving a wide range of issues, including "... land use, land protection, resources utilization, hazard mitigation, development, amenity, recreation and conservation ...", yet these are within the compass of the holistic geomorphological investigation, an approach advocated by studies such as Cooke's *Geomorphological Hazards in Los Angeles* (Cooke, 1984). That the conflicting requirements of amenity, recreation and conservation require a careful management balance is advocated in this volume by Gunn (Chapter 12); while the geomorphological implications of resources utilization are illustrated by Douglas *et al.* (Chapter 18) with particular reference to logging in tropical rainforest.

While the issues involved in land management may be complex, solutions are not necessarily so. McClintock *et al.* (Chapter 7) and González *et al.* (Chapter 11) suggest that simple techniques, requiring data which the planner would have readily available, can produce results which are highly appropriate for local planning issues. McClintock *et al.* illustrate this point using the US soil conservation curve number method as a means of evaluating land use effects on groundwater recharge. In the wider context, this approach raises the question of whether the "engineering hydrology" approach, of providing simple and understandable data without setting out a full understanding of the processes involved, is appropriate for the planning audience. In the context of environmental change, which may radically alter process magnitude and frequency, it may be argued that there is a need to elaborate on process and potential change whether the planner wishes it or not!

A further complication is that different environmental issues assume perceived prominence at different spatial scales. For example, at global and regional scales, issues of global warming, deforestation, ecosystem dynamics, environmental pollution (including "acid rain"), land degradation and its specific form, desertification, are matters of international concern and, in some cases, action. Management choices may be wide, but are circumscribed by the need for concerted action. Geomorphological input may be broad-brush and somewhat general in its approach. At the local scale, however, issues of, for example, erosion, slope failure, deposition and flooding are of more immediate concern to the land owner or land manager. The cause of the problem is often seen as less important than remedial or preventative action, however much the geomorphologist may argue that without detailed knowledge of cause, a lasting and appropriate solution may be difficult to achieve. The "site survey" approach of the geomorphological consultant is therefore often deemed adequate. A systematic framework for mangement input is frequently not present, nor even considered. The political global/regional framework and the local planning environment are rarely interlinked in reality, far less underpinned by appropriate principles for geomorphological investigation.

The Political and Planning Process

The political and planning process has profound implications for land management, although as Lee (1993) points out, planning and management are not synonymous. For example, with particular reference to the UK coastal zone, Lee notes that the UK planning system has largely failed so far to take into account the dynamic nature of the coastline, a problem exacerbated by a lack of co-ordination between land use planning and coastal defence strategy.

Hazards have conventionally been regarded as a matter for the developer, and not the planner. Doornkamp (Chapter 3) takes up this issue with specific reference to legislation, policy and insurance aspects of ground instability. This raises the question of the incorporation of physical components into planning strategies, particularly as few planners have a grounding in earth science, and conversely few geomorphologists are well versed in the intricacies of the planning system. Both Doornkamp and Jones (Chapter 2) cite the example of the UK Department of the Environment's recent approach to the use of earth science information in the planning system; presently by a combination of broad national reviews, development of applied earth science mapping, and formulation of planning policy guidance notes. The effectiveness of this approach has yet to be assessed, but is significant in focusing the planner's attention on the need to take geomorphological hazard into account in development. In this respect, the UK legislative system is some way behind state legislation in USA and in many European countries, notably France and Italy.

Strategies

Geomorphological strategies for land management are also wide-ranging, and only a selection may be presented in a volume such as this. Here again, significant differences in approach and philosophy often pertain in developed and developing areas. Different economic status and social values, and different political and societal pressures, may govern what can and may be done in the face of geomorphological hazard; hypothetical choice rarely matching up to economic and technical feasibility in developing areas.

Methodological approaches vary from the "traditional" field monitoring of process at the local scale to hypothetical modelling at all scales; from simple field instrumentation to relatively sophisticated use of "information technology". Different methodological approaches to a similar problem may yield significantly different forms of output, as witnessed by two contrasting papers on wood fires in dry Mediterranean environments: Walsh *et al.* (Chapter 17) show how field monitoring can highlight land use and management variables at the local scale in northern Portugal; while De Vliegher *et al.* (Chapter 13) investigate the use of remote sensing with geomorphological data and statistical information for setting up a Geographical Information System (GIS) to estimate fire hazard in central Greece. The use of GIS as a tool in assisting land management decisions is also demonstrated for landslide hazard prediction, by Dikau and Jäger (Chapter 4) and for National Parks management, by Gunn (Chapter 12).

The utility of modelling strategies in land management is demonstrated by a range of applications (e.g. Chapters 4, 10, 15 and 16). At the regional scale, the applicability of a geomorphological approach to pre-project environmental impact assessment for regional master plans is demonstrated by González *et al.* (Chapter 11). In contrast, at the local scale, the necessity to model the dynamic element of geomorphological process into management considerations is demonstrated by Downs (Chapter 15) in a practical way with respect to river channel adjustments.

ENVIRONMENTAL GEOMORPHOLOGY: PERSPECTIVE AND PROSPECT

Environmental geomorphology (applied geomorphology in a new guise?) appears, on balance, to be alive and well. Jones (Chapter 2) charts the rise of applied geomorphology in the British case, and suggests that an outwardly healthy view of the situation within the UK should be tempered with some caution. A "sustainable applied geomorphology" requires, Jones argues, the abandonment of the notion of a "pure-applied" dichotomy, a greater measure of interaction with other scientists and potential clients, and proactive marketing of potential expertise.

Setting national, if general, considerations aside, the truly international context of geomorphologists' involvement in matters of environmental concern is illustrated by the output of the Second International Conference on Geomorphology, held at Frankfurt in 1989. Two separate *Supplementbands* of *Zeitschrift für Geomorphologie* (numbers 83 and 87) are devoted to papers in applied geomorphology, while numerous others appear in theme *Supplementbands* from the Frankfurt meeting. In a review paper from the same meeting however, Coates (1990) underlines the constraints that affect the environmental geomorphologist operating in a consultancy capacity. These may include a lack of flexibility in approach, due to prior definition of the problem; a restrictive time-frame; artificial spatial boundaries for the study; and publication constraints.

But, taking on board Jones's argument, geomorphologists need now to reflect on whether the message is targetting the audience? Are geomorphologists putting the case for environmental geomorphology effectively and efficiently? What should be the approach? In a general consideration of "environmental geography", Cooke (1992:132) asserts that geomorphology ". . . commonly only entertains human activity where people manipulate variables in complex physical systems, and it usually ignores cultural, economic and managerial contexts, and fundamental feedback mechanisms." Cooke argues that we as physical geographers will have to shift our ground; to pose different research questions, and to communicate more effectively with a range of environmental practitioners. To succeed, Cooke argues, requires a shift of emphasis towards a more political and social context; though without prejudicing the distinctive nature of physical geographical research contributions. Cooke proposes that effective contributions may be made through approaches which recognize and analyse key environmental issues before the public agenda is set; which promote integrated human–physical research within active environmental issues and the public and private agencies responsible for them; and which seek out the lessons of history and apply them effectively in management strategies.

We may accept the maxim that human activity alters geomorphological response; sometimes to dampen the magnitude and spatial scale of response, but often to alter response progressively and disadvantageously in human terms. Prediction of the nature and scale of response is therefore critical in land management. While many contributions, both in this volume and elsewhere, illustrate complex, physically-based or "blue skies" approaches to geomorphology and land management, the major issue of communicating such information to planners and managers remains. We hope that the wide geomorphological and geographical range of the present volume highlights the practical application of geomorphology to environmental management. This in turn brings into focus, for developers and policy makers alike, the utility and necessity of geomorphological input into environmental risk management in a changing environment.

REFERENCES

Alexander, D. (1993). *Natural Disasters*, UCL Press, London.

Blaikie, P. and Brookfield, H. (1987). *Land Degradation and Society*, Methuen, London.

Coates, D. R. (1990). Perspectives of environmental geomorphology. *Zeitschrift für Geomorphologie Supplement-Band*, **79**, 83–117.

Cooke, R. U. (1984). *Geomorphological Hazards in Los Angeles*, Allen and Unwin, London.

Cooke, R. U. (1992). Common ground, shared inheritance: research imperatives for environmental geography. *Transactions of the Institute of British Geographers (New Series)*, **17**, 131–151.

Eden, M. J. and McGregor, D. F. M. (1994). Deforestation and the environment. In P. A. Furley (Ed.), *The Forest Frontier: Settlement and Change in Brazilian Roraima*, Routledge, London, pp. 86–110.

Flenley, J. R. (1988). Palynological evidence for land use changes in South-East Asia. *Journal of Biogeography*, **15**, 185–197.

Goudie, A. S. (1990). The global geomorphological future. *Zeitschrift für Geomorphologie Supplement-Band*, **79**, 51–62.

Hooke, J. M. (Ed.) (1988). *Geomorphology in Environmental Planning*. Wiley, Chichester.

Lee, E. M. (1993). The political ecology of coastal planning and management in England and Wales: policy responses to the implications of sea-level rise. *Geographical Journal*, **159**, 169–178.

Mannion, A. M. (1991). *Global Environmental Change: A Natural and Cultural Environmental History*, Longman, Harlow.

Smith, K. (1992). *Environmental Hazards: Assessing Risk and Reducing Disaster*. Routledge, London.

Thomas, D. S. G. and Allison, R. J. (Eds) (1993). *Landscape Sensitivity*, Wiley, Chichester.

Thornes, J. B. (Ed.) (1990). *Vegetation and Erosion: Processes and Environments*, Wiley, Chichester.

Thornes, J. B. and Brunsden, D. (1977). *Geomorphology and Time*, Methuen, London.

Wijkman, A. and Timberlake, L. (1984). *Natural Disasters: Acts of God or Acts of Man?* Earthscan, London.

2 Environmental Change, Geomorphological Change and Sustainability

DAVID K. C. JONES

Department of Geography, London School of Economics, UK

ABSTRACT

Geomorphological studies have developed against a background of environmental change but future accelerated rates of change under the influence of global warming, population development and economic growth, indicate the need for more well-focused geomorphological advice regarding potentially adverse consequences. This chapter addresses this broad issue from a British perspective, emphasizing the need for work that is relevant to policy formulation, especially with respect to current concerns regarding sustainability. The chapter emphasizes that significant changes have also occurred regarding the nature of geomorphology as a discipline and the academic and commercial environments within which geomorphology is practised. Using the growth and subsequent decline of engineering geomorphology as a lesson for the future, the chapter advances a number of suggestions for a sustained applied geomorphological contribution to land management.

INTRODUCTION

The title of this anthology is so broad as to allow inclusion of an amazingly varied spectrum of material. To write an introductory piece for such a potentially eclectic collection is therefore a daunting task, with all the attendant problems of emphasis, omission and balance. The pragmatic solution would be to indulge in the frequently adopted ploy of introducing an illustrative case study and then appending a concluding section beginning with the by now immortal phrase "it therefore follows that . . .", which often turns out to be far from the case. Hopefully, a more useful and appealing alternative is to offer a brief reflection of the potential challenges and opportunities for geomorphology provided by a world that is changing in so many respects.

In contemplating the potential future development of geomorphology, particularly the applied aspects of the subject, two intertwined threads emerge which are encompassed by the terms *environmental change, geomorphological change* and *sustainability*. The more obvious is the line of argument concerning the likely

Geomorphology and Land Management in a Changing Environment. Edited by D. F. M. McGregor and D. A. Thompson.
©1995 John Wiley & Sons Ltd

geomorphological consequences of Global Environmental Change (GEC) and their potential significance in terms of sustainable development. Herein lies an increasingly recognized challenge to geomorphology and one that provides an excellent opportunity for the subject to further consolidate its position as an applied discipline of relevance in land management. The second strand concerns the changing character of geomorphology as an academic discipline, the changing environment within which geomorphology is practised and developed, and the form in which the applied aspirations of geomorphologists are capable of being sustained. It is argued here that the first cannot be discussed meaningfully in isolation from the second.

ENVIRONMENTAL CHANGE AND GEOMORPHOLOGICAL CHANGE

The subject of Global Environmental Change (GEC) has permeated "Western" culture and is the focus of debate within a wide range of academic disciplines. It is now recognized as a classic example of an "elusive hazard" (Kates, 1985) in that it is cumulative, diffuse, insidious and slow-acting at first, although potentially capable of developing a momentum that may prove difficult to counter in the later stages. It is not a new phenomenon and clearly arises out of the changing interrelationships between human societies and the natural/physical environment that have continued to evolve since the Industrial Revolution—the so-called "Great Climacteric" of Burton and Kates (1986). Neither is it newly recognized as of significance to environmental management debates, having been highlighted by two important studies over two decades ago (SCEP, 1970; SMIC, 1971).

Unfortunately, as is the case with all newly identified hazards, recognition of a "problem" tends to stimulate overreaction. This has certainly been the case with GEC, for the last two decades have witnessed a plethora of wild exaggerations, catastrophic predictions, doomsday scenarios and statements of pure geofantasy. Predictions have included the widespread inundation of coastal lowlands and the apparently "sudden" submergence of coastal cities, the possible extinction of some island states, changed atmospheric circulation resulting in the increased frequency and intensity of tropical revolving storms and mid-latitude depressions, massive biospheric disruption, the wholesale collapse of socio-agricultural systems and the creation of huge displaced populations (environmental refugees). Geomorphologists have, quite sensibly, largely stayed aloof from this level of debate, confining themselves to pointing out (i) that environmental change has been a normal characteristic of the geosystem, particularly during the Quaternary (Goudie, 1992), (ii) that the "greenhouse effect" is an essential long-term feature of the earth's atmosphere, (iii) that human influences are, for the most part, merely modifying the rate of change and, more recently, (iv) that environmental change is not necessarily harmful nor bad, for GEC may result in benefits/opportunities for some geographical areas, or sectors of economies, and that certain nation states may even deem the benefits to outweigh the costs (Jones, 1993a), at least in the short term.

More recently there have been significant improvements in the modelling of future emissions, changing composition of greenhouse gases in the atmosphere and the consequences in terms of climate change (Houghton *et al.* 1990, 1992; Wigley and

Raper, 1992), which provide a much better base for futurology, although the uncertainties involved, together with the complexity and magnitude of the task, remain daunting. Scientifically respectable predictions of global warming and eustatic sea-level change to AD 2050 have narrowed markedly in range over recent years and there is even a fair degree of consensus to AD 2100 based on "most-likely" policy responses. But of greater importance for those concerned with land management, hazard potential and landform change, have been the initial attempts to translate global-level predictions into regional consequences in terms of climatic parameters; a process that has been termed the "regionalization of GEC" (Jones, 1993a). This is an extremely difficult task, as the recently published attempts for the United Kingdom (Department of the Environment, 1991; Warrick and Barrow, 1991; Hulme *et al.*, 1993) have revealed, for there exist great uncertainties when it comes to predicting important parameters such as seasonal rainfall patterns, storminess and storm rainfall intensities. However, the pace of change is great and increasingly refined predictions will continue to emerge over the coming decade, despite the fact that proof of a pronounced phase of global warming may have to wait 15–30 years.

Concerns about the potential effects of GEC have already stimulated well-developed, high-profile research momentums on the atmospheric, hydrospheric and biospheric aspects of climate change which have yet to be adequately complemented in terms of geomorphological consequences where, with the exception of coastal areas, research has been fitful and fragmentary. It is to be hoped that this reflects lack of data and the currently prevailing scale of uncertainty (see below) rather than lack of interest, because here is the contemporary debate and the imminent research agenda. While explanations of past changes in environmental conditions and their effects on landform development are important, the utility of this information to decision-makers whose main concern is with future changes is not always clear, especially as the circumstances of the past appear to them wholly different to those of the near future. It is also true that failure to become involved in the current debate about the possible future consequences of climate change will merely serve to reinforce a widely held, but misinformed, view that geomorphological changes are exceedingly slow and, therefore, of little relevance to human-centred management systems concerned with the rapid pace of anthropogenically-stimulated contemporary environmental change.

The main potential geomorphological consequences of global warming have been detailed by Goudie (1990) and include the following more obvious examples:

(i) changes in vegetation cover and climatic-induced alterations to agricultural practices could result in increased soil erosion, altered patterns of runoff, siltation and increased flood hazard, all of which have implications for resources management (reservoir storage, water supplies, soil conservation and so on);

(ii) changes to the frequency, magnitude and geographical extent of tropical revolving storms and mid-latitude depressions could increase flooding and exacerbate erosion of both inland and coastal areas;

(iii) changed patterns of storm rainfall could result in inland flooding and erosion;

(iv) changing patterns of rainfall may result in either increased runoff, with associated erosion, flooding and siltation problems, or drought-accentuated low discharges and the disturbance of building foundations due to clay shrinkage;

(v) changing temperature characteristics at high elevations and high latitudes will alter the distribution of ice and snow, resulting in the extinction of numerous small mountain glaciers; and variations in the duration and volume of snow-lie;

(vi) the extent of permanently frozen ground (permafrost) will diminish, creating expanded thermokarst conditions and releasing large quantities of methane which could considerably reinforce global warming (Bell, 1982);

(vii) raised sea-level will result in complex changes in the patterns of wave energy, erosion, sediment movement and sediment deposition along coastlines, with some areas suffering beach narrowing and accelerated cliff erosion.

Such a catalogue of possible consequences, which is by no means exhaustive, while useful in pointing out the potential for geomorphological change, fails to indicate the spatial and temporal aspects of change as related to specific areas. This is of importance, for awareness of the general propensity for change is of limited value to decision-makers concerned with questions regarding the significance of future events, such as:

(i) What are the likely changes in ground conditions and hazard potential over specific periods of time and where will the scale of change be greatest?

(ii) Will there be threshold conditions at which points rates of change will quicken and potential cost escalate?

(iii) How significant will the forecast changes be from a human perspective and will the results be beneficial or detrimental?

(iv) How can the adverse effects be averted or minimized and will the cost of carrying out such actions exceed the losses that would flow naturally from environmental change?

To begin the process of answering these questions requires a level of detail yet to be provided by regional assessments of climatic change, modified in the light of local circumstances (for example, tectonic influences on sea-level change) and the variable influence of management practices. Until recently, relatively little attention has been paid to this scale of analysis for reasons that are obvious. In Britain, for example, the major review of possible impacts published by the Department of the Environment (1991) scarcely mentioned geomorphological consequences, except for some comments on soil erosion and an oblique reference to coastal erosion. The British Geomorphological Research Group/Royal Geographical Society Conference of 12 November 1992 explored the subject in greater detail, using the time-frame 1992–2050 as a suitable compromise between the temporal horizons normally adopted by planning and prediction, and revealed a greater focus on the potential issues but disappointingly little hard data (see Beven, 1993; Boardman and Favis-Mortlock, 1993; Doornkamp, 1993; Heathwaite, 1993; Jones, 1993b; Pethick, 1993; Shennan, 1993). What did emerge, however, was a general consensus on three major points:

(i) Landform changes will reflect local conditions of climate, topography, geology, hydrology, and land use. Thus the climatic influences of global warming may be exacerbated, negated or eclipsed by other factors acting at the local scale. To predict such conditions over periods of 50–100 years requires a highly detailed picture of future circumstances not presently available. It follows, therefore, that an incremental approach is required with initial predictions of ground responses undertaken at the regional scale (generalized), followed by more detailed local investigations. The most satisfactory solution would be achieved by employing regional-scale analysis to indicate possible adverse local conditions which could then be thoroughly investigated at the site-specific scale.

(ii) Inland ground conditions in the British Isles are to varying degrees influenced by human activity. Predicting future land use patterns into the next century is impossible, so the likely geomorphological consequences of climate change can only be identified in the most general terms. Indeed, over much of the country the potential scale of human influences easily exceeds the scale of likely change arising from climate alteration over the period in question. Thus the significance of climate-driven changes likely to occur over the next century can, for the most part, be determined by management decisions, thereby highlighting the need for geomorphological information and scientifically substantiated scenarios.

(iii) The geomorphological consequences of global warming over the next century or so may be significant in certain areas but are unlikely to be spectacular or catastrophic, unless reinforced by ill-conceived land management strategies.

The conclusions as to the significance of local conditions and human influences in determining the location and magnitude of change due to global warming is widely applicable, although what may be defined as "local" will vary with terrain conditions, as will the necessary intensity of anthropogenic factors. There is nothing particularly new in this. The development of geomorphology has taken place against a backdrop of environmental change and the growth of applied geomorphology stems from the recognition that the interaction between human activities and the physical environment is a two-way process capable of prediction and manipulation. What has changed in the case of the GEC debate is the appreciation of the potential pace, scale and significance of impending change and the realization that human activities are the driving force behind the change. There is, therefore, a greater awareness of potential consequences and an increased receptiveness to advice, both of which arise from a sense of urgency driven by uncertainty as regards the future. As a result, considerable new opportunities are presented for the incorporation of geomorphological advice in management debates, but the work has to be properly formulated. The research agenda must focus on the extent to which erosion, deposition and earth surface hazards could change as a consequence of climatic change, the likely significance of such changes and the extent to which various alternative land management practices may exacerbate or minimize the consequences. The emphasis should be on the identification of anticipatory measures designed to control unacceptable changes but bearing in mind that "acceptability" is determined by socio-political and economic considerations. The work, therefore, must be forward-looking and intimately interrelated with land management strategies.

SUSTAINABLE DEVELOPMENT

Contemporary discussions about the potential effects of environmental change inevitably result in references to *sustainability* and *sustainable development*. In recent years these concepts have emerged as powerful influences on thinking about the long-term exploitation of resources and, more generally, in evaluations of the desirable relationships between economic and environmental systems, largely because of growing concerns about the future well-being of the human species. The concept of sustainability emerged first in the context of perceived human plundering of natural resources and gained prominence with the publication of the Bruntland Report (WCED, 1987), but has come to be modified in light of the envisaged threat of GEC. It is a simple idea at heart, morally correct, involving sentiments which have been clearly enunciated by the UK Secretary of State for the Environment, Mr John Gummer, in a recent document (Department of Environment, 1993) as "Sustainable Development simply means growing in ways for which future generations will thank us. It does not mean being against development. That would do our grandchildren no favours. It means instead developing in such a way that we respect the delicate balances on which our lives depend, and protect and enhance the great variety in which nature abounds." As is to be expected, such ideas have attracted much ill-informed rhetoric, as well as growing interest, from a wide range of natural scientists, social scientists and policy makers but, as yet, little from geomorphologists. Failure of geomorphologists to consider the notions of sustainability and sustainable development could prove disadvantageous in the short term, for they are attractive concepts to many despite being flawed in terms of vagueness, internal contradictions and operational impracticality.

The concept of sustainable development is now widely held to be imprecise and vague: indeed Redclift (1991) considers that its very strength lies in its vagueness. Depending on the perspective adopted, sustainable development is about meeting human needs without compromising future generations, maintaining economic growth, conserving natural capital, or combinations of these (Redclift, 1991). What is important here is that the definition of one of the many sub-sets ("Sustainable Economic Development") refers to the optimum level of interaction between three systems—the economic, the social and the ecological/natural—a level which, according to Barbier (1989), is achieved through the dynamic and adaptive process of trade-offs. Thus underlying this branch of thinking about sustainability is the recognition that knowledge accumulated in the natural sciences ought to be applied to economic processes. Some argue that a co-evolutionary perspective is emerging in which economic development is viewed as a process of adaptation to a changing environment, while itself being a source of environmental change. There remain, however, severe differences of opinion as to whether the consequences for the natural environment should be minimized (i.e. physical conservation or stable ecological equilibrium with little attention to human needs) or merely carefully monitored so that adverse affects are kept within acceptable bounds with respect to future needs. These notions are of fundamental relevance to those concerned with the future management of land, soil and water. While many earth scientists would tend to feel more in sympathy with the former position, it should be recognized that there are many policy makers who favour the latter, as is clearly illustrated in the statement from Pearce and Turner (1990:42) ". . . the issue, then, is how we should treat natural environments in order that they can play their part in sustaining the economy as a source of improved standard of living."

It is important, therefore, that those geomorphologists interested in environmental issues, resources development, environmental hazards and landform conservation, should begin to frame their work within the context of sustainability, for this is a subject firmly within the "attention frame" of influential decision-makers. But at the same time, it is essential to note that sustainability means different things to different people. A recent review of the literature has revealed over 70 different definitions of sustainability (Holmberg, 1992), indicating that there is no single paradigm, no unified purpose, no common goal and, indeed, no agreement amongst the interested parties, although it would be dangerous to argue that no such consensus will emerge in the future. It is an ongoing debate, and one that geomorphologists should become involved with.

LAND MANAGEMENT

The title of this collection of essays does not contain the word "sustainability" but instead focuses on "land management". It is necessary to leave aside for the moment the question of what is actually meant by "land management" (but see page 31), in order to consider first the term "management".

Earth scientists have frequently been disappointed and dismayed by the apparent lack of attention paid to their actual or potential contributions in management issues, thereby resulting in calls for greater involvement: indeed, this volume is a clear example of the phenomenon. Information on process operation, predictions of possible outcomes arising from ill-considered practices and carefully produced hazard-zoning maps often appear to be totally disregarded by those responsible for making decisions, to the extent that conspiracy theories abound and management decisions are criticized, at least in private, for being based on ignorance and vested interests. Conversely, one of the major criticisms levelled against geomorphologists, together with other natural scientists, is that they often refer to "management" without having any clear idea as to what it means or involves. This is not surprising, as what constitutes management is very variable, complex, sometimes vague and muddled, and almost inevitably politicized. Geomorphologists' appreciation of the processes involved in socio-political decision-making are understandably rudimentary. As a consequence, the processes of management are usually portrayed diagrammatically in geomorphological texts, with particular emphasis placed on the structure and interrelationship of decision-making bodies or agencies (see Cooke and Doornkamp, 1990), or the potential for scientific (that is geomorphological) inputs into policy formulation (see Figures 2.1 and 2.2), but without reference to the actual nature of the decision process. These diagrams are clearly over-simplifications of a very complex process and fail to indicate the vast array of other relevant criteria that have to be considered. It is also not enough simply to state that in the human domain, to quote Cooke (1992), ". . . environmental conditions and processes are transformed into hazards and resources: they become 'threats', 'public goods' and 'exploitable assets.' All of these simple terms refer to exceedingly complex notions which are culturally defined and therefore vary between individuals and groups so that the consensus changes through time and over space.

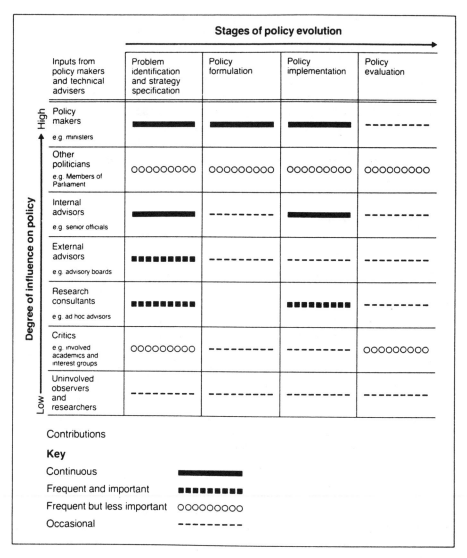

Figure 2.1 Stages and levels of policy involvement as portrayed by Sewell and Coppock (1976) and subsequently reproduced by Jones (1983) and Cooke and Doornkamp (1990). This remains a useful diagram as it shows the various levels of input into policy formulation and the potential significance of geomorphological advice. Lower-level decision-making has the potential to include greater inputs from scientists

At the most basic level, the management of the above phenomena can best be understood in terms of the three basic elements of control theory (Dunsire, 1978):

—the setting of goals, whether explicitly or implicitly;
—the gathering and interpretation of information; and
—action to influence human behaviour or physical phenomena, or both.

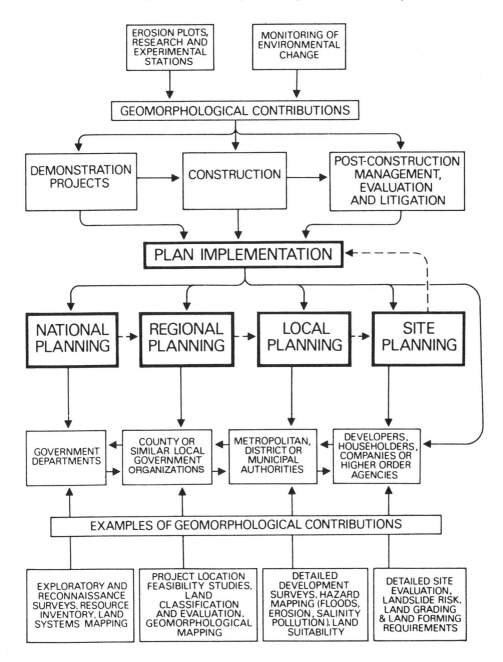

Figure 2.2   The relations between planning scales, the hierarchy of management agencies and potential geomorphological contributions to decision-making (Cooke, 1982). This diagram has the effect of reducing planning decision-making to minimal proportions, thereby contributing to a false sense of simplicity

Management involves decisions about choices, which usually entail trade-offs. The processes by which decisions are taken are sometimes immensely complex, frequently based on inadequate information and involving choices which appear "flawed" from particular perspectives or with hindsight, represent compromises about goals, scales and time-frames, and reflect variable institutional frameworks. It is, almost inevitably, an incremental process which can be envisaged as lurching toward the solution of problems that are both poorly defined and subject to change over time.

When viewed from this perspective, the subject of "land management" can be seen to be immensely complex, involving as it does a wide range of issues including land use, land protection, resources utilization, hazard mitigation, development, amenity, recreation and conservation (see later discussion in this chapter). The introductory details for the symposium that led to this publication referred to *"proper management"* but what is proper in view of the competing interests? Who decides what is to be managed or the objectives of the management? What criteria are to be used to make these decisions and to assess the outcomes? What values are to be placed on differing data and competing objectives? And who decides who should decide? These are questions that geomorphologists rarely consider—indeed geomorphologists have tended merely to be *reactive*, responding to requests for information on what exists (current conditions) or what could happen if certain developments were to occur (environmental assessments), thereby supplying *baseline* data within the context of what has come to be known as the *decision-advice process*.

This role is fine in as far as it goes, except that to be influential requires being asked to contribute to discussions by giving advice and this, in turn, depends upon decision-makers being aware that questions need to be asked, and whom to ask. The requirements here are for profile and publicity. But to have a higher profile requires a *proactive* stance, and this, in turn, requires not only quality of output and good market research, but also an informed understanding of how natural science information is used in decision-making involving the interaction between the human and natural systems—a complex, two-way process that is beginning to be referred to as "the political ecology of management" (Lee, 1993). It also requires some appreciation of the complex and imperfect character of "management" and some involvement in broader management debates, hence the need for consideration of the issue of "sustainable development".

CHANGE IN GEOMORPHOLOGY

There is only one past, but many possible futures. To what extent is geomorphology capable of switching from establishing the details of the past and explaining phenomena, to helping to foresee and shape the future?

Immediately, it is necessary to draw a distinction between geomorphology and geomorphologists. Geomorphology continues to be a healthy, vibrant, multi-disciplinary subject informing, and being informed by, adjunct disciplines. There are numerous scientists and professionals who now claim to have an interest in, or to use, geomorphological information and/or techniques in their work, and the term "geomorphological" is coming into even-wider usage. Geomorphologists *sensu stricto*, by contrast, still preponderantly divide their allegiances between geology and geography for historic reasons. Those with allegiances with geography (e.g. in Britain) may well have an advantage in contributing to studies concerned with managing and adjusting to future environmental change, although this will depend upon the "state of health" of geography as a discipline in the country concerned; for example, diverse character and good internal interrelationships could prove advantageous. It is not feasible to generalize further and so the rest of this discussion will focus on Britain as an example.

It is widely appreciated that geomorphology in Britain has been transformed over the last 30 years, largely due to the so-called "quantitative revolution", the "process revolution" and the application of a wide range of increasingly sophisticated techniques. Comparing 1962 with 1992 reveals five major changes:

(i) *long-term landform evolution*, otherwise known as *regional/historical geomorphology* or *palaeogeomorphology*, has declined from pre-eminence to minimal proportions, leaving the field largely to geology;

(ii) studies of the *near past* (that is, the Quaternary) have greatly increased, become more scientific, continued to be genuinely inter-disciplinary and benefitted from a wide range of dating techniques—although detailed examination of the Holocene is only now underway;

(iii) *process studies* have expanded dramatically to a position of pre-eminence;

(iv) *applied studies* have reached considerable significance, increasingly better informed by improved information on landform evolution, process operation and rates of change; and

(v) marked parochialism has been replaced by a well-developed set of international linkages, culminating in the establishment of the International Association of Geomorphologists, which facilitate better flows of information and co-operation.

Geomorphology has, therefore, developed an "infrastructure" potentially capable of responding to the challenges posed by GEC and a level of technical expertise to match. But as geomorphology has changed, and will continue to do so in the future, so too has the environment for applied work. The evolution of applied geomorphology in Britain may well contain important lessons with regard to the future involvement of geomorphologists in land management issues and is, therefore, worthy of brief consideration.

The development of applied geomorphology in Britain from 1960 to the present displays a distinctiveness in each of the three decades. Briefly these are as follows. First, the 1960s were the period of "exasperation and aspiration" for many geomorphologists of the time—predominantly academics in Geography Departments—as they sought ways of making their subject of practical value. The sense of frustration that prevailed at this time is captured by the first edition of Cooke and Doornkamp's *Geomorphology in Environmental Management* (1974) which emphasized *applicability* but was short on *application*. The feelings of exasperation were understandable: geomorphology is the study of the earth's surface, human activity is focused on the earth's surface, so the potential relevance is obvious. However, geomorphologists of the time were both divided as to the desirability of becoming involved in commercial activities and ill-placed to compete in the market place: they were, by and large, isolated and parochial, without contact networks in the commercial world or professional associations, and with relatively little to sell, for as Clayton was later to remark (1980), ". . . the relevance, or at least the utility of much of our geomorphological knowledge seems pretty slender." Indeed, the scope for potential involvement appeared minimal, for this was the period when technocentrism was at its zenith and it was widely believed that the application of technology and engineering could free human activity from the constraints imposed by nature—a view aptly summed up by Chorley (1971): ". . . man's activities and patterns of life are universally becoming progressively divorced from the physical conditions that immediately surround him." In summary, therefore, a favourable market had not been established for the little relevant expertise that geomorphologists had to offer.

The second decade—the 1970s—in marked contrast, witnessed the birth of applied geomorphology in Britain. A number of different strands of development have been identified in the literature (e.g. Jones, 1980, 1983; Gregory, 1985), the most dramatic being the sudden and unanticipated involvement with engineering. The fortuitous circumstances that led to this liaison are by now well known and need little elaboration here. It can be argued that the opportunity arose largely due to the progressive change in attitude and aptitude displayed by geomorphologists coinciding with the repercussions arising from the widespread over-confident application of technocentrism in the 1950s and 1960s, an approach which lays considerable emphasis on the ability of engineering to dominate or control "natural forces" and to "engineer away" difficulties. This "engineering fix" was partly to blame for a number of costly and embarrassing delays to construction projects in the 1960s and early 1970s which, together, contributed to the desire amongst engineering geologists to improve predictive ability regarding potentially problematic sites so that hazard-loss reduction could be achieved by adjustments or avoidance. As chance would have it, this desire coincided with the first uses of morphological and geomorphological mapping to describe landslide terrains, and so the potential for mutual benefit was obvious. However, it has to be recognized that subsequent developments owed much to the efforts of a single consultant engineering geologist, Peter Fookes, without whose energy, vision, drive and contact network, relatively little would have been achieved during the decade. Thus, to simplify, there was now a *product*, a *market* and a *catalyst*. This favourable combination resulted in a period of rapid development, during which time a small group of academic geomorphologists were able to undertake a series of, by now, well publicized high-profile, consultancy-led geomorphological investigations both in the UK (e.g. The Taff Vale Trunk Road (Brunsden *et al.*, 1975)) and overseas (e.g. the Dharan–Dhankuta Highway Project (Brunsden *et al.*, 1975)); the Bahrain Surface Materials Resources Survey (Doornkamp *et al.*, 1978; Brunsden *et al.*, 1979; Cooke *et al.*, 1982); and the Suez City Survey (Cooke *et al.*, 1982)). These, and other, investigations not only helped establish the three basic planks of applied geomorphology, the "3Ms" of mapping, monitoring and modelling beloved by later authors, but also focused attention on:

(i) the important interrelationship between site and situation; and
(ii) the need to match management systems to geomorphological systems in dynamic environments.

By the end of the 1970s applied geomorphology appeared to have come of age. The first advertisements for academic posts in "applied geomorphology" had begun to appear and taught courses were proliferating within universities. The spirit of optimism, founded in the first half of the decade by Dearman and Fookes (1974) when they predicted the dramatic expansion of the new specialism "engineering geomorphology", even went as far as to the establishment of a specialist company, Geomorphological Services Limited (GSL), in 1979 to cope with the anticipated pressures of as growing market.

The optimism of the 1970s proved to be well founded, for the 1980s were to witness the dramatic expansion and diversification of applied geomorphological studies and the rapid broadening of participation in consultancy and contract work. Applied work was no longer the preserve of the fortunate few. Some indication of the pace and scale of this development can be gained from comparing the 1974 and 1990 editions of Cooke and Doornkamp's *Geomorphology in Environmental Management*, although this understandably fails to show the full range of involvement, especially as regards coastal studies, river management, pollution investigations and land management, as well as changing degrees of participation in the management process, including contributions to public enquiries and in litigation. It is clear that whatever reservations academic geomorphologists originally had experienced regarding involvement in commerical activities had quickly evaporated in the light of the opportunity gains of such relationships, thereby releasing much previously pent-up energy.

One major new development out of several, was the participation of geomorphologists in the research programmes funded by the UK Department of the Environment. This opportunity was only provided because of the existence of GSL and resulted in the "*Review of Research on Landsliding in Great Britain*" over the period 1984–87 (GSL, 1987; Jones 1990, 1993b; Jones and Lee, 1994), the applied earth science mapping of the Torbay area (Doornkamp, 1988; GSL, 1988), the Ventnor landslide study (GSL, 1991; Lee *et al.*, 1991a,b,c) and the yet to be completed "*Review of Erosion, Deposition and Flooding in Great Britain*". The range of reports, maps, databases and recommendations flowing from this body of work have proved of undoubted value in considerations of land management, most obviously in terms of input into the formulation of Planning Policy Guidance Note (PPG 14) *Development on Unstable Land* (Department of the Environment, 1990). But once again it is necessary to identify the important role of specific individuals in helping to generate the work, in this case Drs David Brook and Brian Marker of the Land Stability Branch, Minerals Planning Unit, DoE, and to emphasize the powerful combination of "new needs", "new products" and "new catalysts".

THE DEMISE OF ENGINEERING GEOMORPHOLOGY: A LESSON FOR FUTURE PROGRESS?

The dramatic growth and diversification of applied work in Britain during the 1980s tended to conceal the problems faced by the engineering geomorphology sector. The subject failed to take off in the spectacular fashion predicted by Dearman and Fookes (1974) and there was no explosive growth in the numbers of graduates entering engineering firms, although a number of distinguished individuals did make this transition. Although the definitive history of GSL has yet to be written, it is no secret that the company found it exceptionally difficult to grow on geomorphological work *sensu stricto* and was increasingly forced to diversify into hydrology, structural geology (using remote sensing) and site work. In the end the "climate change" in the economy led to the still viable and expanding company being taken over by Rendel Geotechnics in 1988 and becoming fully merged with the new parent organization in 1991. The experience of a decade in the market-place had, therefore, revealed that demand for geomorphological advice was still inadequate to sustain such a venture, although similar units focusing on coastal management issues have subsequently fared rather better.

Three obvious explanations can be put forward to account for the disappointing performance of the engineering geomorphology sector:

(i)   the decline in project work in overseas developing areas with inadequate indigenous geomorphological information, due to the difficulties of funding, in part reflecting falling oil revenues;
(ii) growing international competition in the engineering sector leading to the pruning of bids by the removal of perceived "frills" such as geomorphological investigations; and
(iii) two major recessions in a decade.

But Griffiths and Hearn (1990) identify a number of other factors of relevance to this discussion:

(i)   the continuing resistance to geomorphology displayed by a majority of civil engineers who still tend to brand geomorphology as "too academic" and "arty" a discipline, practised by specialists with no knowledge of engineering design and, therefore, no understanding of how their information could be put to use. In other words, the practicability and value of employing geomorphologists continues to be questioned;
(ii) an over-emphasis on the virtues of morphological, geomorphological and hazard mapping, which has resulted in the neglect of other forms of contribution. As a consequence, there is continuing poor perception of the utility of geomorphological expertise, which has tended to be used purely to provide preliminary base-line data, thereby denying the potential for other benefits through continued involvement in projects, and participation in design modification;
(iii) the failure of certain mapping exercises and studies to yield information of value to engineering design; and
(iv) a perceived inadequacy in the current training of geomorphologists with respect to a career in the engineering sector; namely
      (a) the heavy emphasis on process studies which does not fit graduates for "site work";

(b) the general decrease in the proportion of graduates with an adequate understanding of geology—thereby raising the old debate as to whether or not geomorphology's close relationship with geography is a hindrance to progress; and

(c) the general decline in landscape and landform interpretation skills. Neglect of landforms has indeed been a feature of geomorphology education in recent years and it is useful to note the definition of engineering geomorphology put forward by Hutchinson in 1979: ". . . the purpose of engineering geomorphology is to achieve an understanding of the nature of landscapes sufficient for engineering works to be carried out safely, predictably and economically within them. It starts with the premise that the earth's surface is, in general, a sensitive indicator of the more recent geological events, and that its morphology thus constitutes a most valuable source of information."

So, is it the market or the product that is the problem, or a combination of the two? If it is the product, then it is up to academic geomorphologists and the BGRG to take steps to resolve the problem, otherwise engineering geomorphology will become wholly subsumed within engineering geology. Certainly the reorganization of geology departments in UK universities and the relatively few remaining academic linkages between departments of geography and geology, suggest that this process is inevitable unless action is taken by the small number of institutions favourably placed to foster such links.

Griffiths and Hearn's criticisms are undoubtedly well-informed and carry some truth, pointing as they do to the type of problems that normally emerge when attempting to interrelate two very different disciplines. But other questions must also be asked:

(i) to what extent has the involvement of geomorphologists in engineering projects actually proved a success in terms of better design or reduced costs?

(ii) how many "extra vitamins" are actually added to engineering decision-making by the employment of suitably trained geomorphologists, or is more to be gained by providing engineering geologists with some geomorphological training?

These are not easy questions to answer for several reasons:

(i) hindsight reviews of engineering programmes are rarely undertaken and even more rarely publicized, especially if mistakes have been made;

(ii) while it is easy to indicate the direct costs of an impact or failure, it is virtually impossible to indicate whether alternative strategies or approaches would have fared any better; and

(iii) apportioning "blame" or "credit" is extremely difficult because there are numerous contributions towards any decision and the final design will reflect many incremental modifications; thus geomorphological contributions often become subsumed by later decisions. As a consequence, claims that mapping exercises led to the re-siting of major structures or the choice of new alignments or the abandonment of one site in favour of another, have to be treated with great scepticism. Usually such outcomes are the consequence of long and involved decision-making which *may*, to some degree, have benefited from geomorphological inputs.

Thus, while individual geomorphologists may consider involvements with projects as "successful" or "beneficial", in reality it is the client's view that counts, especially in terms of perceived cost-effectiveness. Feedback remains patchy and imprecise on this subject and there has yet to be published a detailed and objective hindsight review of any one of the major projects involving significant geomorphological advice. The nearest approximation to date is Hearn's (1987) thesis on the Dharan–Dhankuta Road Project in Eastern Nepal, which revealed that the significant and repeated geomorphological inputs had indeed been greatly valued by the client, although hindsight suggested that the inputs could have been framed differently in order to make them more "user-friendly" for the engineers. Even in this case, however, there had developed a view that the contributions could have been more effectively incorporated into design by either:

(i) having geomorphologists work in combination with engineering geologists during the preliminary investigations rather than in isolation; or
(ii) employing engineering geologists with adequate training in suitable geomorphological skills; an option which was not available in the mid-1970s but exists today and appears to be preferred to the employment of geomorphologists with some training in geological skills.

The potential for increased involvement of geomorphologists in land management decisions is, therefore, dependent on how others assess the value of geomorphological contributions and not self-evaluation nor internalized assessment made within the group of specialized practitioners.

The pattern of evolution of engineering geomorphology focuses attention on the importance of "products", "niches", "catalysts" and "market forces". Growth was achieved while the potential of a new approach was being explored but inevitably resulted in competition with well-established professional networks and interests, so that when momentum faltered, much of the expertise was quickly claimed by adjunct disciplines as attempts were made to return to the *status quo*. It follows, therefore, that any increase in the involvement of geomorphologists in other aspects of land management must be securely based on the production of a steady flow of distinctively trained personnel if it is to be sustainable.

On a more positive note, however, it has to be recognized that geomorphological considerations are now well established within engineering geology. It also should be noted that many examples of the use of geomorphological principles in land management now exist within the engineering/planning/geological/hydrological literature which bodes well for the future. The recent examples of UK Government funded work discussed here clearly indicate the potential for future developments, while at the same time focusing attention on the fact that the incorporation of "geomorphological principles" in land management will be a gradual, incremental process which has to build slowly on a solid platform of satisfactory achievement.

During the 1980s the UK Department of the Environment/Welsh Office sponsored research into landslide potential mapping in the South Wales Coalfield, in order to build upon and extend previous landslide surveys in the area. The study was undertaken by the engineering firm, Sir William Halcrow & Partners, and used geomorphological approaches (Figure 2.3) to establish the relationship between landsliding and the 20 factors that were considered likely contributors to slope instability (Sir William Halcrow & Partners, 1986). Four factors were eventually found to be important—slope angle, superficial deposit type, superficial deposit thickness and groundwater potential—and these were combined in a simple algorithm to define "landslip potential" through a range of values from zero to 518. As planning authorities have a relatively limited range of available responses to planning applications, it was decided to restrict cartographic portrayal to six zones, but grouped into four categories (Figure 2.4):

(i)   areas of active landsliding;
(ii) areas of dormant landsliding;
(iii) areas of "some landslip potential" with LP values in the ranges 121–240 and 241–518; and
(iv) areas with "little landslip potential" with LP values of 0–32 and 33–120.

The resultant maps provide a good basis for defining landslip hazard and form the basis of a zoning scheme that can readily be understoood by planners and easily communicated to the general public, for the four main categories can be translated as follows: "areas where landsliding is occurring"; "areas where landsliding has occurred"; "areas where landsliding may occur" and "areas where landsliding is unlikely to occur". This information is capable of being employed to determine the outcome of planning applications and to advise developers along the lines indicated in Figure 2.5 (Siddle et al., 1987). The possibility that this approach will become more widely adopted in landslide-prone areas of the UK indicates that geomorphological criteria and approaches could become increasingly applied in the context of land management issues.

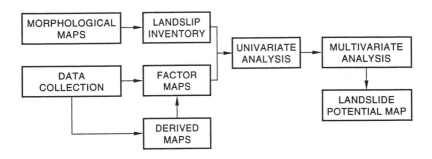

Figure 2.3 Procedure used for assessing landslip potential in Rhondda Borough (after Sir William Halcrow and Partners, 1986)

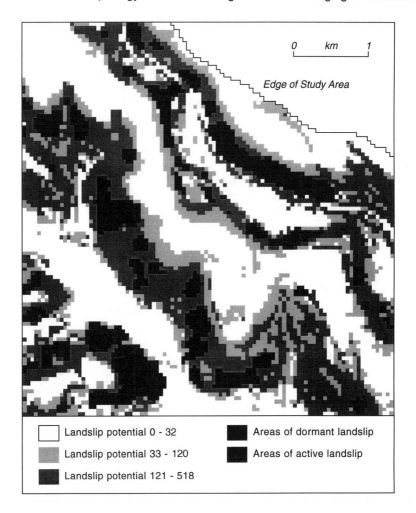

Figure 2.4   Landslip potential map of part of Rhondda Valleys (after Sir William Halcrow and Partners, 1986)

The late 1980s study of the unstable 12-km long Undercliff at Ventnor, Isle of Wight (Geomorphological Services Limited, 1991; Lee *et al.*, 1991a,b,c; Jones and Lee, 1994) represents something of a landmark for geomorphological involvement in land management in the UK. The whole belt of country was mapped geomorphologically at a scale of 1:2500 and patterns of historic movement related to the morphological units identified. This resulted in the production of a 1:2500 scale *Ground Behaviour Map* which, in turn, was used to create a *Planning Guidance Map* which zoned the area with respect to constraints on development and levels of required ground investigation. The two especially unusual aspects of the project were the production of a free public information leaflet which included advice to residents living in the potentially unstable terrain regarding good and bad maintenance procedures

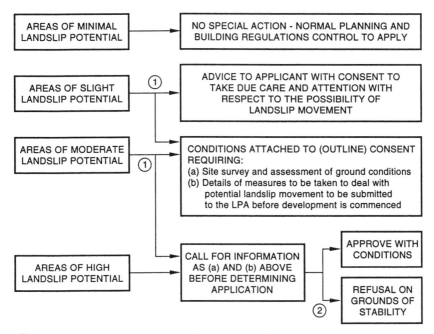

Figure 2.5 The possible interrelationship between landslip potential maps and development control as established in the Rhondda Valleys Study (after Siddle *et al.*, 1987)

(Figure 2.6) and the establishment of a "Landslide Shop" which was open for a period of months in order to provide information and advice to residents concerned about ground movements. Both of these innovations were highly successful and indicate the potentially diverse ways in which geomorphological information can be publicized.

A SUSTAINABLE APPLIED GEOMORPHOLOGY

The previous discussion has sought to show that geomorphology has evolved rapidly in recent decades at the same time as concerns with environmental conditions have grown. Contemporary geomorphology is intellectually and technically better equipped than ever to engage in debates regarding the potential effects of environmental change on the surface of the earth, and the recent expansion and diversification of applied geomorphological contributions to land management have always been undertaken against a background of environmental change, so the challenge of the near future merely represents a change in pace and scale. However, the extent to which

30

DON'Ts

1 Don't block or alter ditches or drains.

2 Don't allow water to collect or pond.

3 Don't shift your water or soil problems downslope to your neighbours.

4 Don't landscape the slope without notifying the Local Authority.

5 Don't clear vegetation off slopes without replanting.

DO's

6 Check roof drains, gutters and downspouts to make sure they are clear.

7 Clear drainage ditches and check them frequently during winter.

8 Make inspections during winter– this is when problems can occur.

9 Watch for water back-up inside the house at sump drains and toilets, since this indicates drain or sewer blockage.

10 Watch for wet spots on the property.

11 Consult an expert if unusual cracks, settling or land slippage occurs. Inform Local Authority of any problems.

12 Regularly inspect scarp slopes for potential rockfalls or loose debris.

13 Regularly inspect swimming pools and ponds for leaks and repair if necessary.

Figure 2.6 Advice to residents of Ventnor, Isle of Wight, regarding suggested good and bad maintenance procedures (after Geomorphological Services Ltd, 1991; Lee *et al.*, 1991a)

geomorphological involvement will continue into the future must be open to question for a number of reasons.

First, the recent expansion in applied work has displayed much variety in terms of scale, scope, approach and purpose. As a consequence, there is virtually no coherence within applied geomorphology, as has been amply illustrated by various texts claiming to cover the field. Some of the work takes the form of "site specific" investigations concerned with controlling ground movements or process operation. Such studies usually seek to constrain responses or "stop things happening" and are probably best termed *ground management*, despite the fact that geomorphologists often appear disinclined to use the term "ground". Ground management is clearly one of the main preoccupations of soil conservationists and engineering geologists and, by extension, engineering geomorphologists. But there also exist a huge variety of other studies concerning such subjects as hazard audits, environmental assessments, pollution studies, solute monitoring and so on, which are far better labelled aspects of *environmental management* or *environmental geomorphology*. The term *land management* would appear to encompass both of these areas, as well as inviting contributions in the fields of landscape conservation, landscape architecture, landform aesthetics, insurance, and so on, which have, to date, been largely excluded from consideration by geomorphologists. This is to be welcomed, for these new developments will undoubtedly provide further stimulation and may also require new techniques and approaches. For example, in order to conserve or enhance inland landscape character for reasons of improving amenity or protecting "heritage", future geomorphologists may well be required to advise on how to maintain or stimulate erosion at specific sites and may even become embroiled in debates as to costs and benefits of erosion. It is important to recognize, however, that as diversification increases, the result will be the proliferation of different strands of "applied geomorphology" that are, to varying degrees, distinctive and separate. This process is wholly necessary and satisfactory for the continued health of geomorphology as a discipline, but it does mean that applied geomorphology will probably not survive for much longer as a distinct entity, but will fragment because of lack of cohesion and the absence of a unifying philosophy. This will be entirely desirable as it will reflect the notion that application is part of the ethos of the subject and not something unusual, special or demeaning. Just as the term "applied geology" has been discarded as irrelevant and superfluous, then so too should "applied geomorphology" in the near future. The incorporation of applied studies as a natural aspiration of geomorphology and the final removal of the "pure–applied" dichotomy will prove important steps in helping to broaden participation in environment management debates.

The second concern focuses on the future source of geomorphological advice. The earlier discussion concerning the progressive demise of engineering geomorphology indicated that any perceived need to involve specialist geomorphologists in projects could be removed by incorporating some geomorphological studies in the training of engineering geologists. The same threat exists in other areas. Geomorphology is such a potentially broad subject as to not be the divine preserve of any single academic group, such as the geographical geomorphologist in the UK. Any desire of existing geomorphologists to maintain the *status quo*, while at the same time seeking to improve the extent and quality of geomorphological advice in land management debates, will require much vigilance and increased profile on the part of both individuals and groups (for example, BGRG). It will require the final abandonment of parochialism in favour of interaction with other scientists and potential clients through joint discussion meetings, publication in non-geomorphological journals, appearances on the media, popularization of the subject, and so on. The core geomorphological community is too small to stay aloof. The question remains, however, as to whether there will be enough active geomorphologists *sensu stricto* to combat substitution and fulfil the potential.

The third and final concern relates to the marketing of potential expertise. The experience gained during the creation of a market niche for applied geomorphologists in the 1970s revealed not only the need for recognized demands, valued products and catalysts, but also that established contact networks had to be broken into, new working practices learned, communications improved and trust established (Brunsden *et al.*, 1978). It is still true that the geographical geomorphologist remains on the fringes of the consultant/contract community, for there is still a marked tendency on the part of potential clients to turn to geologists/engineers for advice on ground conditions, hydrologists for water and pedologists for soil, leaving geomorphologists as the "port of last resort". Overcoming these long-established and deeply entrenched practices will prove difficult unless it can be pointed out that mistakes are currently being made, or opportunities foregone, or unnecessary costs are being incurred. Geologists do not make good sculptors so why should geomorphologists make the best land management advisors? It is up to geomorphologists to argue their case in a pro-active manner, otherwise the advice will be given by other experts. The environment is indeed changing and so too must geomorphologists if they want to continue to be involved in contemporary and future debates. There is undoubtedly a potential demand for well-informed and properly focused advice, stimulated by the uncertainties of GEC. Catalysts also exist to facilitate developments. The question that remains is whether geomorphologists can provide the required products, a question that will be addressed by the other contributions to this volume.

REFERENCES

Barbier, E. (1989). *Economics, Natural Resource Scarcity and Development*, Earthscan, London.

Bell, B. R. (1982). Methane hydrate and the carbon dioxide question. In Clark, W. C. (Ed.), *Carbon Dioxide Review*, Oxford University Press, Oxford.

Beven, K. (1993). Riverine flooding in a warmer Britain. *Geographical Journal*, **159**, 157–161.

Boardman, J. and Favis-Mortlock, D. T. (1993). Climate change and soil erosion in Britain. *Geographical Journal*, **159**, 179–183.

Brunsden, D., Doornkamp, J. C., Fookes, P. G., Jones, D. K. C. and Kelly, J. M. H. (1975). Large-scale geomorphological mapping and highway engineering design. *Quarterly Journal of Engineering Geology*, **8**, 227–253.

Brunsden, D., Doornkamp, J. C. and Jones, D. K. C. (1978). Applied geomorphology: a British view. In Embleton, C., Brunsden, D. and Jones, D. K. C. (Eds) *Geomorphology: Present Problems and Future Prospects*, Oxford University Press, Oxford, pp. 251–262.

Brunsden, D., Jones, D. K. C. and Doornkamp, J. C. (1979). The Bahrain Surface Materials Resources Survey and its application to planning. *Geographical Journal*, **145**, 1–35.

Burton, I. and Kates, R. W. (1986). The Great Climacteric, 1748–2048: the transition to a just and sustainable human environment. In Kates, R. W. and Burton, I. (Eds), *Themes from the Work of Gilbert F. White*, University of Chicago Press, Chicago, pp. 339–360.

Chorley, R. J. (1971). The role and relations of physical geography. *Progress in Geography*, **3**, 87–110.

Clayton, K. M. (1980). Geomorphology. In Brown, E. H. (Ed.), *Geography: Yesterday and Tomorrow*, Oxford, pp. 167–180.

Cooke, R. U. (1982). The assessment of geomorphological problems in dryland urban areas. *Zeitschrift für Geomorphologie*, **44**, 119–128.

Cooke, R. U. (1992). Common ground, shared inheritance: research imperatives for environmental geography. *Transactions of the Institute of British Geographers, New Series*, **17**, 131–151.

Cooke, R. U. and Doornkamp, J. C. (1974/1990). *Geomorphology in Environmental Management*, Clarendon Press, Oxford.

Cooke, R. U., Brunsden, D., Doornkamp, J. C. and Jones, D. K. C. (1982). *Urban Geomorphology in Drylands*, Clarendon Press, Oxford.

Dearman, W. R. and Fookes, P. G. (1974). Engineering geological mapping for civil engineering practice in the United Kingdom. *Quarterly Journal of Engineering Geology*, **7**, 223–256.

Department of the Environment (1990). *Planning Policy Guidance Note 14: Development on Unstable Land*, HMSO, London.

Department of the Environment (1991). Parry, M. L. (Ed.) *The Potential Effects of Climate Change in the United Kingdom*. First Report of the UK Climate Change Impacts Review Group, HMSO, London.

Department of the Environment (1993). *UK Strategy for Sustainable Development: A Consultation Paper*, HMSO, London.

Doornkamp, J. C. (1988). *Applied Earth Science Background: Torbay*. Geomorphological Services Limited, Newport Pagnell.

Doornkamp, J. C. (1993). Clay shrinkage induced subsidence. *Geographical Journal*, **159**, 196–202.

Doornkamp, J. C., Brunsden, D. and Jones, D. K. C. (1978). *Geology, Geomorphology and Pedology of Bahrain*, Geobooks, Norwich.

Dunsire, A. (1978). *Control in a Bureaucracy: The Execution Process*, Vol. 2, Martin Robertson, Oxford.

Geomorphological Services Limited (1987). *Review of Research into Landsliding in Great Britain*. Report to Department of the Environment, Geomorphological Services Limited, Newport Pagnell.

Geomorphological Services Limited (1988). *Applied Earth Science Mapping for Planning and Development: Torbay, Devon*. Report to Department of the Environment, Geomorphological Services Limited, Newport Pagnell.

Geomorphological Services Limited (1991). *Coastal Landslip Potential Assessment: Isle of Wight Undercliff, Ventnor*, Department of the Environment, London.

Goudie, A. S. (1990). The global geomorphological future. *Zeitschrift für Geomorphologie Supplement-Band*, **79**, 51–62.

Goudie, A. S. (1992). *Environmental Change* (3rd edn), Clarendon Press, Oxford.

Gregory, K. J. (1985). *The Nature of Physical Geography*, Edward Arnold, London.

Griffiths, J. S. and Hearn, G. N. (1990). Engineering geomorphology: a UK perspective. *Bulletin International Association of Engineering Geology*, **42**, 39–44.

Hearn, G. J. (1987). *An evaluation of geomorphological contributions to mountain highway design with particular reference to the Lower Himalayas*. Unpublished PhD thesis, University of London.

Heathwaite, A. L. (1993). Disappearing peat—regenerating peat? The impact of climate change on British peatlands. *Geographical Journal*, **159**, 203–208.

Holmberg, J. (Ed.) (1992). *Policies for a Small Planet*, Earthscan, London.

Houghton, J. T., Jenkins, G. L. and Ephramus, J. J. (Eds) (1990). *Climate Change: The IPCC Scientific Assessment*, Cambridge University Press, Cambridge.

Houghton, J. T., Callender, B. A. and Varney, S. K. (Eds) (1992). *The Supplementary Report to the IPCC Scientific Assessment*, Cambridge University Press, Cambridge.

Hulme, M., Hossell, J. E. and Parry, M. L. (1993). Future climate change and land use in the United Kingdom. *Geographical Journal*, **159**, 131–147.

Hutchinson, J. N. (1979). *Engineering in a Landscape*. Inaugural lecture, Imperial College, London.

Jones, D. K. C. (1980). British applied geomorphology: an appraisal. *Zeitschrift für Geomorphologie Supplement-Band*, **36**, 48–73.

Jones, D. K. C. (1983). Environments of concern. *Transactions of the Institute of British Geographers*, New Series, **8**, 429–457.

Jones, D. K. C. (1990). Grounds for concern: landsliding in Great Britain. *Structural Survey*, **9**, 226–236.

Jones, D. K. C. (1993a). Global warming and geomorphology. *Geographical Journal*, **159**, 124–130.

Jones, D. K. C. (1993b). Slope instability in a warmer Britain. *Geographical Journal*, **159**, 184–195.

Jones, D. K. C. and Lee, E. M. (1994). *Landsliding in Great Britain*, HMSO, London.

Kates, R. W. (1985). Success, strain and surprise. *Issues in Science and Technology*, **2**, 46–48.

Lee, E. M. (1993). The political ecology of coastal planning and management in England and Wales: policy responses to the implications of sea-level rise. *Geographical Journal*, **159**, 159–178.

Lee, E. M., Doornkamp, J. C., Brunsden, D. and Noton, N. (1991a). *Ground Movement in Ventnor, Isle of Wight*. Department of the Environment, London.

Lee, E. M., Moore, R., Brunsden, D. and Siddle, H. J. (1991b). The assessment of ground behaviour at Ventnor, Isle of Wight. In Chandler, R. J. (Ed.) (for Institution of Civil Engineers), *Slope Stability Engineering Developments and Applications*, Thomas Telford, London, pp. 189–194.

Lee, E. M., Moore, R., Burt, N. and Brunsden, D. (1991c). Strategies for managing the landslide complex at Ventnor, Isle of Wight. In Chandler, R. J. (Ed.) (for Institution of Civil Engineers), *Slope Stability Engineering Developments and Applications*, Thomas Telford, London, pp. 201–206.

Pearce, D. and Turner, R. K. (1990). *Economics of Natural Resources and the Environment*, Harvester Wheatsheaf Press, Hemel Hemstead, UK.

Pethick, J. (1993). Shoreline adjustments and coastal management: physical and biological processes under accelerated sea-level rise. *Geographical Journal*, **159**, 162–168.

Redclift, M. (1991). The multiple dimensions of sustainable development. *Geography*, **76**, 36–42.

SCEP (1970). Report of the study of critical environmental problems. In *Man's Impact on Global Environmental Problems*, MIT Press, Cambridge, MA.

Sewell, W. R. D. and Coppock, J. T. (1976). Achievements and prospects. In Coppock, J. T. and Sewell, W. R. D. (Eds), *Spatial Dimensions of Public Policy*, Clarendon Press, Oxford, pp. 257–262.

Shennan, I. (1993). Sea-level changes and the threat of coastal inundation. *Geographical Journal*, **159**, 148–156.

Siddle, H. J., Payne, H. J. and Flynn, M. J. (1987). Planning and development control in an area susceptible to landslides. In Culshaw, M. G., Bell, F. G., Cripps, J. C. and O'Hara, M. (Eds), *Planning and Engineering Geology*, Geological Society, Engineering Geology Special Publication 4, pp. 247–253.

Sir William Halcrow & Partners (1986). *Rhondda Landslip Potential Survey*. Department of the Environment.

SMIC (1971). Report on the study of man's impact on climate. In *Inadvertent Climate Modification*, MIT Press, Cambridge, MA.

Warrick, R. A. and Barrow, E. M. (1991). Climate change scenarios for the UK. *Transactions of the Institute of British Geographers, New Series*, **16**, 387–399.

WCED. (1987). *Our Common Future*, World Commission on Environment and Development, Oxford University Press, Oxford.

Wigley, T. M. L. and Raper, S. C. B. (1992). Implications for climate and sea-level of revised IPCC emissions scenarios. *Nature*, **357**, 293–300.

Part 2

GROUND INSTABILITY AND LAND MANAGEMENT

3 Legislation, Policy and Insurance Aspects of Landslip and "Subsidence" in Great Britain

JOHN C. DOORNKAMP

Department of Geography, University of Nottingham, UK

ABSTRACT

Ground instability has become of increasing concern to local authority planners in the UK (through the issue by the Department of the Environment of PPG *14 Planning Policy Guidance Note 14: Development on Unstable Land*), in particular local authority engineers, developers faced with unexpected ground problems, and insurers faced with massive claims by property owners against "subsidence".

The contribution made by geomorphologists in each case has been significant, ranging from the compilation of the National Landslide Data Bank, through specific site investigations, to the assessment of ground instability in the context of insurance.

The way in which ground instability is treated in legislation, in the development of administrative policies, and amongst insurers is defined. The continuing role of geomorphologists needs to be supported by more theoretical research into the identification of marginal stability states.

INTRODUCTION

Ground instability, including landslip, is a "material consideration" in the UK planning process and it has become the substance of legal debate. Since the 1970s both landslip and "subsidence" (taken in the insurance sense of surface movements relating to superficial processes, such as clay swelling and shrinking, that adversely affect building foundations) has been the cause of expensive losses to insurance companies. These factors represent a change in the administrative, legislative and management environments of many professional groups. At the same time, changes in the natural environment appear to have increased the problems faced by these groups as a result of their effects on ground instability. These circumstances provide new research challenges for the geomorphologist.

Geomorphology and Land Management in a Changing Environment. Edited by D. F. M. McGregor and D. A. Thompson.
© 1995 John Wiley & Sons Ltd

GROUND INSTABILITY ISSUES

The Planning Process

There is no one specific piece of legislation which refers solely, or even principally, to the role of slope instability in planning or development control. However, *Planning Policy Guidance Note 14: Development on Unstable Land* (PPG 14), issued to all local government planning departments by the Department of the Environment (DoE) in 1990, clearly identifies ground instability as a *material consideration* in the planning process. As such it can be applied to individual planning applications.

This same Guidance Note makes it clear that it is the planning system which determines whether or not a proposed development should proceed (under the Town and Country Planning Act 1990); and that for certain types of development it is the Building Regulations (as contained within the Building Act 1984) that are used in order to assess the suitability of the design of the building (including its foundations) for safe construction (including design against ground failure). Lest any confusion should exist in the minds of developers, PPG 14 makes it clear (para. 20) that it is not the responsibility of a local authority to investigate ground conditions at any site other than that which it intends to develop for its own purposes.

Development Control

It is the responsibility of the local planning authority to produce *Structure Plans* and *Unitary Development Plans*, which set out strategic planning policies. These may include specific policies for dealing with known areas of instability, including, for example, areas of coastal landsliding and rapid coastal erosion. In most circumstances express (specific) planning permission is required for construction to take place. The decision whether or not to grant planning permission must be made in accordance with the development plan unless material considerations indicate otherwise (Town and Country Planning Act 1990, s.54A). The Town and Country Planning Act, in effect, introduces a presumption in favour of any development proposals which are in accordance with the development plan.

Consideration of Landsliding in the Planning Process

Some of the buildings that have become vulnerable to landsliding were built before planning control was established in 1947. However, it is clear that the planning system has, since that date, allowed building in areas where there are potential problems associated with landsliding. As a result developments have proceeded in landslide-prone locations (e.g. along the coast at Durlston Bay, Dorset, and at Downderry, Cornwall (Coard *et al.*, 1987), and inland at Gipsey Hill, London (Allison *et al.*, 1991) and Brierley Hill, West Midlands (Thompson, 1991)). On occasions this has led to calls for publicly funded coast protection works (e.g. at Durlston Bay) or public funds for the repair of damage to adjacent property (e.g. at Gipsey Hill).

The existing planning system is entirely capable of taking account of landsliding. That it has not always done so reflects the prevailing view that the occurrence of hazards such as landsliding is a problem for the owner, developer or insurer rather than the planner; and the widespread, but false, view that instability problems are difficult to predict and therefore most easily and cheaply accommodated by maintenance and remedial measures in response to damaging events (Jones and Lee, in press).

Within this context there is, therefore, a clear need for information about the nature of ground stability within any area of planning concern. Where development is proposed on unstable or potentially unstable land, the planning authority should ensure (PPG 14, para. 22) that the following issues are adequately addressed by the proposal:

—the land is physically capable of being able to cope with the development;
—the possibility that there may be adverse effects from instability on the development;
—the possibility that the development may have an adverse effect upon the stability of adjoining land.

The general sentiment here is that ground stability should be considered at all stages of the planning process. In this context PPG 14 advises that coastal authorities having jurisdiction over coastlines known to be subject to instability may wish to consider the introduction of a presumption against development in those coastal areas (PPG 14, para. 29). Recent well-publicized cliff failures (e.g. at Scarborough, Yorkshire, and at Black Gang Chine on the Isle of Wight) may reinforce this view.

Such policies clearly need to be supported by surveys of the physical constraints on land use within the area which identify the locations of known sites of instability, and locations of potential instability. The latter poses for the geomorphologist a difficult but challenging subject for research.

Building Regulations

Building regulations are made by the DOE and Welsh Office to secure "the health, safety, welfare and convenience of persons in and about the building" (The Building Act 1984, s.1(1)) and provide a complementary mechanism to the planning system for addressing instability issues during development. The 1991 Building Regulations drew the building industry's attention to the problems that landslides and subsidence may cause to a building and the surrounding area: "The building shall be constructed so that ground movement caused by: (a) swelling, shrinkage or freezing of the subsoil; or (b) land-slip or subsidence, in so far as the risk can be reasonably foreseen, will not impair the stability of any part of the building" (Requirement A2).

LEGAL ISSUES

Under the Building Regulations the case of *Anns* v. *London Borough of Merton* (1978) AC 728 "...established the liability of local authorities to owners or occupiers of premises which were defective because of negligent construction and negligent inspection by the local authority" (Blackler, 1990).

As a direct result of this ruling, insurers and local authorities have paid out substantial sums. However, in an historic judgement, the Law Lords in *Murphy* v. *Brentwood District Council* (1990) 3 WLR 414 (a case which involved consideration of ground stability) decided that their conclusion in Anns was wrong. The details of this decision have been explored extensively in *Building Law Monthly* (1990) and the conclusions reached by the Law Lords have an important bearing on the legal status of decisions made under the Building Regulations in respect of unstable land.

Legal Responsibilities of the Landowner and Developer

Within common law the "natural" rights which protect land from damage arising out of misuse of neighbouring land include *the right of support*, i.e. if excavations on an adjoining property cause land across the boundary to subside then the neighbour responsible for the works is liable for the damage caused.

In *Goldman* v. *Hargrave* (1967) 1 AC 645 the Privy Council decided that in relation to both natural and man-made hazards the landowner or occupier was under a general duty to his neighbour to remove or reduce such hazards if he knew of the hazard and of the consequences of not reducing or removing it.

The case of *Leakey* v. *National Trust for Places of Historic Interest or National Beauty* (1978) 2 WLR 774, in conjunction with the subsequent ruling by the Court of Appeal (*Leakey* v. *The National Trust* (1980) 1 QB 485), provides the clearest statement to date on the landowner's responsibility for a landslide. The case concerns a slope failure in a mound located on National Trust land called Burrow Mump. Natural erosion of Burrow Mump over a number of years has led to "soil and rubble" falling from the mound onto land owned by the plaintiffs and threatening their houses. The original case notes recall that the falls were due to natural weathering and the nature of the soil. In the case notes it is stated: "... from 1968 at the least the defendants knew that the instability of their land was a threat to the plaintiffs properties because of the real possibility of falls from it of soil and other materials."

It appears that the very dry summer of 1976 and the subsequent wet autumn created a new crisis: a large crack opened in the mound just above the houses of two of the plaintiffs. When advised of the danger, the National Trust, the case notes record, replied, "... that, as it was a natural movement of land, they had no responsibility for any damage caused."

A few weeks later a large quantity of earth, and some tree stumps fell from the bank of the mound onto the plaintiffs' property. The plaintiffs accordingly brought an action in nuisance calling for an abatement of the nuisance and for damages. In 1978 the court decided in favour of the plaintiffs but the defendants chose to appeal against the decision.

The basis of the appeal, as recorded in the case record, is: "... that O'Connor J (who had originally tried the case) had been wrong in law in holding that the natural movement of land in its natural state could consistute a nuisance and in holding on the facts as he had found them, that defendants were liable for the natural movement of their land."

It was the view of the National Trust that they should not be liable for any damages caused to a third party by the failure of a slope as a result of natural causes. At the time of this appeal the defence counsel made the point that this was the first time in English law where an owner had been held liable for damage caused by natural processes causing material to encroach on an adjoining property. In reply, the plaintiffs' case was that nuisance was involved because there had been a failure to take reasonable steps to prevent harm to adjoining land or premises once the landowner had knowledge of the danger.

The 1980 appeal by the National Trust was dismissed because the court felt that an occupier of land owed a general duty of care to a neighbouring occupier in relation to a hazard occurring on his land whether such a hazard was natural or man-made. This is a fundamentally important decision as far as landslides and landslide hazards are concerned.

In addition to all of the above there are the legal responsibilities which exist during site development, and the codes of practice which apply to various engineering bodies.

As development on more marginal land occurs it is possible to foresee an increasing number of cases coming before the courts which involve issues of ground stability. These are likely to bring increased opportunities for professional geomorphologists to have a significant role in providing expert evidence.

Unstable Ground and Insurance

Insurance is designed to help to mitigate the effects of damaging events, but it may not do very much to reduce the vulnerability to that event. The basic aim of insurance is to spread the risk of loss over as large a population as possible (that is, the losses of the few are paid out of the premiums of the many).

Several distinctions need to be made in respect of insurance practice. In the UK it is usual for property insurance to cover damage in respect of "subsidence and landslip", though some exceptions may occur such as an exclusion clause which relates to damage caused by coastal erosion. It should be noted that in this context "subsidence" refers to superficial ground movement (for example, as caused by the shrinking and swelling of clays) and not to ground depressions caused by mining or underground workings.

In the UK, insurance related to landsliding is almost without exception taken out as part of the normal insurance for buildings (Edwards, 1988). However, as shown by *Batty* v. *Metropolitan Property Realisation Ltd* (1978) QB 554 CA, there have been cases where the ground may be damaged whilst the house itself remains physically intact and it is not immediately apparent to what extent insurance would cover the situation.

Landslides, though widespread within the UK (Figure 3.1), nevertheless are to be found only in those areas that provide suitable conditions for ground instability (for example, undercut slopes, locally high pore-water pressures, coherent over less-coherent strata) (see Jones and Lee, in press, for a fuller review). In this respect they do not fit the normal condition for insurance that the risk (i.e. ground instability) is spread across all areas with an equal chance of occurrence everywhere.

Landsliding as a process is not amenable to frequency analysis in the same way as is possible with river discharge events, for example. The function of a landslide is to arrive at a slope that is in stable equilibrium with its surroundings. It does not

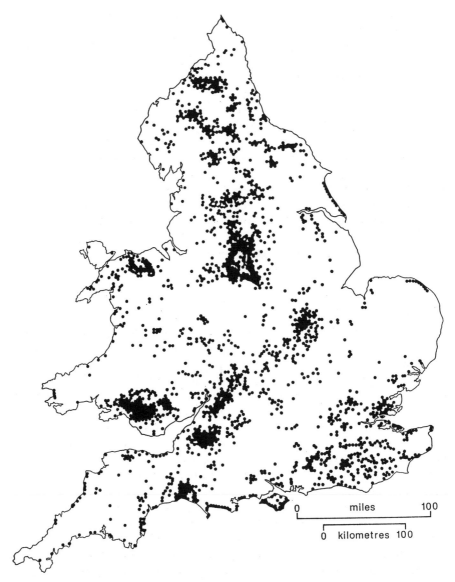

Figure 3.1 The location of recorded landslides in England and Wales (derived from the National Landslide Data Bank prepared for the Department of the Environment by Geomorphological Services Limited)

(normally) have a time-based pattern of recurrences. To this end landslides are not capable of being analysed (in an actuarial sense) in terms of the chances of an occurrence of set magnitude at a defined statistical frequency. Not only is this impossible for single landslides, it has yet to be shown possible, within the UK, for whole areas of ground instability. Whilst the tendency for landslides to be more frequent in periods of heavy rainfall is generally accepted, no one has yet found it possible to attach a statistical frequency–magnitude statement to this.

In practice, the cost of claims for the consequences of ground movement is far greater in respect of clay-shrinkage than it is for landslides.

The average cost of subsidence claims appears to be about £10 000 per property. For example, the Annual Report for 1990 issued by Royal Insurance, a major property insurer, states that the cost of £126 million arises out of claims from about 12 000 properties (i.e. an average of £10 000 per claim).

The processes of clay-shrinkage (and hence the associated experience of property damage) are no more equally distributed across the country than are landslides. They are locationally dependent upon the presence of expansive clay soils. Once again, therefore, there is not an equal chance, across the whole country, of a damaging event occurring. This provides a problem in terms of traditional actuarial practice which assumes that there will be such an equal distribution.

In terms of the statistical magnitude–frequency analysis of clay-shrinkage events there is a closer parallel with river (flood) discharge analysis than was the case with landslides. Clay-shrinkage is climatically triggered (as is flooding) and therefore may be expected to display a degree of predictability in magnitude–frequency terms. The problem, of course, is that these past trends and frequencies may not be repeated in the future if global warming takes place. The statistical frequency of one in 1000 years for the 1975–76 drought may become, over the next 50–100 years a once in 10 years (or less) event (Doornkamp, 1993).

The high cost associated with the subsidence phenomenon, which has been felt by most of the major property insurers, has led to a number of managerial reactions.

Areas which have a high claims record in the post-drought periods of 1975–76 and 1988–92 are now required to pay a higher premium for their buildings insurance by some insurers. They have become disadvantaged by their claims record. A differential premium rating scheme has been introduced by most domestic property insurers in accordance with their perception of the relative risk of clay-related ground movement. The Legal & General, for example, in 1991 introduced six risk zones represented by six premium bands carrying premium rates varying from 18p per £100 insured (for the least risk areas) to 40p per £100 insured (for the greatest risk areas). This compares with an earlier flat rate of 22p. In addition they raised the excess for subsidence from £500 to £1000.

It is pertinent to note that the introduction in 1971 of insurance cover against landslip and subsidence, on domestic insurance policies in the UK, has put additional pressure on the legal aspects. This reflects the desire to recover losses from others involved in the property, whether as builder, developer, designer or professional advisor.

From this discussion it is clear that there are likely to be opportunities within the insurance world for professional geomorphologists to assist in the assessment of unstable ground in respect of insurance claims, and in providing expert evidence in those cases where the manner and cause of ground failure is in dispute.

THE SCIENTIFIC ADVANCES

During the same 20-year period that these legislative, planning policy and insurance aspects of ground instability have been coming to the fore, there have been significant advances in our understanding of ground instability in the UK. Of relevance here are the advances which have increased our understanding of the distributional aspects of instability and clay-shrinkage related subsidence.

The most comprehensive work in this field has been that of the *Review of Landsliding in Great Britain* (which includes the National Landslide Data Bank and a portfolio of 1:250 000 map sheets), and the work currently being undertaken by the British Geological Survey to establish a comprehensive Geographical Information System (GHASP) on ground subsidence based on postcode sectors.

In addition there have been a number of local surveys that have played an important role in providing information to the planning (local government) community. These include studies of landslip potential in the Rhondda Valleys of South Wales (Sir William Halcrow & Partners, 1988) and in Ventnor on the Isle of Wight (Geomorphological Services Limited, 1991).

The research into landslide potential mapping undertaken by Sir William Halcrow & Partners (Consulting Engineers) within the Rhondda has pioneered efforts to translate and communicate the results in such a way that they can be utilized in planning decision-making and incorporated into local planning policy. The local planning authority uses the *Landslip Potential Maps* produced during this survey as a prime source of information on instability. Proposed development sites will be located on the maps and the landslip potential category assessed. Where this process indicates a potential for landsliding, the developer is required to provide a *Stability Report*, either before the application is considered or as a condition of the granting of an outline planning consent (Sir William Halcrow & Partners, 1988).

For developments which require a Stability Report, the planning authority will advise the developer that the report must be prepared by a competent person who is appropriately qualified and has experience of stability problems.

The problems faced by the local community in Ventnor have had to be defined in terms of an understanding of contemporary ground behaviour (Figure 3.2) within an extensive belt of landslipped ground (Lee *et al.*, 1991a,b,c; Geomorphological Services Limited, 1991). The importance of geomorphological mapping (Figure 3.3) to this project cannot be stressed too much. This allowed the framework of landslide units to be established. After that it was possible to relate building damage and movement rates to mapped geomorphological units. There appears to be a strong relationship between the cause of damage (differential vertical and horizontal movement, rotation, tension, forward tilt and ground heave) and a particular geomorphological setting. This indicates that each geomorphological unit identified within the landslide complex has its own characteristic range of stress conditions affecting structures and a characteristic type of damage.

Understanding the geomorphology of the landslide complex at Ventnor has proved to be the key to understanding the nature and pattern of contemporary movements, and was used to form the basis for a 1:2500 scale *Ground Behaviour Map*. This map summarizes the nature, magnitude and frequency of contemporary processes and their impact on the local community. It forms the basis for landslide management strategies that can be applied within the context of a zoning framework that reflects the variations in stability rather than a blanket approach to the problem.

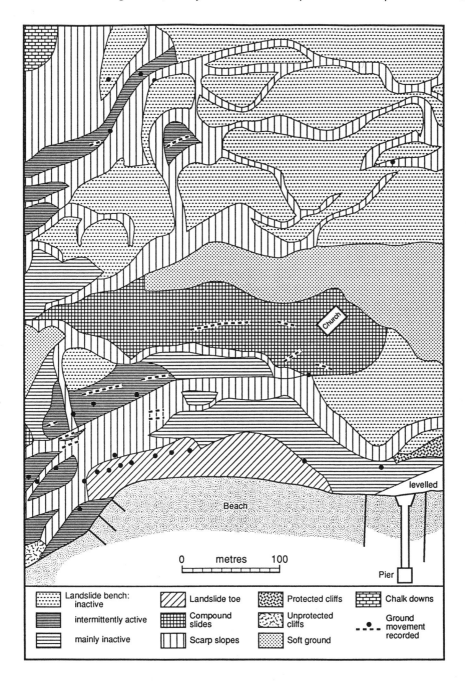

Figure 3.2 Contemporary ground behaviour within a part of the Ventnor area, Isle of Wight (after Lee *et al.*, 1991c)

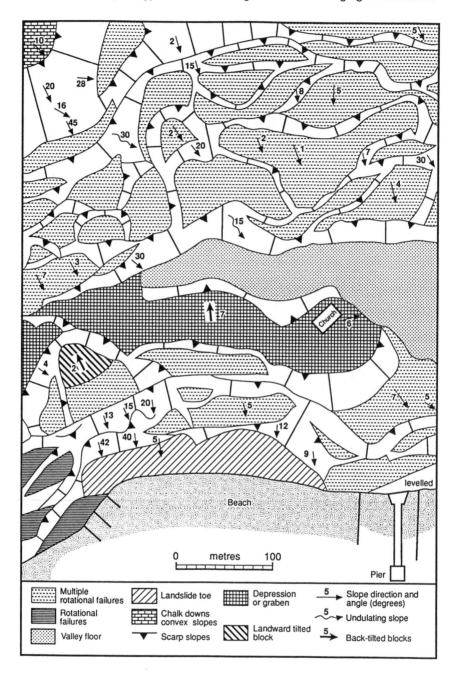

Figure 3.3 Geomorphology map on which Figure 3.2 is based (after Lee *et al.*, 1991c)

During the Ventnor study it was recognized that there were considerable opportunities to minimize future damage to new development by incorporating the knowledge of ground behaviour within the existing planning framework. For this purpose a 1:2500 scale *Planning Guidance Map* was produced which relates categories of ground behaviour to forward planning and development control. The map indicates that different areas of the landslide complex need to be treated in different ways for both policy formulation and the review of planning applications. Areas were recognized which are likely to be suitable for development, along with areas which are either subject to significant constraints or mostly unsuitable.

In a broader context, the Ventnor study provides a useful framework for the formulation of planning policies in coastal areas prone to landsliding, erosion and flooding through its approach to understanding:

—the dynamics of the appropriate physical system;
—the nature, frequency and cause of the hazards;
—the ways in which problems can be best investigated and managed to reduce the likelihood of a damaging event or minimize the impacts resulting from such events;
—the most appropriate ways of addressing the issues within the planning system, to ensure proper precautions are taken to minimize risks.

All of these, either singly or in combination, provide important topics for research.

Within the planning context there is more scope for a geomorphological appraisal of ground conditions, perhaps as a precursor to sub-surface investigations, than perhaps in any other aspect of applied landslide investigations.

OVERVIEW

There are four important parameters at work in the legislative, policy (including both planning and engineering) and insurance arena, as far as ground instability is concerned, each of which is caught up in one or more changing environments. These are as follows:

—the legal/policy/financial environment has forced various professional groups to accept that ground conditions are an important component of their professional activities. *The institutional environment has been changing, and continues to change.*
—the reason why this is the case is that built structures (including domestic properties) are affected by (and in some cases provoke) land instability, causing damage, costs, and a desire for financial compensation. *The man–land relationship is changing where new landslides occur or active landslide sites retreat towards existing properties (e.g. in association with active cliff retreat at the coast).*
—research into ground instability has, from the geomorphological point of view, seen significant advances in the definition of the location of unstable ground and in the definition of landslide systems within at least one major urban area. There have

also been moves to improve our ability to define the potential for further landslide activity. *The scientific basis for the study of ground instability has been changing.* —climatic events over the past 20 years, including periods of intense drought as well as some extreme rainfall events and intense coastal storms, have served to maintain *a dynamic and changing ground stability environment.*

There is considerable potential for future research as a result of the interaction of these key background trends. Some of these have been identified within the discussion above.

The *Review of Landsliding in Great Britain* demonstrated something of the regional variation in landslide problems around the country and highlighted the need to develop improved methods of landslide hazard and risk assessment in order that land instability can be taken into account in land use planning and development decisions.

The assessment of *existing* areas of unstable ground is well within the competence of many (whether they be geomorphologists, engineering geologists, geotechnical engineers, or soil engineers) *once the fact of instability has been recognized.*

What is required at the research level is a greater ability to identify slopes *on the margins of instability.* This is crucial to many of the professions referred to above. Research into slope threshold states still offers ample opportunities. As yet the scientific community has been unable to provide a satisfactory set of guidelines for the recognition of marginally stable slopes. Our geomorphological theory is weak without it, and many others (including those in the legal, planning and engineering professions) need it.

ACKNOWLEDGEMENTS

The formative stages of this study began with a contract from the Department of the Environment (awarded to Geomorphological Services Limited) to Review Research into Landsliding in Great Britain. Since the submission (1986–87) of the reports associated with this project, further work has been carried out, including investigations on behalf of insurance companies, local authorities and consulting engineers. During the course of this work help has been received from a number of colleagues including Prof. R. U. Cooke, Prof. D. Brunsden, Prof. D. K. C. Jones, Dr J. S. Griffiths, and especially Mr E. M. Lee. Valuable advice during many discussions has also been received from Dr D. Brook and Dr B. M. Marker of the Department of the Environment. To all of these I extend my thanks.

REFERENCES

Allison, J. A., Mawditt, J. M. and Williams, G. T. (1991). The use of bored piles and counterfort drains to stabilize a major landslip—a comparison of theoretical and field performance. In *Slope Stability Engineering Developments and Applications (15–18 April 1991, Isle of Wight)*, Institution of Civil Engineers, pp. 347–354.

Blackler, A. (1990). Life after Murphy: thoughts from the battlefield. *Building Law Monthly*, Sept. 1990.

Building Law Monthly (1990). *Murphy* v. *Brentwood District Council*—The judgements and their implications. *Building Law Monthly*, Monitor Press.

Coard, M. A., Sims, P. C. and Ternan, J. L. (1987). Coastal erosion and slope instability at Downderry, south-east Cornwall—an outline of the problem and its implication for planning. In Culshaw, M. G., Bell, F. G., Cripps, J. C. and O'Hara, M. (Eds), *Planning and Engineering Geology*, Geological Society, Engineering Geology Special Publication No. 4, pp. 529–532.

Doornkamp, J. C. (1993). Clay-shrinkage induced subsidence. *Geographical Journal*, **159**, 196–202.

Edwards, G. H. (1988). *Subsidence, Landslip and Ground Heave: With Special Reference to Insurance*, The Chartered Institute of Loss Adjusters, London.

Geomorphological Services Limited (1991). *Coastal Landslip Potential Assessment, Isle of Wight Undercliff, Ventnor*. For the Department of the Environment.

Jones, D. K. C. and Lee, E. M. (in press). *Landsliding in Great Britain*, HMSO, London.

Lee, E. M., Moore, R., Burt, N. and Brunsden, D. (1991a). Strategies for managing the landslide complex at Ventnor, Isle of Wight. In Chandler, R. J. (Ed.) (for Institution of Civil Engineers), *Slope Stability Engineering: Developments and Applications (15–18 April 1991, Isle of Wight)*, Thomas Telford, London, pp. 201–206.

Lee, E. M., Moore, R., Brunsden, D. and Siddle, H. J. (1991b). The assessment of ground behaviour at Ventnor, Isle of Wight. In Chandler, R. J. (Ed.) (for Institution of Civil Engineers), *Slope Stability Engineering: Developments and Applications (15–18 April 1991, Isle of Wight)*, Thomas Telford, London, pp. 189–194.

Lee, E. M., Doornkamp, J. C., Brunsden, D. and Noton, N. H. (1991c). *Ground Movement in Ventnor, Isle of Wight*, Geomorphological Services Limited for the Department of the Environment.

Sir William Halcrow & Partners (1988). *Rhondda landslip potential assessment: Planning guidelines*. Report to the Department of the Environment, Welsh Office.

Thompson, R. P. (1991). Stabilization of a landslip on Etruria Marl. In *Slope Stability Engineering Developments and Applications (15–18 April 1991, Isle of Wight)*, Institution of Civil Engineers, pp. 375–380.

4 Landslide Hazard Modelling in New Mexico and Germany

RICHARD DIKAU and STEFAN JÄGER
Department of Geography, University of Heidelberg, Germany

ABSTRACT

A project to understand the distribution, kind and extent of landslide processes in New Mexico was begun as part of a co-operative agreement between the US Geological Survey, Instituto di Ricerca per la Protezione Idrogeologica (IPRI) of the Italian National Research Council, the New Mexico Bureau of Mines & Mineral Resources, the New Mexico Highway Department and the Department of Geography, University of Heidelberg. New Mexico was chosen because of the joint interest of scientists and engineers in these agencies, because of the paucity of information about landslide processes in semi-arid and arid areas, and because aerial photographs are available for the entire state. A project examining the relation between landslide distribution, geology and slope using computer-assisted methodology is in progress.

Digital data sets of all New Mexico developed by these investigations and a Digital Elevation Model provide an opportunity to explore physiographic and regional landform subdivisions in relation to landslide processes for very large areas. A computer-derived classification of landforms in the entire state has been prepared. The digital method provides adequate patterns for most of the major landform types of the state. The spatial combination with different kinds of landslides shows close relationships to specific landforms. It has been used to derive preliminary spatial landslide hazard models based on topographic information in the entire state.

A similar methodology has been applied to hazard modelling in a landslide-prone escarpment landscape near Frankfurt, Germany. A regional landslide hazard map of this area is based on detailed landform morphometry data. Here, spatial landslide forecasting can be improved by high-resolution morphometric analysis and by time series information from landslide inventories for the last 100 years. Studies in both test areas serve to satisfy the need for hazard aspects in a "hazard, vulnerability and risk" strategy.

INTRODUCTION

This chapter describes approaches to developing landslide hazard models at different temporal and spatial scales, based on two examples, namely New Mexico, USA and south-west Germany, where significantly different data availability and data resolution exist. In both test areas, special attention has been given to the integration of

Geomorphology and Land Management in a Changing Environment. Edited by D. F. M. McGregor and D. A. Thompson.
©1995 John Wiley & Sons Ltd

morphometric factors in the hazard model. The spatial results of our study are landslide hazard probability maps with grid resolutions of 20 and 200 m respectively. A temporal component has been included in the German test area. It includes a rainfall/landslide relationship for the last 100 years using the cumulative departure from mean annual effective precipitation. It can be shown that major landslide activities are coupled with increasing trends of this index.

According to Varnes (1984) and UNDRO (1991) a natural hazard is defined as ". . . the probability of occurrence within a specific period of time and within a given area of a potentially damaging phenomenon" (Varnes, 1984: 10). This requires integration of spatial and temporal models by assessing controlling factors (such as shear strength) and triggering factors (for example, precipitation); and necessitates a maximum of knowledge about the process mechanics. Furthermore, this definition implies that a landslide hazard is based on a physical event which has impacts on the social and economic structures of a society. It is obvious that worldwide there exist only very limited areas where all necessary information to delineate a true natural hazard model in the sense of Varnes (1984) is available.

In the last three decades a growing number of temporal and spatial landslide hazard models have been developed. These modelling approaches aim at the identification of areas with specific probabilities for future landslide events by evaluating the spatial probability for future slope instability (Hansen, 1984; Hartlen and Viberg, 1990). Geographical Information System (GIS) techniques and statistical methods have been used to combine and to evaluate basic data, which are assumed to be direct or indirect causative factors and triggers for landsliding. However, despite high-quality research results, there remain serious problems in prediction quality and in transforming the results into planning and policy practice.

Therefore, following the most recent reviews, existing research is focused on five major topics: (1) the dualism of analytical (site specific) and areal (regional) modelling (Fleming and Varnes, 1991; Hutchinson, 1992); (2) strategies to reduce uncertainties in spatial hazard assessments by including soil mechanical data and probability models into regional estimations (Mulder, 1991; Hutchinson, 1992; Shu-Quiang and Unwin, 1992; Wadge et al. 1993); (3) strategies to include time and landform evolution into hazard models (Brunsden, 1987; Hutchinson, 1992); (4) strategies to apply regional hazard models in planning practice (Styles and Hansen, 1989; Brabb, 1991; Jones, 1992); and (5) approaches to evaluate the objectivity of the data and models involved (Kienholz, 1978; Siddle et al., 1991).

Landslide hazard assessment has close connections to land management and to a changing climatic and human environment. As stated in review articles by Sidle et al. (1985) and Crozier (1986) of the effects of various land management activities, there is a general agreement that deforestation, vegetation conversion, road construction and residential development reduces soil strength parameters and the stability of slopes. However, a proper frequency–magnitude analysis is necessary to quantify the influence of these factors, especially with respect to changing climatic triggering conditions. Despite the lack of sufficient data in landslide research to evaluate a changing climate, even for the historic time-scale, there is some empirical evidence that wetter conditions in terms of higher effective precipitation lead to higher landslide probabilities and to increasing areas of higher landslide potential.

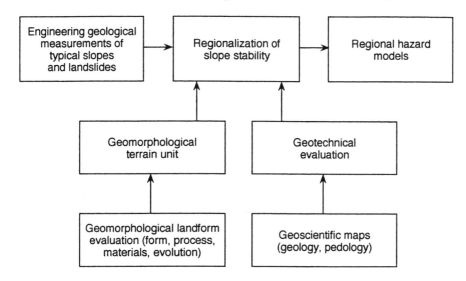

Figure 4.1 Structure of a regional slope stability modelling approach by integrating geomorphological terrain units and geotechnical data

In a situation faced with necessities to evaluate impacts of a changing global climate and increasing human developments on environmental systems, landslide hazard evaluation remains therefore a primary task of applied geomorphology.

Based on these statements we proposed a conceptual structure for regional landslide hazard modelling, which is focused on the research task of regionalization of slope stability (Figure 4.1).

This conception needs to develop a methodology to evaluate regional hazard probabilities using:

(1) the concept of geomorphological terrain units (GTU) including landform morphometry, processes, materials and landform evolution;
(2) geotechnical properties derived from geological and pedological maps; and
(3) geotechnical measurements of typical slopes and landslides.

This approach follows closely a conception published by Styles and Hansen (1989) and Hutchinson (1992). The authors stated that such an approach implied definition of units which will possess an equal probability of failure and similar environmental factors throughout their individual extent. Furthermore, a GTU can be characterized not only by homogeneous spatial properties but also by an equal probability of failure history, derived from geomorphological analysis of landform evolution. Thus, a GTU can be based on attributes of different complexity, which, however, are very diverse in character, objectivity, and spatial variability. Therefore, to reduce uncertainties in temporal and spatial landslide assessment, the key problems of the objectivity and adequacy of the process factors have to be solved.

This chapter follows the conception shown in Figure 4.1 as part of a continuing project to develop a methodology for landslide hazard modelling in time and space. The GTU introduced here is primarily based on landform morphometry. A wide variety of morphometric factors are used in slope stability and landslide hazard analysis, ranging from simple slope angle and slope height attributes to complex patterns of landforms and drainage channels (Rib and Liang, 1978; Cooke and Doornkamp, 1990). Therefore, including landform morphometry in a hazard model follows the hypothesis that appropriate morphometric factors or indices are directly related to mass movement processes.

A second approach to landslide hazard modelling, illustrated in the German test area described in this chapter, is the integration of temporal aspects, that is the occurrence of major landslide events. The approach is based on the assumption that the supply of groundwater is an essential causative factor for landsliding in the basin. Steingötter (1984) showed that five years of precipitation above the long-term annual mean led to the failure of more than 200 slopes in December 1981. However, the relation between precipitation and major landslide activity in the last 100 years showed that the five-year excess precipitation was not a sufficient criterion to explain years with major landslide activity. We assume that the amount of rainfall alone is not a sufficient criterion to assess critical thresholds of the climatic conditions triggering landslides (Crozier and Eyles, 1980). Therefore, to calculate effective precipitation we used the Thornthwaite model for potential evapotranspiration (PET). The moisture balance is derived from the difference of precipitation and PET.

THE STUDY AREA

The German study area Rheinhessen is located in the Tertiary Basin of Mainz, south-west Germany (Figure 4.2) and comprises about 1000 km^2.

Geomorphologically, the area is characterized by cuesta scarp landforms. Bedrock geology consist of clays, sand and marls of Oligocene age which are covered by Miocene marls and limestones and Plio-Pleistocene sand, gravels and loess. In parts of the area this situation is well documented by geological maps at 1:25 000 scale (e.g. Wagner and Michels, 1930). Vertically, the slopes can be subdivided into a sequence of meso-scale form elements of the plateau, convex scarps, straight frontslopes, concave footslopes and the scarp foreland. The horizontal structure shows sequences of spur crests, valleys and small drainage ways of zero to third order (Dikau, 1989). The mean annual precipitation (1959–86) is about 520 mm (rain gauge station Bingen/Büdesheim), indicating the driest region in Germany. The slopes are largely covered by vineyards. Landslides have occurred throughout the basin for centuries (Krauter and Steingötter, 1983). The main causative factor for landsliding in the area is the clay-rich Oligocene material. According to a landslide inventory (see the next section) the mean depth of the slip surfaces reaches about 4.5 m. Geotechnical parameters of the Middle and Upper Oligocene formations show low angles of internal friction ($< 10°$).

The climatic conditions in December 1981/January 1982 caused 200 landslides throughout the basin. The event was triggered by above-average precipitation

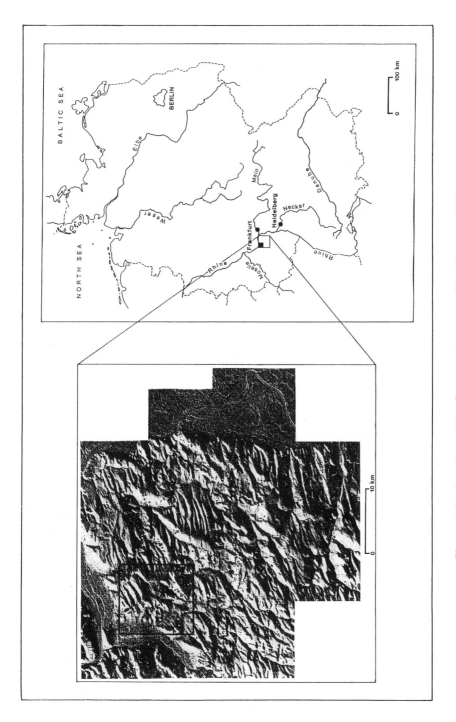

Figure 4.2 Location of the German study area Rheinhessen (RH)

from September 1981 to January 1982, when 22.6 mm fell on melting snow cover of 18 cm from 28 December 1981 to 1 January 1982 (rain gauge station Bad Kreuznach, Deutscher Wetterdienst, Trier).

The New Mexico study area comprises the entire state with $c.\ 314\,000\ km^2$. According to Fenneman (1928), the physiographic classification of New Mexico is characterized by three major divisions (the Interior Plains, the Intramontane Plateau and the Rocky Mountain System (Figure 4.3)), indicating a high diversity of landforms and related geological features.

PREVIOUS WORK

In both test areas previous work comprises basic data acquisition and first approaches to develop spatial landslide hazard models. The physical environment of the test areas is documented in data sources listed in Table 4.1.

In the German test area the first slope stability map was published by Krauter and Steingötter (1983), delineating potentially unstable areas by a manual combination of landslide locations with slope and bedrock geology at 1:50 000 scale. First approaches to transform this model into a digital form using digital terrain models and GIS technologies were presented by Dikau (1990) for a 12 km² test area at the western boundary of the basin. In a further stage of the project we adopted this methodology to a larger area of the basin and included a spatial and temporal landslide inventory into the hazard modelling procedure (GLA, 1989; Jäger and Dikau, 1994). The morphometric model is described in Dikau (1989, 1994).

In New Mexico the development of regional hazard models has been accomplished in several stages. Landslides and features associated with landslides have been mapped from aerial photographs and transformed into a computer-based inventory by Brabb *et al.* (1989) and released in four map sheets at 1:500 000 scale by Cardinali *et al.* (1990). The inventory contains more than 9000 landslide deposits and related features including data which are available from geological and engineering literature and state reports. The classification of landslides refers to Varnes (1978). The inventory contains 24 different landslide types, including 14 types of deep-seated landslides, eight types of shallow landslides and two rockfall types. As stated by Cardinali *et al.* (1990), the inventory resulted from a broad-scale inspection of the state based on 1:31 500 and 1:58 000 aerial photograph interpretation and was plotted on the 1:100 000 topographic maps of the state which were reduced photographically to maps at 1:500 000 scale. These maps were manually digitized. Concerning the uses and limitations of the inventory, the authors stated that the maps are suitable for regional planning and to identify broad areas where landslide processes are or have been concentrated, and where more detailed studies are needed to determine the hazard. First attempts to identify spatial hazard areas have been published by Brabb *et al.* (1989). Hazard assessments based on landslide distribution, geology and slope angle using GIS technologies are in progress. These approaches include methodologies to derive different hazard categories by logistic regression analysis for probabilities of occurrence of deep-seated and shallow landslide deposits on polynomials of the

57

Figure 4.3 Location of the study area New Mexico (NM) (state numbered 4)

1 = Arizona
2 = Utah
3 = Colorado
4 = New Mexico
5 = Texas

Table 4.1 Data sources of the German (RH) and the New Mexico (NM) test areas

Data source	Coverage	RH	NM
Geological map 1:25 000	70%	x	
Geological map 1:500 000	100%		x[a]
Digital elevation models			
100 m resolution	100%		x[b]
20 m resolution	30%	x[c]	
40 m resolution	100%	x[c]	
Meterological records (1850–present)		x[d]	
Spatial landslide inventory		x[e]	x[f]
Temporal landslide inventory		x[e]	
Reports, maps, etc.		x[g]	x[h]

[a]Dane and Bachmann (1965); [b]Brabb *et al.* (1989), USGS (1990); [c]Landesvermessungsamt Rheinland-Pfalz (Ordnance Survey Rheinland-Pfalz); [d]Deutscher Wetterdienst (German Meteorological Survey); [e]GLA (1989) (Geological Survey Rheinland-Pfalz), Jäger and Dikau (1994); [f]Brabb *et al.* (1989); [g]Jäger and Dikau (1994); [h]Cardinali *et al.* (1990).

slope index. The investigation presented in this chapter continues with this work by emphasizing morphometric model parameters.

FACTOR MAPS AND STATISTICAL METHODS

The methodological approach of this chapter has three aspects to it. First, from the data sources contributing factor maps were derived on two spatial resolution levels. Secondly, different statistical methods were applied to assess different landslide hazard categories. Thirdly, time series analysis was used to relate precipitation data with landslide events over a period of the last 100 years.

The major aim of the spatial approach is to use morphometric factors to assess different hazard categories. These factors can be allocated to different scale levels, depending on the scale of the geomorphological phenomena investigated or related to the scale of the model applied. We selected the five factors shown in Table 4.2. The factor selection in the German test area is based on a goodness-of-fit testing using a maximum likelihood procedure. The test included the factors slope angle, relative slope position, curvature, drainage area and lithology. The main explanatory

Table 4.2 Morphometric factors used to derive geomorphical terrain units and to model spatial landslide hazard categories

Reference number	Factor	Number of factor classes	Applied in test area	
			RH	NM
1	Slope angle	3	x	
2	Relative slope position	4	x	
3	Slope angle distribution	4		x
4	Relief (range of elevation)	6		x
5	Profile type	4		x

factors are the slope angle and the relative slope position that have been selected for the hazard model. Factors 1 and 2 have been derived from a local moving window operation including 3×3 grid cells (Dikau, 1989).

In New Mexico we decided to use a regional morphometric classification system developed by Hammond (1964) for the entire United States. The technique used in this chapter to classify landforms and terrain units (the two terms are used synonymously) follows closely the technique used by Hammond. The method involves moving a square window of about 92 km^2 (9.6×9.6 km) across 1:250 000 scale US Army Map Service topographical maps. In each window Hammond estimated three morphometric factors. The combination of these factors could provide as many as 96 geomorphological terrain units (subclasses), which are classified into 24 types and five maintypes. The maintypes are: (1) plains, (2) tablelands, (3) plains with hills and mountains, (4) open hills and mountains, and (5) hills and mountains. This classification approach was transformed into a computer-based procedure using the Defence Mapping Agency (DMA) digital elevation model (DEM) which is now distributed by the US Geological Survey (USGS, 1990). First results and a landform map at 1:1 000 000 scale have been published by Dikau *et al.* (1991).

In New Mexico the delineation of these basic terrain units and their relation to selected landslide types are emphasized in this study. These units are related to a meso- and macro-scale level, ranging in size from approximately 1 to 10 000 km (see Dikau, 1992). In terms of relating landform morphometry to landslide locations, our basic research task here is not to operate on individual slopes. The aim is to delineate higher-order units from local morphometric factors based on the frequency distribution of these factors within a specified unit area.

The morphometric factors are defined as follows (see Table 4.2):

(1) Slope angle: derived from 20-m DEM as first derivative of elevation in a moving window containing 3×3 grid cells (*factor 1*) (classes: $<7°$; $7°-15°$; $>15°$).
(2) Relative slope position: derived from 20-m DEM by adding the parameters height distance to drainage divide (hdd) and height distance to drainage channel (hdc). Normalizing this value by hdd/(hdd + hdc) gives the relative position of each DEM point on the slope with values between 0 (top of slope) and 1 (footslope) (*factor 2*) (classes: 0–0.2 (top); 0.2–0.5 (upper midslope); 0.5–0.8 (lower midslope); 0.8–1.0 (footslope)).
(3) Slope angle distribution: percentage of areas within a 9.6×9.6 km moving window where slope angle is $<8\%$ (*factor 3*) (classes: $<20\%$; 20–50%; 50–80%; $>80\%$; code: A–D).
(4) Relief: range of elevation within a 9.6×9.6 km moving window (*factor 4*) (classes: <30.5 m; 30.5–91.4 m; 91.4–152.5 m; 152.5–304.8 m; 304.8–914.4 m; >914.4 m; code: 1–6).
(5) Profile type: percentage of areas where slope angle is $<8\%$ in either upland or lowland within a 9.6×9.6 km moving window (*factor 5*) (classes: $>75\%$ in lowland; 50–75% in lowland; 50–75% in upland; $>75\%$ in upland; code: a–d).

In the German test area logistic regression analysis has been applied. The statistical method selected in the New Mexico test area is a univariate failure rate analysis.

To derive relative landslide hazard categories based on classes of terrain units, a simple data normalization model has been applied by division of percentages of landslides associated with a particular terrain unit (FDL) by the real extent of that unit (FDA) as

$$FR = \frac{FDL}{FDA}$$

The values can be used to denote a failure rate, FR, indicating the relative importance of this attribute to the occurrence of landslides relative to the entire study area.

The spatial modelling approach in the German test area is based on the landslide locations of the event in December 1991 (Landslide database II; GLA, 1989; Jäger and Dikau, 1994). The New Mexico study includes only the "earth flow and earth slump" landslide classes with more than 1.6 km in maximum dimension. These data have not been classified according to the temporal occurrence of the event, which means that landslides of any age were included in the analysis.

Archive data of landslide occurrence of the last 100 years and climatic records have been used for the present study to assess the influence of climatic triggering factors in the German study area. The precipitation data have been provided by the Deutscher Wetterdienst and are related to the meteorological station Alzey. The landslide data are based on an inventory of the state Geological Survey (Landslide database I; GLA, 1989; Jäger and Dikau, 1994). A principal problem with the archive data used is that the information density decreases with increasing age of the landslide event. This may lead to bias in the temporal data. For this study only data for the period 1890–1990 have been selected.

It is important to emphasize the significant difference between the landslide inventories used. In the German study area the event included in the analysis can be properly dated within a time series of landslide and precipitation events. With the existing data this is not possible for New Mexico, where no dating information is available for individual landslides of the inventory.

The spatial resolution of the data sources is different in the two test areas. In both cases we used the resolution of the digital elevation models for all factor maps, i.e. in Germany a 20-m grid and in New Mexico a 200-m grid. For data storage and analysis we used the raster-based Geographical Information System GRASS. The statistical models were calculated by the commercial computer software package SAS.

RESULTS

The spatial landslide hazard models are shown in Figures 4.4 and 4.5. In the German test area the slope gradient and the relative slope position factor were included in the logistic regression analysis. The model calculates the probability of each factor class combination and the number of predicted landslide locations expressed as grid cells (Table 4.3). In this analysis these locations are related to grid cells of 20×20 m. The predicted probabilities range between 0 and 1 and can be directly expressed as hazard category (low/high probability = low/high hazard category) (see Brabb

Table 4.3 Results of the logistic regression procedure for the German test area. The hazard categories have been classified according to Table 4.4

Slope gradient (degrees)	Relative slope position	Landslides observed (grid cells)	Landslides predicted (grid cells)	Probability predicted	Hazard category
0–7	Foot-slope	34	31	0.000 504	Very low
0–7	Lower mid-slope	44	38	0.001 017	Very low
0–7	Upper mid-slope	10	15	0.000 437	Very low
0–7	Top	12	16	0.000 183	Very low
8–15	Foot-slope	96	98	0.027 513	Moderate
8–15	Lower mid-slope	510	507	0.054 023	High
8–15	Upper mid-slope	202	204	0.023 933	Moderate
8–15	Top	71	70	0.010 181	Low
>15	Foot-slope	0	1	0.019 814	Low
>15	Lower mid-slope	7	17	0.039 205	High
>15	Upper mid-slope	30	23	0.017 218	Low
>15	Top	9	6	0.007 295	Low

et al., 1989; Mark, 1992). However, to get simpler map classes we grouped the probability values into four landslide hazard categories according to the scheme in Table 4.4. These categories are plotted in Figure 4.4, which covers the north-western part of the entire basin (compare Figure 4.1). The rectangle in Figure 4.4 delineates the area of the landslide hazard map published by Dikau (1990).

The results of the New Mexico modelling approach are shown in Table 4.5 and Figure 4.5. The univariate failure rate analysis indicates that only five terrain unit subclasses are significantly related with large earth flow and earth slump landslides. Over 50% of these landslides are located on subclasses B5a and B5b, which are characterized by high percentages of gently sloping land in close proximity to areas with high local relief. The highest failure rate (FR = 39.0) is found in unit C6b, which is a unit surrounding the core areas of the high mountain systems. According to the definition of the morphometric factors (see the previous section) this unit has, within the moving window, (1) 50–80% slope angle of <8%, (2) a local relief of >914.4 m and (3) a profile type where 50–75% of gentle slopes (<8% slope angle) are in lowland. The failure rates have been grouped according to Table 4.4.

The results of the relationship between precipitation and temporal landslide occurrence in the German test area are shown in Figure 4.6. The major landslide events

Table 4.4 Classification of landslide hazard categories based on probability values (compare Table 4.3) and failure rate values (compare Table 4.5)

Test area Rheinhessen, Germany		Test area New Mexico, USA	
Probability	Landslide hazard category	Failure rate	Landslide hazard category
<0.001	Very low	<1	Very low
0.001–0.02	Low	1–5	Low
0.02–0.03	Moderate	5–20	Moderate
>0.03	High	>20	High

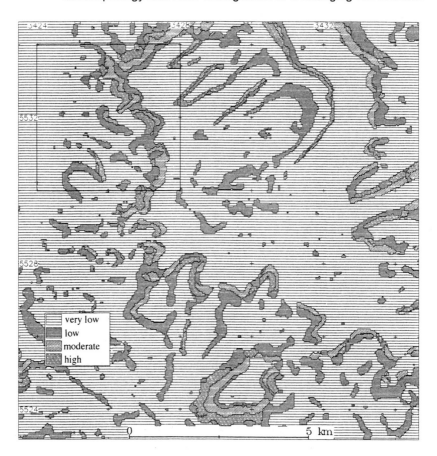

Figure 4.4 Section of the landslide hazard map of the German test area Rheinhessen. Hazard categories are shown in Tables 4.3 and 4.4. The rectangle indicates the hazard map published by Dikau (1990)

Table 4.5 Frequency distribution of geomorphical terrain unit subclasses and selected landslides (earth flows and earth slumps > 1.6 km in width) in relation to failure rates (FR) for the New Mexico test area

Terrain unit (selection)			Earth flow and earth slump	
Type	Subclass	%	%	FR
Plains with hills or mountains (PHM)	A4a	13.2	—	—
	A5a	7.1	—	—
	B5a	10.3	31.6	3.1
	B5b	2.7	23.1	8.4
Open hills and mountains (OHM)	C5a	3.7	16.9	4.6
	C5c	1.6	19.3	12.3
	C6a	1.4	—	—
	C6b	0.2	6.3	39.0

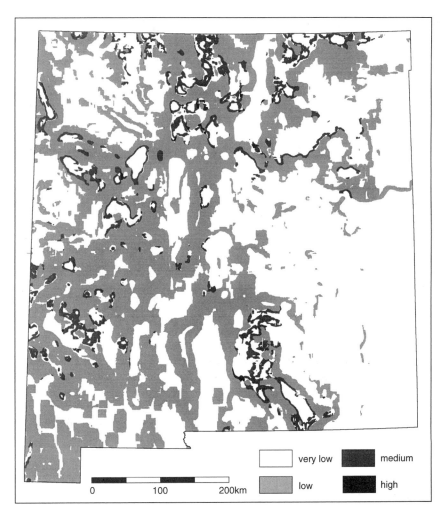

Figure 4.5 Landslide hazard map of New Mexico. Hazard categories are shown in Tables 4.3 and 4.4

are indicated by the bars up from the base of the figure. These events occurred in 1924, 1930, 1941, 1963, 1968 and 1981/82 (December/January). The cumulative departure from the mean moisture balance (CDEP) (solid line in Figure 4.6) and the successive years having a moisture balance above mean (SJAM, bars down from top in Figure 4.6) are calculated from effective precipitation using yearly PET values which were calculated based on daily and monthly temperature and rainfall records. The mean PET value is 661 mm, the mean effective precipitation is − 136 mm, indicating predominantly dry conditions for the period 1890–1990.

The trend of CDEP reflects a climatic cycle with predominantly wet conditions in the periods 1921–32, 1964–70 and 1976–87. Between 1933 and 1964 the long-term trend is negative indicating the dryer part of the cycle. Not all major landslide

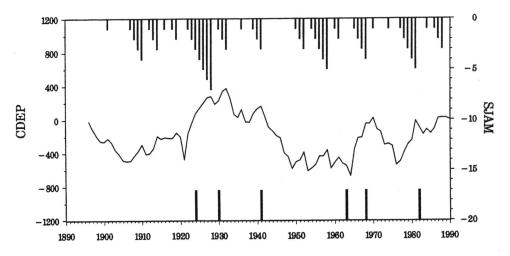

Figure 4.6 Relationships between effective precipitation and landsliding in the German study area Rheinhessen. CDEP = Cumulative departure from mean moisture balance (solid line); SJAM = successive years having moisture balance above mean (bars from top). Major landslide events = bars up from base

events follow increasing cumulative departure periods. The landslide events in 1924, 1940, 1968 and 1982 show a close correlation with increasing CDEP trends, while the 1963 event occurred at the end of the dryer cycle. If we assume that high CDEP values indicate a high recharge of groundwater, the 1930 event can also be correlated with wet conditions, despite the fact that it occurred one year after a decline of the CDEP factor.

DISCUSSION AND CONCLUSIONS

As reviewed in the first section of this chapter, a variety of spatial landslide hazard modelling techniques are described in the literature, ranging from simple empirical methods to complex statistical approaches using different numbers of direct or indirect factors, which may then be expressed as maps. As Jennings *et al.* (1991) stated, the disadvantage of the univariate approach is that it can be rather open-ended because the hazard categories can never be assured of having the optimal solution. Therefore, Jennings *et al.* (1991) prefer a logistic regression model to achieve a prediction success of >70%. However, independently from the modelling approach, a crucial problem in spatial landslide hazard assessments remains the verification of the model results. As Hutchinson (1992) stated, to check properly the true reliability of landslide hazard assessment maps there is currently only one possibility, that is the passage of time; in other words, checking hazard map categories with future landslide events. On the other hand, a statistical model based on spatial landslide data of *past* events could be an appropriate method to reduce the degree of uncertainty of landslide hazard assessments. Therefore, the temporal occurrence of landslides remains a crucial research objective.

As the two spatial landslide hazard maps in Figures 4.5 and 4.6 show, the simple univariate failure rate analysis and the more complex logistic regression results in grouped hazard categories, whose reliability needs to be tested. For this, a statistical model based on spatial landslide data of past events is an appropriate method to verify hazard categories. In the German test area, this topic is the subject of ongoing research.

In terms of relating landslide locations with reproducible geomorphological terrain units and terrain unit factors we applied two different approaches. The German case study relates to a *local* overlay operation of 20×20 m grid cells, whose factor values have been derived by a moving window of 3×3 cells. In New Mexico the geomorphological terrain unit has been derived by *regional* operations based on morphometric factor maps in 200 m resolution and a 9.6×9.6 km moving window operation. Therefore, the two regional hazard maps are different in terms of content and scale of the geomorphological terrain units.

The results of the temporal occurrence of landslides in the German study area correspond well with relationships between cumulative departure of annual precipitation and major landslide activity in California reported by Leighton *et al.* (1984; cited in Wiggington and Hickmott, 1991) and Wiggington and Hickmott (1991). There are indications that in the study area this relationship to the long-term trends of cumulative department values (Church and Miles, 1987) can be used as a first basis for an assessment of impacts of an expected climatic change on the activity of landsliding. However, one problem for the proper application of this concept is the lack of appropriate historical landslide data and their causative factors for larger areas. Further research is therefore of high importance in both study areas, especially through attempts to intensify the temporal components (dating) and by reducing bias in the archive data sets.

ACKNOWLEDGEMENTS

The authors are grateful to Prof. E. Krauter, Geological Survey of Rheinland-Pfalz, for helpful discussions and for providing comprehensive landslide data and unpublished reports. Earl E. Brabb and Robert K. Mark, US Geological Survey, graciously provided landform modelling software, comprehensive data, and the opportunity for an inspiring research stay in Menlo Park, California, gratefully funded by the Deutsche Forschungsgemeinschaft.

This chapter is part of the EC Climatology and Natural Hazards programme EPOCH CT90-0025 (CERG) on "The temporal occurrence and forecasting of landslides in the European Community".

REFERENCES

Brabb, E. E. (1991). The world landslide problem. *Episodes*, **14** (1), 52–61.
Brabb, E. E., Guzzetti, F., Mark, R. and Simpson, R. W. (1989). The extent of landsliding in northern New Mexico and similar semi-arid regions. In Sadler, P. M. and Morton, D. M. (Eds), *Landslides in a Semi-arid Environment: Studies from the Inland Valleys of Southern California*, Inland Geological Society of Southern California, Riverside, pp. 163–173.

Brunsden, D. (1987). Principles of hazard assessment in neotectonic terrain. *Memoirs of the Geological Society of China*, **9**, 305–334.

Cardinali, M., Guzzetti, F. and Brabb, E. E. (1990). *Preliminary maps showing landslide deposits and related features in New Mexico: U.S. Geological Survey in cooperation with the Research Institute for Hydrogeological Protection in Central Italy, New Mexico Bureau of Mines and Mineral Resources, New Mexico Highway Department*. US Geological Survey Open File Report 90-293, 1:500 000, Menlo Park, California.

Church, M. and Miles, M. J. (1987). Meteorological antecedents to debris flow in southwestern British Columbia. Some case studies. *Geological Society of America Reviews in Engineering Geology*, **7**, 63–79.

Cooke, R. U. and Doornkamp, J. C. (1990). *Geomorphology in Environmental Management*, Oxford University Press, Oxford.

Crozier, M. J. (1986). *Landslides: Causes, Consequences and Environment*. Croom Helm, London & New York.

Crozier, M. J. and Eyles, R. J. (1980). Assessing the probability of rapid mass movements. *Third Australian—New Zealand Conference on Geomechanics, Wellington 1980*, **2**, 47–51.

Dane, C. H. and Bachmann, G. O. (1965). *Geologic Map of New Mexico*, scale 1:500 000, US Geological Survey, Albuquerque.

Dikau, R. (1989). The application of a digital relief model to landform analysis in geomorphology. In Raper, J. (Ed.), *Three Dimensional Applications in Geographical Information Systems*, Taylor and Francis, London, pp. 51–77.

Dikau, R. (1990). Derivatives from detailed geoscientific maps using computer methods. *Zeitschrift für Geomorphologie Supplement-Band*, **80**, 45–55.

Dikau, R. (1992). Aspects of constructing a digital geomorphological base map. *Geologisches Jahrbuch*, **A 122**, 357–370.

Dikau, R. (1994). Computergestützte Geomorphographie und ihre Anwendung in der Regionalisierung des Reliefs. *Petermanns Geographische Mitteilungen*, **138**, 99–114.

Dikau, R., Brabb, E. E. and Mark, R. M. (1991). *Landform Classification of New Mexico by Computer*. US Geological Survey, Open File Report 91-634, map scale 1:1 000 000, Menlo Park, California.

Fenneman, N. M. (1928). Physiogeographic divisions of the United States. *Annals of the Association of American Geographers*, **18**, 261–353.

Fleming, R. W. and Varnes, D. J. (1991). *Slope Movements*. Geological Society of America Centenary, Special Vol. 3, pp. 201–218.

GLA (1989). *Geologisches Landesamt Rheinland-Pfalz, Rutschungs-Kataster*. Author Krauter, E., unpublished, Mainz.

Hammond, E. H. (1964). Analysis of properties in landform geography: An application to broad-scale landform mapping. *Annals of the Association of American Geographers*, **54**, 11–19.

Hansen, A. (1984). Landslide hazard analysis. In Brunsden, D. and Prior, D. B. (Eds), *Slope Instability*, Wiley, Chichester, pp. 523–602.

Hartlen, J. and Viberg, L. (1990). General report: Evaluation of landslide hazard. *Proceedings of the Fifth International Symposium on Landslides*, Lausanne, pp. 1037–1057.

Hutchinson, J. (1992). Landslide hazard assessment. *Proceedings of the Sixth International Symposium on Landslides*, Christchurch, NZ, pp. 3–35.

Jäger, S. and Dikau, R. (1994). The temporal occurrence of landslides in south Germany. In Commission of the European Community (Ed.), *Programme EPOCH, Contract 90 0025: Temporal occurrences and forecasting of landslides in the European Community, Final Report*, Part II, Vol. 1, pp. 509–559.

Jennings, P. J., Siddle, H. J. and Bentley, S. P. (1991). A comparative study of indirect methods of landslip potential assessment. In Chandler, R. J. (Ed.) (for Institution of Civil Engineers), *Slope Stability Engineering: Developments and Applications (15–18 April 1991, Isle of Wight)*, Thomas Telford, London, pp. 143–148.

Jones, D. K. C. (1992). Landslide hazard assessment in the context of development. In McCall, G. G. H., Laming, D. J. C. and Scott, S. C. (Eds), *Geohazards*, Chapman and Hall, London, pp. 117–141.

Kienholz, H. (1978). Maps of geomorphology and natural hazards of Grindelwald, Switzerland, scale 1:10 000. *Arctic and Alpine Research*, **10**, 169–184.

Krauter, E. and Steingötter, K. (1983). Die Hangstabilitätskarte des linksrheinischen Mainzer Beckens. *Geologisches Jahrbuch*, **C34**, 3–31.

Mark, R. K. (1992). *Map of debris-flow probability, San Mateo County, California*. US Geological Survey, Miscellaneous Inventory Series, Map I-1257-M.

Mulder, F. (1991). *Assessment of Landslide Hazard*, Nederlandse Geographische Studies, No. 124, Royal Dutch Geographical Society, University of Amsterdam.

Rib, H. T. and Liang, T. (1978). Recognition and identification. In Schuster, R. L. and Krisek, R. H. (Eds), *Landslides Analyses and Control*, Special Report 176, pp. 34–79, Washington.

Shu-Quiang, W. and Unwin, D. J. (1992). Modelling landslide distribution on loess soils in China: an investigation. *International Journal of Geographical Information Systems*, **6**, 391–405.

Siddle, H. J., Jones, D. B. and Payne, H. R. (1991). Development of a methology for landslip potential mapping in the Rhondda Valley. In Chandler, R. J. (Ed.) (for Institution of Civil Engineers), *Slope Stability Engineering: Developments and Applications (15–18 April 1991, Isle of Wight)*, Thomas Telford, London, pp. 137–142.

Sidle, R. C., Pearce, A. J. and O'Loughlin, C. L. (1985). *Hillslope Stability and Land Use*, AGU, Water Resources Monograph Series, No. 11, Washington.

Steingötter, K. (1984). *Hangstabilitäten im linksrheinischen Mainzer Becken. Ingenieurgeologische Untersuchungen und kartenmäßige Darstellung*. Unpublished PhD Thesis, University of Mainz.

Styles, K. A. and Hansen, A. (1989). *Geotechnical Area Studies Programme: Territory of Hong Kong*, Geotechnical Control Office, Hong Kong, GASP Paper XII.

UNDRO (1991). *Mitigating Natural Disasters. Phenomena, Effects and Options*. United Nations Disaster Relief Co-ordinator, United Nations, New York.

USGS (1990). *Digital Elevation Models, Data Users Guide 5*, United States Department of the Interior, US Geological Survey, Reston, VA.

Varnes, D. J. (1978). Slope movement, types and processes. In Schuster, R. L. and Krisek, R. J. (Eds), *Landslides—Analysis and Control*. Transportation Research Board, National Research Council, Special Report 176, Washington, DC, pp. 11–33.

Varnes, D. J. (1984). *Landslide Hazard Zonation: A Review of Principles and Practice*. Unesco, Paris (for the International Association of Engineering Geology).

Wadge, G., Wislocki, A. P. and Pearson, E. J. (1993). Spatial analysis in GIS for natural hazard assessment. In Goodchild, M. F., Parks, B. O. and Steyaert, L. T. (Eds), *Environmental Modelling with GIS*, Oxford University Press, Oxford, pp. 332–338.

Wagner, W. and Michels, F. (1930). *Geologische Karte von Hessen*, scale 1:25 000, Blatt Bingen-Rüdesheim, Darmstadt.

Wigginton, W. B. and Hickmott, D. (1991). The Sargent landslide and the long-term groundwater fluctuations in California hillsides. In Chandler, R. J. (Ed.) (for Institution of Civil Engineers), *Slope Stability Engineering: Developments and Applications (15–18 April 1991, Isle of Wight)*, Thomas Telford, London, pp. 61–66.

5 Mass Movement Hazard in the Garhwal Himalaya: The effects of the 20 October 1991 Garwhal Earthquake and the July–August 1992 Monsoon Season

LEWIS A. OWEN, MILAP C. SHARMA and RICHARD BIGWOOD
Departments of Geography and Geology, Royal Holloway, University of London, UK

ABSTRACT

Mass movements induced both by shaking during the 20 October 1991 Garhwal earthquake and by heavy rainfalls during the 1992 monsoon season in the Bhagirathi and Jumna catchment areas, Garhwal Himalaya, were studied to assess their role as natural hazards. Damage to humans and their belongings resulting from the earthquake was concentrated within villages where building design was poor. Avalanching was the major mass movement process that occurred during the earthquake and during the heavy monsoonal rains, and was greatest in the lower reaches of the valleys where rivers are actively eroding steep rock and debris slopes and where road construction has cut into slopes. These processes, however, caused little damage to villages. Inventories of both the earthquake and rainfall-induced mass movements were used to characterize the different types and distribution of mass movements. The extent and type of damage, ground conditions, geology and geomorphology were mapped in order to produce hazard maps for the region and to identify areas of greatest risk. During the earthquake extensive fissuring developed along the main highway. This was mapped in order to identify unstable areas which are likely to fail in the future.

INTRODUCTION

On the 20 October 1991, an earthquake of magnitude 6.5 (M_b; USGS, 1991) shook the Garhwal Himalaya (30.738°N, 78.792°E; Figure 5.1) and initiated over 200 mass movements. The effects on the population living in the mountains were studied in November 1991 to assess the hazard and to aid in the mitigation of future events. This included a study of building damage and an examination of the characteristics of earthquake-induced mass movements. These effects were compared, during the monsoon season of 1992, with mass movements produced by heavy rainfalls, in order to produce a comprehensive landslide hazard map for the Bhagirathi valley in the

Geomorphology and Land Management in a Changing Environment. Edited by D. F. M. McGregor and D. A. Thompson.
©1995 John Wiley & Sons Ltd

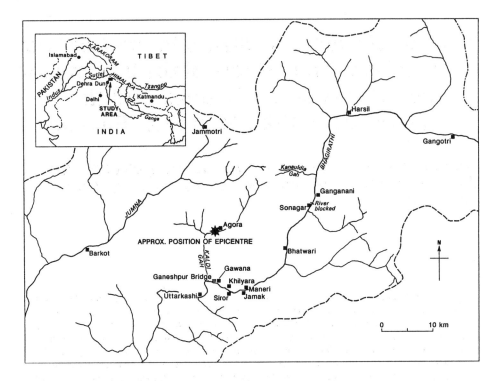

Figure 5.1 The location of the earthquake epicentre, main villages and rivers in the study area

Garhwal Himalaya. The geomorphology of the region was, therefore, studied in order to identify the factors and processes responsible for the calamity. This involved the determination of the extent of the damage resulting from the earthquake, as well as the factors responsible for, and the damage resulting from, mass movements induced by heavy rainfall.

GEOMORPHOLOGICAL SETTING

The Garhwal Himalaya is situated within the Central Himalayas, northern India, in the collision zone between the Indian and Asian continental plates. Two major east–west trending geological sutures delimit the region: the Main Central Thrust to the south and the Indus-Tsangpo Suture to the north (Valdiya, 1988). The main rock types include schists, psammites, phyllites, gneiss and granites. The Garhwal Himalaya is situated within the Central Seismic Gap of the Himalaya region and until October 1991 the Garhwal Himalaya had experienced little seismic activity during the last 200 years (Seeber and Gornitz, 1981). To the west in Kashmir and to the east in Bihar, in contrast, quakes measuring 8.6 and 8.4 on the Richter scale occurred in 1905 and 1934 respectively (Ambraseys *et al.*, 1981).

The mountain summits exceed 6000 m a.s.l. while the valley floors lie at less than 1000 a.s.l. Above 4500 m most of the valleys are glaciated, some of the glaciers exceeding 28 km in length, e.g. the Gangotri Glacier. The region is drained by the Jumna and Bhagirathi Rivers, the latter being considered as the main source river of the Ganges.

The climate of the region is influenced by the Indian monsoon which produces heavy rainfall during June to August each year. The region becomes more arid towards the north because the monsoon is inhibited by the high mountains. There is a strong altitudinal control on vegetation with a treeline at an elevation of approximately 4000 m. There is much evidence for recent anthropogenic deforestation in the southern part of the region. Glacial, mass movement, glaciofluvial and fluvial are the dominant geomorphological processes in this region. These help produce deep valleys, vast thicknesses of superficial sediments and high sediment loads in the rivers.

METHODS

The Bhagirathi and Jumna catchment areas were studied shortly after the earthquake (20 November to 20 December 1991), and throughout the following monsoon season (20 July to 10 September 1992). The area was examined by driving and walking along the main Bhagirathi and Jumna valleys, and by walking along their tributary valleys.

The Earthquake Study

Details of casualties and damage resulting from the earthquake were collected from the local authorities in Uttarkashi so as to establish the distribution and intensity of damage (Table 5.1 and Figure 5.2). Study areas were chosen in which the factors responsible for the varying degrees of damage could be examined in detail. The distribution and style of fissuring along the Bhagirathi highway between Gangotri and Uttarkashi was recorded.

Landscape changes which had occurred during the earthquake were studied in detail. Most landscape changes were produced by mass movements resulting in modification of slopes. Therefore a mass movement inventory was made and the position of each failure was mapped (Figure 5.3 and Table 5.2). Varnes' (1978) classification for mass movements was adopted.

Table 5.1 List of the main information recorded for the fatalities and damage in each village resulting from the 20 October earthquake

Village code:	Village name:
Location. Eastings:	Northings:
No. of buildings totally destroyed:	No. of buildings partially damaged:
No. of fatalities:	No. of large animals killed:
No. of small animals killed:	
Comments:	

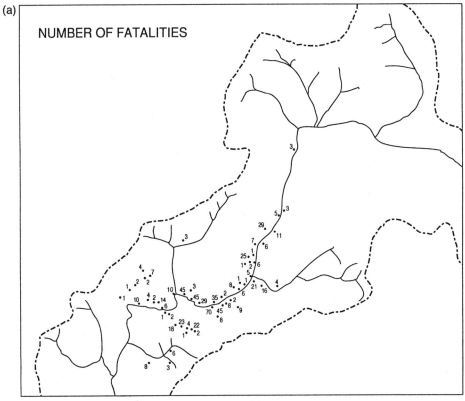

(a) NUMBER OF FATALITIES

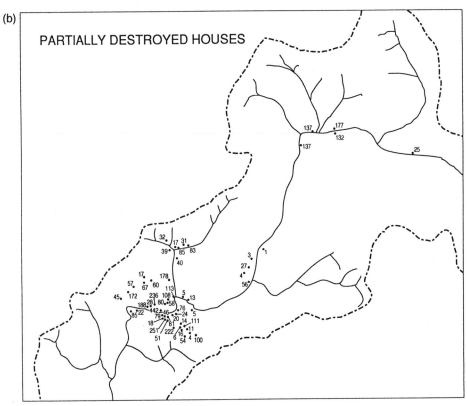

(b) PARTIALLY DESTROYED HOUSES

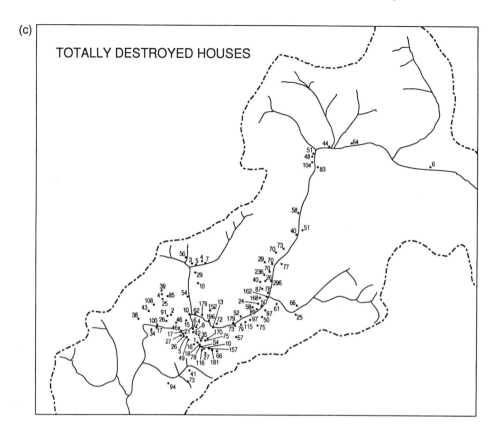

Figure 5.2 The numbers and distribution of: (a) fatalities; (b) partially destroyed houses and (c) totally destroyed houses in the Garhwal Himalaya resulting from the 20 October 1991 earthquake

The Monsoon Study

The distribution of mass movements induced by monsoonal rainfall during the 1992 season was mapped on a scale of 1:50 000 on slopes throughout the Bhagirathi valley between Gangotri and Uttarkashi (Figures 5.4 and 5.5). Care was taken to distinguish new monsoonal-induced mass movements from reworked and resedimented mass movements produced during the 1991 earthquake. An inventory of mass movements was produced to characterize the types of rainfall-induced failures and the degree of reworking of mass movements induced by the 20 October earthquake (Table 5.3).

Detailed geological maps were constructed at a scale of 1:50 000 to provide information on lithology and structure (Figure 5.6). Additional detailed geological information was also recorded for each of the failures in the mass movement inventory (Table 5.3). Slopes were classified using the slope stability characteristics of Crozier (1984) (Figure 5.5) and these were plotted on 1:50 000 scale base maps. The thickness

74

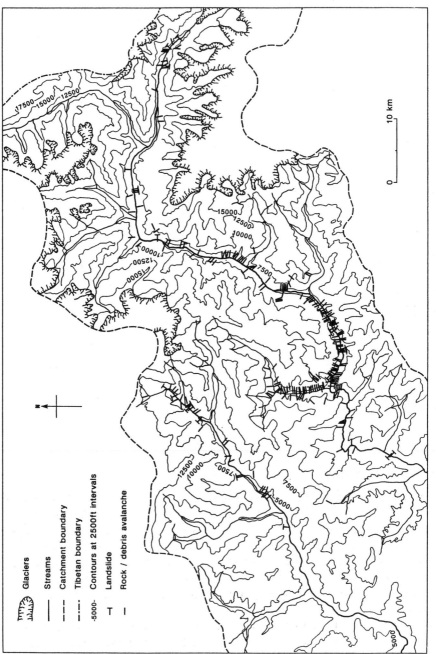

Figure 5.3 The distribution of landslides and rock avalanches formed during the 20 October 1991 Garhwal earthquake

Table 5.2 List of the main information recorded in the inventory for earthquake-induced mass movements

Landslide code:				
Location.	Eastings:		Northings:	
Landslide type:				
Dimensions of excavation.		Width:	Length:	Depth:
Maximum angle of failed slope:				
Runout distance:				
Volume of accumulated debris:				
Does debris reach the village?				
Comments:				

Table 5.3 List of the main information recorded in the inventory for monsoon-induced mass movements

Landslide code:				
Location.	Eastings:		Northings:	
Landslide type:				
Dimensions of excavation.		Width:	Length:	Depth:
Maximum angle of failed slope:				
Runout distance:				
Volume of accumulated debris:				
Does debris reach the village?				
Geology.	Lithology:		Structure:	
Hydrology:				
Ground conditions:				
Vegetation:				
Regolith.	Thickness:		Texture:	Composition:
Human modification of slope:				
Additional comments:				
Map of landslide				

and characteristic of regolith was also mapped on a scale of 1:50 000 using the index shown in Figure 5.7. Figures 5.5 to 5.7 show examples of these maps for a selected area in part of the Bhagirathi east of Uttarkashi. These maps were compiled together with information on the distribution and size of settlements to produce hazard maps at a scale of 1:50 000 using four categories of hazard based on Crozier (1984) (Figure 5.8). A hazard map for the whole of the Bhagirathi valley between Gangotri and Uttarkashi at a scale of 1:50 000 was then drafted which is reduced and summarized in Figure 5.9.

RESULTS

The Earthquake Study

Village Damage

Village damage occurred by the total or partial collapse of buildings. The great loss of life was attributed to the earthquake occurring at 3.05 a.m. when most

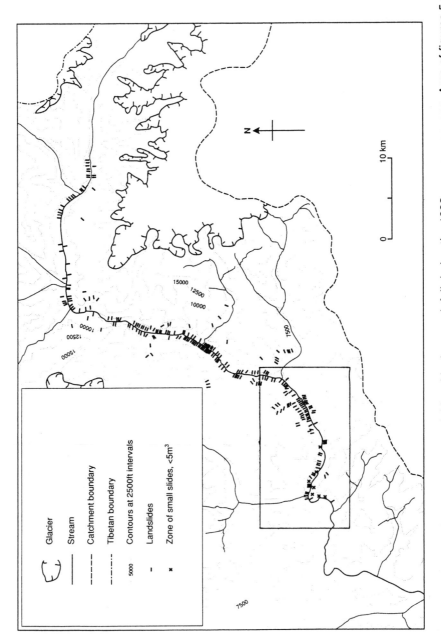

Figure 5.4 The distribution of mass movements initiated by heavy rainfall during the 1992 monsoon season. Area of figures 5.5 to 5.8 indicated by box

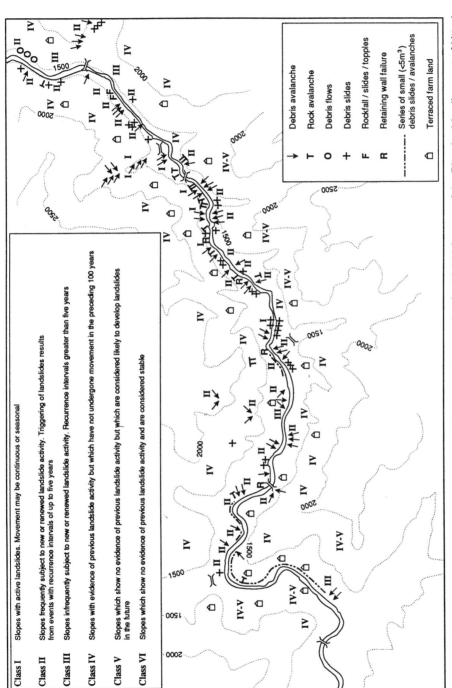

Figure 5.5 Landslide location and landslide susceptibility mapped at a scale of 1:50 000 for part of the Bhagirathi valley east of Uttarkashi. The classification of landslide susceptibility is based on Crozier (1984)

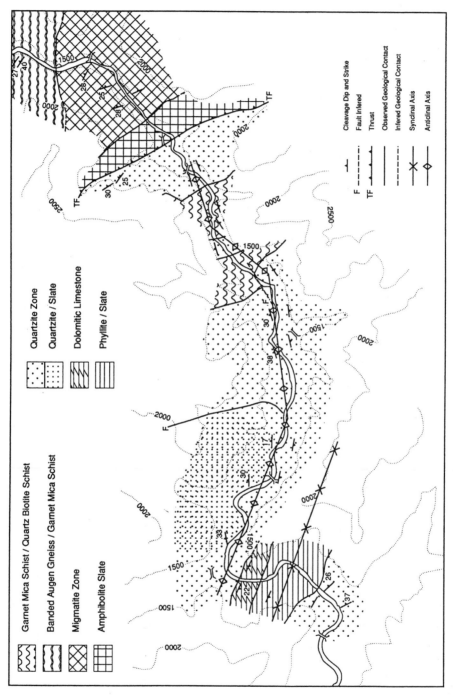

Figure 5.6 Geology mapped at a scale of 1:50 000 for part of the Bhagirathi valley east of Uttarkashi

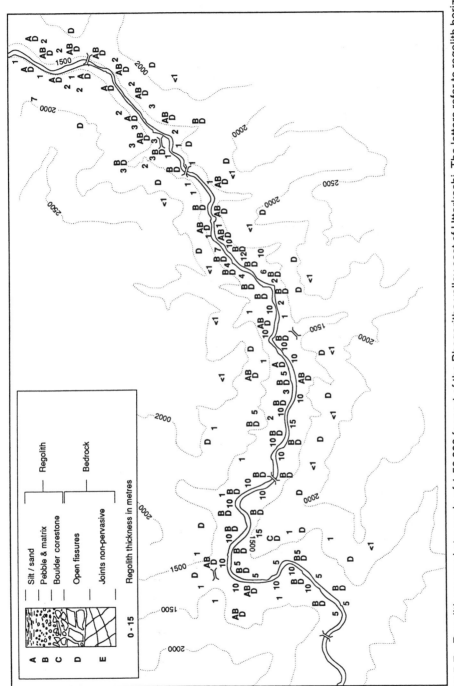

Figure 5.7 Regolith mapped at a scale of 1:50 000 for part of the Bhagaritha valley east of Uttarkashi. The letters refer to regolith horizons e.g. $\frac{AB}{D}$ is horizon A and B overlying horizon D, horizon C is absent

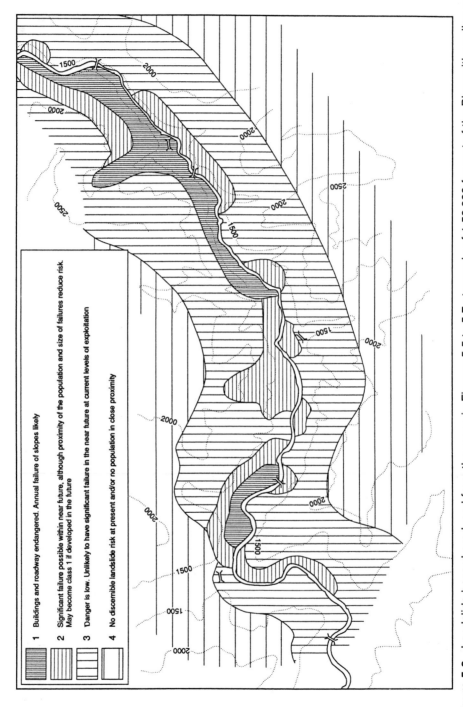

Figure 5.8 Landslide hazard produced from the maps in Figures 5.5 to 5.7 at a scale of 1:50 000 for part of the Bhagaritha valley east of Uttarkashi

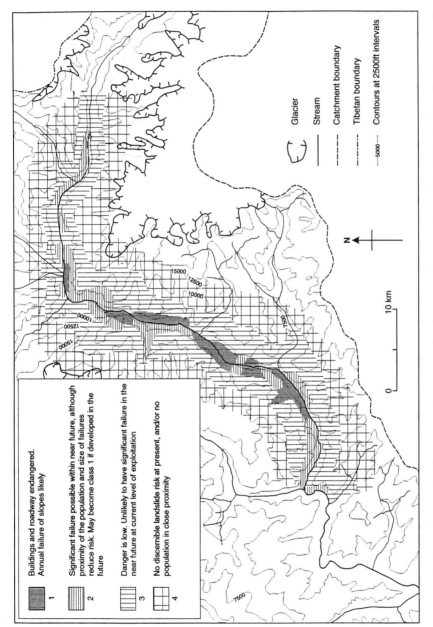

Figure 5.9 Landslide hazard compiled from mapping at a scale of 1:50 000 for the whole of the Bhagirathi valley between Gangroti and Uttarkashi

Legend:

Glacier

Stream

Catchment boundary

Tibetan boundary

—5000—— Contours at 2500ft intervals

1 Buildings and roadway endangered. Annual failure of slopes likely

2 Significant failure possible within near future, although proximity of the population and size of failures reduce risk. May become class 1 if developed in the future

3 Danger is low. Unlikely to have significant failure in the near future at current level of exploitation

4 No discernible landslide risk at present, and/or no population in close proximity

people were indoors and asleep. Many people escaped injury by exiting their houses soon after the earthquake began. Others were not so lucky, being trapped in their homes because doors jammed during the initial motion. In addition, huge numbers of cattle died because they are kept indoors during the cold autumn and winter nights. The dead animals remained buried under rubble for several days and began to rot leading to unbearable smells and the spread of disease. Table 5.4 lists, and Figure 5.2 shows, the distribution of fatalities and damage resulting from the earthquake.

Some villages (e.g. Jamak) were totally destroyed, while adjacent villages experienced little damage. Most villages were built on gently dipping (5°–10°) terraced alluvial fans which are flanked by steep valley sides. Their lower reaches are eroded and truncated by the main river, and form steep cliffs. These fans comprise stratified sands and gravels. These were relatively dry during the month of October when rainfall is scarce and little irrigation is being undertaken. There was no evidence of liquefaction of sediment, but a few small fissures developed on some of the adjacent hillsides. Damage within each fan was spatially random. Fan thickness did not influence the degree of damage—thick fans suffered as much as thin ones.

The main factor influencing variations in village damage was building design and construction. Four main construction types were recognized:

1. traditional designs in small buildings constructed of wood. These are used to store grain, but few people live in these and cattle are usually not kept in them. These structures suffered little or no damage.
2. traditional designs with walls constructed of masonry enclosed in a wooden framework. No mortar is used in the walls; rather, large stones form the inner and outer faces and spaces are filled with smaller stones and sands. The roofs consist of meshwork of wooden beams upon which the thick slates are placed. Vertical and horizontal beams help support the roof. These constructions suffered little damage because the ground vibrations were accommodated within the wooden beams. Partial collapse of the roof occurred in some of the buildings, but was very restricted in its extent.
3. modern buildings constructed of concrete and breeze blocks. Steel cables are used to reinforce the concrete pillars which forms the corners, doorways and beams of the building. The spaces between these are filled with breeze blocks and cement. A concrete slab reinforced with steel wire forms the roof. Most of these buildings suffered little damage, except for partial cracking of the outer layers of cement.

Table 5.4 Summary of fatalities and damage resulting from the 20 October earthquake

Total number of villages:	107
Number of totally destroyed buildings:	6723
Number of partially damaged buildings:	4190
Number of fatalities:	598
Number of large animals killed:	397
Number of small animals killed:	184

4. buildings constructed of a combination of traditional and modern designs. The walls are made of traditional masonry with few if any wooden beams. A modern concrete slab roof is placed on top of the walls. The masonry walls support the roof. This was the least stable design and damage occurred by total collapse of the walls which allowed the roof to fall. This type of failure accounted for the majority of the fatalities.

The villages which suffered most damage mainly comprised buildings of the last design. The biggest centre of population, Uttarkashi, is dominated by modern buildings and consequently suffered little damage. Few settlements were damaged by avalanching, as most were situated on alluvial fans from unstable slopes where avalanching occurred.

Fissuring

Shaking during the earthquake produced extensive fissuring along the main Bhagirathi Highway, but elsewhere fissuring was limited. The extent and style of fissuring was mapped along the Bhagirathi Highway between Gangotri and Uttarkashi to identify unstable stretches of road (Figure 5.10). The frequency of fissures decreased away from the epicentre of the earthquake. Certain stretches of road, however, had very high concentration of fissuring associated with subsidence. These were most common where deep excavations into steep debris and bedrock slopes had been made to construct the road.

Mass movements initiated by earthquakes

Table 5.5 shows the number and size of mass movements identified in the study area. Avalanching, involving both rock and superficial sediment, was the main geomorphological process that occurred during the earthquake. Debris flows and slides were also recognized, but were few in number. The distribution of mass movements is shown in Figure 5.3. This shows that the distribution of avalanching was highly localized, being confined to the lower reaches of the valley where recent active fluvial erosion had produced steep slopes. All the mass movements were initiated on slopes steeper than 45° and most had runout distances of less than 100 m. In addition, there is a negative correlation between the number of failures and the volume of material that failed.

The Monsoon Study

There was no recorded building damage induced as a consequence of heavy rainfall during the monsoon season. Where rainfall-induced mass movements advanced over roads, however, they caused considerable damage to road surfaces and inconvenience to traffic. Figure 5.4 shows the distribution of mass movements along the Bhagirathi catchment. The numbers and total volume of material transported by each type of process are listed in Table 5.5. Avalanches were the most common process, comprising 70% by volume of the debris moved by mass movement processes during the monsoon

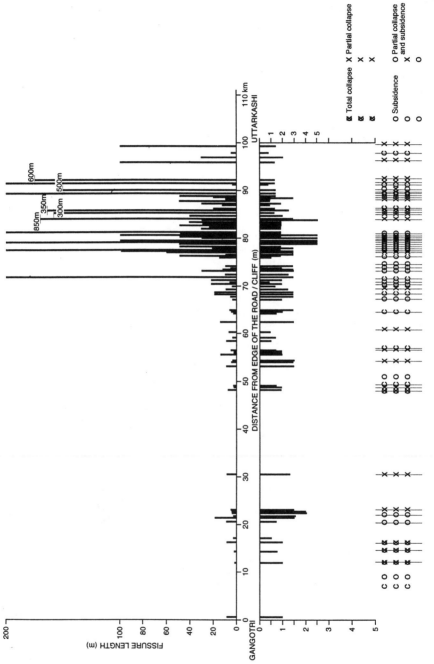

Figure 5.10 The distribution of fissures and subsidence along the Bhagirathi road between Gangotri and Uttarkashi

Table 5.5 Summary of the volumes of debris produced as a result of earthquake-induced rock and debris avalanches, debris flows and landslides; the number and volumes of debris in failures >250 m^3; and the percentage of mass movements that reached the river

Process	No.	Total volume (m^3)	No. >250 m^3	Volume >250 m^3 (m^3)	% volume reaching the river
Earthquake-induced					
Rock avalanche and falls	99	11 073	9	6760	59
Debris avalanches	68	5075	3	2855	54
Debris flows	5	15	—	—	80
Slides	11	345	—	—	83
TOTAL	183	16 508	12	9615	69
Rainfall-induced					
Rock avalanche	79	6914	5	1650	51
Rockfalls	20	590	—	—	50
Debris avalanches	173	8279	6	2650	59
Debris flows	19	1198	—	—	84
Debris slides	69	1455	—	—	58
TOTAL	360	18 436	11	4300	60

season; 23% of the material was transported by just 11 failures (3% of the total number of failures). Mass movements were confined to the lower slopes of the valleys and were most abundant in regions where river and road construction was actively undercutting valley slopes. From Figure 5.9, which summarizes the results from the 1:50 000 scale hazard maps for the Bhagirathi valley, it can be seen that highest hazard is located in the lower reaches of the valley slopes. This is where rivers are actively undercutting slopes, regolith is thickest, the gully density is greatest, and most settlements and roads are located. Failures were most abundant within gneiss, quartzite and schist (Figure 5.9).

DISCUSSION AND CONCLUSIONS

Damage to humans, their animals and property resulting from the earthquake was primarily due to poor building design. This damage was concentrated in particular villages where buildings were poorly constructed. The damage was not related to ground conditions or the distance from the epicentre, however there was little damage in villages more than 50 km away from the epicentre. Fissuring produced by the earthquake was common along the highways and was related to steepened artificial excavations produced during the construction of the road.

Mass movement was the main geomorphological process induced by the earthquake and heavy rains during the monsoon. There was strong altitudinal control on distribution of mass movement processes. Figure 5.11 is a schematic diagram of the altitudinal distribution of processes within the Garhwal Himalaya. It highlights the areas particularly susceptible to slope failure during the earthquake. Avalanching was the most common type of mass movement and its distribution was confined to the

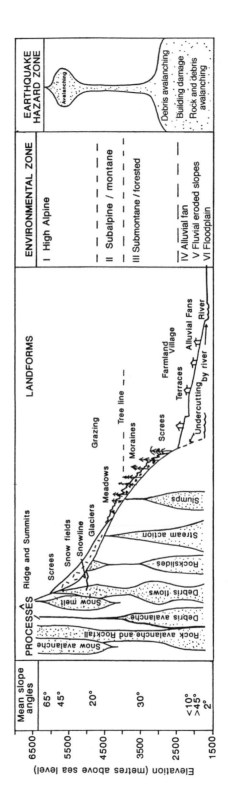

Figure 5.11 The altitudinal variation of geomorphological processes and landforms, and the altitudinal distribution of earthquake hazard in the Garhwal Himalaya. Note that the variation in the thickness of the process columns (stippled) is a relative measure of the magnitude and frequency of the process

steep (>45°) slopes in the lower reaches of the valley (Figure 5.9). Both earthquake-induced and rainfall-induced mass movements coincide with the steepest slopes along the lower reaches of the valley slopes (Figures 5.9 and 5.11). These steep lower slopes are probably the result of recent fluvial erosion. Brunsden *et al.* (1981) noted a similar situation in the Low Himalaya of eastern Nepal. Failures result in little damage to villages because they are located on alluvial fans away from steep slopes. Extensive damage, however, resulted from earthquake- and rainfall-induced mass movements which occurred along particular stretches of the roads located adjacent to steep natural or artificial slopes. Areas of highest hazard occur along the north–south reach of the Bhagirathi where the river is antecedent, active fluvial erosion is greatest and the valley is gorge-like. In addition, there is a monsoon control because heavy rains are less intense in the upper east–west trending section of the Bhagirathi valley.

The magnitude of monsoon-induced mass movements was greater than the earthquake-induced mass movement. If, however, the earthquake had occurred during the monsoon season the ground would have been wet and the number and size of mass movements would have been greater. There is a need for more studies of this nature to compare the effects of the varying magnitude and seasonal incidence of earthquakes. In addition, the results of the study on the monsoonal rainfall-induced mass movements represent only one season's study. Monsoonal rainfall totals, and hence sediment yields, vary considerably from year to year so that this study should be regarded as semi-quantitative.

Future planning and mitigation of hazards should concentrate on the regions classified as high risk (classes 1 and 2) in Figure 5.9. Recommendations for the mitigation of future earthquake hazards should include improved building design, and the location of villages, buildings and roads away from steep rock and debris slopes (specifically more than 250 km away from slopes >45°). A practical solution to reduce failures bordering roads would be to control more strictly the levels of deforestation. High denudation rates make it impractical to reinforce valley sides with buttresses or walks because they are likely to undergo the same mobilization as the country rock and regolith.

ACKNOWLEDGEMENTS

This project was supported by NERC grant GR3/8384. Thanks are due to Justin Jacyno for drafting the figures, and to Edward Derbyshire who carefully reviewed the paper.

BIBLIOGRAPHY

Ambrasey, N., Larsen, G., Moinfar, A. and Pennington, W. (1981). The Pattan (Pakistan) earthquake of 28 December 1974: field observations. *Quarterly Journal of Engineering Geology*, **14**, 1–16.

Brunsden, D. and Jones, D. K. C. (1984). The geomorphology of high magnitude–low frequency events in the Karakoram Mountains. In Miller, K. (ed.), *International Karakoram Project*, Cambridge University Press, Cambridge, pp. 343–388.

Brunsden D., Jones, D. K. C., Martin, R. D. and Doornkamp, J. C. (1981). The geomorphological character of part of the low Himalaya of Eastern Nepal. *Zeitschrift für Geomorphologie Supplement-Band*, **37**, 25–42.

Crozier, M. J. (1984). Field assessment of slope instability. In Brunsden, D. and Prior, D. B. (Eds), *Slope Instability*, Wiley, Chichester, pp. 103–142.

Derbyshire, E. and Owen L. A. (Eds) (1989). Quaternary of the Karakoram and Himalayas. *Zeitschrift für Geomorphologie Supplement-Band* **76**.

Oldham, R. D. (1899). Report on the Great Earthquake of 12th June 1897. *Memoirs of the Geological Survey of India*, **29**, 1379.

Owen, L. A. (1988). Neotectonics and glacial deformation in the Karakoram Mountains and Nanga Parbat Himalaya. *Tectonophysics*, **163**, 227–266.

Seeber, L. and Armbruster, J. (1981). Great detachment earthquakes along the Himalayan arc and long-term forecasting. *Maurice Ewing Series, American Geophysical Union*, **4**.

Seeber, L. and Gornitz V. (1981). River profiles along the Himalayan arc as indcators of active tectonics. *Tectonophysics*, **92**, 335–367.

Selby, M. J. (1988). Landforms and denudation of the High Himalaya of Nepal: results of continental collision. *Zeitschrift für Geomorphologie Supplement-Band*, **69**, 133–152.

Valdiya, K. S. (1988). Tectonics and evolution of the central sector of the Himalaya. *Philosophical Transactions of the Royal Society of London*, **A326**, 151–175.

Varnes, D. J. (1978). Slope movements and types and processes. In *Landslides: Analysis and Control*, Special Report 176, Transportation Res., Board Nat. Acad. Sci., Washington, DC. pp. 11–33.

United States Geological Survey (1991). *Preliminary Determination of Earthquake Epicentres*. US Department of the Interior Geological Survey, Washington, DC.

6 The Landslide Hazard in North China: Characteristics and Remedial Measures at the Jiaoshuwan and Taishanmiao Slides in Tian Shui City, Gansu Province

EDWARD DERBYSHIRE and XINGMIN MENG
Department of Geography, Royal Holloway, University of London, UK and Geological Hazards Research Institute, Gansu Academy of Sciences, Lanzhou, People's Republic of China

ABSTRACT

The Tian Shui region lies between the Loess Plateau and the Tibetan Plateau, in Gansu Province, China. It is a rich source of information on landslides in loess-covered terrain. This chapter considers two recent case studies from the environs of Tian Shui city. Both landslides involve Neogene argillites as well as the thick superincumbent loess drape.

The Jiaoshuwan landslide has been a brickyard quarry site since the Qing Dynasty (19th century), and repeated artificial oversteepening has affected the toe slope. Slope was remodelled during house construction in the 1990s and 1980s. This impeded several natural springs. However, the artificial excavation of the slope materially reduced the safety factor of the slope as a whole. Cracks appeared above the headwall in 1985, and the August 1990 rainfall event accelerated movement to a rate of 13 mm/day. A temporary retaining wall has acted as a "stay of execution" as works continue in an effort to minimize the effect of this threatening slide upon a densely-packed urban area.

Urban expansion in the Taishanmiao slide area has also led to modification of the original slope (itself part of an ancient landslide). Slight deformation was noted in 1985 but, following the August 1990 rains, many houses and one factory showed material damage; and by October 1990 the movement rate had reached maxima of 17 mm/hour and 77 mm/day.

The basic reason for the reactivation of the Jiaoshuwan landslide is human modification of the slope and its drainage. The Taishanmiao slide is also substantially the product of human action, but the ambient groundwater situation here is much closer to critical. Both slides were ultimately triggered by the same rainfall event, and both pose formidable problems in terms of mitigation strategies, some of which are described.

Geomorphology and Land Management in a Changing Environment. Edited by D. F. M. McGregor and D. A. Thompson.
©1995 John Wiley & Sons Ltd

INTRODUCTION

The western margin of the Loess Plateau of China in eastern Gansu Province is a mountainous bedrock landscape mantled by loess of Quaternary age which varies in thickness by more than 300 m. The combination of steep slopes, variable but frequently very heavy summer monsoonal rains, seismic activity, and a loess mantle which is metastable to varying degrees, makes the two principal cities of Gansu Province, Lanzhou and Tian Shui, two of the most seriously landslide-threatened cities in China (Figure 6.1).

Gansu Province is mountainous, about three-quarters of its total area of 400 000 km^2 lying above the 1000 m contour. The sites of more than 40 000 landslides are known, the area affected making up about 27% of the total area of the Province (Figure 6.2). Landslides have been the cause of many serious disasters affecting the human population over many centuries (Wang and Derbyshire, 1988; Wang et al., 1991). The Tian Shui region lies in the sub-humid/semi-arid transition. Mean annual temperature is 10 °C, annual precipitation is 580 mm, with an average potential evaporation of 1294 mm, and there is, therefore, a considerable moisture deficit. Up to 70% of the annual precipitation is usually concentrated in the months June to September (Figure 6.3). Moreover, according to the records for the past 40 years, the maximum daily and hourly precipitation occurs in July and August and may make up to 65% of the annual total (data from Tian Shui Meteorological Station).

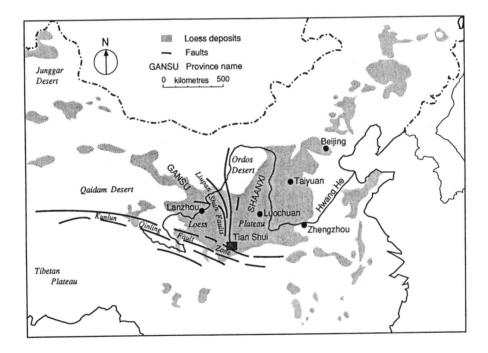

Figure 6.1 Distribution of thick loess (> 10 m) and Helan Shan and Liupan Shan–Qinling fault zones in central and northern China

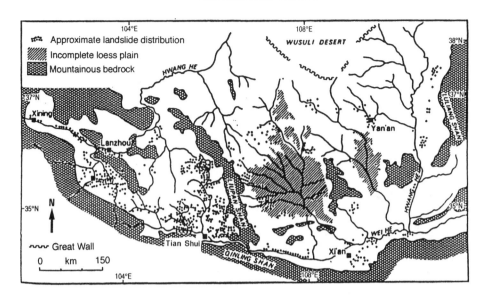

Figure 6.2 Distribution of landslides in Gansu Province (after Derbyshire *et al.*, 1991)

The landscape around Tian Shui is characterized by high loess-covered ridges ("liang" in Chinese), loess-draped hills, and deep valleys (Figure 6.4). The city is built on a series of river terraces of the Wei River (principal tributary of the Yellow River) and the Qi River (which flows into the Wei). These terraces are confined within a narrow east–west structural basin with an overall gradient towards the east. To the

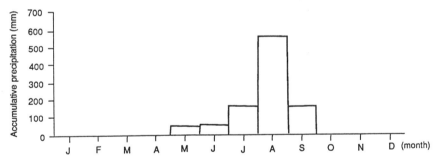

Accumulative precipitation of rain storms (⩾25 mm) between 1950s and 1980s

Figure 6.3 Accumulative precipitation of rain storms in Tian Shui region between 1950s and the 1980s (data from the Tian Shui Meteorological Station)

north and south are mountains with altitudes of 1300–1600 m, while the lowest river terraces lie at 1100–1200 m, i.e. relative relief is of the order of 200–400 m. The mountain slopes range in steepness from 15 ° to 40 °.

With the great rise in population and the development of industry and agriculture in recent decades, the pressure on land for crop production and industry has greatly

Figure 6.4 Gorge of the Wei River just north of Tian Shui city, showing thick loess cover and recent landslide in loess

increased. In order to secure a livelihood, the local people have had to excavate slopes and cut down trees so as to make space for houses and arable land which, in some places, is irrigated. Such activities have changed the dynamic equilibrium on slopes, and added to the serious landsliding activity which occurs under natural conditions. This chapter presents a case study of two typical landslides in Tian Shui city (second city of the Gansu Province, with a population in excess of one million) which were caused essentially by a combination of human activity and heavy rainfall.

THE 1990 SLIDE EVENTS

On 11 August 1990, a heavy rainstorm occurred at Tian Shui. A total of 107 mm of rain fell in two and a half hours, giving rise to floods, debris flows and landslides. Some 22 people were killed, and substantial economic losses were incurred in this very poor region, the total estimate being 50 million Chinese yuan (about £5 million). One of the most serious failures occurred above a factory which makes structural steel. Here, the foot of the slope had been excavated during the construction of the factory, and the gentle surface at the top of the slope had been under channel irrigation for many years. The landslide movement occurred within only a few seconds, destroying six large workshops and killing seven people. Normally more than 300 people worked in the plant but most escaped because, just prior to the slope collapse, the electrical power supply to the factory had been inadvertently cut, so that almost all the workers had gone back to their homes (Derbyshire, 1992). Less spectacular, but much more widespread, are many sites, including ancient landslides, which have the potential for reactivation during heavy rainfall events, especially where slopes have been modified by human action. Many of the slopes around Tian Shui, in fact, are made up of surfaces of multiple slide events ranging in age from a few years to several thousand years.

The two case studies considered here are particularly hazardous situations because they are located very close to the centre of the city. Both are sites of relict landslides, the Taishanmiao slide having been triggered by the earthquake of AD 1654 which had a magnitude of 8 (Richter) (Tian Shui Annals). Both landslide sites became an increasing threat as a result of excavation of the base of the old slide masses in the process of extending the area available for dwelling houses. One important effect of this was to impede the groundwater exits when constructing house foundations. The violent rainfall event in August 1990 caused a rapid rise in the groundwater table of 2–4 m and the two old landslides began to move. Initial movement was very slow but by October of 1990 it had become quite rapid, the maximum rate recorded being 77 mm/day (unpublished records of the Geological Hazards Research Institute, Gansu Academy of Sciences). This points to the gradual softening of the slide material under the action of groundwater. It was noted that the cracks above the backwall had extended to the flanks of the slide and the bulging and thrust shears at the toe of both slides were more prominent. It was evident that were the two landslides to accelerate suddenly, over 2000 local residents would be threatened. As a short-term measure during November 1990, two temporary retaining walls consisting of boulders were built at the toe of both landslides, and several drainage wells were dug across the slide masses by the Geological Hazards Research Institute (GHRI). These measures reduced the rate of movement to about 1 mm/day, and thus provided valuable time for more ambitious remedial work to be planned and executed. Detailed engineering geological surveys were then undertaken, including series mapping (1:2000 and 1:500 scale maps of topography, engineering geology, groundwater level and landslide deformation), 27 boreholes, the excavation of 37 inspection wells with an average depth of 7 m, soil mechanical tests, and water chemical analyses. To control the landslides a construction plan was then designed by the team of GHRI, in consultation with the senior author and a team working under a European Community contract. The construction was handled by the Tian Shui No. 1 and No. 2 construction companies. This plan was successfully implemented by June 1992, at a cost of 6 million Chinese yuan (about £600 000). The event is noteworthy, because it is the first time any local government body in Gansu Province has spent so much money in an attempt to control landslides.

MATERIAL AND ENVIRONMENTAL CHARACTERISTICS AFFECTING THE JIAOSHUWAN AND TAISHANMIAO LANDSLIDES

Tian Shui city is situated at the junction of the east–west Qinling fault system and north–south Helan Shan–Liupan Shan fault structures (Figure 6.1). Since the Lower Pleistocene, the Qinling fault system has been very active with evidence of uplift of

the Qinling Mountains by as much as 2700–3200 m, at an average rate of
1.4–1.6 mm/year (Gansu Geological Bureau, 1985). The bedrock, which is mainly
Neogene argillite, has been folded and severely shattered. Neotectonic movements
are still active in the Tian Shui area. Since the beginning of written records, 52
earthquakes with magnitudes of over 6 (Richter) have been recorded. The average
rate of uplift of the Tian Shui area has been estimated at 0.6–0.8 mm/year (Gansu
Seismic Bureau, 1987).

The Jiaoshuwan and Taishanmiao landslides lie on the southern and north-eastern
slopes, respectively, of Fengjia Mountain (1438 m), a ridge (Chinese: "*liang*") situated
immediately north of the centre of Tian Shui city (Figure 6.5). The strikes of the
two slopes are NE67 ° and NW42 ° respectively. The second terrace of the Qi River
lies at 1178 m, so that the relative relief hereabouts is 250 m. Slope steepness ranges
between 10 ° and 30 °. Fengjia Mountain is made up of Upper Pleistocene Malan
loess and Middle Pleistocene Lishi loess resting on Neogene lacustrine argillites (the
red clay). Some small thrust faults and folds are present within the area affected by

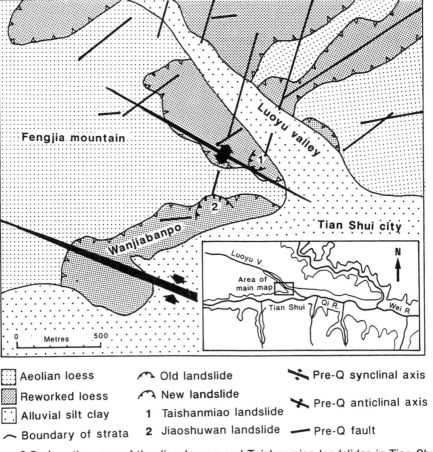

Figure 6.5 Location map of the Jiaoshuwan and Taishanmiao landslides in Tian Shui
city, Gansu Province

landslides. Specifically, one fold which affects the argillite (the "Taishanmiao fold") has clearly influenced the Taishanmiao landslide, the axis of which runs in a north-westerly direction. Some of the faulted bedding planes in the argillite are of neotectonic origin and, with a strike of NE19 °–30 °, they differ significantly from those due to the landslide movement. The Jiaoshuwan and Taishanmiao slides are located on the western and the eastern limbs of the Taishanmiao fold, respectively.

Malan loess, with an average thickness of 10 m, caps the mountain. It is characterized by a loose fabric, with large voids ratios (0.90–1.12), a high coefficient of collapsibility (0.13) and low bulk densities (mean: 1.45 g/cm^3). The natural moisture content is around 17%. The underlying Lishi loess is jointed and contains several palaeosols. Bulk densities are around 1.7 g/cm^3 and natural moisture contents range up to 20%. The Neogene lacustrine argillite is red-brown and grey-green in colour and is often intercalated with several units of grey-white sandy clay, characterized by relatively high bulk densities (mean: 2.10 g/cm^3), a high plasticity index ($I_p > 17$) and low shear strengths, as well as extensive joint systems. This argillite is widespread in the Tian Shui area. It is rich in illite and smectite, the mechanical properties of which make it susceptible to slope failure. When saturated, it displays very low strength, but it is very hard when dry. The local people describe it as "dry like knife, wet like cream". The upper 1–2 m of the argillite is usually weathered, so that shear strengths are much lower (residual internal friction angle 7 ° and cohesion 0.5 kPa).

CHARACTERISTICS OF LANDSLIDES

Jiaoshuwan

On the south slope of Fengjia mountain there is a series of loess landslides of different ages, amongst which the relict Jiaoshuwan–Wangjiabanpo slide is the largest, with a length of 200 and a width of 900 m (Figure 6.6). The Jiaoshuwan landslide of 1990 was a reactivated part of an old slide, the slide area having been 23 000 m^2 (length 150 m, width 170 m). With a backwall altitude of 1247 m and a toe at 1204 m, the relative relief is 43 m. The average thickness of the slide mass was 16 m, and the mean slope angle 18 °. It mainly consists of loess and some 1–5 m of shattered argillite caused by former landslide movements. The loess in the upper part of the slide mass is much looser than *in situ* loess, and contains many fissures and cracks, some of which are striated. Moisture contents in the loess increase from top to bottom. Loessic silts are mixed with the shattered argillite, and brecciated into random-shaped fragments, some with striae and polished surfaces. The shattered argillite reaches a maximum thickness of 5 m near the toe of the landslide, and gradually thins towards the backwall. This indicates that the shattered argillite was disrupted and mixed with the loess as it moved along the surface of the bedrock. The toe of the landslide now rests on top of the second terrace of the Qi River (Figure 6.7).

The main slip surface is located at the bottom of the shattered argillite, indicating that the 1990 slide utilized an old shear zone, some 5–20 cm thick, consisting of grey-green, yellow-grey and red-brown clays. In boreholes and pits the shear zone material is in a condition ranging from plastic to saturated. Groundwater levels do not coincide

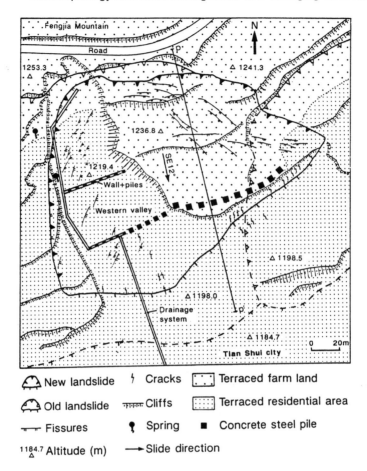

Figure 6.6 Reactivated area of the Jiaoshuwan landslide and the major controlling structures. p–p' is the cross-section shown in Figure 6.7

with the slip surfaces to any significant degree. The slip surface has been determined over a wide area, its striae striking at SE12 ° and dipping at 13 °.

On the western part of the landslide there is a 40–70 m wide step-shaped valley caused by artificial excavation in recent decades. The average thickness of the slide mass in the valley is 6 m, made up of artificially-infilled loessic silts (of house foundations), loess, and fragmented argillite. The slip surface has not here been affected by human activity.

Beginning with the rainy season of 1985, fissures began to develop above the backwall of the reactivated landslide and continued to enlarge. The whole slide mass appears to have subsided by approximately 0.7 m between 1985 and 1990. The rainstorm of 11 August 1990 accelerated the movement to a maximum rate of 13 m long and 0.3 m wide. All the deformation phenomena strongly suggest that the landslide had reached a critical condition. Only the temporary retaining wall (November 1990) delayed the potential catastrophe.

97

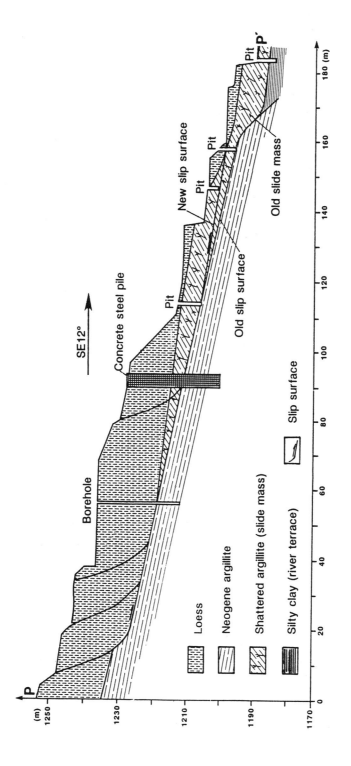

Figure 6.7 Cross-section of the Jiaoshuwan landslide

Taishanmiao

The Taishanmiao landslide, located on the west side of the Luoyu valley, has been a hazardous location for many centuries, having repeatedly suffered from irregular floods and mud flows along the Luoyu valley. Excavation of the slopes since the 1960s as part of a programme to build houses for the burgeoning local population included the cutting of a series of large steps in the slope. Thousands of people now live there. In addition, a heavily-used main road was constructed across the middle part of the landslide. Thus the morphology of the old landslide has been completely altered. This posed some difficulties during the investigation of the landslide, especially with respect to determination of the exact outline of the slide and location of boreholes at optimal locations.

The relict landslide is 110 m long and 1600 m wide, with an average surface slope of 15 °, a relative relief of 30 m, an average slide mass thickness of 6 m, and a slide direction of NE58 °. There are two slip surfaces within the landslide, one on the contact surface between loess and argillite, and the other along the bedding planes within the argillite. Thus, two potential surfaces of movement are present, one on the surface of the bedrock and one below this surface.

In 1985, slight deformation, fissuring and tilting of house walls were reported. The small scale of the features, however, caused little concern. During the severe storm of August 1990, the landslide began to move retrogressively. The maximum area of

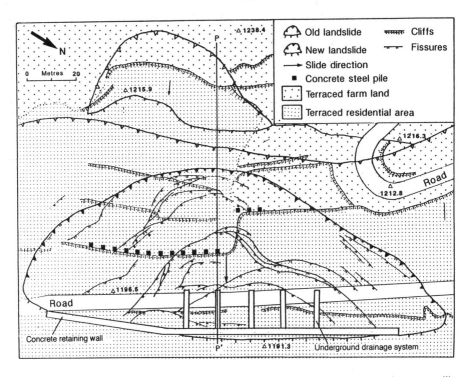

Figure 6.8 Reactivated area of the Taishanmiao landslide and the major controlling structures. p–p′ is the cross-section shown in Figure 6.9

deformation was about 10 000 m² (length 67 m, width 176 m: Figure 6.8). Within the reactivated landslide area all domestic premises and the workshops of the Tian Shui Electricity Equipment Factory were damaged. In October 1990 the slide accelerated to 17 mm/hour. Many people were now threatened and the potentially numerous (several hundred) refugees were at risk of being without shelter.

The reactivated Taishanmiao landslide consisted of infilled loessic silt, loess and shattered argillite. The artificial fill materials, 0.5–3 m thick, included loessic silt, bricks and human rubbish. Underneath the surface fill of loessic silts is 3–4 m of loess: it is loose and homogeneous and contains many landslide-induced fissures. Argillite, brecciated by landsliding to a depth of 1–4 m, makes up the lower part of the slide mass (Figure 6.9). Some blocks are striated and polished.

The slip surface reactivated in August 1990 was the second of the relict slip surfaces (situated within the shattered argillite). With a gradient of 16 ° and a strike (measured from striae on the slip surface) of NE57 °–59 °, the failure zone was found to be 10–30 thick and to consist mainly of clay, of which the natural moisture content was around 25%.

According to the movement gauges set up inside the inspection pits by the GHRI team between September and December 1990, there was no perceptible movement along the first slip surface (contact plane between loess and bedrock). This was because the shattered argillite had been saturated by groundwater, and the outcrop of the second slip surface (at the toe of the landslide) had been cut by mechanical excavation. Thus the whole slide mass, made up of both loess and shattered argillite, was induced to move. Data from monitoring gauges show that the Taishanmiao landslide was a typical retrogressive landslide.

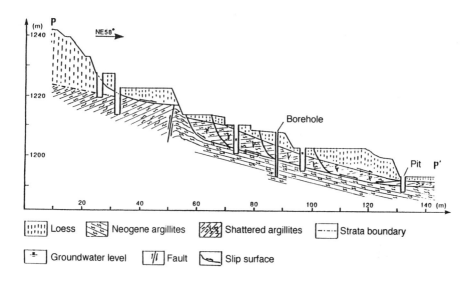

Figure 6.9   Cross-section of the Taishanmiao landslide

LANDSLIDE CONTROL

Tian Shui is one of the most earthquake-susceptible areas of Gansu Province. During the three-month field work period, starting on 16 September 1990, on which this chapter is based, three earthquakes with a magnitude of over 3 (Richter) were recorded; although the monitoring records suggest that they had no perceptible effect on the two landslides. It is for this reason that all control designs at these two sites include provision for earthquakes with magnitudes of up to 8 (Richter).

Landslide Control at Jiaoshuwan

Given that the principal reason for the reactivation of the landslides was human excavation and blocking of groundwater exits, the control design measures included the following.

1. A row of 10 concrete and steel piles was built at the toe of the landslide to resist the sliding forces, the size of individual piles ranging between $4 \times 4 \times 27$ m and $4 \times 4 \times 11$ m (Figure 6.8).
2. An underground drainage system with a cross-section of 2×5 m and a length of 129 m was set up in the middle of the western valley of the landslide where groundwater was concentrated (Figure 6.10). The drainage trenches were filled with boulders, and filter layers placed on their flanks, consisting of pebbles on the outside, coarse sands in the middle and fine sands in the core. The bottom of the drainage trenches are lined with concrete and are cut below the slip surface.

Figure 6.10 One major trench (right of centre) making up part of the drainage system in the middle of the western valley of the Jiaoshuwan landslide, April 1992

This drainage serves not only to reduce the water content in the slide mass but also to create a resistance against the sliding forces.

3. In order to avoid secondary slides in the western valley, two relatively small rows of concrete steel piles combined with retaining concrete walls were installed. At the back of the retaining walls, filter layers similar to those in the underground drainage system were installed.

4. An extensive drainage system consisting of channels was engineered on the slope surface to direct rainfall water.

5. After these measures had been completed all cracks on the slope surface were filled and tamped to minimize infiltration.

Landslide Control at Taishanmiao

Because of the retrogressive nature of the Taishanmiao slide and the concentration of groundwater in the lower part of the slide mass, control design measures were mainly concentrated in the lower half of the feature. They were as follows.

1. A concrete retaining wall was built at the toe, with an underground drainage system consisting of five branches, each being $2 \times 7 \times 15$ m (Figure 6.11). It is thus a similar structure to that used in the western valley of the Jiaoshuwan landslide.

2. In order to avoid the failure of the upper (artificially cut) part of the slide, a row of 22 concrete steel piles, each $2 \times 2 \times 12$ m, was built.

3. An extensive drainage system was structured on the surface of the slope.

4. All cracks on the slope surface were filled and tamped.

Since the completion of all these measures in June 1992, no further deformation of the two landslides has been recorded by a series of SINCO digital inclinometers and ETM (Electron Theodolite Machine)-operated monitoring nets (Figure 6.12).

CONCLUSION

Many recent investigations have shown that almost all new landslides or reactivated relict mass failures affecting centres of population in Gansu Province have been triggered, or at least influenced, by human activities. However, public awareness is currently very low, even in mountain areas where many landslides occur every year. This general lack of awareness of the landslide threat renders such communities even more vulnerable.

Clearly, the development of an educational strategy and the design of a long-term programme to mitigate landslide disasters are urgent priorities in Gansu. The urgency is graphically illustrated by the way liberties are still taken with the land by local people. For example, slopes are excavated for building purposes without any rational plan or slope protection precautions, and waste water is casually released where no drainage system exists.

Although, by 1989, a series of long-term protection measures against landslides and debris flow hazards in Lanzhou city had been formulated together with a team

102

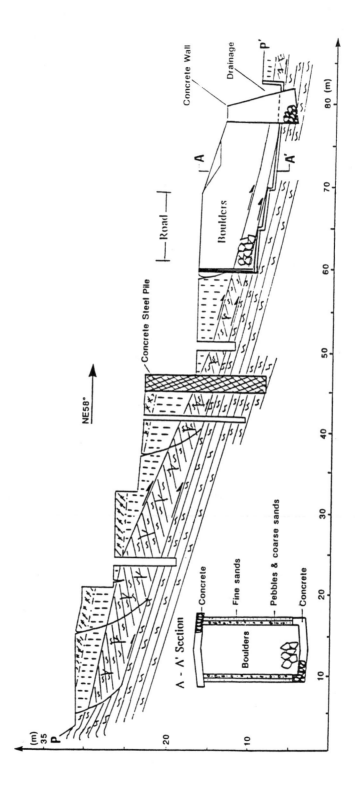

Figure 6.11 Major controlling structures at the Taishanmiao landslide, shown in cross-section. See Figure 6.8 for location

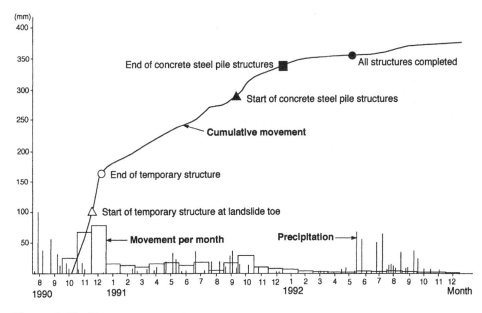

Figure 6.12 The movement of Jiaoshuwan landslide in relation to precipitation and controlling structures

from the European Community (Derbyshire *et al.*, 1991), this applies only to the environs of Lanzhou city, capital of the Province, leaving most of Gansu Province (with an area similar to that of France) in need of the same kind of work.

Attempts to control landsliding are rare in Gansu because of the high cost of such operations. The most common response is simply to remove houses or even whole villages if they are seriously threatened. However, this is a difficult operation in many cases because of the problem of finding a safe alternative location, the resistance of rural populations to any kind of move and, of course, the ever-present cost factor acting as a powerful disincentive. In cases like Jiaoshuwan and Taishanmiao, it is thus not surprising that local authorities often turn to landslide control measures.

Gansu remains one of the poorest provinces in China. The financial cost of controlling landslides as big as those described here in one and the same year are clearly beyond the region's long-term gross productivity. Accordingly, other strategies must be sought, including detection of potentially dangerous landslide slopes before they are mobilized. In the long-term, this is clearly better economy than any post-failure strategy. This must now be addressed, and the fatalistic attitudes enshrined in the traditional saying "there is enough money to buy coffins but not money enough to buy medicine" dispelled.

REFERENCES

Derbyshire, E. (1992). Engineering in Quaternary sediments: case studies from western Europe and eastern Asia. *Quaternary Proceedings*, **2**, 33–48.

Derbyshire, E., Wang, J. T., Jin, Z.X., Billard, A., Egels, Y., Kasser, M., Jones, D. K. C., Muxart, T. and Owen, L. A. (1991). Landslides in the Gansu loess of China. *Catena Suppl.*, **20**, 119–145.

Gansu Geological Bureau (1985). Report of Tian Shui geological structures (in Chinese).

Gansu Seismic Bureau (1987). Report of Tian Shui seismic investigation (in Chinese).

Wang, J. and Derbyshire, E. (1988). EC launches project on landslides and debris flow in Chinese loess. *Episodes*, **11**, 131–132.

Wang, J., Derbyshire, E., Meng, X. and Ma, J. (1991). Natural hazards and geological processes: an introduction to the history of natural hazards in Gansu Province, China, XIII INQUA. In Liu Tungsheng (Ed.), *Quaternary Geology and Environment in China*, Science Press, Beijing, pp. 285–296.

Part 3

HYDROLOGY AND
LAND MANAGEMENT

7 Assessing the Hydrological Impact of Land Use Change in Wetland Watersheds: A Case Study from Northern Ohio, USA

KEITH A. McCLINTOCK*, JONATHAN M. HARBOR and
TIMOTHY P. WILSON
*Department of Geology and Water Resources Research Institute, Kent State
University, USA*

ABSTRACT

One important contribution that geomorphologists can make to land management is to develop techniques that empower non-specialists to make rational planning decisions within the context of a changing environment. For example, existing hydrological models can be used to estimate the potential hydrological impacts of land use change, but are usually so complex and data intensive that they are beyond the scope of local planners. To help planners manage changing environments we have developed a simple method to provide an estimate of long-term changes in storm water runoff volumes and groundwater recharge that result from land use change. The method is based on the US Soil Conservation Service's curve number method, and provides results that are highly appropriate for local planning needs. For a wetland watershed in north-eastern Ohio the method predicts a 43%–373% increase in average annual storm water runoff volumes when natural woodland is converted to high-density residential uses, compared to a 97%–202% average increase in storm water runoff volumes for individual, large storms. Runoff volume change estimates also provide a measure for the change in groundwater recharge caused by varying land use patterns. For the wetland watershed studied here, land use change produces a 14%–100% decrease in groundwater recharge. This work highlights the potential significance of land use change in controlling water supply and wetland survival, and illustrates a useful initial impact assessment technique that can be used by land use planners to manage changing environments.

INTRODUCTION

"Wetlands are among the most important ecosystems on the earth" (Mitsch and Gosselink, 1986:3), notably because they help maintain the quality and supply of surface and ground waters, and in many areas reduce flooding. Wetlands also help filter contaminants from surface water, furnish habitat for wildlife, and provide

---

*Present address: West Chester County Department of Planning, White Plains, NY, USA.

Geomorphology and Land Management in a Changing Environment. Edited by D. F. M. McGregor and D. A. Thompson.
©1995 John Wiley & Sons Ltd

educational and recreational areas for many individuals. Despite their importance, wetlands are often viewed as "mosquito infested" areas of little or no economic benefit to the landowner and, as a result, a vast majority of the wetlands in the United States have been destroyed. For example, over 90% of all wetlands in Ohio have been destroyed to date (Mitsch and Gosselink, 1986).

To protect wetlands, the US government has regulated land uses by limiting construction activity within defined wetland boundaries (Section 404 permit of the Clean Water Act 1977). However, the survival of wetlands not only relies on conditions within the wetland boundaries, but also on processes operating within the watersheds surrounding the wetlands. The wetland watershed is defined as the area which can potentially contribute surface water runoff and sediment to the wetland body. The hydrology of a wetland watershed is the most important determinant for maintaining wetlands and wetland processes (Mitsch and Gosselink, 1986), and development within the watershed may disrupt input of water, nutrients and sediment to the wetland. Thus, in order to ensure the continued survival of wetlands, the integrity of the wetland hydrologic regime, including the surrounding watershed, must be considered when development is proposed for areas near wetlands.

Although there is considerable interest in wetland protection, efforts to assess potential impacts of land use change have been hindered by the lack of a practical assessment method. Existing methods can be used to assess the impact of land use change on individual storms, but do not address longer-term impacts. A method that could provide quick, general estimates of the long-term potential hydrologic impact associated with changes in land use would be invaluable to planners and local regulators because it would allow them to regulate development in wetland watersheds in a manner which minimizes the disruption of beneficial processes in the adjacent wetland.

This study illustrates the use of a new method for long-term impact assessment, taking as an example a wetland watershed in Hudson, Ohio, USA (Figure 7.1). By applying the method to a range of historical and expected/planned land uses within this watershed, the model provides insight into the effects which various land use change scenarios will have on the long-term surface water input to the wetland, as well as local groundwater recharge.

METHODOLOGY FOR SIMPLE IMPACT ASSESSEMENT

Existing hydrologic models, such as those developed by the US Department of Agriculture (1986), the Environmental Protection Agency (SWMM; Huber *et al.* 1988), the United States Army Corps of Engineers (STORM and HEC-1 1974, 1985) and various other private organizations, are designed to determine how various changes in watershed characteristics affect the water and sediment supplied to a body of water, in this case a wetland. One way to determine this is to numerically route surface water runoff generated by individual storms through a watershed. This allows the effects of variations in structures that control flow, such as grass-lined channels and retention ponds, and variations in land use to be calculated. Therefore, the impacts of known historical changes and planned changes in land use can be determined for individual

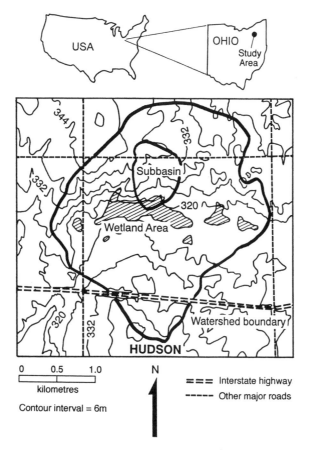

Figure 7.1 Location of the study site. Detailed map shows wetland watershed boundary, wetland areas, major roads, and sub-basin location. Wetland Areas based on the National Wetland Inventory (NWI) Map (Twinsburg Quadrangle)

storm events, such as the 50-year recurrence interval storm. There are two important limitations with this approach. First, although some models are suitable for use in continuous (long-term) simulations, generally they are suitable only for individual storm events. These models do not provide information on long-term changes in groundwater recharge and downstream water supply. Second, the models are complex and require experience and time to master their usage. They are usually beyond the scope of local planners, and very few planning agencies can afford skilled consultants to use these models. In order for a hydrologic method to be most useful to local planners, it must be rapid and easy to employ. In this context, we sought to develop a simple method that local planners could use to address the basic question, "What will the impact of a change in land use be on long-term surface water runoff volumes?"

Surface water runoff models are based on hydrologic abstraction principles. In the US, the most frequently used hydrologic abstraction technique is the Soil Conservation Service's curve number (CN) method (Kibler *et al.*, 1991). The curve number method provides a way to estimate the surface water runoff generated by a 24 hour rainfall amount, on the basis of land use and soil type characteristics. The hydrologic abstraction technique, though often buried in complex models, is very straightforward and is suitable for use with a simple spreadsheet on a personal computer.

In our new approach the CN method is used to determine runoff depths from daily precipitation data over many years (Harbor, 1994). This differs from the traditional use of the method to determine runoff only for individual extreme events (single-day design storms). To use this new method local planners need only assemble basic information, such as daily precipitation, soil type distribution, and present and predicted land use. With curve numbers for past, present and future land uses, daily runoff depths are determined and used to provide long-term average estimates of runoff volume. Results can be produced in a few hours, depending on the size of the watershed, and provide an initial estimate of the relation between land use and volume of runoff. This straightforward technique allows planners to assess changes between various real and hypothetical land use scenarios simply by changing the curve number used in the analysis. Although this method produces results that can be utilized for local planning ordinances and for hydrologic sensitivity analyses, the results are not sufficiently accurate to make detailed hydrologic predictions. A full description of the method can be found in Harbor and Wilson (1992) and Harbor (1994).

LIMITATIONS OF THE METHOD

The method developed here should only be used to provide insight into the relative hydrologic impacts associated with land use change. Results produced by this method are not to be confused with storm runoff estimates for individual design storms, which are developed and used in hydrologic design. Certain elements of the Soil Conservation Service's (SCS) curve-number method were simplified for this study. For example, the SCS curve-number technique is designed to predict storm water runoff generated for each land use region, which are then summed to produce a total amount of runoff. Our method makes use of area-weighted curve numbers which produce a runoff amount for average land use conditions within the watershed. Several elements of the SCS curve-number method are not used in this method. They include antecedent moisture conditions, periods of the year during which ground surfaces are frozen (which result in increased rates of storm water runoff), and precipitation in the form of snowfall. A more detailed discussion of the limitations and procedure of the SCS curve-number technique can be found in US Department of Agriculture (1985, 1986) as well as various hydrology text books (e.g. Viessman et al., 1989; Singh, 1992).

STUDY AREA

The study site is located in Hudson Township, Summit County, north-eastern Ohio (Figure 7.1). Hudson Township was selected because it is a rapidly developing area with extensive planned and in-progress development occurring in wetland watersheds.

Realizing the importance of wetlands and their many benefits, Hudson Township officials want to protect wetlands while allowing continued development and economic growth.

The surficial deposits of Hudson Township consist mainly of poorly drained glacial and lacustrine materials that were deposited by the Wisconsinan ice sheet approximately 12 000 years ago. Glacial deposits cover approximately two-thirds of Ohio, and in this area overlie sandstone and shale bedrock (Ritchie and Steiger, 1990). The landscape is typical of many glaciated areas in the mid-west United States, characterized by low relief and poorly drained soils. The gently rolling topography, poorly drained soils, and sustained periods of wetness combine to provide extensive areas of wetlands within a landscape that was dominantly forested before clearing for agriculture. Almost 35% of Hudson Township consists of soils that are hydric or have hydric components, and these soil types are well suited to wetland plants and wildlife (Ritchie and Steiger, 1990).

The wetland and surrounding watershed selected for this study is located just north of the village of Hudson (Figure 7.1). The wetland watershed covers an area of 5.4 km² and has experienced rapid encroachment by residential development in the last 20 years. Low-density residential developments now nearly surround a palustrine emergent, scrub/shrub and forested (broad leaf deciduous), saturated/semi-permanent/seasonal wetland. The wetland, as defined on the US Fish and Wildlife National Wetland Inventory (NWI) map, is shown on Figure 7.1. This wetland has been artificially drained by a large culvert, which is common of many wetlands located near agricultural and urban areas. Portions of the wetland have been set aside as a recreational area (Darrow Road Park), but this does not protect these portions of the wetland from the adverse impacts of development in its watershed, such as increased sediment and non-point source pollutant loadings.

Development within the watershed could potentially alter ground and surface water sources and flow characteristics. Underlying the wetland and its watershed is a 6–12 m thick layer of clay till containing isolated lenses of sand and gravel, which overlies sandstone bedrock (Harbor and Wilson, 1992). The clay forms an impermeable layer, which isolates the wetland from the regional water-table. Therefore, the Darrow Road Park wetland is largely supported by surficial runoff and flow through the near-surface soils, rather than by the regional flow system (Harbor and Wilson, 1992). With this geological setting, development within the wetland watershed has the potential to alter local surface water and shallow groundwater sources and flow characteristics, which may in turn disrupt the hydrologic regime of the wetland.

To assess the impact of historical and predicted land use change on the amount of runoff generated in the watershed five reasonable land use scenarios were selected: pre-settlement woodland, pre-development agriculture, low-density residential areas with wooded corridors, low-density residential areas without wooded corridors, and high-density residential areas. The Summit County Soil Survey (Ritchie and Steiger, 1990) provided the distribution and characteristics of the soils located in the wetland watershed. The majority of the soils have low permeability, which is typical of soils developed on glacial till deposits common in the northern mid-west United States (Ritchie and Steiger, 1990). Land use distributions and hydrologic soil groups for the watershed were used to determine reasonable curve-number values for each scenario.

The pre-settlement (*c.* 1800) condition of this watershed was, for the most part, wooded. Using the US Soil Conservation Service's method, a curve number of 75 is appropriate for this land cover, based on historical descriptions of the area (Izant, 1985). Pre-development land use classification was based on aerial photographs of the watershed taken on 4 May 1960. In 1960, most of the watershed was covered by agricultural fields with areas of woodland, brush and meadows crossed with roads and an occasional home. The overall curve number for the watershed in 1960 is 79. Aerial photographs from 1990 show the watershed had been converted to low-density residential development with wooded corridors left between houses. An overall curve number of 82 was calculated for this low-density residential condition. These conditions represent the actual historical land uses for the Darrow Road Park watershed. However, to illustrate potential impacts of future development, we considered two additional changes in land use, although such land uses have not been proposed for the study area. In the first scenario, the wooded corridors between individual houses are removed. This results in a curve number of 84. The second scenario considers the conversion of the watershed into a high-density residential community, which has a curve number of 88.

RESULTS AND DISCUSSION

The effects of changes in the land use scenarios for the Darrow Road Park watershed were determined using our application of the SCS curve number method, in conjunction with daily rainfall data for the period 1960–84, from the Akron weather station. Average values for the depth of runoff produced by each land use category, for the 1960–84 period, are given in Table 7.1. The average annual rainfall for the 1960–84 period was 90.2 cm, ranging from a high of 111.5 cm in 1972 to a low of 60.4 cm in 1963. A small portion of the annual records shows significant year-to-year variability in runoff depths (Figure 7.2), but patterns of relative runoff as a function of land use remain consistent throughout the period. For pre-settlement (wooded) conditions the predicted average annual runoff depth was 2.4 cm (a high of 7.0 cm in 1979 and a low of 0.2 cm in 1963), and for pre-development conditions the predicted average runoff was 3.9 cm (a high of 9.0 cm in 1979 and a low of

Table 7.1 Impact of land use change on storm water runoff depths, based on 1960–84 average daily rainfall (PS = pre-settlement, PD = pre-development, LD1 = low-density residential area with wooded corridors, LD2 = low-density residential area without wooded corridors, and HD = high-density residential area)

Land use	CN	Average runoff 1960–84 (cm/year)	(%) Increase in runoff over pre-settlement conditions	(%) Increase in runoff over undeveloped conditions
PS	75	2.44	0	—
PD	79	3.91	60	0
LD1	82	5.59	129	43
LD2	84	7.11	192	72
HD	88	11.53	373	195

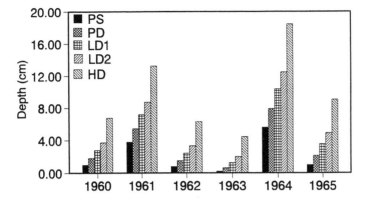

Figure 7.2 Impact of land use change on storm water runoff depths for 1960–65 (PS = pre-settlement, PD = pre-development, LD1 = low-density residential area with wooded corridors, LD2 = low-density residential area without wooded corridors, and HD = high-density residential area)

0.7 cm in 1963). For the three other land use scenarios, predicted annual runoff depths were markedly higher than pre-developed conditions, increasing by 43% for low-density residential areas with wooded corridors, 72% for low-density residential areas without wooded corridors, and 195% for high-density residential areas (Figure 7.3).

The increase in annual runoff depth from pre-development to low density with wooded corridors is relatively low (43%) as compared to the increase from pre-settlement to low-density residential areas with wooded corridors (129%) (Figure 7.3).

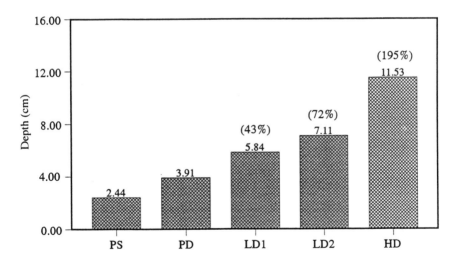

Figure 7.3 Impact of land use change on storm water runoff, given as depths and percentage increases compared to pre-development conditions. Based on 1960–84 average daily rainfall. (PS = pre-settlement, PD = pre-development, LD1 = low-density residential area with wooded corridors, LD2 = low-density residential area without wooded corridors, and HD = high-density residential area)

One usually associates an increase in impervious surfaces (such as roads, driveways and roof tops) with marked increases in runoff. The moderate increase in runoff in this case results from the fact that pre-developed conditions were largely agricultural fields which remained fallow for long periods of the year, during which high rates of runoff occurred. The increase in impervious surface area in the low-density residential setting is largely offset by the wooded corridors and green spaces left between streets and homes, but does result in a 43% increase in runoff from pre-development conditions. When the wooded corridors are removed from the analysis (LD2), the runoff increases by 72% relative to the pre-development level. Therefore, the conversion of agricultural areas to low-density residential development, with sensible design to maintain green space and wooded corridors, results only in a minimal increase in surface water runoff depths.

Estimated runoff depths can also be used to determine the change in runoff input into the wetland, by multiplying the runoff depth by the watershed area (Figure 7.4). A long-term average increase of 48 000 l/day/km^2 in storm water runoff volume occurs when the watershed is converted from pre-developed conditions to low-density residential conditions with wooded corridors. As the watershed is converted to low-density residential without wooded corridors and to high-density residential conditions, storm water runoff volumes increase to 87 000 and 207 000 l/day/km^2, respectively. The results show that very significant increases in runoff inputs to the wetland occur as a result of land use changes.

The change in runoff volume calculated by this method also provides an initial estimate of the maximum decrease in groundwater recharge that might occur as a result of historical and predicted changes in land use. The maximum decrease in

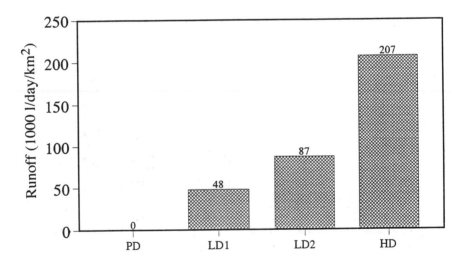

Figure 7.4 Impact of land use on storm water runoff input to the Darrow Road Park wetland. Numbers represent the increase in runoff volume compared to pre-development conditions. Based on 1960–84 average daily rainfall (PD = pre-development, LD1 = low-density residential area with wooded corridors, LD2 = low-density residential area without wooded corridors, and HD = high-density residential area)

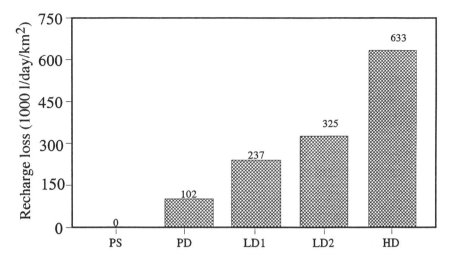

Figure 7.5 Volume of groundwater recharge lost as a function of development type, based on 1960–84 average daily rainfall (PS = pre-settlement, PD = pre-development, LD1 = low-density residential area with wooded corridors, LD2 = low-density residential area without wooded corridors, and HD = high-density residential area)

groundwater recharge predicted for these land use scenarios is compared to pre-development conditions in Figure 7.5, expressed as the average daily volume decrease in groundwater recharge per square kilometre of land surface subject to land use change. This is a maximum estimate of the decrease in recharge and is calculated assuming no change in volume of water lost through evapotranspiration. In practice, if vegetative cover is removed during development, evapotranspiration may decrease. Thus a portion of the increase in runoff may result from a decrease in evapotranspiration, rather than from a decrease in recharge. Typical recharge rates for this area range from 219 000 to 731 000 l/day/km^2 (Howell, 1976; Richards, 1981; Kammer, 1982; Patzke, 1986; US Geological Survey, 1990). A change from wooded conditions to high-density residential conditions may reduce groundwater recharge by as much as 633 000 l/day/km^2 (Figure 7.5), thus land use change may entirely eliminate ground water recharge in some situations.

POTENTIAL IMPACT ON THE WETLAND

These results support the obvious notion that changes in land use in a wetland watershed can cause marked changes in runoff and recharge. The increase in surface water runoff, and corresponding decrease in groundwater recharge, may cause an erratic hydrologic regime within the wetland. The increase in runoff during storm events will most likely flood the wetland, while water levels in the wetland will potentially decline during dry spells as a result of a decrease in recharge from local soil and groundwater. This is especially true for wetlands such as the Darrow Road Park area which is drained by a large culvert (183 cm in diameter) that was installed for agricultural purposes. Much of the capacity to store flood water between rain events is essentially lost due to the culvert. The predicted result of development in the wetland system is that the wetland may receive enhanced surface water supply during, and shortly after, rain events, but cannot store the excess water for drier periods between storms. As yet we have no objective way to assess the impact this will have on wetland ecology, however it is likely that there will be significant differences between the species adapted to continuously wet conditions and those adapted to a post-development flood and drought regime.

SCS TR-55 ANALYSIS

In the US, most community ordinances regulating storm water discharge are based on individual storm events of specific recurrence intervals. Therefore, it is important to know if individual storm events show the same level of impact as the long-term average measures predicted by our method. If so, individual storm events would be a sufficient estimate of the level of hydrologic impact associated with changing land use environments. To evaluate this, the SCS TR-55 (US Department of Agriculture, 1986) method was used to determine the total volume of storm water runoff generated for a series of individual storm events for a sub-basin within the Darrow Road Park watershed. The results are compared with the long-term averages, which are the basis for our method.

The sub-basin chosen for this comparative analysis is 0.34 km^2 in size and is located directly north of the wetland (Figure 7.1). Four land use scenarios (wooded, pre-development (agricultural), low-density residential areas (half acre lots), and high-density residential areas (one-eighth acre lots)) were used with the SCS TR-55 method to calculate the runoff resulting from a series of individual storm events at the 2, 5, 10, 20, 50 and 100 year recurrence intervals. Both total storm water runoff volumes (Table 7.2) and peak discharge rate estimates (Table 7.3) were produced for each recurrence interval for each land use scenario.

Table 7.2 Comparison of storm water runoff volumes as a function of land use (PD = pre-development, LD = low-density residential area, and HD = high-density residential area)

Land use	Percentage increase in total runoff volume using individual storm events (recurrence intervals)						Percentage increase in total runoff volume based on daily rainfall data (this study)
	2 years	5 years	10 years	20 years	50 years	100 years	
(a) From PS wooded conditions							
PD	39	27	23	20	17	15	60
LD	77	55	46	41	35	31	140–192
HD	118	83	68	60	51	45	373
(b) From PD pre-developed conditions							
LD	27	22	19	17	15	13	43–72
HD	57	43	37	33	28	26	195

Table 7.3 Impact of land use change on peak discharge based on the US Soil Conservation Service's TR-55 method (PD = pre-development, LD = low-density residential area, and HD = high-density residential area)

Land use	Estimated peak discharge (m^3/s) using individual storm events (recurrence intervals) (SCS TR-55 method)					
	2 years	5 years	10 years	20 years	50 years	100 years
PD	0.74	1.27	1.93	2.38	3.00	3.54
LD	0.71	1.22	1.61	2.01	2.49	2.92
HD	1.27	2.01	2.58	3.11	3.79	4.36

Peak discharge rates are predicted to decline by between 4% and 21% when the sub-basin is converted from pre-developed agricultural conditions to low-density residential conditions (Table 7.3). This decrease occurs because in agricultural fields the time needed for runoff to travel from the most distant part of the watershed to its outflow point, known as the time of concentration (Tc), is relatively short. As a result, the runoff is quickly routed through the small channels between crop rows. However, when low-density residential areas are constructed, large areas that were previously maintained as agricultural fields, are converted to grass lawns, resulting in longer Tc values. Because longer times of concentration result in lower peak discharges, peak discharges are lower for low-density residential conditions than for pre-development conditions. When the sub-basin is converted to high-density residential, peak discharges increase (27% to 73%) from pre-developed conditions. This increase in peak discharge results from a decrease in the times of concentration, which is due to the decrease in green space between individual homes coupled with an increase in impervious surfaces.

Although peak discharges decrease slightly during the change from the pre-developed to low-density residential conditions, the total storm water runoff volumes increase by 13% to 27%. This increase is much smaller than the volume increase predicted by our method based on daily rainfall data. Our model predicts an average annual storm water runoff based on daily rainfall data increases of 195% for conversion of pre-developed conditions to low-density residential conditions. This comparison suggests that using individual storm events, even the 100-year recurrence interval storm, underestimates the volume of storm water runoff when compared with average annual runoff volumes. Interestingly, a large percentage of the runoff produced during a year is not the result of large storm events, but rather the sum of runoff generated during minor precipitation events that produce runoff more frequently as the watershed becomes increasingly developed. It is this increase in the number of events producing runoff, in combination with greater runoff volume from the individual events, that explains why estimates based on daily rainfall data are larger than estimates based on single storm events.

MINIMIZING IMPACT BY DESIGN AND PLANNING

In order to prevent flooding and erosion of downstream areas, many community ordinances in the US require new developments to be designed to prevent or minimize increased storm water runoff. Most ordinances often require new developments to be designed to prevent peak runoff discharges from exceeding pre-development rates. However, these ordinances do not consider the increase in storm water volume associated with development. As our results show, the total storm water runoff volume must be controlled in order to minimize disturbance to groundwater recharge and to local wetland systems. Therefore, a natural extension of existing ordinances would be to amend storm water ordinances to require design of new developments to prevent total storm water volumes from exceeding pre-development levels. This would effectively help to reduce flooding and erosion problems, and would help to minimize non-point source pollutants. Such regulations would fulfil the requirements of the US Environmental Protection Agency's National Pollutant Discharge Elimination System (NPDES) regulations, because reducing runoff volumes is a very effective means of reducing non-point source pollutants. Methods to reduce storm water runoff volumes include landscaping for on-site detention, increased green space between structures, sand filters, porous pavements, and infiltration trenches and basins. These methods help to increase infiltration before water can become storm water runoff. Further descriptions and design of such structures can be found in Commonwealth of Virginia (1990), Goldman *et al.* (1986), Galli (1990), and Stahre and Urbonas (1990).

FUTURE WORK

This study illustrates the use of a practical method to assess the hydrologic impacts of land use change in a wetland watershed. The method is accessible to planners, and can help them make rational decisions in their attempt to manage changing environments. Although this method makes use of a technique central to many advanced hydrologic models, complete empirical verification of the predictions in this example would require a long-term study of actual storm water runoff from the study area.

The results show that changes in land use within a wetland watershed have significant impacts on the timing and quantity of runoff. However, this change is not the only impact associated with land use change. Urban development often increases the levels of non-point source pollutants (US Environmental Protection Agency, 1983), which may result in a decrease in water quality within the wetland system. Therefore, a future research goal is to determine the relation between changes in land use and the amount of sediment and chemicals delivered to a wetland system from its surrounding watershed, with the aim of developing guidelines for development practices to reduce rates of sedimentation.

ACKNOWLEDGEMENTS

The research reported here was supported by The Ohio Board of Regents, Urban University Program, Northeast Ohio Inter-Institutional Urban Research Consortium, and the Department of Geology and the Water Resources Research Institute at Kent State University. The trustees and officials of Hudson Township assisted in our efforts to obtain funding and information for the project. We would also like to thank Sharen Keattch and Kirk Gregory for their technical assistance, and Dr Abdul Shakoor and Dr Yoram Eckstein for their comments on an initial draft of this paper.

REFERENCES

Commonwealth of Virginia (1990). *Best Management Practices Handbook—Urban*, Virginia Department of Conservation and Recreation, Division of Soil and Water Conservation.

Galli, J. (1990). *Peat–Sand Filters: A Proposed Stormwater Management Practice for Urbanized Areas*, Metropolitan Washington Council of Governments.

Goldman, S., Jackson, K. and Bursztynsky, T. (1986). *Erosion & Sediment Control Handbook*, McGraw Hill, New York.

Harbor, J. (1994). A practical method for estimating the impact of land use change on surface runoff, ground water recharge, and wetland hydrology. *Journal of the American Planning Association*, **60**, 91–104.

Harbor, J. and Wilson, T. (1992). *Managing urban development in wetland watersheds in Northern Summit County, Ohio*, Unpublished Research Report, Kent State University.

Howell, L. (1976). *Groundwater resources of Brimfield Township, Portage County, Ohio*. Unpublished MS thesis, Kent State University.

Huber, W., Dickenson, R., Roesner, L. and Aldrich, J. (1988). *Stormwater Management Model User's Manual, Version 4*, US Environmental Protection Agency, Athens, GA.

Izant, G. G. (1985). *Hudson's Heritage*. Kent State University Press, Ohio.

Kammer, H. (1982). *A hydrologic study of the Ravenna Arsenal, Eastern Portage and Western Trumbull Counties, Ohio*. Unpublished MS thesis, Kent State University.

Kibler, D., Jennings, M., Louis, G., Tschantz, B. and Walesh, S. (1991). Microcomputer Software in Urban Hydrology. *Hydata*, September 1991, 27–32.

Mitsch, W. and Gosselink, J. (1986). *Wetlands*, Van Nostrand Reinhold, New York.

Patzke, J. (1986). *Evaluation of natural recharge rates within the Upper and Middle Mahoning River basins, northeastern Ohio*. Unpublished MS thesis, Kent State University.

Richards, S. (1981). *A hydrologic study of South Russell and adjacent areas*. Unpublished MS thesis, Kent State University.

Ritchie, A. and Steiger, J. (1990). *Soil Survey of Summit County, Ohio*, United States Department of Agriculture, Soil Conservation Service, Washington, DC.

Singh, V. (1992). *Elementary Hydrology*, Prentice Hall, Englewood Cliffs, NJ.

Stahre, P. and Urbonas, B. (1990). *Storm-Water Detention for Drainage, Water Quality and CSO Management*, Prentice Hall, Englewood Cliffs, NJ.

US Army Corps of Engineers (1974). *Urban Stormwater Runoff—STORM, Computer Program 723-58-L2520*. The Hydrologic Engineering Center, US Army Corps of Engineers, Davis, CA.

US Army Corps of Engineers (1985). *Flood Hydrograph Package HEC-1*. The Hydrologic Engineering Center, US Army Corps of Engineers, Davis, CA.

US Department of Agriculture, Soil Conservation Service (1985). *SCS National Engineering Handbook*, Section 4, Hydrology.

US Department of Agriculture, Soil Conservation Service (1986). *Urban Hydrology for Small Watersheds*, Engineering Division, Technical Release 55.

US Environmental Protection Agency (1983). *Results of the National Urban Runoff Program*, Washington (NTIS #PB84-185552).

US Geological Survey (1990). *Geohydrology, Groundwater Quality, and Simulated Ground Water Flow, Geauga County, Ohio*, Water Resources Investigations Report 90-4026.

Viessman, W., Lewis, G. and Knapp, J. (1989). *Introduction to Hydrology* (3rd edn), Harper & Row, New York.

8 Impact of Source Area Liming on the Hydrochemistry of an Acidic Headwater Stream in Upland Wales

CHRISTOPHER SOULSBY*
National Rivers Authority, Northumbria and Yorkshire Region, UK

and

BRIAN REYNOLDS
Institute of Terrestrial Ecology, Bangor Research Unit, University College of North Wales, UK

ABSTRACT

Acid surface waters are characteristic of large parts of upland Wales, particularly where commercial forestry is the dominant land use. The elevated levels of aluminium found in acid surface waters have contributed to the degradation of aquatic ecosystems and the loss of salmonid fisheries in headwater streams. Although the long-term solution to acidification requires a reduction in international emissions of acidic oxide pollutants, liming the hydrological source areas of upland catchments has been shown to be effective in reducing stream acidity and aluminium levels, thus improving conditions for salmonids in the short-term. Indeed, source area liming has been recently recommended by the Forestry Commission as an integral part of afforestation schemes in acid-sensitive upland areas. This chapter presents data from a source area liming experiment at Llyn Brianne in upland Wales. Data were collected over a period of six years to examine the impact of lime application on stream water quality. Fortnightly spot samples and hourly sampling during storm events demonstrated that although liming decreased stream acidity and aluminium concentrations, some detrimental hydrochemical effects also occurred. These include increased levels of colour, dissolved organic carbon and iron. If liming became a widespread land management technique in acid-sensitive upland areas such changes are likely to have important implications for the ecology of upland streams and may jeopardize potable rural water supplies which often receive minimal treatment. The results of this study suggest that further research is needed before source area liming is recommended as a standard means of mitigating acidification in upland catchments.

INTRODUCTION

A major challenge to geomorphologists is the need to utilize the extensive body of scientific knowledge accumulated in relation to catchment solute processes in the

---

Present address: Department of Geography, University of Aberdeen, UK.

Geomorphology and Land Management in a Changing Environment. Edited by D. F. M. McGregor and D. A. Thompson.
©1995 John Wiley & Sons Ltd

management of water quality problems (Walling and Webb, 1986). Fresh water acidification is one of the most serious contemporary water management issues in the British uplands and predictions of future levels of atmospheric deposition indicate that it is likely to remain so for the next few decades (Ormerod *et al.*, 1990). Acid waters occur when catchments are unable to buffer the impact of acid deposition due to the dominance of base-poor rocks and acid soils. Surface waters are acidified as a result and concentrations of toxic aluminium species increase (UKAWRG, 1989). Consequently, salmonid fisheries and macroinvertebrate populations are often damaged.

Extensive areas of upland Wales have been severely affected by acidification and the resulting damage to Welsh fisheries is estimated to have produced an economic loss of £5 million to fishery owners, with a potential revenue loss, if acidification continues, of up to £25 million (Milner and Varallo, 1990). The base-poor Lower Palaeozoic geology of the Welsh uplands has given rise to strongly acid soils that produce extremely acid-sensitive catchments (Hornung *et al.*, 1990a). Moreover, the afforestation of extensive moorland areas with exotic conifers earlier this century has significantly increased levels of acid deposition by enhancing dry and occult deposition to tree canopies (Ormerod *et al.*, 1989). Streams draining afforested catchments are therefore often more acidic than adjacent streams draining moorland areas, giving land management a central role in the acidification issue in Wales (Stoner, *et al.*, 1984).

The severe consequences of acidification in Wales are such that much effort has been directed at developing palliative management options. Long-term solutions depend upon international reductions in the emission of polluting acid oxides of sulphur and nitrogen produced by fossil fuel burning. However, it is likely to be several decades before the impact of international emission control agreements, such as the European Community's Large Combustion Plant Directive (88/609/EEC), produce noticeable improvements in water quality (Jenkins *et al.*, 1990).

To achieve more rapid results, various land management options have been considered (Hornung *et al.*, 1990b). Catchment liming has been shown to be an effective short-term strategy for ameliorating acid surface waters in some areas (Warfvinge and Sverdrup, 1988). Liming increases the acid neutralizing capacity of catchment soils resulting in increased stream pH and calcium levels, with a concomitant reduction in concentrations of toxic aluminium (Jenkins *et al.*, 1991). Consequently, liming has been useful in restoring salmonid fisheries in acidified areas where fish stocks have been depleted (Underwood *et al.*, 1987; Tervet and Harriman, 1988). Indeed, Ormerod and Edwards (1985) suggest that the cessation of agricultural liming for pasture improvement may have contributed to increased stream acidity in parts of upland Wales during the last century.

The most cost-effective method of liming is to target application to the hydrological source areas of headwater catchments (Waters *et al.*, 1991). This minimizes the amount of lime used whilst ensuring that stream water is neutralized during storm episodes when the most acidic conditions occur (Davies *et al.*, 1992). Source area liming has therefore been advocated by the Forestry Commission as an integral part of afforestation schemes in acid-sensitive parts of the UK (Forestry Commission, 1991).

Notwithstanding the value of liming as a management tool, increasing criticism has been directed at its use. Hydrological source areas are often characterized by peatlands of high conservation value, and liming has been shown to cause the loss of some sensitive plant species (Woodin and Skiba, 1990). Moreover, most streams that have been acidified since fossil fuel burning increased in the last century, would to some extent be naturally acidic with an ecology adapted to such conditions; liming is a major perturbation which, whilst restoring fisheries, may have negative impacts on other organisms (Weatherley, 1988). Consequently, there is a need to fully appraise the impact of source area liming before it is widely adopted as a management option.

As part of an ongoing National Rivers Authority investigation into environmental acidification at Llyn Brianne in Mid-Wales, catchment liming experiments have been carried out (National Rivers Authority, 1992). Results from an experiment where lime was applied to the hydrological source areas of a moorland catchment are reported here. The effectiveness of this particular treatment in reducing the acidity and aluminium toxicity of stream water has been described by Donald and Gee (1992), whilst the impact on stream ecology was evaluated by Weatherley and Ormerod (1992). This chapter focuses on the increased concentrations of dissolved organic carbon (DOC) and iron which occurred after liming and the impact that these had on stream colour. Changes are observed for two years after lime application and include the monitoring of hydrochemical changes during storm episodes. The results of the study have important implications as increasing concern has been expressed about the problem of discoloration of potable water supplies abstracted from streams draining peat-dominated upland catchments (Kay *et al.*, 1989). This is unpopular with consumers who prefer clear water and can cause staining in pipe systems. Moreover, it can lead to the violation of European Community regulations on water quality. Such changes can also adversely affect the ecology of aquatic organisms in upland streams by reducing light penetration or causing precipitation of iron-rich deposits on the stream bed, thus disrupting freshwater habitats.

STUDY AREA

The Llyn Brianne area lies in the headwaters of the river Tywi in Mid-Wales and has been the location for a major acidification study described by Gee (1990) (Figure 8.1). The climate is dominated by westerly frontal systems with mean annual precipitation exceeding 2000 mm. Rainfall is acidic with a mean pH of 4.9 and annual hydrogen ion (H^+) deposition of 0.8 kg/ha/year (Donald *et al.*, 1990). The area is underlain by base-deficient Lower Palaeozoic mudstones and shales that have given rise to strongly acidic peats, stagnopodzols and stagnogleys. Catchment streams are therefore usually acidic, particularly at high flows when hydrological pathways in the upper soil horizons generate acid, aluminium-rich runoff (Soulsby, 1992; Soulsby and Reynolds, 1993).

A moorland catchment at Llyn Brianne (CI2) was chosen as the site for a source area liming experiment (Figure 8.2) The impact of liming on stream chemistry was assessed by monitoring pre- and post-liming conditions, together with those of an

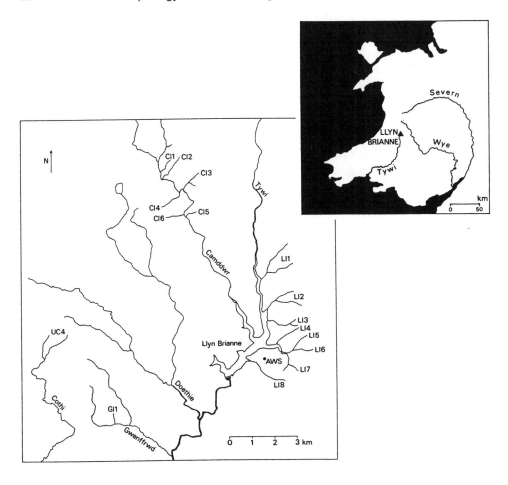

Figure 8.1   Location of Llyn Brianne and the experimental catchments CI2 and CI6

unlimed moorland control catchment (C16). The characteristics of the two catchments are shown in Table 8.1.

Approximately 80 tonnes of lime (CaCO$_3$) were applied to the hydrological source areas of CI2 in June 1988. The period during and after lime application was warm (mean monthly temperature of 14°C) and dry, with only 15.6 mm of precipitation falling in the last 20 days of June. The 5-ha area targeted for liming was identified using an application of TOPMODEL which predicted likely source areas on the basis of topography (Waters *et al.*, 1991). Lime was applied to 50% of the predicted source areas to minimize costs. Manual spreading was used to ensure even distribution, thus giving an application rate of 15–20 tonnes/ha on 7% of the catchment. The limed area was dominated by valley-bottom peat soils of the Crowdy Series (Rudeforth *et al.*, 1984). These were around 1 m deep.

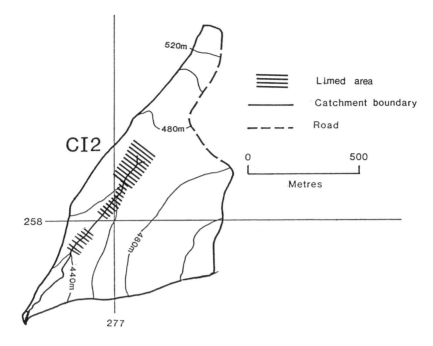

Figure 8.2   The CI2 catchment showing location of limed hydrological source area (shaded)

Table 8.1   Characteristics of the study catchments

	CI2 limed	CI6 control
Catchment area (ha)	59	72
Mean precipitation (mm)	2059	1937
Altitudinal range (m)	430–530	330–450
Soil coverage (%)		
peats	48.7	30.7
stagnohumic gleys	15.3	22.3
humic gleys	10.2	—
stagnopodzols	15.3	30.1
brown podzolics	5.8	—
rankers	4.7	16.9

METHODOLOGY

Chemical monitoring between 1985 and 1990 included the collection of weekly or fortnightly stream water samples from both study catchments. Additionally, over 20 storm events were sampled automatically from each stream between 1986 and 1990 using a Rock and Taylor Ltd sampler triggered by a tipping bucket rain gauge at rainfall intensities of 4 mm/hr. Samples were analysed using standard methods (Allen, 1989) for pH and, after 0.45 μm filtration, iron, DOC and colour (in Hazen units).

Samples were filtered on return to the laboratory and analysed the following day to an accuracy of ±5% for each parameter. After 1986, stream flow was also continuously monitored in each stream; stage was measured at 15-minute intervals with a pressure transducer and ratings were developed by gauging stable channel sections.

To evaluate the impact of liming on the chemistry of runoff draining from the limed source area, three tensionless tray lysimeters were inserted below the upper 5 cm of peat where high hydraulic conductivities produce rapid water movement through and over the soil surface. These were emptied fortnightly and samples were bulked prior to analysis. The samplers were installed and allowed to equilibrate for three months before sampling began in November 1987. Monitoring continued until September 1989.

RESULTS AND DISCUSSION

Impact of Liming on Peat Runoff Chemistry

Runoff from the peat source area was strongly acidic prior to liming and iron and DOC concentrations remained below 1 and 7 mg/l respectively (Figure 8.3 and Table 8.2). Lime application produced a marked increase in all three determinands. The pH of peat runoff increased immediately with levels initially fluctuating between 5.5 and 7.0, before steadying around 7.0 and never falling below 6.3. The primary cause of this initial pH rise was the dissolution of lime spread on the peat surface. However, a proportion of calcium from the lime will also be retained on soil ion exchange sites, thus ensuring buffering over a longer time-scale. (Warfvinge and Sverdrup, 1988; Waters et al., 1991).

In comparison to pH, the increase in iron and DOC exhibited a slight lag before concentrations rose to 4.3 and 75 mg/l respectively in August (weeks 6–10). Thereafter, concentrations declined markedly, following August and September which were exceptionally wet in 1988 (Walsh, 1992), before rising again during the dry autumn; with iron reaching a peak of 8.6 mg/l in late November 1988 (week 20) and a second DOC peak of 60 mg/l occurring in December (week 22). Concentrations of both species declined throughout the rest of the winter before again increasing during the summer of 1989.

The initial increase in DOC concentrations during the first summer was probably due to increased levels of humic substances produced by a flush of decomposition as soil microbial activity was stimulated by the increase in soil pH (Haynes and Swift, 1988). The increase in DOC is also likely to play a role in the observed increase in iron. The mobilization of iron in upland catchments is regulated by two main mechanisms; complexation by organic macromolecules (Grieve, 1984a) and reduction processes in anaerobic soils (Reid et al., 1981). Concentrations of DOC and iron were correlated ($r^2 = 0.296$, significant at $p < 0.01$) in peat runoff, suggesting organic complexation is important in this case. However, the limed source areas were rapidly covered (within several weeks) by iron- and organic-rich ochreous precipitates. These may have been caused by the saturation of iron-organic complexes or by oxidation of reduced iron in the high-pH, oxygen-rich surface of the limed source

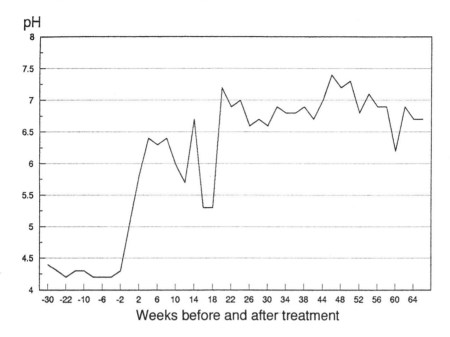

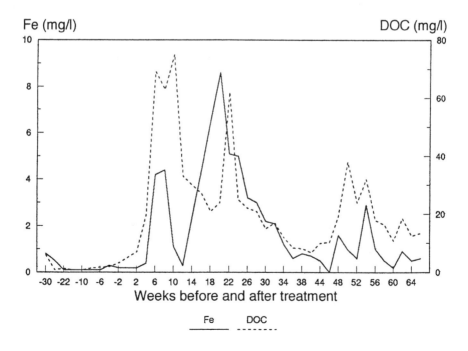

Figure 8.3 Chemistry of peat runoff before and after the liming treatment

(a)

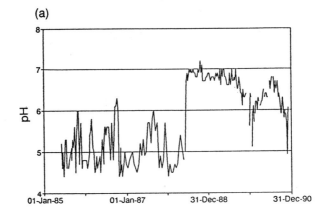

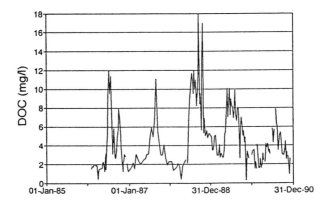

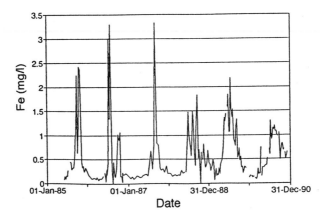

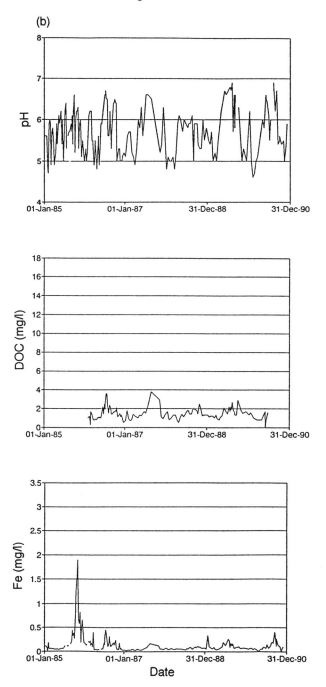

Figure 8.4 Chemistry of (a) limed Cl2 and (b) unlimed Cl6 catchments sampled between 1985 and 1990. Liming occurred in June 1988

Table 8.2 Arithmetic mean pH, Fe and DOC concentrations in soil water draining from peat surface horizon in Cl2

		Pre-liming	Post-liming
pH	Mean	4.3	6.2
	Range	4.2–4.3	5.3–7.4
DOC (mg/l)	Mean	2.0	25.4
	Range	0.8–6.0	6.8–75.0
Fe (mg/l)	Mean	0.2	1.8
	Range	0.1–0.8	0.1–8.6

area. It is therefore possible that reduced iron, mobilized in peat and gley soils, was precipitated as it reached the source area as return flow. In the absence of detailed studies on the mechanisms of iron transport in this catchment such explanations must, however, remain tentative.

The increase in DOC and iron is clearly most marked immediately after liming as the increases during the second summer were much more modest. Hughes *et al.* (1990) show that DOC and iron in the soil water of a stagnopodzol in upland Wales exhibited summer peaks due to accelerated decomposition during higher summer temperatures and drier soil conditions. Given the low DOC peak in the exceptional summer drought of 1989, the results imply that the major flush of decomposition is relatively short-lived. Unfortunately, the lack of summer sampling in the pre-liming period makes interpretation of the second summer peaks more difficult, though concentrations of both solutes appear to remain high.

Impact of Liming on Stream Water Chemistry

Annual Patterns

Prior to liming, the stream pH in CI2 was generally below 5.0 during the winter and up to pH 6 during the summer (Figure 8.4). This seasonal variability primarily reflects the relative importance of catchment hydrological pathways; with relatively well-buffered groundwater dominating during the summer and runoff from the surface horizons of the acid peat soils prevailing in winter. Immediately after lime application, runoff from the hydrological source areas increased stream pH to 7.0 and sustained levels above 6.5 until the winter of 1989 (Table 8.3). High flows following heavy rainfall in January and February 1990 produced the first signs of re-acidification with pH falling below 5.5. Stream pH remained above 6.0 over the following summer, though it dropped below 5.0 in December 1990. The pH of the untreated CI6 showed no comparable changes over this period, though high pH values were detected during base flows in summer droughts of 1989 and 1990.

Levels of DOC in CI2 were also characterized by seasonal fluctuations in the pre-liming period varying between 2 mg/l in the winter and spring and 12 mg/l in the summer and autumn. Such seasonal patterns have been reported for other upland streams, and the late summer/early autumn peak is explained by the flushing of soluble

Table 8.3 Arithmetic mean pH, Fe and DOC concentrations in CI2 stream waters before and after liming in June 1988

		pH	DOC (m/l)	Fe (mg/l)
1985	Average:	5.06	na	0.681
	Range:	4.4–6.0		0.076–2.430
1986	Average:	5.12	3.62	0.388
	Range:	4.4–6.3	0.007–3.304	0.4–12
1987	Average:	5.08	3.49	0.408
	Range:	4.5–6.0	1.5–11.1	0.092–3.33
1988[a]	Average:	4.80	1.90	0.197
	Range:	4.4–5.4	0.4–2.5	0.142–0.272
1988[b]	Average:	6.87	9.04	0.799
	Range:	6.7–7.2	4.8–18.0	0.003–1.84
1989	Average:	6.45	4.44	0.624
	Range:	6.1–7.0	0.3–10.1	0.065–2.19
1990	Average:	6.19	3.45	0.543
	Range:	4.92–6.8	0.9–7.9	0.08–1.3

[a]1988 samples prior to liming.
[b]1988 samples after liming.

decomposition products accumulated over the summer (McDonald *et al.*, 1989). The stimulation of soil decomposition immediately after lime application gave very high stream DOC concentrations during the summer of 1988 which were sustained well into the winter. Mean concentrations remained higher than pre-liming during 1989 and 1990 indicating that increased biological activity was sustained, though the liming-induced enhancement of decomposition lessens each year. The unlimed control catchment shows much lower DOC concentrations in the pre-liming period, though similar seasonal variations are clearly apparent. There is no evidence of any increase in DOC during 1989 and 1990 which is surprising in such hot weather though dry soil conditions may have limited microbial activity (Paul and Clark, 1989).

Temporal variations in iron reflected those of DOC prior to liming with a winter minimum of <0.2 mg/l and a summer/autumn maximum of 2–3 mg/l. After liming, mean iron concentrations increased, although peak summer levels remained below those measured previously. The reason for this reduced summer maximum is difficult to explain. The precipitation of iron-rich deposits on the limed source area is one possibility; however, it is also likely that some iron in stream water may have been present in organic complexes or inorganic colloids that were >0.45 μm in size and thus not filterable. Iron concentrations in CI6, like DOC, were much lower than CI2, although seasonal fluctuations are evident as are anomalously high concentrations in 1985. The lower DOC and iron concentrations in CI6 possibly reflect the lower coverage of anaerobic peaty soils.

The increased DOC and iron concentrations detected in stream water after liming remained below those measured in peat runoff. This implies that runoff from the limed source area was diluted by inputs from other sources in the catchment. This is likely as only 7% of the catchment was limed, though considerably larger areas drain into the source area (Figure 8.2). Unfortunately, insufficient data were collected to disaggregate the influence of limed and unlimed areas on stream chemistry. It is also possible that some iron and DOC was precipitated prior to reaching the stream channel. The latter process would help explain the observed formation of ochreous deposits on the source area after liming.

Storm Event Responses

The effects of changing controls on DOC release and iron mobilization were particularly apparent when solute dynamics were observed during storm events. Space precludes a full comparison of the characteristics of each storm event here. However, two storms which exemplify the major hydrochemical differences observed for events in the pre- and post-liming periods, regardless of storm characteristics or antecedent conditions are discussed. Prior to liming, the storm response of DOC and iron was positively correlated with flow due to their transport into streams by storm hydrological pathways in the upper soil horizons. Figure 8.5 shows the DOC and iron response during a storm in September 1987. Both DOC and iron concentrations peak close to the storm hydrograph peak. In contrast, a storm event in November 1988 (Figure 8.6) shows a response that was typical of the post-liming period. Both DOC and particularly iron peak early on the rising limb of the storm hydrograph, with levels declining at the storm peak. This hysteresis is probably explained by the flushing of iron-rich and organic-rich precipitates from the limed source area and stream channel. Note that concentrations of both solutes were also higher during post-liming events.

IMPLICATIONS FOR WATER QUALITY MANAGEMENT

The findings of this investigation demonstrate that although source area liming is an effective short-term land management strategy for increasing the pH of acidified surface waters, marked changes to other water quality parameters can occur. The presence of elevated levels of DOC and iron has two main implications; first in relation to the quality of water supplies in rural regions, and second for the ecology of upland streams.

The colour of stream water is usually primarily determined by the concentration of organic matter of which DOC is an important component (McDonald et al., 1989). Colour is an important parameter in quality standards for drinking water as discoloured water is aesthetically unacceptable once its colour exceeds 15 Hazen units and requires extensive treatment by filtration and coagulation. Moreover, DOC can react with other chemicals such as chlorine to produce complex compounds such as trihalomethanes which may have health implications (Water Research Centre, 1986). Iron concentrations too can discolour water, cause taste problems and can stain and precipitate within pipe systems. In most public water supply situations, treatment prior to distribution would remove such problems. However, Buckley and Keil (1990) estimate that over 20 000 private supplies in Wales receive only simple treatment of filtration and disinfection after direct abstraction; these supplies are predominantly located in remote upland areas that are sensitive to acidification.

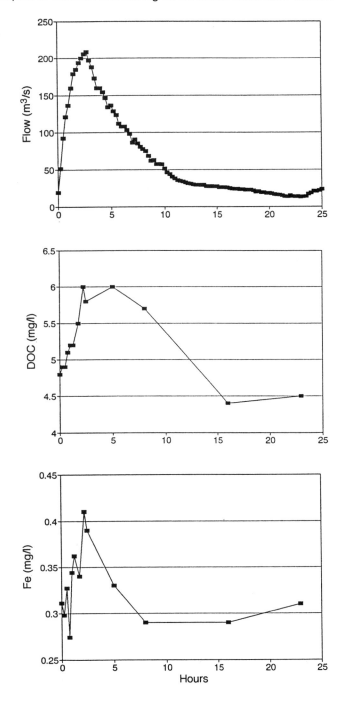

Figure 8.5 Response of DOC and Fe during a pre-liming storm event on 23 September 1987

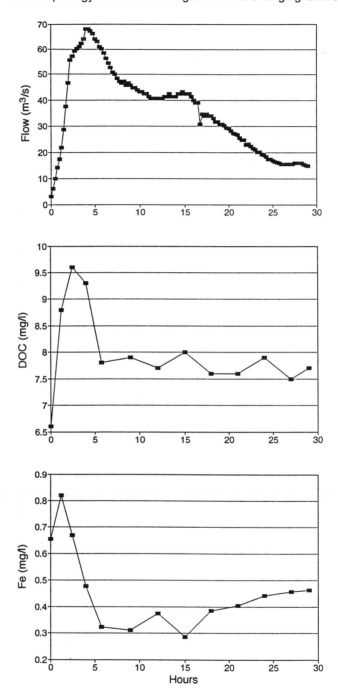

Figure 8.6   Response of DOC and Fe during a post-liming storm event on 8 November 1988

Two European Community Directives are of relevance to the quality of water supplies in acidified areas. The Surface Water Directive (75/440/EEC) relates to the quality of surface waters abstracted for drinking water and the Drinking Water Directive (80/778/EEC) pertains to the quality of drinking water at the point of consumption. Both directives include the parameters of colour, iron and pH. The Surface Water Directive stipulates higher recommended and lower mandatory standards, whilst the the Drinking Water Directive specifies guidelines and, more importantly, statutory maximum admissable concentrations (MAC) which should not be exceeded. Table 8.4 shows that both the mean post-liming colour and iron concentrations of CI2 exceeded the mandatory standard and MAC of the Surface and Drinking Water Directives respectively. Although mean iron concentrations exceeded standards prior to liming, the percentage compliance rate decreased after liming as did that of colour (Table 8.5). Thus, it appears that catchments like CI2 with a hydrology resulting in high percentage coverage of anaerobic soils and naturally high DOC and iron concentrations, may be particularly susceptible to water quality problems after liming.

The increases in DOC and iron may also have implications for the ecology of upland streams. The DOC derived from catchment soils is an important component in the carbon cycle of aquatic ecosystems and may constitute an additional nutrient source that could disrupt nutrient dynamics (Grieve, 1984b). In addition, high concentrations of iron can be toxic to some species and its precipitation on the stream bed could seriously damage the habitat of stream invertebrates.

It is clear that many issues remain unresolved with regard to catchment liming; this study has demonstrated the potential deterioration in the quality of water supplies. The magnitude of the impact on downstream abstractions will not be clear until

Table 8.4 Impact of liming on stream water quality in relation to water quality standards of EC Directives

	pH	Colour (Hazen)	Fe (mg/l)
Directive			
Surface Water	—	20	0.3
Drinking Water	6.5–9.5	20	0.2
CI2 pre-liming mean	5.06	10	0.447
CI2 post-liming mean	6.54	48	0.615

Table 8.5 Percentage compliance of CI2 samples with EC water quality standards

	Colour	Fe
Pre-liming		
Surface Water Directive	100%	68%
Drinking Water Directive	100%	48%
Post-liming		
Surface Water Directive	24%	21%
Drinking Water Directive	24%	16%

large-scale, long-term liming experiments have been carried out on larger catchment systems. Moreover, such land management practices are set against a background of environmental change; patterns of acid deposition are changing as emissions of sulphur dioxide decreases whilst emissions of nitrogen oxides continue to increase (Gilham *et al.*, 1992). Overarching such changes in air quality are the uncertain impacts of climatic change and the implications for the hydrological and hydrochemical processes in upland catchments (Arnell and Jenkins, 1992). Clearly, there remains an urgent need to understand solute processes in relation to land management and environmental change over the coming decade.

ACKNOWLEDGEMENTS

The authors are grateful to the National Rivers Authority field and laboratory staff for the data collection. The Llyn Brianne Project was funded by the Department of Environment, Welsh Office, NRA and NERC. The views expressed are entirely the authors' own and not necessarily those of the NRA.

REFERENCES

Allen, S. E. (1989). *The Chemical Analysis of Ecological Material* (2nd edn), Blackwell, Oxford.

Arnell, N. A. and Jenkins, A. (1992). *Implications of Climate Change for the National Rivers Authority*, NRA R&D Project 358 Report, NRA, Bristol.

Buckley, C. B. and Keil, L. (1990). Acid deposition—drinking water quality and health. In Edwards, R. W., Gee, A. S. and Stoner, J. H. (Eds), *Acid Waters in Wales*, Kluwer, Dordrecht, pp. 145–158.

Davies, T. D., Tranter, M., Wigington, P. J. and Eshleman, K. N. (1992). Acidic episodes in surface waters in Europe. *Journal of Hydrology*, **132**, 25–69.

Donald, A. P. and Gee, A. S. (1992). Acid waters in upland Wales. *Environmental Pollution*, **78**, 141–148.

Donald, A. P., Stoner, J. H., Reynolds, B., Oldfield, F., Rippey, B. and Natkanski, J. (1990). Atmospheric deposition. In Edwards, R. W., Gee, A. S. and Stoner, J. H. (Eds), *Acid Waters in Wales*, Kluwer, Dordrecht, pp. 39–44.

Forestry Commission (1991). *Forest and Water Guidelines*, HMSO, London.

Gee, A. S. (1990). Introduction to Welsh Studies. In Edwards, R. W., Gee, A. S. and Stoner, J. H. (Eds), *Acid Waters in Wales*, Kluwer, Dordrecht, pp. 1–10.

Gilham, C. A., Leech, P. K. and Eggleston, H. S. (1992). *UK Emissions of Air Pollutants*, Report LR 887 (AP), Warren Spring Laboratory, Stevenage.

Grieve, I. C. (1984a). Relationships among dissolved organic matter iron and discharge in a moorland stream. *Earth Surface Processes and Landforms*, **9**, 35–41.

Grieve, I. C. (1984b). Concentrations and annual loading of dissolved organic matter in a small moorland stream. *Freshwater Biology*, **14**, 533–537.

Haynes, R. J. and Swift, R. S. (1988). Effects of lime and phosphate additions on changes in enzyme activities, microbial biomass and levels of extractable N, S and P in an acid soil. *Biology and Fertility of Soils*, **6**, 153–158.

Hornung, M., Le-Grice, S., Brown, N. and Norris, D. (1990a). The role of geology and soils in controlling surface water acidity in Wales. In Edwards, R. W., Gee, A. S. and Stoner J. H. (Eds), *Acid Waters in Wales*, Junk, Dordrecht, pp. 55–66.

Hornung, M., Brown, S. J. and Ranson, A. (1990b). Amelioration of surface acidity by catchment management. In Edwards, R. W., Gee, A. S. and Stoner, J. H. (Eds), *Acid Waters in Wales*, Junk, Dordrecht, pp. 311–328.

Hughes, S., Reynolds, B. and Roberts, J. D. (1990). The influence of land management on DOC concentrations and its effect on the mobilization of Al and Fe in podzolic soils in Mid-Wales. *Soil Use and Management*, **6**, 137–144.

Jenkins, A., Whitehead, P., Cosby, B. J. and Birks, H. J. B. (1990). Modelling long-term acidification: a comparison of with diatom reconstruction and the implications for reversibility. *Philosophical Transactions of the Royal Society (Series B)*, **327**, 435–440.

Jenkins, A., Waters, D. and Donald, A. (1991). An assessment of terrestrial liming strategies in upland Wales. *Journal of Hydrology*, **124**, 243–261.

Kay, D., Boon, R. and Crowther, J. (1989). Coloured waters in Wales: spatial and temporal trends. In *Proceedings of the 2nd British Hydrological Society Symposium*, British Hydrological Society, London, pp. 1.49–1.57.

McDonald, A. T., Edwards, A. M. C., Naden, P. S., Martin, D. and Mitchell, G, (1989). Discoloured runoff in the Yorkshire Pennines. In *Proceedings of the 2nd British Hydrological Society Symposium*, British Hydrological Society, London, pp. 1.59–1.63.

Milner, N. J. and Varallo, P. V. (1990). Effects of acid deposition on fish and fisheries in Wales. In Edwards, R. W., Gee, A. S. and Stoner, J. H. (Eds), *Acid Waters in Wales*, Junk, Dordrecht, pp. 121–144.

National Rivers Authority (1992). *Llyn Brianne Acid Waters Project Final Report*, NRA, Cardiff.

Ormerod, S. J. and Edwards, R. W. (1985). Stream acidity in some areas of Wales in relation to historical trends in afforestation and the use of agricultural limestone. *Journal of Environmental Management*, **20**, 189–197.

Ormerod, S. J., Donald, A. P. and Brown, S. J. (1989). The influence of plantation forestry on the pH and aluminium concentration of upland Welsh streams: A re-examination. *Environmental Pollution*, **62**, 47–62.

Ormerod, S. J., Weatherley, N. S., Merrett, W. J., Gee, A. S. and Whitehead, P. G. (1990). Restoring acidified streams in upland Wales: a modelling comparison of the effects of liming and reduction in sulphate deposition. *Environmental Pollution*, **64**, 67–85.

Paul, E. A. and Clark, F. E. (1989). *Soil Microbiology and Biochemistry*, Academic Press, New York.

Reid, J. M., MacLeod, D. A. and Cresser, M. (1981) Factors affecting the chemistry of precipitation and river water in an upland catchment. *Journal of Hydrololgy*, **50**, 129–145.

Rudeforth, C. C., Hartnup, R., Lee, J. W., Thompson, T. R. E. and Wright, P. S. (1984). *Soils and Their use in Wales*, Soil Survey of England and Wales, Harpenden.

Soulsby, C. (1992). Hydrological controls on acid runoff generation in an afforested headwater catchment at Llyn Brianne, Mid-Wales. *Journal of Hydrology*, **138**, 431–448.

Soulsby, C. and Reynolds, B. (1993). Influence of soil hydrological pathways on stream aluminium chemistry at Llyn Brianne, Mid-Wales. *Environmental Pollution*, **81**, 51–60.

Stoner, J. H., Gee, A. S. and Wade, K. R. (1984). The effects of acidification on the ecology of streams in the upper Tywi catchment in West Wales. *Environmental Pollution, Series A*, **35**, 125–157.

Tervet, D. J. and Harriman, R. (1988). Changes in pH and calcium after selective liming in the catchment of Loch Dee, a sensitive and rapid-turnover loch in south west Scotland. *Aquaculture and Fisheries Management*, **19**, 191–203.

Underwood, J., Donald, A. P. and Stoner, J. H. (1987). Investigations into the use of limestone to combat acidification in two lakes in west Wales. *Journal of Environmental Management*, **24**, 29–40.

United Kingdom Acid Waters Review Group (1989). *Acidity in United Kingdom Freshwaters*, HMSO, London.

Walling, D. E. and Webb, B. W. (1986). Solutes in river systems. In S. T. Trudgill (Ed.), *Solute Processes*, Wiley, Chichester, pp. 251–327.

Walsh, R. P. D. (1992). Climate and Hydrology. In *Llyn Brianne Acid Waters Project*, National Rivers Authority, Cardiff, pp. 13–21.

Warfvinge, P. and Sverdrup, H, (1988). Soil liming as a measure to mitigate acid runoff. *Water Resources Research*, **24**, 701–712.

Water Research Centre (1986). *Health Aspects of Organics in Drinking Water*, TR231, Water Research Centre, Medmenham.

Waters, D. J., Jenkins, A., Donald, A. and Staples, T. B. (1991). Terrestrial liming in upland Wales: the importance of hydrological source areas. *Journal of the Institute of Water and Environmental Management*, **5**, 336–341.

Weatherley, N. S. (1988). Liming to mitigate acidification in freshwater ecosystems: a review of biological consequences. *Water, Air and Soil Pollution*, **39**, 421–437.

Weatherley, N. S. and Ormerod, S. J. (1992). The biological response of acidic streams to catchment liming compared to the changes predicted from stream chemistry. *Journal of Environmental Management*, **34**, 105–115.

Woodin, S. and Skiba, U. (1990). Liming fails the acid test. *New Scientist*, March 1990, 50–54.

9 Potential Effects of Climate Change on Agricultural Production and the Hydrology of Drained Grassland in the UK

A. C. ARMSTRONG

and

D. A. CASTLE
ADAS Soil and Water Research Centre, Cambridge, UK

ABSTRACT

Climate change due to increased CO_2 concentrations can be expected to lead to increases in both mean temperatures and rainfall amounts. The impact of these potential effects on the hydrology and agricultural production of grassland is investigated using a tripartite model. The first part generates a synthetic meteorological record from an existing data set. This synthetic record is used to model the soil water balance, which is then input into a simple grass growth model to predict the basic productivity of grass under the changed regime. The model is applied to data derived from a drainage experiment at North Wyke, Devon, for which the grass growth model has been validated under current conditions. The shape of the response surface is shown for various changes in both temperature and rainfall amounts. These show that grass growth increases more in response to increases in temperature than in rainfall. Because of the feedback between available crop water supply and actual transpiration, mean soil moisture deficits in summer do not increase sharply, although total transpiration rates do increase. The increase in temperature leads to greater grass growth, although the decrease in grass production in mid-summer due to moisture shortage still remains. Relating soil moisture status to grazing potential permits the evaluation of the grazing period, and again the model shows that in a warmer environment both the start and end of the grazing season are extended, both by the greater growth of grass and the lengthened period of soil moisture deficit.

INTRODUCTION

Possibly the greatest of all anthropogenetic changes to the environment is global warming due to an increased CO_2 content of the atmosphere (Houghton *et al.*, 1990; Leggett, 1990). Changes in the global climate will change the local climate, and one

---

Geomorphology and Land Management in a Changing Environment. Edited by D. F. M. McGregor and D. A. Thompson.
©1995 John Wiley & Sons Ltd

immediate consequence will be changes to the hydrological cycle (UKCCIRG, 1991). The relative importance of surface flow, through-drainage, and macropore flow will change as the degree of soil structural development changes in response to different (probably greater) soil moisture deficits, and these will lead in turn to changes in the patterns of nutrient leaching (Armstrong *et al.*, in press). In the long term these changes may be given physical expression in the landscape, as the geomorphological system adjusts to altered hydrological regimes.

Patterns of agriculture production and activity will also be affected by these changes to the environment, as they respond to differing temperatures and soil water regimes (Parry *et al.*, 1988; Bennett, 1989). These will, however, be the result of a number of interlocking processes, in which the productivity of agricultural crops interacts with hydrology, land management actions, and the socio-economic context (Loveland *et al.*, 1994).

Changes to the climate can thus affect the short-term look of the landscape as land use decisions and land management actions react to the changed opportunities and constraints, but it can also affect the long-term hydrological and geomorphological nature of the landscape as first soils and then the whole geomorphological system respond to the altered environmental inputs. Detailed study of the impacts of climate change on the current landscape–geomorphological system thus have a potential to inform debates about past changes, as well as to guide the policy makers who plan for the future.

This study considers the potential impact of changes on one part of the complex web of the physical landscape, focusing on the issues of the performance and utilization of grazed grass swards. To do this, it uses a grass growth model that includes the explicit consideration of climatic variables on both soil physical condition and grass physiology. The sensitivity of the modelled system to various assumptions about the magnitude of the climate change can then be investigated. The study of sensitivities is necessary until better estimates of the magnitude of the changes are available from climate modelling studies. There are thus three components to the study:

- the derivation of input data that reflect the changes to the climate,
- a model that describes the physical impact of these changes, and
- a model to describe the effects on grass growth and utilization.

In practice, these last two stages cannot be completely separated, because of the important feedback between crop growth and actual transpiration by the crop.

This study uses the combined hydrologic and grass growth model, SWARD (Dowle and Armstrong, 1990; Armstrong *et al.*, 1993), for the study of drainage effects in grassland, and validated for the North Wyke drainage experiment (Armstrong & Garwood, 1991; Tyson *et al.*, 1992). Because of this strong experimental basis to the model, the numerical experiments that are reported in this chapter were all performed within the context of the same site at North Wyke in Devon. The climate at this site is characterized by moderately high rainfall, annual average 1060 mm, with a strong winter maximum (Wilkins, 1982). The soil is a clay pelo-stagnogley of the Hallsworth series (see Armstrong and Garwood, 1991 for a complete description). This model has already been used for a study of the impact of a single climate change scenario on grass production (Armstrong and Castle, 1992).

CLIMATE INPUT DATA

Changes to the mean climate cannot be immediately translated into daily weather values suitable for modelling, and so some scheme must be used to create these values, the climate inverse problem (Kim *et al.*, 1984). The solution adopted for this study, which is just one of the many possible, is to adjust current weather data to meet altered means. Possible alternatives available include the use of stochastic weather generators to provide synthetic weather sequences of analogue climates or of GCM outputs. In the scheme adopted, daily temperatures are all altered by the same absolute amount, and daily rainfall by the same percentage amount. This has the advantage of being simple, but carries with it the assumptions that the structures within the data are similar. Thus, to produce, for example, a greater rainfall amount, it assumes more rainfall each rain day, not more rain days.

Potential evapotranspiration (PET), which is input to the model as a calculated value, is a particular problem, as it is a function not only of both radiation and temperature but also of cloudiness and windiness, variables for which we do not have good predictions. In order to reflect the relative importance of circulation and temperature variables, simple linear regressions, using climatic data from Smith (1976), were used to identify the relationship between mean monthly temperature and mean monthly PET rates for the agroclimatic regions of the West of England. A series of regressions, one for each month, gave the mean daily rate of evaporation as a linear function of mean monthly temperature. These give coefficients that reflect the relative importance of temperature and circulation effects on PET, being higher in summer than winter. Table 9.1 shows the values derived, and the correlation coefficients of the relationship. From these values the current PET values were adjusted upwards to bring them into line with the changed temperatures.

Table 9.1 Increases in monthly potential evapotranspiration rates due to a one degree increase in temperature, derived, using regression analyses, from climate data quoted by Smith (1976). The correlation coefficient between temperature and PET is also given ($n = 17$)

Month	Increase in PET (mm/day)	Correlation coefficient
Jan.	0.046	0.86
Feb.	0.079	0.92
Mar.	0.093	0.91
Apr.	0.171	0.95
May	0.211	0.91
June	0.276	0.95
July	0.221	0.93
Aug.	0.228	0.93
Sept.	0.186	0.93
Oct.	0.066	0.79
Nov.	0.062	0.75
Dec.	0.053	0.87

SOIL WATER BALANCE MODELLING

The meteorological data (both for current and revised climates) were then input into a simple soil water balance model. The soil was represented as a single store, 1 m deep, with a porosity of 50%, and so capable of storing a maximum of 500 mm of water. This store was then partitioned into four components:

(i) free draining water, which is removed by drainage above field capacity (FC);
(ii) readily available water which is removed without restraint by the crop between field capacity and wilting point (WP);
(iii) less readily available water which is removed with increasing difficulty by the crop between wilting point and permanent wilting point (PWP); and
(iv) unavailable water below PWP.

Although it is possible to define these points in terms of absolute water content (or in terms of the tension required to reach these water contents), it is computationally convenient to define them all in terms of the Soil Moisture Deficit that they represent. For the current model we define FC (SMD = 0) as a profile moisture content of 475 mm, WP as a deficit of 75 mm and PWP as a deficit of 175 mm. The 25 mm of "free" water above field capacity reflects 5% of the soil volume (drainable porosity) above a mole drain depth of 500 mm, which could be removed by drainage. These values were all chosen in the light of the physical properties of the soil at North Wyke, given by Armstrong and Garwood (1991).

The state of the soil moisture (B_t) is calculated from the simple balance equation:

$$B_t = B_{t-1} + R_t - ET_t - D_t \qquad (9.1)$$

where R_t is rainfall in time t, ET_t is the actual evapotranspiration, and D_t is the drainage rate.

The actual evapotranspiration rate is equivalent to the potential rate until the wilting point is reached. Between wilting point (WP) and permanent wilting point (PWP), the actual ET is calculated from the potential reduced by the size of the deficit below wilting point, and below permanent wilting point it becomes zero:

$$
\begin{array}{lll}
ET_{act} = ET_{pot} & B_t > WP & (9.2a) \\
ET_{act} = ET_{pot}(B_t - PWP)/(WP - PWP) & WP < B_t < PWP & (9.2b) \\
ET_{act} = 0 & B_t < PWP & (9.2c)
\end{array}
$$

The drainage rate is calculated from the height of the water table using the Hooghoudt (1940) drainage equation. Water table height, h is calculated from the total water content above field capacity (FC) divided by the drainable porosity, f:

$$h = (B_t - FC)/f \qquad (9.3)$$

and the drainage rate is then given by:

$$D_t = (4Kh^2 + 8Khd)/L^2 \qquad (9.4)$$

where K is the hydraulic conductivity of the soil, L is the drain spacing, and d is the "effective" depth of soil below the drain.

The derivation and use of this equation is discussed by, among others, ILRI (1973) and Smedema and Rycroft (1983). Although for this study, the model was run for the soil in a drained state, the same model can represent the natural undrained state by always setting the drainage component (D_t) to zero.

If equation (9.3) predicts a water table at the surface, water cannot enter the soil, and so becomes direct runoff.

GRASS GROWTH MODEL

The model considers a daily grass herbage balance:

$$W_t = W_{t-1} + G_t - S_t - R_t \qquad (9.5)$$

where W_t is the weight of herbage on day t, G_t is the growth of herbage, S_t is the senescence and R_t is the removal.

This inclusion of removal as the last term ensures that the management of the sward is an integral part of the model, which therefore needs to include either the grazing rules or the cutting regime. For the purpose of this chapter, the sward is defined as grazable if the SMD is greater than 25 mm, and the stocking rate adjusted to the herbage available. The rate of grass removal, R_t, is then calculated assuming a constant rate of grass intake per grazing animal. Although the results presented in this chapter were derived under continuous grazing, the model can also accommodate both rotational grazing and cutting. More complicated interactions between grass availability and the management of the sward (particularly the satisfaction of both grazing and conservation requirements for a fixed herd size) could perhaps be considered at the risk of an increase of model complexity, but these have not been included at this stage.

The rate of grass growth is predicted from the function:

$$G_t = G_{max}F(JW)f(N)f(T)f(B) \qquad (9.6)$$

in which a potential maximum is multiplied by four limiting functions that each varies between 0 and 1; where J = radiation, W = crop weight (a surrogate for leaf area index), N = nitrogen fertilizer supply, T = temperature and B = soil water balance.

The potential rate, G_{max}, is defined as 0.25 t/ha/day (Parsons and Johnson, 1985). It is possible that as a result of the "direct fertilization effect" of enhanced CO_2 levels that a higher value for this constant might be appropriate (Kimball, 1983; Strain and Cure, 1985), but such an interaction has not been explored in this study.

The photosynthesis interaction, $f(JW)$, depends on the availability of both radiation and herbage to intercept it. Where the radiation is non-limiting, then the growth rate depends on the crop standing weight:

$$f(W) = 1 - \{(W - W_{opt})/W_{opt}\}^2 \qquad (9.7)$$

where the optimum crop weight, W_{opt} is 5 t/ha (Dowle and Armstrong, 1990). When crop weight is non-limiting, then the effect of radiation is given by a similar function:

$$f(J) = 1 - \{(J - J_{opt})/J_{opt}\}^2 \qquad (9.8)$$

Where both are limiting, then $f(JW)$ is the product of $f(J)$ and $f(W)$. By reducing the crop weight, grazing or cutting reduces the photosynthetic efficiency of the crop. This interaction emphasizes the need to consider the management of the grass crop as a component of the model.

The nitrogen component of the growth curve is an empirically derived function for the overall annual nitrogen application rate. For the purposes of this study, it is assumed that nitrogen is non-limiting.

The form of the relationship between grass growth rate and water supply shows a limitation due both to water in excess (waterlogging) and in shortage (drought) (Figure 9.1). The exact form of the relationship has been difficult to establish experimentally, and so a series of straight lines has been widely used (e.g. Feddes, 1988), to estimate the depression of growth rate outside the optimum range, field capacity to wilting point. This form has a maximum between field capacity and wilting point, and drops to zero at both complete saturation and permanent wilting point. As grass growth rate is depressed by water shortage, so the actual evapotranspiration is also proportionately reduced.

The results from this model are a daily sequence of water balances and grass standing crop weights (Figure 9.2). The total grass growth, the pattern of growth and the magnitude of the drainage effect are predicted with reasonable success (Table 9.2). The predicted stocking rates, and the start and end of the grazing season were also predicted moderately well by this model (Dowle and Armstrong, 1990). It was thus considered reasonable to use the model for the study of climate change impacts on grass growth and utilization.

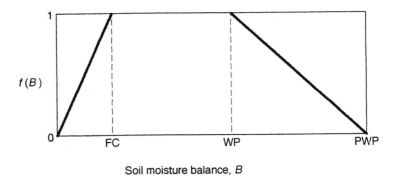

Soil moisture balance, B

Figure 9.1 Interaction between grass growth rate and soil moisture balance, B. The function f(B) in equation 9.6

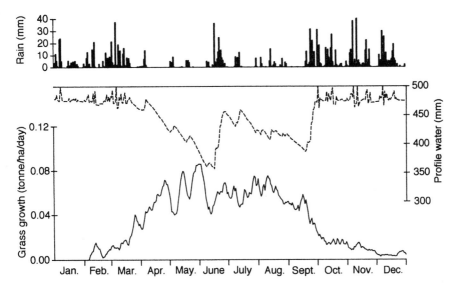

Figure 9.2   Example output from the model. Results from one year showing rainfall inputs, soil moisture balance and daily grass growth rate, for a drained sward at North Wyke, Devon

Table 9.2   Grass dry matter yields predicted by the SWARD model and recorded at the North Wyke experiment under four weekly cutting (after Dowle and Armstrong, 1990, Table 5)

	Undrained		Drained	
Cut	Predicted	Observed	Predicted	Observed
1	0.9	1.2	2.0	1.6
2	1.6	1.6	1.8	1.8
3	1.7	1.7	2.0	1.9
4	1.6	1.8	1.7	1.9
5	1.6	1.3	1.6	1.3
6	0.8	0.8	0.8	0.8
Total	8.2	8.4	9.9	9.3

CLIMATE CHANGE SCENARIOS

An initial series of experiments with the model considered the effect of only a single climate change scenario (Armstrong and Castle, 1992). Assuming a 3 °C increase in mean temperature, and a 10% increase in winter rainfall and a 10% decrease in the summer, it was possible to show that although the impact of climate change was to increase the productivity of grass, it also shifted the main peak of production forward in the year, and increased the size of the drop in productivity in the summer due to soil moisture deficit.

However, because of the uncertainties in the climate change predictions, it is also important to investigate the sensitivity of these results to variations in the assumed magnitudes of the climate change effects. Consequently, this study examined the impacts of a range of change effects:

- temperature changing from current to +5 °C; and
- rainfall changing between −10% and +25%.

This was done by encapsulating the model within a loop in which the rainfall and temperature change parameters were varied systematically, and then running it for a 10-year test period. It is one of the characteristics of this sort of exercise that it generates an enormous amount of output, so it is necessary to examine the shape of the response surface in order to identify the effects.

RESULTS: HYDROLOGY

Predicted changes in the soil water budget are summarized in a series of pie-charts in Figure 9.3. The total rainfall input is lost by one of three routes: by evapotranspiration, by drainage and by direct surface runoff. The direct surface runoff, which arises when rain falls on a soil with the water table already at the surface, is the component affected most. Under current conditions, it is about 4% of the total rainfall, in line with the observation by Armstrong and Garwood (1991). This component therefore increases to 7% of the total as rainfall increases, but also decreases as the increase in temperature increases the rate of evapotranspiration. This component will thus diminish if the increase in temperature is accompanied by a

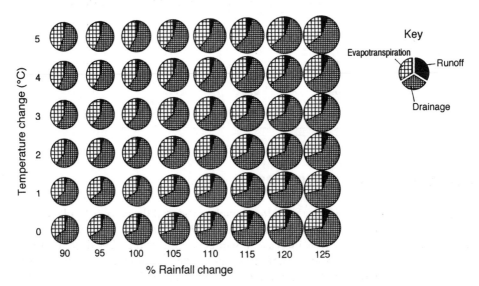

Figure 9.3 Components of the mean soil moisture balance (evapotranspiration, surface runoff and drainage) in response to changes in temperature and rainfall amounts

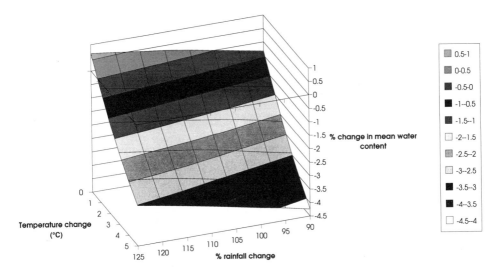

Figure 9.4   Change in mean profile water content in response to climate change variables, expressed as a percentage of the current value

decrease in rainfall. Such a prediction, however, does not take into account the possible change of rainfall pattern to a more convectional regime, in which more high-intensity summer storms may generate significantly greater amounts of surface runoff (UKCCIRG, 1991).

The results can be compared with predictions for the Semois basin in Belgium given by Bultot *et al.* (1988). They used a scenario in which temperature increased by 2.9 °C and rainfall increased by 54 mm (close to 5%). They predicted an increase in total runoff of 37 mm, whereas this model predicts an increase of 21 mm. In view of the detailed differences between the models, and the different physical situations they represent, the agreement in direction and rough order of magnitude is encouraging.

The response surface for the mean profile water content (Figure 9.4) shows a strong dependency on temperature which overrides the large shifts in assumed rainfall amounts. This is the reflection of the fact that the soil is, under both the current and the altered climates, largely saturated for much of the winter. Increases in rainfall cannot, therefore, be accommodated within the soil, and the effect will be an increase in winter runoff, not a greater storage of water in the soil. Bultot *et al.* (1988) report similar findings.

RESULTS: AGRICULTURE

The impacts of climate change on patterns of grass growth are equally dominated by temperature effects (Figure 9.5). The effect of a 25% increase in rain is less than 3% growth, whereas the effect of a 25% increase in temperature is as much as 18%. This result is perhaps surprising considering how sensitive grass production is to soil water supply. However, the drainage advantage is also maintained, as the all-important

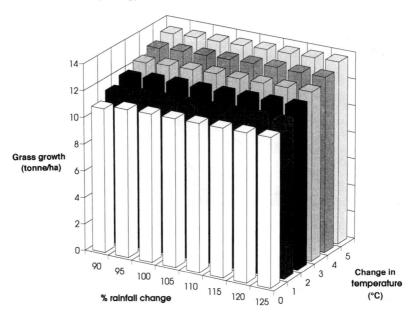

Figure 9.5   Response of mean total grass growth to climate change variables

effect of drainage in improving on early season growth is retained. It is also noticeable that the response surfaces do not appear to reach a maximum. For the range of responses examined, and hence for the reasonable expectations for the climate, the future of grass farming, in the West of the UK at least, is not threatened.

However, the response of the farming system is more complicated when examined in terms of the length of the growing season (Figure 9.6). This important variable reflects the farmer's ability to utilize the grass that is grown. An extended grazing season is probably the most important reason for draining grass, and not the change in total grass grown. Here, there is a big effect due to rainfall, as increases in rainfall, particularly those leading to waterlogged conditions in the early part of the year, restrict the accessibility of the land for grazing. Consequently, increases in winter rainfall are reflected in a direct reduction in the length of grazing period. However, the earlier onset of the soil moisture deficit in spring, in response to the greater evaporative demand, and so the effect of increased temperatures, is always to extend the grazing season.

The conclusion from these two results shows that the bigger impact of climate change is in terms of the management options available to the farmer. Furthermore, detailed examination of the results from a single scenario by Armstrong and Castle (1992) also suggests that the effect of climate change will be to emphasize the mid-season decrease in grass availability. Although both the total length of the grazing season and the amount of grass available will increase, new management actions may be required to utilize that production.

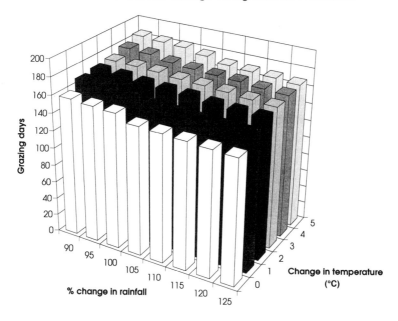

Figure 9.6 Response of mean length of grazing season to climate change variables

CONCLUSIONS

These results have demonstrated the use of a fairly simple model to investigate the responses of the soil-hydrological system, and its use by agriculture, to changes in the climate. However, these responses can be complicated. Nevertheless, two major hydrological impacts are clear: that the winter period will be increasingly wetter, with surface runoff amounts increasing even in the drained state; and that in the summer, the hydrological system will be dominated by increased evapotranspiration. The degree of contrast between winter and summer will thus be enhanced. This effect will be further emphasized if, as is sometimes asserted, summer rain in a warmer climate will be more convectional, and hence more intense, than at present. It seems inevitable that the result will be more "flashy" stream responses, which may result in a change in the form of the river channels.

The hydrological impact that will have the greatest impact on grassland farming will be the earlier onset of the soil moisture deficit, which to the farmer means an earlier start to the grazing season. Although the greater temperatures will lead to increases in grass production, grazing will have to be maintained over a longer period, and more frequently over drought-stressed summer periods of grass shortage.

These results have shown that even where the soil physical system, for example the soil moisture deficit, changes in a relatively predictable way, the effect on agricultural management is more complex. The length of the grazing season, which is a critical factor in the management of swards in UK, is much more sensitive to the changes in climate than either grass growth or the SMD alone. This at least is one of the areas where the effects appear to be additive.

The results presented here are all restricted to a single site. It is now necessary to extend them to a range of conditions, embracing both a variety of soil types and a range of geographical locations. However, to do so simply by altering parameters is dangerous, and so the exercise needs to be undertaken in conjunction with the assessment of model performance at other locations for which validation data are available. Only when such data have been assembled and the model validated, can the extension to broader spatial pattern be addressed.

ACKNOWLEDGEMENTS

Financial support from the UK Ministry of Agriculture, Fisheries and Food is gratefully acknowledged. We are grateful to Mr J. Cochran, of the Meteorological Office, for suggesting the scheme for revised PET estimates.

REFERENCES

Armstrong, A. C. and Castle, D. A. (1992). Potential impacts of climate change on patterns of production and the role of drainage in grassland. *Grass and Forage Science*, **47**, 50–61.

Armstrong, A. C. and Garwood, E. A. (1991). Hydrological consequences of artificial drainage of grassland. *Hydrological Processes*, **5**, 157–174.

Armstrong, A. C., Castle, D. A. and Tyson, K. A. (1993). SWARD: a model of the growth and utilisation of grazed grass swards to predict the economic return from drainage. *Transactions, 2nd Workshop on crop-water models, 15th International Congress on Irrigation and Drainage (ICID)*, The Hague, The Netherlands, 1993.

Armstrong, A. C., Matthews, A. M., Portwood, A M., Addiscott, T. M. and Leeds-Harrison, P. B. (in press). Modelling the effects of climate change on the hydrology and water quality of structured soils. In Rounsevell, M. (Ed.), *Proceedings, NATO Advanced Research Workshop: Soil Responses to Climate Change: The Implications for Natural and Managed Ecosystems*.

Bennett, R. M. (Ed.) (1989). *The "Greenhouse Effect" and UK Agriculture*, CAS Paper 19, Centre for Agricultural Strategy, Reading.

Bultot, F., Coppens, A., Dupriez, G. L., Gellens, D. and Meulenberghs, F. (1988). Repercussions of a CO_2 doubling on the water cycle and on the water balance—a case study for Belgium. *Journal of Hydrology*, **99**, 319–347.

Dowle, K. and Armstrong, A. C. (1990). A model for investment appraisal of grassland drainage schemes on farms in the UK. *Agricultural Water Management*, **18**, 101–120.

Feddes, R. A. (1988). Modelling and simulation in hydrologic systems related to agricultural development: state of the art. *Agricultural Water Management*, **13**, 235–266.

Hooghoudt, S. B. (1940). Bijdragen tot de kennis van enige natuurkundige grootheden van de grond, No 7. Algemene beschouwing van het probleem van de detailontwatering en de infiltratie door middel van parallel lopende drains, greppels, sloten und kanalen. *Verslagen van landbouwkundig Onderzoekingen*, **46**, 515–707.

Houghton, J. T., Jenkins, G. J. and Ephraums, J. J. (Eds) (1990). *Climate Change: The IPCC Scientific Assessment*, Cambridge University Press, Cambridge.

ILRI (International Institute for Land Reclamation and Improvement) (1973). *Drainage Principles and Applications*, ILRI, Wageningen, The Netherlands.

Kim, J-W., Chang, J-T., Baker, N. L., Wilks, D. S. and Gates, W. L. (1984). The statistical problem of climate inversion: determination of the relationship between local and large-scale climate. *Monthly Weather Review*, **112**, 2069–2077.

Kimball, B. A. (1983). Carbon dioxide and agricultural yields: an assemblage and analysis of 430 prior observations. *Agronomy Journal*, **75**, 779–788.

Leggett, J. (Ed.) (1990). *Global Warming: The Greenpeace Report*, Oxford University Press, Oxford.

Loveland, P. J., Le Gros, J-P., Rounsevell, M. D. A., de la Rosa, D. and Armstrong, A. C. (1994). A spatially distributed soil, soil hydrological and agroclimatic model for the prediction of climate change in The European Community. *Transactions, 15th World Congress of Soil Science*, **6**, 83–99.

Parry, M. L., Carter, T. R. and Konijn, N. T. (Eds) (1988). *The Impact of Climatic Variations on Agriculture, Volume 1: Assessments in Cool Temperate and Cold Regions*, Kluwer, Dordrecht.

Parsons, A. J. and Johnson, I. R. (1985). The physiology of grass growth on grazing. In Frame, J. (Ed.), *Grazing*, Occasional Symposium No. 19, British Grassland Society, Hurley, pp. 3–13.

Smedema, L. K. and Rycroft, D. W. (1983). *Land Drainage. Planning and Design of Agricultural Drainage Systems*, Batsford, London.

Smith, L. P. (1976). *The Agricultural Climate of England and Wales*, MAFF Technical Bulletin No. 34, HMSO, London.

Strain, B. R. and Cure, J. D. (Eds) (1985). *Direct Effects of Increasing Carbon Dioxide on Vegetation*, United States Department of Energy, Office of Energy Research, DOE/ER-0238, Washington, DC.

Tyson, K. C., Garwood, E. A., Armstrong, A. C. and Scholefield, D. (1992). Effects of field drainage on the growth of herbage and the liveweight gain of grazing beef cattle. *Grass and Forage Science*, **47**, 290–301.

UKCCIRG (United Kingdom Climate Change Impacts Review Group, M. Parry, Chairman) (1991). *The Potential Effects of Climate Change in the United Kingdom*, HMSO, London.

Wilkins, R. J. (1982). The permanent grassland division at North Wyke. In *Annual Report 1981*, The Grassland Research Institute, Hurley, pp. 112–118.

10 Agricultural Terrace Degradation in South-East Spain: Modelling and Management Strategies

DONALD A. THOMPSON
Department of Geography, Royal Holloway, University of London, UK

and

HELEN M. SCOGING
Department of Geography, London School of Economics, UK

ABSTRACT

Reduced management of dryland flood farming systems in south-east Spain, associated with economic change and rural depopulation, has resulted in severe degradation. The stages of degradation include erosion of terraces by rills, gullies and pipes. Field survey and observation of one such system near Turré in the province of Alméria is the basis of a conceptual model of terrace degradation linking topographic hollows, dessication cracking and subsurface flow processes. Temporal evolution of the degrading terraces is discussed. The first stages of computer simulation model operationalization, using a surface flow accumulation by flow line vectors, are described. The aim of the model under development is to identify the location of areas which are *sensitive* to erosion and deposition. These areas should then become the focus of management or conservation strategies.

INTRODUCTION: TERRACE AGRICULTURE IN SOUTH-EAST SPAIN

Dry land or "secano" agriculture, employing flood farming terrace systems, are an important small-scale activity in the most arid regions of Spain. These farms are part of the declining "*minifundia*" system which has suffered from the out-migration of population to urban or coastal tourism related industries over the last 40 years. Following Spain's accession to the European Community in 1986, grant aid from the Common Agricultural Policy (CAP) has contributed to the rapid growth of "*regadio*" or irrigated horticulture, particularly in the south-eastern coastal zone of Andalucia. Economic factors and subsequent rural depopulation have contributed to the neglect

Geomorphology and Land Management in a Changing Environment. Edited by D. F. M. McGregor and D. A. Thompson.
©1995 John Wiley & Sons Ltd

of flood water terrace systems, which has led to severe degradation by internally and externally generated geomorphic processes. The main process of degradation on abandoned *secano* systems is piping (López-Bermúdez and Romero-Díaz, 1989). Field observation in Alméria province since 1988 has suggested that large-scale degradation by pipes and gullies can occur within two to three years. The period 1988–93 has also witnessed a major effort to rehabilitate old degraded terrace systems and the establishment of new terraces on previously unused land. This renewed interest in terrace farming may also be due to CAP funding and makes understanding of the process–form interactions on terraces of considerable practical importance.

This chapter examines the processes of degradation on a flood farming terrace system near Mojácar in the Provincia de Alméria, Andalucia (Figure 10.1). The stages of degradation include the erosion of individual terraces by rills, gullies and pipes and subsequently the integration of the terrace erosional system with valley drainage. Field survey and observation is the basis of the development of a conceptual model of terrace degradation. The operationalization of major elements of this model in terms of a computer simulation model is then discussed. The aim of the model being developed is to examine the mechanisms of degradation and their relationship to surface and subsurface processes, the temporal evolution of the terrace system in response to the processes and the spatial localization of erosion. Possible threshold conditions for the development of gullies and pipes are explored. The model can then be used to identify areas that are *sensitive* to

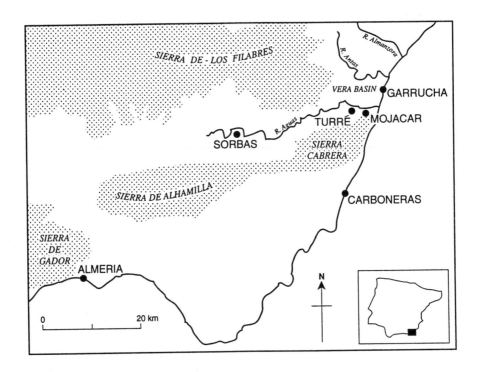

Figure 10.1 Location of the study area

erosion and deposition. These locations should then become the focus of management or conservation strategies.

FIELD CONTEXT: THE VERA BASIN

Geological Setting

The terrace system studied is located in the Vera Basin, one of a series of basins formed at the eastern end of the Betic Cordillera (Figure 10.2). Miocene tectonism created the conditions for marine inundation of the basins and accumulation of Neogene sediments. The basins are bounded by metamorphic nappes of the Nevado/Filabride complex (Harvey, 1987). Marine deposition of gypsiferous marls, sands and mudstones continued in the Pliocene. The topography of the Vera Basin is relatively subdued away from the major river systems, the Rios Almanzora, Antas and Aguas. Incision along these rivers associated with recent tectonics has removed surface gravels and exposed the erodible marls, sands and turbidites giving rise to localized badland formation (Harvey, 1982, 1987).

The terrace system lies approximately 4 km west of Mojácar, near the town of Turré. The soils are derived from gypsiferous Pliocene marls and sands, and sandy turbidites outcrop on the valley sides (Figure 10.2). The total relief of the valley is about 30 m. The soils are characterized by low final infiltration rates (Thornes and Gilman, 1985) which give rise to low ponding times and rapid runoff initiation.

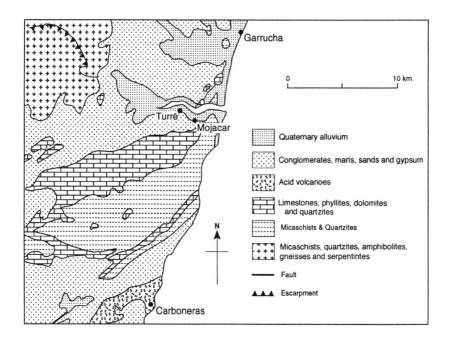

Figure 10.2 Geological setting of the study area

The soils are also subject to slaking, desiccation cracking and the formation of surface crusts (Harvey, 1982).

Climate

The Province of Alméria is in the driest part of Spain, lying in the rain shadow of the Sierra Nevada mountains to the west. Mean annual rainfall falls to less than 200 mm in places and is around 170 mm at Vera (Geiger, 1970). The climate is characterized by intense summer drought between June and September and a winter wet season with two rainfall maxima in October and April respectively. Mean annual rainfall is also highly variable in this region. López-Bermúdez and Romero-Díaz (1989) suggest that inter-annual variability of rainfall in this region is of the order of 35%. There have been two major drought periods in the last 20 years. Mean temperatures for January and July at Alméria are 14 °C and 28 °C respectively. The severe summer drought results in high erosion potentials during the autumn rainfall peak when vegetation cover is minimal.

Terrace Cultivation and Morphology

The terrace systems are mainly used on a rotation basis to grow winter barley and grass. However about 50% of the terraces in any valley system is devoted to the cultivation of tree crops, notably olives, almonds and occasionally figs. Most terraces are also freely grazed by goats during fallow periods. Such unrestricted grazing is likely to be a major cause of accelerated erosion through compaction, reduction of infiltration rates and increased runoff production (Thornes, 1985; Ruiz-Flaño et al., 1992). Terraces become vulnerable to degradation in the medium term when maintenance is neglected and in the short term during periods of fallow when vegetation densities are seasonally low and grazing pressures high.

The terrace system is of the bench type. Maintained terraces are graded to a linear depression just behind the riser (Figure 10.3). Water thus drains across the terrace to the front depression and is then concentrated to a flood diversion channel at the side of the terrace and carried to the next terrace down-valley. During periods of proper maintenance, the terrace equilibrium is maintained by ploughing and regrading of the terrace surface, preservation of terrace risers with stone wall facing and removal of sediment accumulations derived from valley side rill and gully systems. Ploughing disrupts surface crusts and increases final infiltration rates. Times to ponding and total runoff production will therefore be reduced. Ploughing also increases surface roughness and reduces flow continuity with the effect of decreasing potential flow accumulation and shear stress on the terrace surface. The overall effects of maintenance are therefore to increase infiltration rates and reduce runoff accumulation.

Field Survey and Topographic Representation of Terraces

The Turré terrace system was surveyed using theodolite tacheometry. The boundaries of the system were surveyed using theodolite traverse and then each terrace was

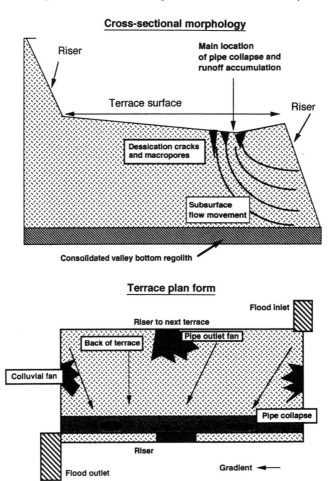

Figure 10.3   Terrace cross-sectional morphology and plan form including location of significant degradation processes

covered with random spot heights to establish terrace topography. The survey points allowed a topographic grid to be generated from the survey points at a resolution of 1 m. Erosional features were surveyed at a higher resolution, 0.1 m, to determine accurate dimensions and morphology. The survey points for the whole terrace system are shown in Figure 10.4, which also shows the locations of major gully and pipe systems.

The treatment of terrace morphology for modelling purposes is discussed with reference to a representative terrace, Terrace 41 (Figure 10.4). Raw survey data are entered into the MAPICS spatial data analysis programme which allows a grid to be derived from the raw survey points. Grid resolution in this case was 1 m × 1 m but is flexible and could be increased with a greater density of ground survey

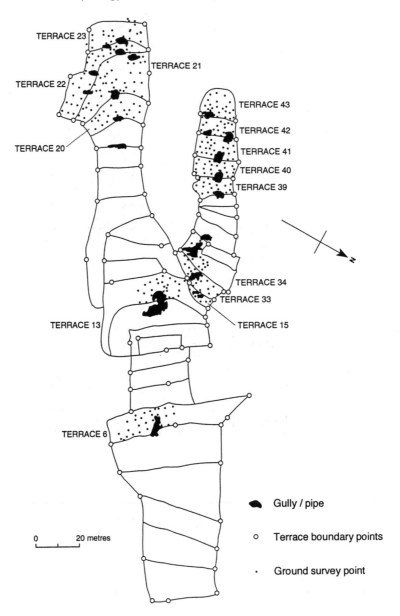

Figure 10.4   Map of the Turré terrace system including location of major pipe/gully features and terrace ground survey points

points. The grid established using MAPICS is used to obtain the direction of potential flow lines on the terrace and to calculate contributing areas to gullies and pipes. The terrace grid survey data are used to establish the flow field. The more detailed mapping of pipes and gullies is utilized to establish the percentage degraded area for each terrace and gully or pipe perimeter length and depth.

STAGES OF TERRACE DEGRADATION

Several stages in the degradation process can be identified on the Turré terrace system. First, decline of management results in localized surface erosion on individual terraces. Specifically, failure to maintain the terrace by ploughing and re-grading leads to surface crusting and accumulation of water behind the riser. Wetting–drying sequences over a complete winter–summer cycle lead to desiccation cracking within the water accumulation zones behind the riser. Measured final ring infiltration rates ranged from 4.0 cm/hr on bare, crusted, fallow terraces to 6 cm/hr on vegetated terraces (grass and stubble). These figures are comparable with those found by Harvey (1982), López-Bermúdez and Romero-Díaz (1989), Gilman and Thornes (1985) and Francis (1986a). Wetted depths of soil seem low, at about 5.0 cm after 30 min, suggesting that large dessication cracks and pores provide the main source of rapid water penetration to the subsurface pipe zone (Harvey, 1982). The marls have low porosity and storage capacities (López-Bermúdez and Romero-Díaz, 1989), particularly on abandoned crusted surfaces, and will produce runoff rapidly at the onset of rainfall. Imeson and Verstraten (1985) noted ponding on crusted marls in south-east Spain after only 1.5 mm artificial rainfall applied at intensities between 2.0 cm/hr and 6.0 cm/hr, i.e. well within the ranges experienced in storms. Surface erosion by sheetwash and rill formation is therefore an early consequence of reduced maintenance or fallow and can cause high rates of soil loss; for example, López-Bermúdez and Romero-Díaz (1989) found rates of 37 mm/year on abandoned marl *secano* terraces. Rill and sheetwash erosion (Figure 10.5) is also active on the valley side slopes adjoining the terraces and is the source of colluvial fans which build across the terrace. The fans (Figure 10.3) distort the topography of the terrace such that runoff will tend to concentrate in the centre of the terrace. Between rainfall events, desiccation cracks are formed in the crusted marl which act as macropores at the start of the next event and give locally high, flux controlled, infiltration rates at certain locations on the terrace. This runoff enters the subsurface zone and is then available for pipe formation.

Secondly, failure to maintain terrace risers results in localized collapse during rainstorms associated with groundwater seepage and pipe development. Differential infiltration results in variable subsurface water flux. Pipes develop via exploitation of subsurface macropores, tree root paths and the contrast in compaction between disturbed terrace soil and the *in situ* valley regolith. The marl soils are liable to dispersion as well as desiccation cracking, both of which are processes fundamental to pipe formation (Gutiérrez *et al.*, 1988). García Ruiz *et al.* (1986) discuss the formation of pipe terraced *secano* systems in La Rioja, showing that pipe formation is associated with the fourth-year rest period of the crop rotation when lucerne is

Figure 10.5 Rill erosion and colluvial fan deposition on the side of a terrace

grown. They show that dimensions of pipes and their collapse features are correlated to the number of irrigations, slope and height of terrace. In non-maintained systems the number of runoff events can be substituted for irrigation events although García Ruiz *et al.* (1986) show that pipe formation may be inherent in the rotation system adopted. At Turré it is thought that the concentration of runoff above the riser is a major causative factor in pipe and pipe-collapse location and localized collapse of the riser. This location has a large potential supply of water to the subsurface zone and, being close to the riser, has a large hydraulic gradient (Jones, 1981; García-Ruiz *et al.*, 1986). A field survey of the system in 1987–88 showed that the preferential location of pipes and gullies on the Turré terraces was at the front-centre of the riser (Figure 10.4). Some terraces had lost up to 15% of their total area by pipe collapse and gullying. Measured pipe diameters were up to 1 m. The threshold for pipe collapse seems to be around 1 m and is probably related to riser height, which ranges from 1 m on the lower part of the system to 2 m in the steeper

Figure 10.6 Pipe collapse damage to a terrace riser

upper valley. Figure 10.6 shows pipe damage to a terrace riser at Turré. In the foreground the riser has also collapsed and a pipe-induced gully has formed. This process is common as the pipes debouch at the base of the riser for reasons of differential porosity and maximum hydraulic gradient. Doline-type collapse features form during high magnitude rainfall-runoff events. Figure 10.7 shows a partially collapsed terrace pipe which will subsequently evolve as a gully.

Finally, once pipes or gullies are established on one or more terraces, morphological feedback (Figure 10.3) focuses subsequent runoff towards the failure zones. Concentrated flow is directed onto the next terrace down-valley by pipes and gullies and, in the absence of remedial measures, a "new" integrated erosional network is eventually established which replaces the "artificial" terraced valley topography.

Morphological Controls of Degradation

Degradation Processes

The stages of terrace degradation at the meso scale in the absence of maintenance have been described in general terms. As noted in Figure 10.4, the location of the most intense erosion in the front-centre of the terrace is clear. On the upper valley terraces there is evidence of linkage between the erosional forms of adjacent terraces (Figure 10.4), suggesting that over several seasons the degraded terraces will be

Figure 10.7 Partially collapsed pipe system at front of a terrace. This system will subsequently evolve as a gully

replaced by a regraded valley floor drainage network. In terms of rate of degradation, therefore, the contributing area to terrace gully/pipe systems is incremented over time as additional terraces and their valley side catchments become integrated into the growing gully drainage system. The rate of degradation should therefore show an accelerating trend.

The back terrace boundary zone is an area where deposition of material eroded from the up-valley adjacent terrace takes place in the form of low angle fans (Figure 10.8). The fans act to disperse flow. Colluvial fans derived from rill and gully activity on the valley sides are also deposited on terraces. In the absence of maintenance the topography of the terrace is adjusted in a manner which enhances flow convergence in the centre-front zone where most collapsed pipes have been observed.

Figure 10.8 Sediment from pipe system breaching the terrace riser has deposited a low-angle sediment fan on the downvalley terrace

Location and Growth of Pipes

The location and rate of terrace degradation by pipes is dependent on high rates of infiltration. During the early period of abandonment or fallow, the magnitude, frequency and intensity of the precipitation control supply of water to incipient pipes. Subsequently overland and rill flow discharge to the infiltration zone determines pipe growth, its magnitude being controlled by terrace contributing areas. The establishment of topographic lows or hollows on the terrace by the processes already discussed, and as a function of terrace design, will collect runoff and concentrate infiltration to preferential locations. The efficiency of water infiltration will depend on macropore dimension and density at the hollow. Surface hollows are thus seen as a pipe-enhancing phenomenon.

Macropore distribution is generally thought to be a decreasing function of distance from the soil surface (López-Bermúdez and Romero-Díaz, 1989). High macropore densities can also increase the surface area available for infiltration (Beven and Germann, 1982). However as surface hollow processes or terrace seepage takes place, new distributions of macropores are generated. These tend to increase connectivity between the hollow generating zone and the seepage face at the base of the terrace riser. Tree roots also provide a discontinuity in the subsoil which can provide a locus for flow concentration and pipe generation. Collapse at this location will cause enlargement of the pipe exit (Figure 10.6).

Conceptual Model of Erosional Processes on Terraces

Terrace design and the operation of hillslope erosional processes result in a tendency for flow concentration in the absence of maintenance. The surface configuration, subsurface soil water potential gradients and material properties are likely to be generated differently on the basis of event magnitude and frequency. The key here is the role of surface topography and the generation of surface hollows which concentrate runoff and water supply to the infiltrating zone. It is proposed that topographic hollow formation, by terrace overland flow and deposition of material derived from the valley sides by rill and pipe processes (Figure 10.5), generate a variable distribution of hydraulic conductivity on the terrace surface. Intra- and inter-season wet–dry periods predispose macropore and desiccation crack formation within these topographic lows. Two process mechanisms can be postulated which are dependent on the magnitude of the rainfall-runoff event.

Low Magnitude Event Model

Low magnitude rainfall events lead to deposition within hollows. Surface flow processes on the terrace will be directed to, or between, surface hollows where temporary storage will take place (Figure 10.9 (a)). Stored runoff will deposit eroded soil. The deposited material is likely to be structurally distinct from the surrounding *in situ* material in two ways: it will have a higher potential for dispersion and a higher solute concentration after inter-event evaporation. Hence hollows will tend to be partially filled with fine, dispersive eroded soil which is prone to desiccation cracking. The hollows will thus become areas of preferential runoff entry to the subsurface zone, allowing pipe initiation processes to be maximized nearby. Hollow desiccation crack formation should therefore be directly associated with pipe location. With a series of low magnitude runoff events the hollows may be filled, leading to surface stability and lowered flow concentrations. This model should be tested in the field by comparing soil dynamic properties in hollows and inter-hollow locations.

High Magnitude Event Model

During high intensity storms, larger flow depths and discharges will be generated on the terrace. Transport-limited sediment load conditions will prevail. Erosion of surface material will tend to increase the flow concentration in hollows (Figure 10.9 (b))

Surface Model - Microscale

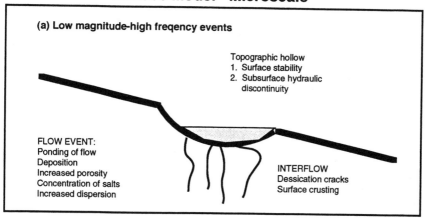

(a) Low magnitude-high freqency events

Topographic hollow
1. Surface stability
2. Subsurface hydraulic
   discontinuity

FLOW EVENT:
Ponding of flow
Deposition
Increased porosity
Concentration of salts
Increased dispersion

INTERFLOW
Dessication cracks
Surface crusting

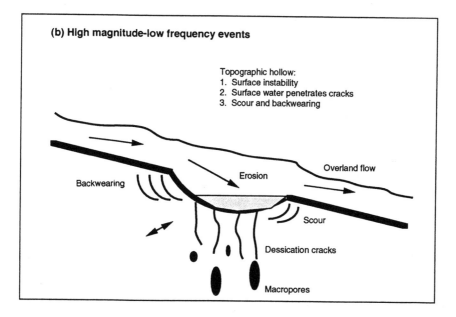

(b) High magnitude-low frequency events

Topographic hollow:
1. Surface instability
2. Surface water penetrates cracks
3. Scour and backwearing

Overland flow

Erosion

Backwearing

Scour

Dessication cracks

Macropores

Figure 10.9 Conceptual model of the relationship between terrace topographic hollow development, degradation and runoff event magnitude: (a) low-magnitude–high-frequency events; (b) high-magnitude–low-frequency events

much in the manner of surface gully initiation (Morgan, 1986). Headcut incision of the upper hollow boundary can be expected as well as scour at the outlet leading to linearization of flow paths and linkage of adjacent hollows. Ponding of flow in hollows will also provide large inputs to subsurface pipes and macropores. This is the basic conceptual model applicable to surface gully initiation in the absence of maintenance. This process can be distinguished from pipe formation in that, under the hollow generating model, pipe initiation is related to low magnitude, high frequency events while gully formation is adjusted to high magnitude events. Pipe growth, however, as opposed to initiation, will also be correlated to high magnitude events.

The hollow evolution model provides the linkage between surface flow processes and the initiation and evolution of pipes at depth. It also covers surface channel initiation. The origin of hollows is both (i) structural, arising from the design of the terrace itself, and (ii) a function of local topographic variations as controlled by past ploughing or terrace maintenance and erosional input from valley sides.

COMPUTER MODEL DEVELOPMENT

Surface Flow Routing and Generation of Contributing Areas

The aim of the preliminary modelling procedures outlined here is to establish areas of maximum *potential* degradation which will be of greatest sensitivity to management inputs.

The first phase of modelling has concentrated on prediction of areas of maximum *potential* morphological change. The field survey of terrace and erosional forms determines the spatial resolution of the model. The first stage is to determine areas of surface flow dispersion and accumulation on the terrace taking into account the topographic complexity of the terrace surface. Results from this model are used to forecast (1) potential zones of surface erosion by sheet wash or rills and (2) areas where infiltration and pipe development are most active. These aims are achieved by determination of the location and direction of flow lines and contributing areas to all cells on the terrace surface. This basic model can then be incremented according to the magnitude of rainfall excess; although it should be noted that the aim is not to model intra-event processes but to consider steady state conditions for mean event magnitudes.

Terrace surface topography is fundamental to the processes acting on the terrace. The surface configuration determines the distribution of (1) erosional energy and (2) the location of hollows and water sources to the subsurface pipe domain. Transport capacity is modelled as a function of cumulated rainfall excess and local topographic gradient. A two-dimensional routing procedure is therefore needed. The terrace surface is defined as a series of topographic grid cells (Figure 10.10 (a)), derived from the field theodolite survey. Flow line vectors are determined as a result of the relative height differences across and down slope in each terrace cell according to the model developed by Scoging (1992) (Figure 10.10 (a)). For each cell in the grid the total across, *Fa*, and down slope, *Fd*, forces are represented as orthogonal axes when projected onto the plane. Their resultant is the flow line vector, *Fp* (Figure 10.10 (b)).

Across cell forces:

$$F1 = \sin a1 . H1 \qquad (10.1)$$
$$F2 = \sin a2 . H2 \qquad (10.2)$$
$$Fa = F1 + F2 \qquad (10.3)$$

(a) Cell dimensions

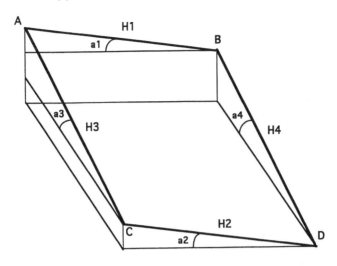

(b) Force vectors

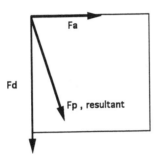

Figure 10.10 Derivation of flowline vectors from topographic cell corner heights. (a) Cell with highest point (A) to lowest point (D). (b) Across, down and resultant flowline vectors derived from corner heights

Down cell forces:

$$F3 = \sin a3 . H3 \tag{10.4}$$
$$F4 = \sin a4 . H4 \tag{10.5}$$
$$Fd = F3 + F4 \tag{10.6}$$

$H1$, $H2$, $H3$ and $H4$ represent the height differences between the adjacent topographic cell corners, and thus scale the vectors by the potential energy component along the opposite cell boundaries (Scoging, 1992). The across cell and down cell boundary height differences define the flow line outlet (Scoging, 1992) into one of eight possible vector directions, with respect to adjacent cells, known as IRECT 1–8 (Figure 10.11),

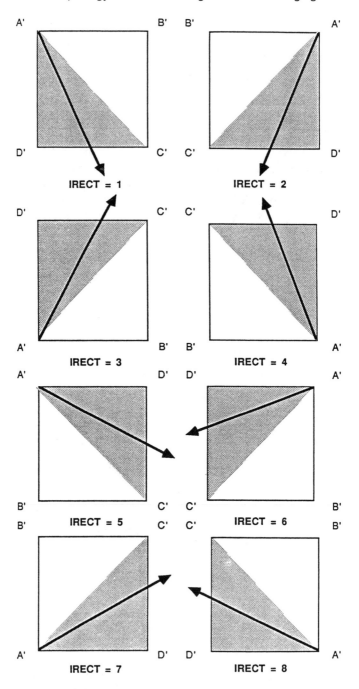

Figure 10.11 Flowline exit categories, IRECT. The eight categories are generated from the cell corner height configuration and the resultant direction of the flowline exit with respect to the surrounding cells

the parameter IRECT specifying the exit boundary for a given cell. The IRECT values for all terrace cells can be used to determine groups of cells linked, by their IRECT outflow categories, by common flow lines. The flow line vectors are assumed to originate from the highest corner of each cell (Figure 10.10 (a), point A) and have a magnitude and direction (in the plane ACD which contains the lowest vertex of the cell, D) determined by the relative heights of the four corners (Scoging, 1992). Using this flow line linkage, the "contributing area" to each cell on the terrace or to a gully or pipe boundary cell can be calculated. Displacement vectors do not represent the actual motion of water, and only the net effect of the forces in the across and down slope directions, denoting magnitude and position change and direction, are calculated. The model therefore indicates areas of flow accumulation or dispersion. Limitations to this model are that it is very sensitive to small height differences and that flow routing within the cell is neglected (Scoging, 1992). However, for management at the sub-terrace scale the model provides a promising two-dimensional approach to the flow routing problem.

Preliminary Results

Operation of the flow line vector model is illustrated using the example of Terrace 41 from the Turré system (Figure 10.4). Figure 10.12 shows the resultant vector

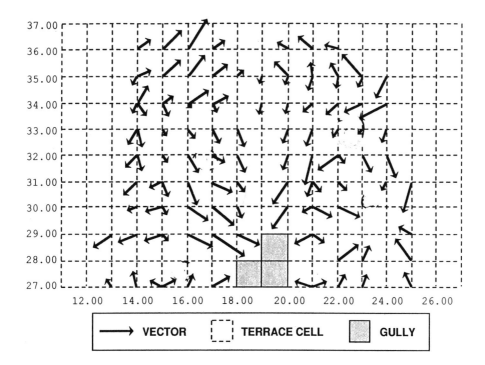

Figure 10.12 Flowline vectors calculated from the topographic survey of Terrace 41. Length of the arrows is an indicator of the height differences within the cell. Direction of the arrow suggests the outlet location for water from the original cell

map for the terrace. The arrows show the direction of flow and their length is indicative of the potential gradient, derived from height differences. Cells with long flow line vectors can thus be interpreted as possessing high transport potential for a given level of runoff. This is derived from the cross or down cell gradients and does not represent the magnitude of discharge, which varies with infiltration rate, precipitation intensity and contributing area. The vectors are large around the shaded gullied cells at the front of the terrace, representing the increased gradients around the gully head. The zone of converging flow vectors on the right-hand side of the terrace represents an incipient hollow associated with piping.

The direction of flow line vectors allows input–output linkages to be made between groups of cells. Thus distinct contributing areas to given terrace locations can be determined. As can be seen in Figure 10.12, distinct areas of flow convergence and divergence can be distinguished. Figure 10.13 shows the contributing areas to specific locations on the terrace; for example, cells 4 and 6, gully boundaries,

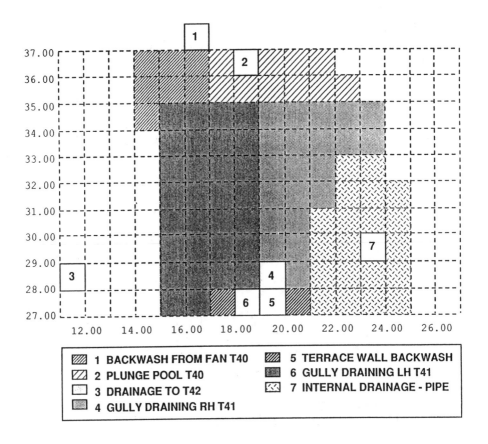

Figure 10.13 Contributing area map for Terrace 41 derived from flowlines. Areas with different shades are contributing terrace areas to specific degradation features. Locations with large contributing areas are likely to be sensitive to degradation processes

can be seen to have large contributing areas and are therefore sensitive to surface runoff. Area 7, a hollow with a large contributing area, is likely to be associated with saturated subsurface conditions and rapid pipe development.

In terms of land management for the terrace systems, repetition of this analysis for the whole terrace locates topographic hollows, which require regrading to reduce flow accumulation and pipe growth, and those gullies, with large contributing areas, which may require urgent conservation measures to prevent growth by headwall retreat. Such management may include ploughing and regrading of the terrace to prevent flow convergence. Most of the major gullies surveyed in 1988 originated from collapse of pipes and would require rebuilding of the terrace riser.

Flow Accumulation and Erosion Potential

A first step towards quantifying flow accumulation and erosion potential for the terrace grid requires distributed infiltration rate data for each terrace, and autographic rainfall data.

The modified Green and Ampt (1911) equation has been shown to be applicable to semi-arid Spanish conditions (Scoging and Thornes, 1980; Scoging, 1982).

$$i = A + B/t \qquad (10.7)$$

where i is the infiltration rate, A and B are parameters and t is time since the start of rainfall. Parameter A, is the final steady state infiltration rate, and is used in a modified form of the Musgrave equation to estimate erosion "potential".

$$q = (p - A).a \qquad (10.8)$$

where q represents discharge per unit time for a given cell or contributing area, p is the precipitation rate per unit time, A is the final infiltration rate and a is the area of cell which is derived from the resolution of the field survey. The erosion potential is then given, for a given cell or drainage area as:

$$E = k\,q^2\,S^{1.66} \qquad (10.9)$$

where E is erosion potential, k is a parameter representing lithological effects on the availability of material for erosion and is set at 0.02 after Thornes and Gilman (1985). S is the gradient of the cell in question. This model allows comparative flow accumulation and erosion potential to be calculated for all cells on the terrace and the identification of potential zones of instability. With cumulative contributing area for gully boundary cells, the most erosionally unstable gully or pipe boundaries may also be identified. The model does *not* simulate erosion rates throughout a storm or allow recalculation of terrace topography at this stage. The aim is to identify unstable areas for remedial management measures and to consider *relative* erosion potentials on adjacent terraces.

Requirements for a Subsurface Model

The subsurface domain presents the greatest modelling problem. The previous sections have described a steady state model for flow accounting on the terrace surface which could give a first estimate of potential instability on the basis of topogaphic survey, infiltration rates and precipitation data. These are all relatively easily obtained. However, this is not the case for the subsurface processes which control pipe growth, a significant process of degradation at Turré. Water enters the subsurface zone via slow infiltration of the surface material or through desiccation cracks. It is then redistributed through the particulate medium according to Darcian principles or via macropores. Growth of macropores by fluid shear stress and solution processes is fundamental to pipe initiation (Jones, 1981).

Building a physically-based predictive model which successfully unites these fundamentally different subsurface flow processes is not yet attainable given the three-dimensional nature of the problem. The macropore systems are dynamic and, as pointed out by Beven and Germann (1982), they can be produced over several seasons and destroyed in one rainstorm by collapse, surface sediment transport or washing in of rain-splashed material.

Macropores result in heterogeneous infiltration rates which will vary by several orders of magnitude. The modified Green/Ampt equation would not be applicable to topographic hollows with desiccation cracks. Turbulent flow models would be required (Beven and Germann, 1982). Darcy's law for flow in unsaturated media can be used as the basis for the distribution of water in the subsurface zone only where the matrix is relatively uniform and where macropores are absent. Darcy's law for matrix flow is given as:

$$V_x = -K(\theta) \cdot (\Delta H / \Delta x) \qquad (10.10)$$

where V_x is the flow velocity in the direction x, $K(\theta)$ is the hydraulic conductivity for given moisture content and $(\Delta H / \Delta x)$ is the gradient of total potential in direction x. Beven and Germann (1982) suggest that macropore flow could be described using Poiseulles flow law where discharge is related to the square of macroporosity. Such a model would require data for the spatial distribution of macroporosity within the whole terrace subsoil zone and some idea of the dynamic properties of macropore distribution and dimensions. In terms of data requirements and parameterization an intra-event model is impractical for present purposes.

DISCUSSION

Field survey and observation have allowed us to postulate the sequence of processes leading to the rapid degradation of agricultural bench terraces in the Turré area (Figure 10.14). The linkage between surface and subsurface processes of degradation seems to be associated with topographic hollows, which are a function of erosional processes and design factors, and are thought to be fundamental in pipe generation. Once gullies and pipes on adjacent terraces become linked via terrace riser degradation,

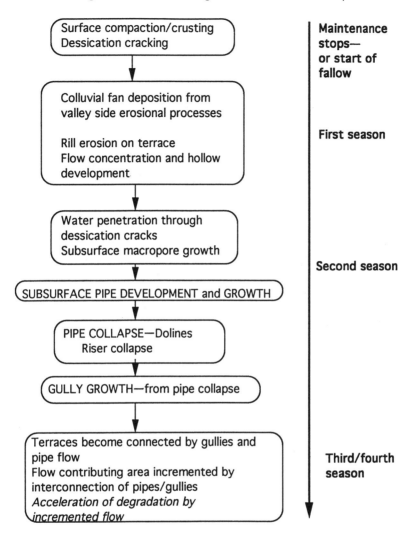

Figure 10.14 Turré terrace degradation sequence based on observation over four seasons

the lower of the terraces becomes subject to accelerated degradation by runoff processes as its contributing area is incremented by the area of the gullied terraces up-valley. Degradation processes thus accelerate over time in an unstable positive feedback loop.

The flow line vector and surface erosion potential models allow erosion-sensitive areas to be located on the basis of topographic field survey, infiltration rates and precipitation data. These relatively simple data requirements have the potential to make this model a useful management tool.

Consideration of the subsurface process dynamics, however, suggest much greater data requirements and an intractable modelling problem at this scale. The principal barriers to the development of the model are (1) the difficulty of collecting data on soil macroporosity, pipe dimensions, hydraulic conductivity and soil water potentials over a large area and through time to establish initial and boundary conditions for the model, (2) the computational problems of solving flow equations over three dimensions numerically and, (3) representing the dynamic process of macropore and pipe growth.

A better strategy for the applied management of terraces is to build up a temporal data base of the following variables:

(1) seasonal soil moisture regimes for terraces as they degrade;
(2) spatial macroporosity distributions for terraces at different stages of degradation;
(3) long-term temporal changes in terrace morphology after abandonment or during fallow periods.

Between site visits in spring 1990 and 1991 major remedial work was carried out on the Turré system. Terraces 20–23 and 39–43 (see Figure 10.4) were completely rebuilt and major repair was carried out on Terraces 13, 15, 33 and 34 to remove gullies and pipe collapse holes. This episode has prevented further monitoring of the features surveyed in 1988 and subsequent development of the model, but provides an opportunity to monitor rates of degradation from a known date of origin and to establish the temporal data record.

ACKNOWLEDGEMENTS

We wish to thank Jeanette Kayes and Gerald Harvey for their assistance in the field, Justyn Jacyno for the maps and the Hostal Regio, Vera for the warm welcome given to us during the field seasons. We also thank Dr Duncan McGregor, Royal Holloway, for his constructive comments during preparation of the manuscript.

REFERENCES

Beven, K. and Germann, P. (1982). Macropores and water flow in soils. *Water Resources Research*, **18** (5), 1311–1325.

Francis, C. (1986). Subsurface hydrology of gully heads (Ugijar Basin). In López-Bermúdez, F. and Thornes, J. B. (Eds), *Estudios Sobre Geomorfologica del sur de Espana*, Universidad de Murcia, Spain.

García-Ruiz, J. M., Lasanta-Martinez, T., Ortigosa-Izquierdo, L. and Arnáez-Vadillo, J. (1986). Pipes in cultivated soils of La Rioja: origin and evolution. *Zeitschrift für Geomorph, Supplement-Band*, **58**, 93–100.

Geiger, F. (1970). *Die Aridität in Südostspanien*. Stuttgarter Geographische Studien, **77**, 1–173.

Gilman, A. and Thornes, J. B. (1985). *Land-use and Prehistory in Southeast Spain*, The London Research Series in Geography, No. 8. George Allen & Unwin, London.

Green, W. H. and Ampt, G. A (1911). Studies on soil physics. 1: the flow of air and water through soils. *Journal of Agricultural Science*, **4**, 1–24.

Gutiérrez, M., Benito, G. and Rodríguez, G. (1988). Piping in badland areas of the middle Ebro basin, Spain. *Catena Suppl.*, **13**, 49–60.

Harvey, A. M. (1982). The role of piping in the development of badlands and gully systems in south-east Spain. In Bryan R. and Yair, A. (Eds), *Badland Geomorphology and Piping*, Geobooks. Norwich.

Harvey, A. M. (1987). Patterns of Quaternary aggradational and dissectional landform development in the Alméria region, southeast Spain: a dry-region, tectonically active landscape. *Die Erde*, **118**, 193–215.

Imeson, A. C. and Verstraten, J. M. (1985). The erodibility of highly calcareous oil material from southern Spain. *Catena*, **12**, 291–306.

Jones, J. A. A. (1981). *The Nature of Soil Piping. A Review of Research*, British Geomorphological Research Monograph, Vol. 3. Norwich.

López-Bermúdez, F. and Romero-Díaz, M. A. (1989). Piping erosion and badland development in south-east Spain. *Catena Suppl.*, **14**, 59–73.

Morgan, R. P. C. (1986). *Soil Erosion and Conservation*, Longman, London.

Ruiz-Flaño, P., García-Ruiz, J. M. and Ortigosa (1992). Geomorphological evolution of abandoned fields. A case study in the Central Pyrenees. *Catena*, **19**, 301–308.

Scoging, H. M. (1982). Spatial variations in infiltration, runoff and erosion on hillslopes in semi-arid Spain. In Bryan, R. B. and Yair, A. (Eds), *Badland Geomorphology and Piping*, Geobooks, Norwich, pp. 89–112.

Scoging, H. M. (1992). Modelling overland-flow hydrology for dynamic hydraulics. In Parsons, A. J. and Abrahams, A. D. (Eds), *Overland Flow Hydraulics and Erosion Mechanics*, UCL Press, London, pp. 89–103.

Scoging, H. M. and Thornes, J. B. (1980). *Infiltration characteristics in a semi-arid environment*. Proceedings of the International Association of Hydrological Sciences Symposium on the Hydrology of Areas of Low Precipitation, Canberra, IAHS-AISH Publication No. 128, pp. 159–168.

Thornes, J. B. (1985). The ecology of erosion. *Geography*, **70**, 222–235.

Thornes, J. B. and Gilman, A. (1985). Potential and actual erosion rates around archeological sites in south east Spain. In de Ploey, J. (Ed.), *Rainfall Simulation, Runoff and Soil Erosion*, Catena Supplement 4, Braunschweig, pp. 91–113.

Part 4

GEOMORPHOLOGY AND LAND MANAGEMENT: ENVIRONMENTAL IMPACT AND ENVIRONMENTAL RISK

11 The Incorporation of Geomorphological Factors into Environmental Impact Assessment for Master Plans: A Methodological Proposal

A. GONZÁLEZ, J. R. DÍAZ DE TERÁN, E. FRANCÉS and A. CENDRERO*
DCITTYM, Division of Earth Sciences, University of Cantabria, Spain

ABSTRACT

The need to carry out environmental impact assessments of master plans is discussed and a general methodology is proposed. The methodology enables the easy integration of geomorphological factors into the process of impact evaluation. Several quantitative and qualitative impact indicators are proposed for the measurement of impacts and for the comparison of alternative plans. The methodology is illustrated through its application to the assessment of impacts in several case studies.

INTRODUCTION

Environmental impact assessments (EIAs) are normally carried out for specific projects or actions, for which several alternative locations have to be compared, or, more often than not, in a location which has already been decided upon. It is thus a case of determining whether the action is environmentally acceptable or not and what safeguards have to be taken in order to prevent negative impacts.

However, very often impacts can be minimized by simply selecting the most appropriate locations for the activities to be carried out in a certain area. The definition of the kinds of activities which will be allowed in the different parts of a territory (municipality, province and so on) is usually made through master plans. Although there are differences between countries, master plans normally regulate the use of land and specify where industrial installations, residential areas, recreational facilities, agricultural developments, conservation zones and so on must be located. Therefore, once a master plan has been established for a certain area, the location of specific

Present address: Graduate Center for Public Policy and Administration, California State University, USA.

Geomorphology and Land Management in a Changing Environment. Edited by D. F. M. McGregor and D. A. Thompson.
©1995 John Wiley & Sons Ltd

developments is fairly well defined and the degrees of freedom for the siting of new projects are very limited. In this sort of situation an EIA can only say "yes", "no" or "yes but with certain restrictions or safeguards". Thus, the master plan represents one among many possible proposals for the use of the territory and it conditions to a great extent each project or development to be carried out in the area.

Different proposals for the distribution of human activities on a territory constitute different ways to use the earth's surface, and, therefore, will have different environmental impacts. According to this, it is desirable to select, among the various possible alternatives, the one with the lowest environmental impact. Thus, EIA of master plans can be a most effective way to prevent undesirable impacts and to reduce the cost of preventive measures, as it will help to assign each activity to the parts of the territory most suitable to sustain it with a minimum impact. The need for EIA for master plans is especially important in those regions where impacts are due mainly to land occupation (Aurenheimer, 1992), as is the case of the coastlands of many parts of Europe, particularly around the Mediterranean.

When it comes to the consideration of geomorphological factors, this is even more apparent. Impacts on the geomorphological environment can be due to (Panizza, 1990, 1992):

(a) destruction or deterioration of geomorphological resources;
(b) interference with geomorphological processes and appearance (or increase) of geomorphological hazards and risks.

The impacts in both cases are best avoided by siting activities where no interference occurs between these and either geomorphological resources or processes, that is, by regulating land occupation and use. The problem of the importance of impacts derived from land occupation has been recognized by several autonomous regional governments in Spain, where recent regional legislation establishes the need to carry out EIAs as an integral part of master plans (Aurenheimer, 1992).

The systematic application of EIA to plans could ensure that future land use would produce the minimum possible impacts on the environment and would also reduce the cost of corrective measures for individual projects, as they would be located in areas with low vulnerability for the kinds of actions considered. Moreover, this type of EIA facilitates the incorporation of geomorphological considerations, as factors such as landforms, materials and surficial dynamics are especially relevant for defining optimum land uses. This does not imply, of course, that EIA for projects would not be necessary, nor that geomorphology should not be considered in it. The aim of the model presented here is simply to extend and improve the process of EIA, by including in it the plans that constitute the general framework within which the different projects have to fit.

GENERAL METHODOLOGICAL CONSIDERATIONS

Two basic types of models are used for the evaluation of environmental impacts. One type could be called "convergent" and it is normally used for the evaluation of the vulnerability of various environmental components for different actions (Steinitz and Rogers, 1975; Varios Autores, 1977). These models start by considering a given environmental component or element (soil, water, air, flora and so on) and try to define how it will be affected by the different activities which are foreseen (Figure 11.1). The vulnerability of these elements is defined in relation to those actions and then the impacts are predicted using various indicators.

When it comes to the evaluation of environmental impacts of master plans, it is better to use a "divergent" type of model. This means that the impact of each activity whose location is going to be regulated in the area under consideration, should be assessed for the different environmental elements in each point of land unit (Figure 11.1). The overall impact of the plan will obviously be obtained by adding up the impacts corresponding to each one of these land units.

In the first case the possible impacts of different activities "converge" over each element, whereas in the second case the impacts from each activity "diverge" towards the various environmental elements.

It follows that environmental impact assessment for master plans requires the prior identification and definition of the existing land units, the determination of their descriptive parameters, the evaluation of those qualities or characteristics which are relevant from the point of view of the impacts they can experience, and the knowledge of their spatial distribution. The first step in EIA of master plans should thus be the mapping, description and diagnosis of land or terrain units.

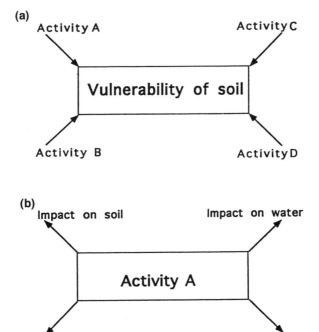

Figure 11.1   (a) "Convergent" and (b) "divergent" models for the evaluation of impacts

Mapping of terrain characteristics for EIA can be carried out following two types of procedures (Cendrero and Díaz de Terán, 1987; McCall and Marker, 1989; Cooke and Doornkamp, 1990; Claver *et al.*, 1991). One group of procedures is based on the representation of integrated, "homogeneous" environmental units, defined on the basis of the different significant environmental elements (Christian and Stewart, 1968; Brown *et al.*, 1971; Cendrero and Trilla, 1983). In the second group of procedures the different environmental elements are represented by means of separate thematic maps, which are later integrated during the evaluation process (McHarg, 1969; Varios Autores, 1977; Environmental Analysis Group, 1980).

METHODOLOGY PROPOSED

The model for EIA of plans proposed here is based on the use of separate thematic maps, and it is schematically represented in the flow diagram of Figure 11.2. It can be seen that once the activities contemplated in the plan have been defined, the environmental elements which can suffer impacts can be identified and thematic maps can be prepared showing the distribution of the different "types" of each "element". Thus, a thematic map will represent the element "vegetation", showing the location and area of the types "oak forest", "prairies" and so on. The map of the element "surficial deposits" will include types such as "sandy alluvial deposits 2–4 m thick", "residual clays over 5 m thick" and so on.

The impact of a given activity on one point of the territory can be obtained using a weighting/scaling method for the aggregation of the impacts on each element considered. The following expression can be used:

$$I_a = \sum_{i=1}^{m} W_{ia} \cdot V_{ia} \tag{11.1}$$

where I_a is the impact of activity "a" on that point; W_{ia} is the weight of element "i" for the overall impact of activity "a" (or contribution of the impact on that element to the total impact); V_{ia} is the value of the type (unit) of element "i" present in the point, in a rank of impacts to be experienced as a result of activity "a" (for instance, in a scale of five terms); and m is the number of elements (thematic maps) considered.

The weights W_{ia} were obtained using the Delphi method of repeated consultations with a group of experts (Balkey, 1968; Ervin, 1974; Eckenrode, 1975; Claver *et al.*, 1991) with the following expressions:

$$R_c = \sum_{i=1}^{n} R_{cj} \tag{11.2}$$

where R_c is the sum of the "n" values assigned to element "c"; R_{cj} is the value given to element "c" by expert "j"; and n is the number of experts consulted.

$$W_c = \frac{R_c}{\sum_{c=1}^{m} R_c} \tag{11.3}$$

where W_c is the weight of element "c"; and m is the number of elements considered. The weights thus obtained were then expressed as percentages.

Values for units in the different thematic maps were derived from consultations with a panel of experts, who ranked them in a scale of five terms.

If the weights are expressed as percentages and the rank is expressed on a scale from 0 (no impact or positive impact) to 4 (maximum negative impact), the impacts for any activity will vary between 0 and 400. If the rank varies between -2 (highly negative) to 2 (very positive) the corresponding value will vary between -200 and 200. Table 11.1 shows the weights and values obtained for the assessment of impacts from low-density urban use, corresponding to the example described below.

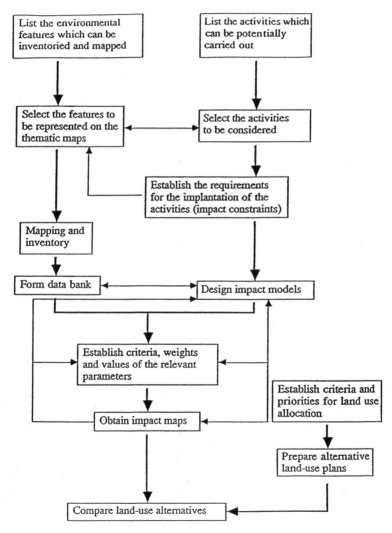

Figure 11.2   Flow diagram of the methodology for EIA of land-use plans (modified from Cendrero and Díaz de Terán, 1987)

Table 11.1 Impact values on different units of the elements considered, for low-density urbanization. 2: maximum positive impact; −2: maximum negative impact; E: unit to be excluded because of very severe impact on the element

Impact values	Elements (weight %)									
	Permeability groundwater (8)	Landforms (8)	Active processes (9)	Soils (12)	Vegetation (14)	Fauna (12)	Slope (14)	Visual landscape (8)	Surface water (12)	Scientific value (13)
2										
1										
0	6	3	6	1	9		1	1, 2	3, 4, 5	1
−1	4, 5	4	3, 4, 5	2, 3, 4, 5, 6, 7	1, 2, 3	1, 2, 3	2	3, 4	1, 2	2
−2	2, 3	1, 2		8, 9, 10, 11	4, 6	4, 5	3	5, 6, 7		3
E	1		1, 2		5, 7, 8	6, 7, 8, 9				4

Simplified legend for the different elements:

Permeability. 1: Beach and estuarine sands and silts; 2: highly permeable surficial deposits over important aquifers; 3: highly permeable karstic formations with important aquifers; 4: moderately permeable surficial deposits over smaller aquifers; 5: moderately permeable rocks such as sandstones with smaller aquifers; 6: impervious or low permeability materials without aquifers.

Landforms. 1: Karstic landforms; 2: small marine terraces; 3: artificial excavations and spoil heaps; 4: other landforms.

Active processes. 1: Areas with semi-permanent waterlogging; 2: coastal areas with intense erosion/sedimentation; 3: landslide areas; 4: areas of compaction and subsidence; 5: flood-prone areas; 6: no important active process.

Soils. 1: Lithosols; 2: rendzinas and luvisols; 3: eutric cambisols; 4: rankers; 5: podsols; 6: histosols; 7: distric cambisols; 8: fluvisols; 9: regosols; 10: humic cambisols; 11: phaeozems.

Vegetation. 1: Artificial prairies and cultivated fields; 2: eucalyptus and pine plantations; 3: heathlands; 4: deciduous indigenous forests (other than oak); 5: oak forests; 6: *Quercus ilex* shrubs; 7: wetlands; 8: vegetated dunes; 9: pioneer vegetation.

Fauna. 1: Cultivated fields with poor fauna; 2: eucalyptus and pine plantations with poor fauna; 3: shrublands with poorly preserved fauna; 4: indigenous forests with large and small mammals and birds; 5: rocky and shrubland areas with well-preserved reptile and bird fauna; 6: beaches and dunes with well-preserved reptile and bird fauna; 7: cliffs with birds' nesting areas or with well-preserved reptile fauna; 8: river margins with well-preserved fauna; 9: estuaries and wetlands with abundant waterfowl.

Slope. 1: <10%; 2: 10-30%; 3: >30%.

Visual landscape. 1: Units with medium quality and low fragility; 2: low quality and fragility; 3: medium quality and fragility; 4: high quality, medium fragility; 5: very high quality, high fragility; 6: low quality, high fragility; 7: medium quality, high fragility.

Surface water. 1: Units with very small streams (order 1); 2: small and medium streams (orders 2 and 3); 3: large streams (order 4); 4: rivers (order 5); 5: units with no watercourses.

Scientific value. 1: No sites of scientific value in the unit; 2: one or more sites of low scientific value; 3: two or more sites of medium scientific value or one of high value; 4: more than one site of high value.

A "point" of the territory can be a pixel, a cell in a square grid (or any other type of grid), or even a unit with an irregular shape, such as a homogeneous integrated unit. The application of the expression described to all the cells or units of the area under consideration will enable the construction of a map of impact for the activity. This task can be greatly facilitated by the use of a Geographical Information System (GIS), which allows the superposition and combination of different maps using units with either "geometrical" of "natural" boundaries.

Once the impact maps for all activities have been outlined, the impact of the plan can be determined by adding the impacts corresponding to the activity in that plan to each unit.

The expression to use would be:

$$I_p = \frac{\sum_{j=1}^{n} I_{aj}}{n} \tag{11.4}$$

where I_p is the impact of plan "p"; I_{aj} is the impact on unit "j" of activity "a" (proposed in plan "p"); and n is the number of units.

If units have irregular shapes and different sizes the individual impacts obtained for each unit should be previously normalized, using a factor which takes into consideration the relative size of units.

$$I_{aj} = I'_{aj} \frac{S_j}{\sum_{j=1}^{n} S_j}$$

where I_{aj} is the corrected impact value; I'_{aj} is the initial impact value; S_j is the area of the unit; and n is the number of units.

The use of this expression implies, obviously, that the whole unit will be subject to the use considered.

It is clear that the plan with the lowest value for I_p will be the most advisable alternative from the point of view of environmental impact. This provides a means to compare different master plans and to determine the one which proposes the distribution of activities that will have the least effect on the environment. The specific projects to be carried out and assessed, once the plan has been approved, will be located in areas which are, in principle, favourable, and they will require fewer, and cheaper, corrective or precautionary measures.

The method described provides a simple and straightforward means of integrating geomorphological considerations into EIA. Geomorphology can be one "element" to be represented in a thematic map, or it can be split into several thematic maps. Probably the best is to have two maps: *geomorphological resources* (soils, surficial deposits, water, sites or landscapes of cultural or scientific interest, and so on); and *geomorphological processes* (including hazards). An independent map of *geomorphological impacts* can be obtained, or, more conveniently, the impacts on geomorphology can be integrated with other impacts, assigning to the element "geomorphology" a weight according to the methods described above.

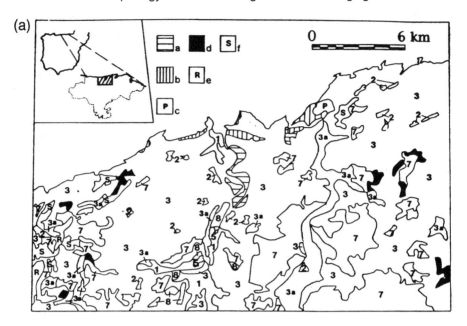

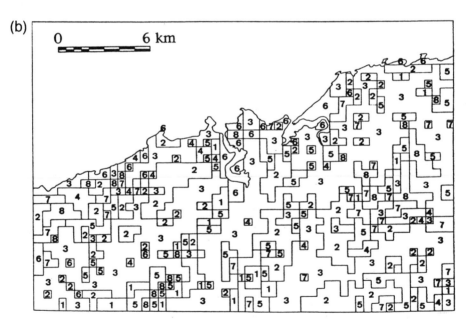

Figure 11.3 Location of the study area (inset). (a) Present land use distributiion. 1: high density urban; 2: low density urban. 3: dairy farming with some agriculture; 3a: agriculture with some dairy farming; 5: industrial park; 7: eucalyptus plantations; 8: quarrying; a: wetlands; b: beaches and dunes; c: dunes with pine woods; d: indigenous forests; e: rocky areas; f: shrublands. (b) proposed distribution of activities according to plan B. 1: high density urban; 2: low density urban; 3: agriculture and dairy farming; 4: extensive cattle-raising; 5: industrial park; 6: natural park; 7: eucalyptus cultivation; 8: quarrying

The method proposed was applied, for instance, to the comparison of impacts derived from different distributions of activities obtained through the application of different sets of criteria, for a master plan for Cantabria, a province of 5200 km² in northern Spain (Cendrero and Díaz de Terán, 1987; Francés *et al.,* 1990a) (Figure 11.3).

The elements of the environment were represented in thematic maps at the 1:50 000 scale, and included: bedrock and surficial deposits, landforms, active processes, soils, depth of regolith, vegetation, fauna (vertebrates), slope, altitude, aspect, visual landscape, population, accessibility, drainage network, and sites of scientific or cultural significance. All maps were transferred to a databank by means of a square grid with 500-cells, and each one of these was described by its Universal Transverse Mercator (UTM) coordinates.

Eight land use activities were selected and characterized in terms of their likely effects on different environmental elements.

Using equations (11.1), (11.2) and (11.3), the overall impact of each activity in each cell of the grid was computed. The impact values obtained for all grid cells and for each activity were grouped into "classes" as shown in Figure 11.4. Cells which could suffer a terminal impact on any environmental element were excluded, appearing as "blanks". Figure 11.5 is an example of the impact map for one activity, low-density urbanization.

A similar procedure was followed to obtain the capacity of units for the activities selected.

The overall "suitability" of one grid cell for an activity was derived by a combination of impact and capacity, using the following expression:

$$A_c = \frac{W_c\, C_c + W_i\, C_i}{W_c + W_i}$$

where A_c is the suitability class, C_c is the capacity class, C_i is the impact class, W_c is the capacity weight, W_i is the impact weight, and $W_c + W_i = 100$.

"Optimum" activities were assigned to each cell using different criteria, representing different combinations of suitability, impact and capacity classes for the activity considered as well as different priorities among activities. Thus, each set of criteria produced a different distribution of activities, representing different land use options or alternatives. Table 11.2(a) lists the criteria corresponding to two such alternatives or "plans". Table 11.2(b) shows the distribution of activities obtained through the application of those criteria, as well as the average impact of each "plan", using expression (11.4). It can be seen that the better of the two alternatives, from the impact point of view, is plan B. Figure 11.3 shows the present distribution of land use in a part of the province and the distribution of land use corresponding to plan B.

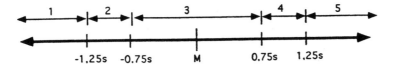

Figure 11.4 Division in classes of impact values obtained using expression (1). M = Mean, s = standard deviation

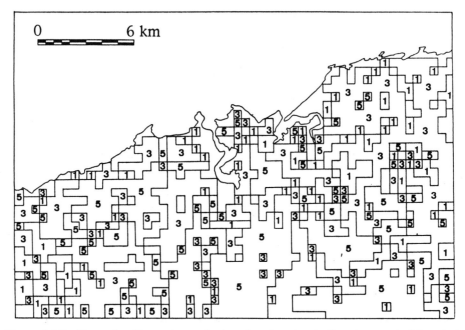

Figure 11.5 Example of impact map for low density urbanization, in a part of the study area. 1: impact classes 1 + 2 (very negative impact); 3: impact class 3; 5: impact classes 4 + 5 (no impact or positive impact). Blank: areas excluded because of terminal impact on some element

Indicators

Another, simpler approach to the assessment of plans, also starting from the identification and mapping of environmental units, can be based on the definition of a series of significant indicators. Several indicators can be used for the description of units, some of them quantitative or semiquantitative and others qualitative. Possible quantitative or semiquantitative (depending on the precision of the available data) indicators are:

- area occupied by the different types of units (especially those worthy of preservation);
- area occupied by units with different "geomorphological problems";
- volume and/or value of geomorphological resource subject to marketing (sand, gravel, water);
- agricultural productivity of the soils;
- geomorphological risk (expressed as expectable losses within a certain time span, in the existing situation);
- existing rate of erosion.

Some of the qualitative indicators that can be used are:

Table 11.2 (a) Criteria for the allocation of land use activities in two alterative plans. (b) Distribution of activities using the criteria indicated and average impact of plans. Activities: 1, high-density urbanization; 2, low-density urbanization; 3, agriculture and dairy farming; 4, extensive cattle raising; 5, industrial park; 6, natural park; 7, eucalyptus cultivation; 8, quarrying

(a)

Plan	Criteria
A	Each point will be devoted to the activity with the highest "suitability" (combination of capacity and impact). If several activities have the same A suitability, the one with the lowest impact will have priority; and if the suitability, impact and capacity are equal, the order of preference for the activities will be: 1, 5, 2, 8, 3, 7, 4, 6
B	Each point will be devoted to the activity with the highest "suitability" (combination of capacity and impact). If several activities have the same B suitability, the one with the lowest impact will have priority; and if the suitability, impact and capacity are equal, the order of preference for the activities will be: 3, 4, 7, 6, 2, 5, 1, 8

(b)

Plan		1	2	3	4	5	6	7	8	Impact
					Activities					
A	%	14.51	22.42	21.59	6.18	3.99	24.30	1.62	5.38	−20 159
	km²	772.7	1194.2	1150.0	328.5	213.5	1294.2	86.7	286.5	
B	%	4.30	11.34	26.06	15.23	4.95	31.13	2.66	4.30	2446
	km²	229.0	604.0	1388.5	810.5	263.7	1657.2	142.2	229	

- soil capability;
- soil erodibility (rank);
- value of the different units for conservation;
- surface or groundwater vulnerability;
- landscape quality and fragility;
- geomorphological hazards (rank).

These indicators can be used for the assessment of impacts. The comparison of alternative plans can be made, for instance, on the basis of:

- area with soils of different productivities which is going to be affected by constructions or other transformations;
- number of sites (or area of units) with different degrees of value for conservation which will be affected;
- volume of resources with an economic value which will be rendered unexploitable;
- area which will experience an increase in erodibility;

- expected volume of eroded material;
- area of high water vulnerability affected;
- expected increase in runoff;
- magnitude and extent of visual impacts;
- area with different types of geomorphological hazards which will be occupied by various activities;
- induced geomorphological hazard/risk.

In particular, the "measurement" of the impact on geomorphological hazards can be made using indicators like:

- area for which the proposed plan will increase slope instability;
- expected increase of runoff and its influence on flood hazard;
- expected increase in erosion;
- area with flood hazard which will be occupied by certain activities;
- area with slope instability hazard that will be occupied;
- area with swelling clays in which constructions are proposed.

To compare alternatives (or to compare the existing situation and the one contemplated in a plan) on the basis of geomorphological hazards, it is possible to use a "risk index" (Cendrero *et al.*, 1987) such as:

$$I_r = V.v/p$$

where:

I_r = risk index;
V = value, in monetary units, of the lives, buildings, structures, utilities and so on, in a given land unit;
v = vulnerability (percentage of the value likely to be destroyed by a dangerous geomorphological event);
p = average periodicity, in years, between dangerous geomorphological events (floods, landslides and so on).

The risk index will therefore be expressed in US$/year, or "potential average yearly losses" to be expected during a certain time-span, and it will provide a monetary indicator of the impact of the plans on geomorphological risks on each map unit. Comparison between the risk indexes obtained for all units and for each alternative plan will provide the means to assess the potential impacts on hazards of the different plans proposed.

The former indicators can be used to compare plans assuming that no specific corrective measures will be taken, and also to compare alternatives which specify such measures. It is quite clear that in the first case the plan with the lowest impact will also be the one which will require less investment for impact mitigation. However, this does not necessarily mean that it will be the most advisable plan. The need of greater expenses for impact mitigation can be compensated by other aspects of the plan, such as a better use of resources with a market value. This should be evaluated by considering how the plans use the "capacity" of the territory.

An example of the incorporation of impact assessment into municipal plans, using this kind of approach, is the planning of the coastal municipality of Suances, in northern Spain (Francés et al., 1990b).

Alternative distributions of land use types proposed by architects were compared in order to select the distribution with the lowest impact, on the basis of the following significant indicators:

- area of soils of capability classes A and B (FAO classification) affected by non-agricultural uses;
- area of potentially unstable slopes which would be subject to different types of construction;
- flood-prone areas devoted to different types of construction;
- extent of aquifer recharge areas affected by potentially polluting activities;
- percentage of units of high visual landscape quality affected by constructions.

The "indicator approach" can also be used to incorporate the consideration of environmental changes into the process of impact assessment of plans. Environmental changes, although usually very difficult to predict, have particular consequences which can be assessed through the establishment of certain scenarios. These scenarios, in turn, can provide the means to develop appropriate indicators useful for EIA. This is the case, for instance, of sea-level rise. Coastal lowlands are in a situation of high potential hazard but high uncertainty with respect to this process, and land use or master plans should take this into consideration.

An analysis of some environmental and economic consequences of sea-level rise on the north coast of Spain has been carried out, considering three different scenarios (Rivas and Cendrero, 1991, 1994). Although not conceived as part of an environmental impact assessment, the results obtained in that work provide the basis for defining certain quantitative indicators which can be applied to EIA of plans.

Areas subject to eventual coastal flooding, considering three possible scenarios (0.5, 1.0 and 1.5 m rise in sea-level), were identified and mapped. The potential losses that would occur in each case have been estimated (Rivas and Cendrero, 1991, 1994). The areas affected and the capital losses would be, respectively, 23.5 km^2 and US$ 820 million; 79 km^2 and US$ 8370 million; 97 km^2 and US$ 9770 million. That is, the average loss in the areas below 0.5 m (23.5 km^2) would be US$ 34.5 million/km^2; in the areas between 0.5 and 1.5 m (55.5 km^2) US$ 136 million/km^2; and in the areas slightly above 1.5 m (18 km^2) US$ 77.8 million/km^2. However, the flooding of certain agricultural or forestry areas and their conversion into coastal wetlands would bring about an increase in biological productivity and could represent a monetary gain of US$ 260 000/km^2/year (Rivas and Cendrero, 1991).

Comparison of alternative master plans for these areas, taking into consideration eventual changes in sea-level, should include the use of indicators such as:

- area subject to hazard under scenarios of 0.5, 1.0 and 1.5 m rise in sea-level which would be occupied by constructions and would eventually require protective measures;
- capital value which would be under risk in case of sea-level rise;

• difference in total biological productivity of intertidal and wetland areas under different land occupation proposals and for the different scenarios.

FINAL COMMENTS

Master plans are the main planning instrument for the regulation of land use. They contemplate a certain distribution of activities within a given area and, consequently, represent a most important conditioning factor in the location of future projects and developments. In that sense, although a plan as such is not a physical action that will produce impacts, it does indeed have very serious environmental impact implications. It is thus important to assess the environmental impact of plans, both to ensure that land use in general is carried out with minimum damage to the environment and to reduce the cost of environmental protection measures.

The method proposed here constitutes a possible way to present a description and a diagnosis of the state of a territory whose use is going to be regulated by a master plan. It also provides a means of comparing the environmental impacts of different plans in order to choose the most appropriate one. This method enables the incorporation of geomorphological factors into the general process of EIA, using both quantitative and qualitative indicators, which can help in the prediction of the environmental effects that a given distribution of land use activities will have. Situations derived from eventual environmental changes can also be contemplated.

It is proposed that EIA of master plans should be made compulsory in the European Union, so that the distribution of land use activities can be regulated on the basis of impact evaluations. This will help in the siting of future projects, reduce the cost of impact mitigation measures and will also, implicitly, introduce impact assessment considerations into smaller projects or actions not presently regulated by national or European norms.

ACKNOWLEDGEMENTS

Critical review by Prof. D. W. Fischer and two anonymous referees was very useful for improving the original manuscript. This chapter is part of the EU Human Capital and Mobility Project (ERBCHRXCT 930311) *Geomorphology and EIA: a network of research in the European Union*. Publication No. 3.

REFERENCES

Aurenheimer, C. (1992). The role of environmental geology within the regional administration. In Cendrero, A., Lüttig, G. and Wolff, F. (Eds), *Planning the Use of the Earth's Surface*, Springer Verlag, Berlin, pp. 443–455
Balkey, N. C. (1968). *The Delphi Method, and Experimental Study of Group Opinion*. Rand Memorandum 5888, P. R. Rand Corporation, Santa Monica, California.
Brown, L. F., Fisher, W. L., Erxleben, A. W. and McGowen, J. M. (1971). *Resource Capability units; their Utility in Land- and Water-Use Management, With Examples from the Texas Coastal Zone*, Geological Circular 71–1, Bureau of Economic Geology, University of Texas at Austin.

Cendrero, A. and Díaz de Terán, J. R. (1987). The environmental map system of the University of Cantabria, Spain. In Arndt, P. and Lüttig, G. (Eds), *Mineral Resources Extraction. Environmental Protection and Land-Use Planning in the Industrial and Developing Countries*, E. Schweizerbat Verlag, Stuttgart, pp. 149–181.

Cendrero, A. and Trilla, J. (1983). La geología ambiental en la evaluación del territorio para usos agrícolas. Il Reunión Nacional de Geología Ambiental y Ordenación del Territorio. Vol. Ponencias, GEGAOT Lérida, Spain, pp. 11–57.

Cendrero, A., Díaz de Terán, J. R., Fernández, O., Garrote, G., González Lastra, J. R., Inoriza, I., Lüttig, G., Otamendi, J., Perez, M., Serrano, A. and Grupo Ikerlana (1987). Detailed geological hazards mapping for urban and rural planning in Vizcaya, Northern Spain. In Wolff, F. (Ed.), *Geology for Environmental Planning*, Special Publication 2, Geological Survey of Norway, Trondheim, pp. 25–41.

Christian, G. S. and Stewart, G. A. (1968). Methodology of integrated surveys. In *Aerial Surveys and Integrated Studies*, UNESCO, Natural Resources Research, Paris, pp. 233–280.

Claver, I., Aguilo, M., Aramburu, M. P., Ayuso, E., Blanco, A., Calatayud, T., Ceñal, M. A., Cifuentes, P., Escribano, R., Francés, E., Glaría, G., González-Alonso, S., Lacoma, E., Muñoz-Rodriguez, C., Ortega, C., Otero, I., Ramos, A. and Sáiz, M. G. (1991) *Guiá Para la Elaboración de Estudios del Medio Físico: Contenido y Metodología*, MOPT, Madrid.

Cooke, R. U. and Doornkamp, J. C. (1990). *Geomorphology in Environmental Management*, Clarendon Press, Oxford.

Eckenrode, R. T. (1975). Weighting multiple criteria. *Management Science*, **12**, 180–192.

Environmental Analysis Group (1980). Environmental survey along the Santander-Unquera coastal strip, Northern Spain, and assessment of its capacity for development. *Landscape Planning*, **7**, 23–56.

Ervin, O. L. (1974). The Delphi method: some applications to local planning. *The Tennessee Planner*, **32**, 1–22.

Francés E, Gómez Orea, D., Cendrero, A., Díaz de Terán, J. R., Fernández, P., Echeverría, G., Escobar, G. and Villarino, T. (1990a). Una metodología para la definición de unidades de diagnóstico en la elaboración de directrices de ordenación territorial a escala regional: el modelo de Cantabria. In *Proceedings, IV Reunión Nacional de Geología Ambiental y Ordenación del Territoria*, SEGAOT-Universidade de Oviedo, pp. 213–224.

Francés, E., Díaz de Terán. J. R., Cendrero, A., Gómez-Orea, D., Villarino, T., Leonardo, J. and Saiz, L. (1990b). Environmental mapping applied to the planning of urban and natural park areas in the north coast of Spain. In *Proceedings, VI International Association of Engineering Geology*, Balkema, Rotterdam, pp. 95–101.

McCall, G. J. H. and Marker, B. R. (Eds) (1989). *Earth Science Mapping for Planning. Development and Conservation*, Graham and Trotman, London.

McHarg, I. L. (1969). *Design with Nature*, Natural History Press, New York.

Panizza, M. (1990). Geomorfologia applicata al rischio e all'impatto ambientali. Un esempio nelle Dolomiti, Italia. *Actas 1 Reunión Nacional de Geomorfología, Tomo 1*, Teruel, Sociedad Española de Geomorfología, pp. 1–16.

Panizza, M. (1992) Geomorphological hazards and environmental impact assessment and mapping. In Cendrero, A., Lüttig, G. and Wolff, F. (Eds), *Planning the Use of the Earth's Surface*, Springer Verlag, Berlin, pp. 101–123.

Rivas, V. and Cendrero, A. (1991). Use of natural and artificial accretion on the north coast of Spain: historical trends and assessment of some environmental and economic consequences. *Journal of Coastal Research*, **7**, 491–507.

Rivas, V. and Cendrero, A. (1994). Human influence in a low-hazard coastal area: an approach to risk assessment and proposal of mitigation strategies. *Journal of Coastal Research*, in press.

Steinitz, C. and Rogers, R. (1975). *The Santa Ana River Basin: An Example of the Use of Computer Graphics in Regional Plan Evaluation*. Report to the US Army Engineering Institute for Water Resources, Fort Belvior, Virginia.

Varios Autores (1977). *Modelo de Procesado de Datos para la Ordenacion Territorial*, CIDS, Santander, Spain.

12 Environmental Change and Land Management in the Cuilcagh Karst, Northern Ireland

JOHN GUNN

Limestone Research Group, Department of Geographical and Environmental Sciences, The University of Huddersfield, UK

ABSTRACT

One of the main problems in the development of land management strategies for karstified limestone terrains is that a significant proportion of the catchment is frequently outside of the area underlain by limestone. Any environmental change in this allogenic area, whether natural or a result of human activity, is likely to have profound impacts on the karst. The problem is well illustrated by the Cuilcagh karst in County Fermanagh, where land use changes in the allogenic catchment have adversely affected Marble Arch, Northern Ireland's only show cave, part of which was opened to the public by Fermanagh District Council in 1985. The Limestone Research Group has been commissioned to investigate the threat and to prepare a land management strategy for part of the show cave catchment which the Council propose to purchase and to designate as a Natural History Park. The project illustrates four ways in which geomorphologists may contribute to land management: identification and mapping of key landform assemblages; evaluation of long-term natural environmental change; assessment of human impacts on landforms and processes; and development of appropriate management strategies. It also provides an opportunity to investigate the utility of GIS in drainage basin management.

INTRODUCTION

This chapter which is based on research commissioned by Fermanagh District Council and the Environment Service—Countryside and Wildlife of the Department of the Environment for Northern Ireland (DoE(NI)), examines land management problems consequent upon environmental changes on Cuilcagh Mountain in County Fermanagh. Although the detail is site specific, the general problem is typical of many other karst areas both in the British Isles and worldwide. In addition the project illustrates four ways in which geomorphologists may contribute to land management:

1. by the identification and mapping of key landform assemblages;
2. by evaluating the natural evolutionary and long-term environmental changes which have produced these landform assemblages;

Geomorphology and Land Management in a Changing Environment. Edited by D. F. M. McGregor and D. A. Thompson.
©1995 John Wiley & Sons Ltd

3. by assessing the influence of human activities on the natural environment in terms of both processes and landforms;
4. by developing appropriate strategies for management of the physical environment.

The Management of Karstified Limestone Terrains

Karstified limestone terrains are frequently areas of high natural beauty and are valued for recreation and tourism. They are also of high scientific value both intrinsically and for the information which they can provide on past environments. Caves are particularly valuable in this respect, acting as repositories for deposits which have long since been removed from the earth's surface. For this reason many karst areas receive some form of statutory protection and in Great Britain about 75% of known cave passage lies within designated Sites of Special Scientific Interest (SSSI). Although this should provide a high degree of protection the SSSI boundaries are generally drawn so as to encompass only land which is underlain by cave passage and which provides direct, autogenic recharge. Unfortunately most active caves also receive allogenic drainage from non-limestone lithologies which extend over a much wider area and any land use change in the wider surface catchment will impact upon the karst area (Hardwick and Gunn, 1990). Hence it is important in karst areas, as in most others, that land management be undertaken on a catchment basis.

THE CUILCAGH UPLAND

Approximately half of Ireland is underlain by Carboniferous Limestone (Figure 12.1) but around 75% of this is lowland karst, much of which is covered by thick superficial deposits such that the limestone has little surface expression. Of the upland karsts, the Burren in County Clare bears a strong imprint of glaciation whereas the north-west plateau karsts, of which Cuilcagh is one, are more typically fluviokarstic (Williams, 1970). Cuilcagh Mountain lies some 20 km south-west of Enniskillen in County Fermanagh (Figure 12.1). The mountain forms a distinctive ridge profile against the Fermanagh skyline, and is a prominent backdrop to much of the county's lakeland scenery. Cuilcagh summit (667 m) is the highest point in the county, and the summit ridge forms the border with County Cavan and the Irish Republic.

LANDFORM ASSEMBLAGES IN THE CUILCAGH UPLAND

Although the area is best known for its karst there are two other main landform assemblages in the Cuilcagh Upland: the boulder fields and mass movements which characterize the summit area, and the peat land of the mid-slopes (Figure 12.2).

Boulder Fields and Mass Movement

The summit ridge of Cuilcagh Mountain is formed of massive Namurian sandstones and gritstones of the Lackagh and Briscloonagh Sandstone Formations. The edge is characterized by cliffs up to 30 m in height and in several places large, intact blocks

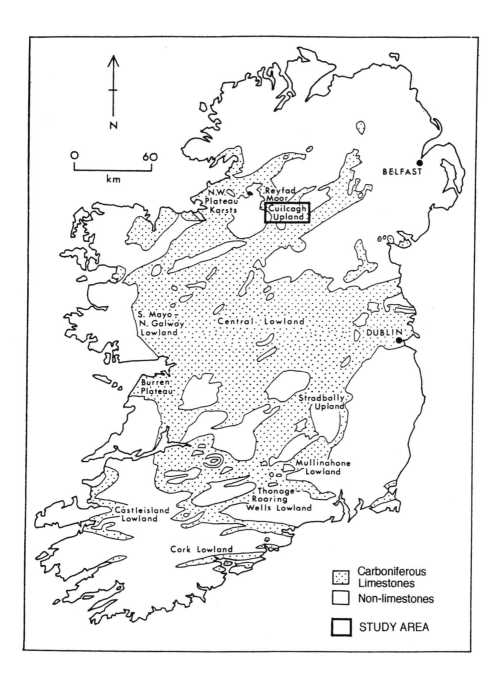

Figure 12.1   The Cuilcagh Upland and limestone outcrops in Ireland (after Williams, 1970)

198

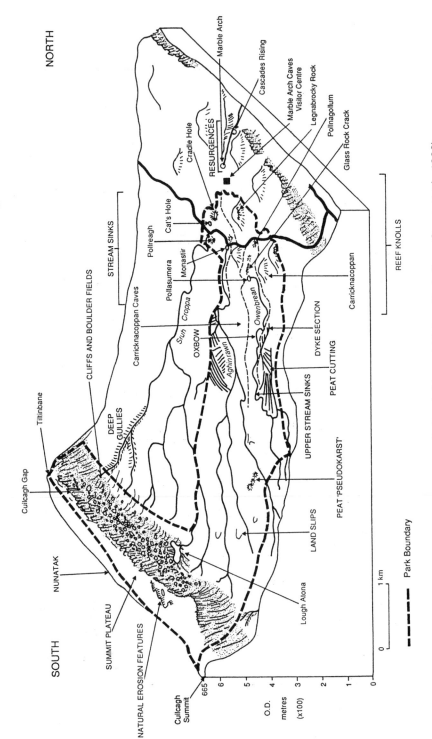

Figure 12.2 Landforms of the Cuilcagh Natural History Park (from Gunn *et al.*, 1993)

have slid forward and are separated from the edge by deep gullies. Beneath these slopes the ground is littered with boulders up to 10 m in long axis which are associated with large-scale mass movement from the edge of the ridge.

Peat Landforms and Drainage

The middle slopes of Cuilcagh Mountain are underlain by sandstones and shales with thin interbedded limestones. These are overlain by thin boulder clay deposits which in turn are covered by 1–3 m of peat forming one of the best examples of a mountain blanket bog ecosystem in Northern Ireland. Of particular geomorphological interest are the extensive areas of piping and associated pseudokarst landforms including depressions with a long axis of up to 10 m and depths of up to 2.5 m. The majority of the pipes are large features (> 20 cm diameter) and contain perennial or seasonal streams which in some cases flow on bedrock floors. They are found both on the gently sloping benches and on the steep slopes at the edge of the benches. Preliminary studies suggest that some have their headwaters in areas of permanent pools on the bog surface and that some at least have formed where peat has grown over the top of small stream channels. Neild (1993) has undertaken a study of piping erosion on Cuilcagh but further work is required to determine the extent and nature of the pipe networks and the processes responsible for their formation. In the higher parts of the peat bog there are a number of small mass movement features which, in the absence of any evidence of past human activities, are presumed to be of natural origin. Rainfall increases with altitude and this may result in greater saturation and higher pore pressures in the peat. Where throughflow lubricates the base of the peat, rotational slumping is likely to result and this is thought to have been the cause of a large flow which occurred in the upper Owenbrean catchment in August 1992 and sent a body of liquid peat several kilometres downstream and through the Marble Arch caves (Walker and Gunn, 1993).

Karst Landforms and Drainage

The sandstones, shales and bog country form the catchment of three large rivers, the Owenbrean, Aghinrawn and Sruh Croppa, which flow down the northern slopes of Cuilcagh Mountain (Figure 12.3). Each river sinks after crossing onto the limestones and flows through the large and extensive passages of Marble Arch cave before rising at the head of the Cladagh Glen (Figure 12.3). The lowest sinks of each river are at Pollasumera, Monastir and Cat's Hole (Figure 12.3) but all three are dry for part of the year, their respective rivers sinking at more recently developed sites some distance upstream. In the case of the Sruh Croppa and Aghinrawn water, tracing has shown that the upstream and downstream sinks are associated with the same drainage system, but part of the Owenbrean's flow is captured by the adjoining Cascades catchment via sinks in its bed at around 500 m and about 1400 m above Pollasumera (Figure 12.3).

Marble Arch cave is the fourth longest in Ireland (c. 6500 m in length) and some 450 m of it forms the only show cave in Northern Ireland, having been opened to the public by Fermanagh District Council in 1985. Since that time it has attracted over 350 000 visitors from all over the world. There are three other major cave systems on the mountain—Shannon Cave (c. 2500 m), the Prod's Pot–Cascades system

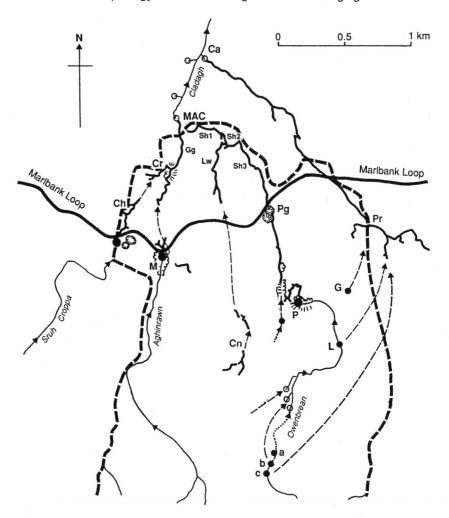

Figure 12.3   Caves and drainage in the Cuilcagh Natural History Park (from Gunn *et al.*, 1993)

(*c.* 4100 m) and Tullyhona Cave (*c.* 1500 m)—and several other smaller sinks, cave passages and risings (Jones, 1974).

In addition to the caves, the lower slopes of the mountain are associated with some of the finest examples of upland karst topography in the British Isles. Major sites include the impressive stream sinks of Monastir and Pollasumera at the end of blind valleys, large collapse dolines at Pollreagh and Pollawaddy, a large karst window (Cradle Hole) and the Marble Arch itself, a remnant section of passage isolated by collapse. In addition, there is a series of mud reef knolls and several small areas of limestone pavement.

LONG-TERM ENVIRONMENTAL CHANGE

Relatively little is known of past environments in the Cuilcagh Uplands but the present landforms have certainly been evolving since at least the early Tertiary. Consideration of these natural changes is an important precursor to examination of more recent, human-induced changes.

Tertiary Environments in the Cuilcagh Area

Mitchell (1985) argues that the modern Irish landscape dates essentially from the Tertiary, when the Cuilcagh area had a tropical climate and large-scale erosion removed substantial amounts of post-Carboniferous sediments. Wilson (1964), using evidence from Magho Mountain, 20 km north of Cuilcagh, claims that up to 200 m of sediment once buried the current topography of Northern Ireland. The more massively bedded mud reef knolls experienced differential erosion and now stand in relief (Figure 12.2). Detailed research has yet to be undertaken but it is considered likely that the inception stage of the larger caves began early in the Tertiary, if not before, and that some of the presently accessible relict passages were formed in this period of massive denudation. A doleritic dyke which was intruded across the lower slopes of the mountain during the Tertiary has very little surface expression except in sections on the Owenbrean and Aghinrawn rivers but is responsible for a major deviation in the course of the Sruh Croppa.

Quaternary Environments in the Cuilcagh Area

Surface evidence of Quaternary environments is poorly preserved in Ireland although both Williams (1970) and Mitchell (1985) claim that the influence of glacial erosion on the landforms of Ireland, and more specifically the limestone uplands, is limited to "trimming" of detail, in an otherwise fluvially and periglacially moulded landscape. Till and moraine on Cuilcagh are believed to date to the last glaciation (the Midlandian); although the ice is thought to have reached only to the 500 m contour leaving the summit area as a nunatak (Kilroe, 1888; Chapman, 1970). Hence, the shattered cliffs, rock pillars, screes and boulder fields below the summit ridge may all be attributed to periglacial (freeze–thaw) weathering. Subsequently Holocene erosion and modification of these landforms has occurred, with many of the blocks and pillars toppling.

In contrast to the paucity of surface material, the active and relict cave passages contain extensive suites of clastic deposits and speleothems which will eventually provide evidence for Quaternary palaeoclimates. The evolution of the Prod's Pot–Cascades and Marble Arch Cave systems provides a useful example of the complex history preserved underground. Water tracing experiments have proved that under low flow conditions the entire flow from the upper Owenbrean catchment feeds the Cascades Rising (via the Prod's Pot–Cascades system). As discharge increases, the sinks are overwhelmed and the excess flow continues downstream for about 1400 m before sinking at Pollasumera and entering the Marble Arch system (Figure 12.3). Prod's Pot also receives concentrated recharge from several small stream-sinks but it is unlikely that these small flows could have produced the large cave passage. Instead, it is probable that at some stage in the past a much higher percentage of water from the Owenbrean flowed in this direction. This is supported by the existence in Marble Arch of speleothems which are being actively redissolved under present-day normal high water conditions and which clearly formed when the system experienced substantially less frequent inundation. The evidence suggests that Prod's Pot–Cascades was originally a much smaller system than Marble Arch. Over time the present-day Ownbrean sinks enlarged, gradually capturing more of the flow with consequent passage growth in the Prod's Pot–Cascades system. The Owenbrean in Marble Arch Cave would have been relatively depleted such that speleothem could accumulate in the no longer active channel. The extensive speleothem growth suggests that this occurred under interglacial conditions, probably somewhat warmer than at present. During one or more subsequent glacial episodes the sinks became fully or partially blocked by sediments which are gradually being removed under present-day conditions. Although at first sight this may seem of purely academic interest it does have considerable potential application and is considered further later in this chapter.

Holocene environmental change was documented by Jones and McKeever (1987) who produced a detailed sedimentology of a sand bank in Skreen Hill Passage. They were able to attribute the sedimentation sequence to post-glacial flood events, which brought in unsorted material, dumping it as the water receded equally rapidly. These sediments were cored, and palynological analysis revealed a detailed vegetative history. A decline in hazel (*Corylus avellana*) was found to coincide with an increase in bryophytes, graminoids and dwarf shrubs, probably reflecting a deterioration in climate at *c.* 6000–5000 BP. Further information was provided in 1987 when an excavation of cave sediments in Pollnagollum by the Ulster Museum revealed human remains. These were radiocarbon dated to *c.* 4500 BP, confirming the presence of humans in the area during the time when woodland was declining. These studies demonstrate the value of cave sediments in revealing palaeoenvironmental information.

Peat accumulation in the area began around 5000 BP as a result of the change to a substantially wetter and cooler climate. Erosion of the peat as a result of human activities is considered below, but it is unlikely that these activities were responsible for the severely eroded surface on the eastern end of the Cuilcagh Mountain summit ridge where there is exposed regolith, gullies and residual peat hags. Natural processes are also thought to have been responsible for the exposed bedrock at the western end of the summit ridge which forms a "sandstone pavement". Eroded sandstone pedestals provide evidence of the former depth of peat. A habitat survey undertaken for the DoE(NI) in 1989 estimated the total area of degraded blanket peat and bare ground to be 8 ha, nearly 25% of the summit area. Initial peat growth on the summit was probably rapid, due to the high rainfall, consequent lower decomposition rates, and a lack of slope erosion. However, there may be an "inherent hydrological instability" (Ratcliffe and Oswald, 1988:52) within a blanket mire, which limits vertical growth. Bower (1962:33) identified such a "natural end point to peat development" as one of the causes of upland erosion in the English Pennines. The presence of a significant break in slope on the north face, where the cliffs and scarp slope begin, may have caused an initial mass movement sequence. Alexander *et al.* (1986) identified a break of slope as an important factor in many Irish bog bursts, causing tension in the surface vegetative layer. They argue that over time the threshold of stability of the peat may be exceeded, leading to a bog burst, without any external stimulus. However, less dramatic mass transport, in the form of headward channel erosion, particularly in such plateau/scarp topographic units, is another possible cause of initial peat erosion. Once erosion by mass movement or gullying was initiated, subsequent erosion is likely to have been rapid, as the summit receives over 2000 mm of rainfall per annum. Bower (1960) claimed that once such erosion thresholds are passed, subsequent peat development is halted as drainage becomes free, and any deposition of organic material is rapidly removed by sheetwash or gully erosion.

ENVIRONMENTAL CHANGES CONSEQUENT UPON HUMAN OCCUPANCE

The oldest evidence of human occupance of Cuilcagh is a poorly preserved Neolithic cairn on the Tiltinbane end of the summit ridge (Figure 12.2), and the earliest human impacts took the form of agricultural forest clearance at this time. Between the summit ridge and the limestone hills there is very little visible evidence of early human use of the land. This is a result of the change to a substantially wetter climate at the onset of the Atlantic period around 5000 years ago which had two important influences. First, the agriculture of the Neolithic farmers would have been detrimentally affected, with crop failure and famine driving people from the uplands. Secondly, blanket peat began to accumulate, burying any field boundaries, settlements, artifacts and all but the largest manifestations of life at these times. The Atlantic climatic decline resulted in a marginalization of agriculture which has effectively left a hiatus between Neolithic and recent (post AD 1500) human impacts. Any forest which had not been cleared was overwhelmed by peat growth as the water table rose, and where the peat has subsequently been removed, tree stumps are often exposed.

In Medieval times population densities were high and land was at a premium. This is evidenced by the re-habitation of crannogs in Lough Macnean Lower, around 600 years after they were first constructed, as defensive farmsteads. Brian Williams (County Archaeologist, pers. comm., 1990) has dated a recently discovered booley house near the upper banks of the Owenbrean River to around this period when transhumance was widely practised in the west of Ireland (Buchanan, 1970). In the more accessible areas of blanket mire, there are old squares and banks, remnants of hand-cutting of turf which still occurs in the area to this day, although to a much lesser degree than in the past. Some of these areas are almost totally overgrown with *Sphagnum* species, which prefer the wetter conditions existing behind the banks and in the hollows. Certainly in the Middle Ages settlement extended considerably higher up the mountain than is the case today, as evidenced by derelict habitations.

Large-scale abandonment of the mid and upper slopes of Cuilcagh probably took place during the 19th century famine and between then and the early 1980s the remoteness of the area and the poor agricultural quality of the land ensured that human impacts were minimal, with relatively low sheep stocking densities and a small amount of hand-cutting of peat for domestic use. The major stimulus for change in the past decade has probably been the European Union. Cuilcagh is a

"Less Favoured Area" and agricultural grants and subsidies are higher than for other more productive environments. Local farmers have taken advantage of grants and subsidies to construct access tracks high up the mountain and to increase stocking densities above those which the bog can support. This has been accompanied by burning of heather to encourage growth of grass. The net result has been a major increase in runoff and erosion, with significant downstream impacts which are considered below.

Whilst overgrazing is spatially the most important human impact, the most visibly prominent and controversial activity is mechanized peat extraction which was made possible by the introduction of Sandinavian compact harvesting technology. The peat extrusion machinery is mounted on large four-wheel-drive tractors, and extraction is now possible over large areas of bog. This damages the land for traditional sheep farming and forces the animals onto smaller areas of grazing, often of lesser quality. Prior to peat extraction extensive drainage works are required and these, together with the compaction of the ground surface during harvesting, change the discharge characteristics of streams draining the affected areas. Between 1982 and 1989 commercial peat cutting affected over 60 ha of the Marble Arch Cave catchment and involved the digging of over 8700 m of new drainage channel and the construction of 6000 m of access track. As yet the main peat pseudokarst areas have not been affected but it seems inevitable that they will be totally destroyed if extraction continues unabated.

DEVELOPMENT OF LAND MANAGEMENT STRATEGIES

During the late 1980s staff at the Marble Arch show cave became concerned that the rapidity and magnitude of flood events was increasing and that this posed a risk to public safety. As mechanized peat extraction was expanding at this time it was felt that this could be the cause of the hydrological changes. Concern over flooding problems and a more general desire to conserve Cuilcagh as an environmental resource, prompted Fermanagh District Council to commission an assessment of the geomorphology and hydrology of the area with particular reference to recent environmental change in the cave's catchment. The assessment has been carried out at three scales:

1. a general review of the Cuilcagh/Marlbank area including development of a GIS and proposals for the establishment of a natural history park;
2. examination of the flooding problem in the Skreen Hill Passage of the Marble Arch show cave and proposals for reduction of the risk to visitors;
3. a small catchment study of the hydrological and geomorphological impact of mechanized peat cutting.

Geomorphology and Land Management on Cuilcagh

When the research project commenced in 1991 there was no statutory protection for any part of Cuilcagh Mountain although it was assessed for designation as an Area of Special Scientific Interest by the DoE(NI) in 1989. Perhaps because small-scale peat cutting for domestic supply has a long history in the area, planning controls were proving (and have continued to prove) ineffective in preventing the larger-scale commercial operations even though the work is technically illegal since no planning permission has been applied for. In view of this, and of the difficulty of controlling farming activities, it became apparent at an early stage of the research that the only way in which effective land management could be exercised was through land ownership. A key portion of the cave's catchment was identified and it was proposed that it be purchased and designated as the Cuilcagh Natural History Park (CNHP) (Figure 12.2). The proposed CNHP will cover some 1140 ha, a further 1220 ha being already part of the adjacent Florence Court Forest Park which is managed by the Royal Society for the Protection of Birds. Together they include a large part of the catchment of the Marble Arch show cave and the two largest peat cutting areas. Funding has been sought from a number of sources including the European Union and the UK Government. The National Heritage Memorial Fund has offered approximately 25% of the sum required but an application to the 1993 LIFE initiative (the European Union instrument for the environment) was unsuccessful. At the time of writing (December 1993) a revised bid is being prepared.

Subsequent to the CNHP initiative, the whole of the Cuilcagh/Marlbank area was included as part of the proposed Fermanagh Caveland Area of Outstanding Natural Beauty (Department of the Environment for Northern Ireland, 1992). In April 1993, the Department of Agriculture for Northern Ireland launched the West Fermanagh and Erne Lakeland Environmentally Sensitive Area (ESA) Scheme which covers most of the northern flank of Cuilcagh Mountain. If the CNHP initiative is unsuccessful then this may provide a means by which the most damaging agricultural impacts can be restricted. However, there was no consultation with geomorphologists and the ESA does not contain any mention of peat extraction and its adverse environmental impacts. A similar lack of geomorphological involvement was apparent in early proposals from the Environment Service—Countryside & Wildlife of the DoE(NI) who indicated in mid-1993 that they were intending to designate an Area of Special Scientific Interest on Cuilcagh, but that only the ecological interest of the area was to be considered in line with the European Union Habitats Directive. Subsequent correspondence from the author and others has led to greater weight being given to earth science conservation. However, even if an Area of Special Scientific Interest is designated it is by no means certain that the area will be managed in a sustainable manner as ". . . official figures show that 200–300 of the UK's 6000 SSSIs are damaged or destroyed each year as 'development' invariably takes precedence over conservation . . ." (Anon., 1993:10). Hence, the CNHP initiative remains the only hope for long-term sustainable land management on Cuilcagh.

The CNHP initiative is of particular interest because its primary focus is geomorphological, although the ecological interests of the area are also of considerable importance. A Management Plan has been prepared which reflects this balance of interest (Gunn et al., 1993). In particular, it is proposed to lease back most of the land in the park to local farmers but to control stocking ratios so as to reduce erosion and consequent downstream impacts. All commercial peat cutting will be prohibited and it is also proposed to investigate methods by which the degraded areas may be rehabilitated. The boundaries of the CNHP have been drawn so as to include the most significant landforms and virtually the whole of the proposed park will fall within the drainage basin of the Marble Arch caves. It was decided to support the CNHP Management Plan by development of a Geographical Information System (GIS) for the Marble Arch Caves catchment and this also provided an ideal opportunity to investigate the utility of GISs for drainage basin management.

The Cuilcagh GIS

The GIS will include details of the key geomorphological and hydrological features on the mountain as well as ecological and archaeological data and information on land use. The aims of the Cuilcagh GIS are to:

1. act as a medium for the collation and collection of appropriate data sets relevant to both the catchment of the Marble Arch Caves and the CNHP from a wide range of sources;
2. act as an inventory for the storage of data in a digital format;
3. allow the integration of data sets;
4. allow the identification of critical areas by the overlaying of different variables;
5. allow the visualization of future effects with respect to management regimes.

As in any GIS which is to be used in drainage basin management, the Cuilcagh GIS will utilize a substantial volume of data, the major features being their varying formats, multi-temporal nature and differing origins. Early in 1991 the Environment Service—Countryside and Wildlife (DoE(NI)) expressed their interest in the Cuilcagh GIS project and as a result have supplied ecological data sets. The Environment Service are also participating in the development of the Northern Ireland Geographical Information System (NIGIS) (Brand, 1988) and subsequently proposed that the Cuilcagh GIS form a pilot study for NIGIS. For this reason the Ordnance Survey for Northern Ireland agreed to supply both a digital topographic map, following a re-survey of part of the Cuilcagh area during the summer of 1991, and a contour map. The topographic survey thus forms the frame of reference and map base of the Cuilcagh GIS. Other data sources for the GIS are listed in Table 12.1.

The data are presently being automated and when the GIS is fully operational, both the overlay and network capabilities of PC ARC/INFO will be exploited in helping to answer the following questions:

1. How has land use changed in the catchment, particularly the extent of peat cutting?
2. How has the drainage network changed?
3. What are the critical areas of the catchment where heavy rainfall is likely to result in rapid runoff into the cave system?
4. Where are the most suitable areas for future peat cutting?
5. What are the likely hydrological impacts of future land use change?
6. What are the relationships between surface landforms/land usage and underground landforms?

Table 12.1   Data available for the Cuilcagh GIS

Survey	Extent	Format	Source
Topographic survey	Catchment	1 : 10 000/1 : 2500 digital map (DXF)	OSNI
Geological survey	Catchment	1 : 50 000 map sheet (Solid and Drift)	GSNI
Contours	Catchment	1 : 50 000 digital map (DXF)	OSNI
Digital terrain model	Catchment	400 points/km², elevations in metres	IOH
Soil survey	Catchment	1 : 50 000/1 : 10 000 map and field sheets	DANI
Hydrological survey	Catchment	Continuous point discharge	LRG
Meteorological survey	Catchment	Continuous point rainfall	LRG
Habitat survey	3500 ha, 225 quadrats	1 : 10 000 maps, notes and reports, RECORDER	CWB, RSPB
Woodland survey	115 ha, 45 sites	1 : 10 000 maps dBase IV	CWB, EAU
Cave survey	All known caves	Maps at various scales	SUI
Aerial photographs	Catchment	1 : 20 000/1 : 10 000 stereo pairs 1982, 1989, 1991	OSNI
Archaeological survey	Catchment	1 : 10 000 map, summary notes	HMB
Landscape ecology	12 × 25 ha grids	1 : 10 000 maps, dBase IV	CWB, UU

OSNI: Ordnance Survey (Northern Ireland); GSNI: Geological Survey for Northern Ireland; IOH: Institute of Hydrology; UU: University of Ulster; DANI: Department of Agriculture for Northern Ireland; LRG: Limestone Research Group, University of Huddersfield; CWB: Department of the Environment for Northern Ireland (Countryside and Wildlife Branch); RSPB: Royal Society for the Protection of Birds; EAU: Environmental Advisory Unit, Liverpool University; SUI: Speleological Union of Ireland; HMB: Department of the Environment for Northern Ireland (Historic Monuments and Building Branch).

A GIS, or any other information system for that matter, is not an end in itself. Its value will arise from the usefulness of its resultant information products which are dependent upon the timeliness, accuracy and completeness of the data and the accessibility of the system. The success of the Cuilcagh GIS as a management tool may, in part, be judged by its ability to answer complex queries such as those above. However, its value will also depend upon the extent to which the system is designed for the benefit of the user since a basic aim of building a GIS must be to meet the needs of the user more efficiently, effectively and equitably.

Flood Risk Reduction in the Marble Arch Show Cave

Water tracing experiments (Figure 12.3 and above) have established that the Owenbrean sink at Pollasumera is the main feeder to Skreen Hill passage, the section of the show cave in which flash flooding is a major problem. A telemetric water-level recorder has been installed at the sink to provide advance warning of any flood events and a check dam has been installed at the end of the show cave to provide flood detention storage. A telemetric water-level recorder has also been installed at this site. In the longer term it is possible that if the sediments which are impeding flow into the upper Owenbrean sinks (see section on Quaternary Environments above) could be removed, then a greater amount of water would once again flow to the Prod's Pot–Cascades system with a concomitant decrease in flow, and hence in flood risk, in Marble Arch. An additional advantage of this would be an increase in flow at the Cascades Rising which is a source of potable supply.

The Hydrological and Geomorphological Impacts of Mechanized Peat Extraction

As the impacts of mechanized peat extraction on upland blanket bog have not previously been investigated, a detailed study has been initiated in a small catchment which is tributary to the Aghinrawn River. The upper parts of the catchment (about 25 ha) are largely natural and the level of grazing is typical of that elsewhere on Cuilcagh. The lower part of the catchment (about 30 ha) has been heavily quarried, the majority of the surface vegetation having been removed. The hydrological and geomorphological characteristics of the upper and lower catchments are being compared with a view to developing predictive mathematical models. The work commenced in January 1993 and is ongoing but it has already become clear that the lower catchment can produce up to three times the peak specific discharge of the upper catchment during individual storm events. Despite this, it is considered that peat extraction alone is unlikely to have changed the overall hydrological regime at the caves since the area so far affected is less than 3% of the catchment area. However, it has probably contributed, along with the more widespread changes resulting from more intensive agricultural activity on the mountain.

CONCLUSIONS

The Cuilcagh uplands form a magnificent environmental resource which has been sculptured by geomorphological processes acting over time-scales of millions to thousands of years. Since the early 1980s human activities have directly and indirectly increased the rate of environmental change in a manner which threatens both the scientific integrity of the landscape and its use as a recreational/touristic resource. Quantification of the geomorphological, as well as the ecological impacts of these activities is an important prerequisite to management. However, as is so often the case, effective management will only be possible if appropriate land use controls can be exercised, ideally through the purchase and establishment of the Cuilcagh Natural History Park. If this can be accomplished then the development of a geomorphologically based management plan and GIS will undoubtedly facilitate future land management efforts.

ACKNOWLEDGEMENTS

The research project on the Cuilcagh Karst is being funded by Fermanagh District Council and by the Environment Service—Countryside and Wildlife of the Department of the Environment for Northern Ireland. However, the views expressed above are entirely those of the author. Christine Hunting (University of Huddersfield) worked on preparation of the GIS from May 1991 to November 1993 with assistance from Sarah Cornelius (Manchester Metropolitan University). Valuable field assistance has been provided by Michelle Gray, Paul Hardwick and Robert Hyland of the Limestone Research Group and the whole project would not have been possible without the enthusiastic support of Richard Watson and the staff at Marble Arch Caves. Figure 12.1 was drawn by Cathy Gunn and Figures 12.2 and 12.3 by Stephen Pratt. This paper is a contribution to the work of the IGU Commission on Environmental Changes and Conservation in Karst Areas.

REFERENCES

Alexander, R. W., Coxon, P. and Thorn, R. H. (1986). A bog flow at Straduff Townland, County Sligo. *Proceedings of the Royal Irish Academy,* **86(B)**, 107–119.

Anon (1993). Conservation in Europe: Can the UK make the grade? *Earth Matters,* **20**, 10–12.

Bower, M. M. (1960). The erosion of blanket peat in the Southern Pennies. *East Midlands Geographer,* **13**, 22–33.

Bower, M. M. (1962). The cause of erosion in blanket peat bogs. A review of evidence in the light of recent work in the Pennines. *Scottish Geographical Magazine,* **78**, 33–43.

Brand, M. J. D. (1988). The geographical information system for Northern Ireland. *Mapping Awareness and Spatial Information Systems,* **2**, 18–21.

Buchanan, R. H. (1970). Common fields and enclosure: an eighteenth century example from County Down. *Ulster Folklife,* **15/16**, 99–118.

Chapman, R. J. (1970). The late-Weichselian glaciations of the Erne basin. *Irish Geography,* **6**, 153–161.

Department of the Environment for Northern Ireland (1989). *Ecological Survey Report for Marlbank and Cuilcagh,* unpublished report, DOE(NI), Belfast.

Department of the Environment for Northern Ireland (1992). *Fermanagh Caveland Area of Outstanding Natural Beauty Proposal,* DOE(NI), Belfast.

Gunn, J., Cornelius, S., Gray, M. and Hunting, C. (1993). *A Management Plan for the Cuilcagh Natural History Park,* Limestone Research Group Report 93/50, University of Huddersfield.

Hardwick, P. and Gunn, J. (1990). *The Impact of Agriculture on the Scientific Interest of Cave SSSI,* Limestone Research Group Report to the Nature Conservancy Council.

Jones, G. Ll. (1974). *Caves of Fermanagh & Cavan,* Watergate Press, Enniskillen.

Jones, G. Ll. and McKeever, M. (1987). The sedimentology and palynology of some postglacial deposits from Marble Arch Cave, County Fermanagh. *Cave Science,* **14**, 3–6.

Kilroe, J. R. (1888). Directions of ice flow in the north of Ireland as determined by the observations of the Geological Survey. *Quarterly Journal of the Geological Society of London,* **44**, 827–833.

Mitchell, F. G. (1985). The preglacial landscape. In Edwards, K. J. and Warren, W. P. (Eds), *The Quaternary History of Ireland,* London, Academic Press, pp. 17–37.

Neild, C. (1993). *An investigation of peat piping on Cuilcagh Mountain, County Fermanagh, Northern Ireland.* Unpublished BSc (hons) dissertation, Manchester Metropolitan University.

Ratcliffe, D. A. and Oswald, P. H. (Eds) (1988). *The Flow Country The Peatlands of Caithness and Sutherland,* Nature Conservancy Council, Peterborough.

Walker, C. and Gunn, J. (1993). A peat flow in the catchment of Marble Arch caves, Ireland (abstract). 3rd International Geomorphology Conference, McMaster University, Programme with Abstracts, p. 267.

Williams, P. W. (1970). Limestone morphology in Ireland. In Stephens, N. and Glasscock, R. E. (Eds), *Irish Geographical Studies,* Queen's University, Belfast, pp. 105–124.

Wilson, R. L. (1964). The tertiary dykes of Magho Mountain, Co. Fermanagh. *Irish Naturalist Journal,* **14**, 254–257.

13 The Use of Remote Sensing, Geomorphological Data and Ancillary Information for the Hazard Mapping of Wood Fires with Some Examples From Greece

B. M. De VLIEGHER, M. De DAPPER
Department of Geography, Universiteit Gent, Belgium

and

P. S. BASIGOS
Forestry Directorate, Nomarchia Messinias, Kalamata, Greece

ABSTRACT

The modelling of wild fire hazard is based upon a combination of multi-temporal field work, remote sensing and GIS. Because of the availability of a different amount and kind of information, the study has been applied in two regions in Greece, each of them characterized by different physical and anthropogeneous landscape phenomena.

The first model is made for south Euboia using limited information, and taking into account a limited number of influencing factors. A hierarchical system indicates the degree of influence: (1) of vegetation; (2) altitude/aspect; and (3) slope/accessibility. The combination of the single hazard for each factor gives the fire hazard. Four hazard classes are differentiated (none to very severe). A second model is in the process of being set up for the eparchy of Pylias (south-west Peloponnese) using highly detailed fire statistics. The hazard is investigated for two aspects of the fire behaviour (temporal and spatial). Some of the first results are discussed.

INTRODUCTION

Wild fires are one of the major problems in Mediterranean regions; they affect about 5000 km² every year (Kailidis, 1992). Yearly, an average of about 900 fires are recorded in Greece, extending over an area of nearly 32 000 ha in total, corresponding to 35.13 ha per fire.

Geomorphology and Land Management in a Changing Environment. Edited by D. F. M. McGregor and D. A. Thompson.
©1995 John Wiley & Sons Ltd

The susceptibility to wild fires is mainly due to:

- the typical Mediterranean climate with dry and hot summers;
- the characteristics of the natural vegetation: vegetation is often adapted to the dry conditions in summer; most of the shrubs found in the typical Mediterranean plant communities are spiny and contain a high content resin and oils;
- the topography;
- the human influence: for thousands of years, men have used and misused fire for their survival (agriculture, hunting, grazing of animals) (Thirgood, 1981; Trabaud, 1981).

At present, fire is mainly used for agricultural purposes and the importance of pastoralism. Fire is used by farmers during the month of October in order to clean the orchards before the harvest of olives. Shepherds set land on fire in order to improve the quality of the grazing land.

AIM OF THE STUDY

This chapter presents the first results of a study concerning the fire hazard in Greece. The study has been applied in two regions: (1) the very southern part of the island of Euboia (central Greece); and (2) the eparchy ("district") of Pylias (south-west Peloponnese) (Figure 13.1). Both areas are characterized by a strong difference in the physical and human aspects of the landscape. The regions were also chosen because of the different amount and kind of available information about the history of fires.

The aim of the research is to model fire behaviour and to acquire some knowledge about the problem of controlling wild fires. Using a different information data set, a fire model is set up for the study regions. A first fire hazard model is made for south Euboia and is based upon a limited data set. The availability of more and highly detailed information for the region of Pylias allows the investigation of other aspects of fire behaviour, namely fire frequency and fire spread. The hazard is investigated based upon the relationship between the history of fires and the physical and human aspects of the study region.

This knowledge and the modelling of fire behaviour will offer more effective control of the wild fires, in particular: (1) the opening of new fire roads; (2) the supply of useful technical equipment (3) the rearrangement of the fire-fighters' locations; (4) information for the public; and (5) better construction of a development and management plan for the natural ecosystem in relation to wild fire behaviours.

LITERATURE REVIEW

The application of remote sensing for forest fire mapping and inventory can be split up into different categories. First, analogue and digital techniques are used for the assessment of the loss by wild fires. Tanaka *et al.* (1983) used Landsat Multi-Spectral

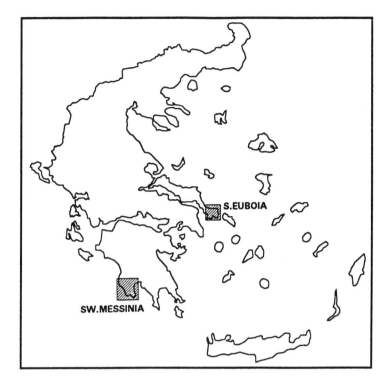

Figure 13.1 Location of the study areas

Scanner data for the classification, mapping and area estimation of devastated land in Japan. Karteris and Kritikos (1992) used Landsat Thematic Mapper data and applied non-supervised and supervised classifications for assessing the forest fire damage on the Holy Mount Athos (Greece). Other satellite information such as NOAA-AVHRR (Advanced Very High Resolution Radiometer) images (3.8 mm band) are used for the detection of worldwide fire activity (Matson *et al.*, 1987).

The automatic classification of burnt land using satellite imagery can, however, cause some mis-classifications because of the spectral overlap between burnt/not-burnt land especially in areas where the vegetation cover is very sparse (Chuvieco and Congalton, 1988; DeVliegher, 1991).

Secondly, the gathering of information on fire fuels by remote sensing is very important, since the availability and the characteristics of the fuels influence fire behaviour a great deal. Numerous studies can be cited using the NOAA-AVHRR multi-temporal data for the differentiation of broad-scale fire fuel classes over large areas (McKinley *et al.*, 1985; Werth *et al.*, 1985).

Thirdly, remote sensing facilitates monitoring of vegetation regeneration, for which the leaf area index is calculated (Diamantopoulos and Paraskevopoulos, 1986), or the normalized difference vegetation index using a multi-temporal data set (Lopez Soria *et al.*, 1988; Dagorne *et al.*, 1990).

Geographical information systems (GIS) are of great help in the monitoring and the mapping of fire risk.

In the past, fire risk models have been set up based upon the fire history of the region. Three different components are calculated: (1) the basic risk, referring to the fire frequency, (2) the cause index, indicating the typology of the cause, and (3) the vegetation index, showing the influence of the plant associations (Anon., 1987). Kailidis and Pantelis (1988) determined the relationship between fires and the climatic conditions using statistical fire data and defined a fire danger rating system for fire spreading.

Using a geographical information system, the relationship between the occurrence of fires and the spatial characteristics of the numerous influence factors can be investigated; this can result in a tool for forest management (Root et al., 1985).

METHODOLOGY

This research is based upon a combination of different techniques—field survey, remote sensing and Geographical Information Systems (GIS)—in which a multi-source data set is stored. The ILWIS (Integrated Land and Watershed Information System, ITC-Enschede) software at PC-configuration is used. Using the GIS, it is possible to search for the relationship between the fire locality and the different fire-influencing phenomena.

The risk or hazard mapping for environmental degradation requires an understanding of the different influencing factors. They are defined based upon the multi-temporal field knowledge and a thematic study is performed according to the availability of information. The factors influencing fire behaviour are: climate, type of vegetation, topography, accessibility of the area and other anthropogeneous factors (proximity to waste dumps and to agricultural land, the influence of tourism, decrease in population, etc.).

The information concerning the vegetation is obtained by applying remote sensing techniques (supervised classification, ratio). Information about the other influencing factors are introduced in the GIS as separate layers by digitizing the existing information (contour lines, road network) or by applying a multiple regression (climate). Information about the fire localities has also been incorporated by digitizing, polygonizing and labelling.

The different thematic maps are combined with the fire maps in order to find the relationship.

FIRE HAZARD MODELLING IN SOUTH EUBOIA (CENTRAL GREECE)

Environmental Setting

South Euboia is very sensitive to environmental degradation, such as that caused by fires. During the period 1981–89, 62 fires were registered in the forest district of Karystos, destroying in total 6165 ha (10% of the district), with an annual total area of loss varying between 23 ha and 4340 ha. Most of these fires occurred towards the end of the dry season (August–October) when high water deficiencies are noted and when vegetation is extremely dry. South Euboia is also characterized by the occurrence of strong northerly winds, the Meltemnia, which are attended by low air humidity and high temperatures.

Available Information

A multi-source and multi-temporal data set is used, consisting of:

- multi-temporal field data on an annual basis for the period 1983–89;
- six topographical maps at a scale of 1:50 000 (Hellenic Army Geographical Service, Athens) indicating the contour lines, hydrographic network, roads and settlements;
- localities of the fires for the period 1 January 1981 to 21 September 1989 on a topographical base map;
- statistical data about the fire (date, site area, owner, type of vegetation);
- satellite image of Landsat Thematic Mapper, scene 182/34-Q1, dated 31 July 1985.

Fire Hazard Mapping

Only one meteorological station is located in the southern part of Euboia. Due to the lack of sufficient data and the importance of microclimates in the region, the influence of climate has been omitted in the hazard model. A thematic study is only made for vegetation, topography and accessibility of the area.

Data Input

Vegetation.   Information about the vegetation is obtained by applying a supervised classification (maximum likelihood) using six Landsat Thematic Mapper bands (exclusion of thermal infrared) and differentiating eight main land cover classes. Due to differences in illumination and in vegetation density and composition, some of the classes are subdivided. The classes which are distinguished are:

- *class 1*: deep water
- *class 2*: shallow water
- *class 3*: burnt land, illuminated side
- *class 4:* burnt land, shaded side
- *class 5: phrygana*, illuminated side
- *class 6: phrygana*, shaded side. The phrygana is composed of small shrubs in general not taller than 50 cm. The shrubs are often spiny and have a windblown shape; leaves are small and leathery or densely grey-hairy.
- *class 7: maquis*. The maquis is a tall (2–3 m high) dense formation of hard leaved, evergreen shrubs
- *class 8*: agricultural land with crops (vines)
- *class 9*: agricultural land without crops (cereals are harvested by the end of June)
- *class 10*: evergreen trees, including irrigated land

- *class 11*: deciduous trees
- *class 12*: bare rocks—limestone
- *class 13*: bare rocks—shale
- *class 14*: built up areas

The commission–omission matrix is given in Table 13.1. It indicates an overlap between the classes phrygana (class 5), burnt land (class 4) and bare rocks (class 13). This is mainly because of the common factor concerning the coverage of the soil: each class is characterized by a poor to extremely low cover. The overlap is due to the fact that the phrygana is characterized by a wide variability; at some places the cover is relatively dense compared to neighbouring zones where rocks (shale) outcrop.

A second overlap is found between evergreen trees (class 10) and deciduous trees (class 11). This is due to the occurrence of phenomena within the class of evergreen trees which reflect the infrared strongly. The class "evergreen trees" is sampled in the irrigated parts of the agricultural zones, in which beside citrus trees surrounded by cypress, clover, sorghum, maize and vegetables are also cultivated.

A third overlap occurs between phrygana (class 6) and evergreen trees (class 10) due to the presence of shadow in both classes. Training samples for class 6 are located along the non-illuminated side of the hill slopes; the influence of shadow is of great importance in the irrigated zones because of the occurrence of cypress fences.

An overlap can also be observed between the bare rocks (class 12) and the built-up areas (class 14). Both classes are characterized by a virtual absence of vegetation.

Other thematic information. The topography is investigated by digitizing the contour lines with 100 m intervals in the hilly regions, and 20 m, 10 m or 5 m intervals in the flat lands and in top zones. After digitization, a digital elevation model is created

Table 13.1 Commission-omission matrix of training areas for vegetation classification

Trained as[a]	Classified as:														
	1	2	3	4	5	6	7	8	9	10	11	12	13	14	Rej.[b]
1	2969	0	0	0	0	0	0	0	0	0	0	0	0	0	32
2	0	264	0	0	0	0	0	0	0	0	0	0	0	0	19
3	0	0	766	38	5	0	0	0	0	0	0	20	0	0	40
4	0	0	12	176	17	0	0	0	0	0	0	0	0	0	0
5	0	0	2	109	1678	14	0	0	0	5	0	30	404	0	1
6	0	0	0	0	1	533	0	0	0	47	0	0	8	0	2
7	0	0	0	0	0	13	146	0	0	22	18	0	0	0	3
8	0	0	1	0	1	0	0	369	0	24	2	3	0	5	14
9	0	0	0	0	0	0	0	0	44	0	0	0	0	0	3
10	0	0	0	0	1	0	0	4	0	86	19	0	0	0	1
11	0	0	0	0	0	0	1	0	0	21	106	1	0	0	1
12	0	0	4	0	19	0	0	0	0	0	0	290	0	70	5
13	0	0	0	0	15	6	0	0	0	2	0	0	161	0	8
14	0	0	0	0	0	0	0	0	0	0	0	17	0	80	3

[a] 1–14: Sample classes (legend see above).
[b] Rej.: rejected.

by means of linear interpolation. The interpolated image is then used as a basic document for the derivation of slope and aspect.

The basic document for the information about the accessibility of the area is the topographical map. The road network is digitized and distances are calculated.

Hazard Mapping

By means of the GIS it is possible to combine the different information layers. Based upon the comparison between the thematic maps and the fire locality map (1981–89), the hazard is calculated. This method is based upon the one described by Chuvieco and Congalton (1989).

The different influencing factors form part of a hierarchical system. By measuring the strength of the relationship between the fire locality and the various landscape phenomena, i.e. the correlation coefficient, the environmental characteristics are ranked. The highest correlation with the occurrence of wild fires in south Euboia is found for the original type of vegetation, followed secondly by the altitude and aspect, and thirdly by the slope and the accessibility of the area.

Each level of the hierarchy is represented by means of a weight. The values of the weights are chosen according to Chuvieco and Congalton (1989). In the present study, the choice of the weights for each factor was derived from the multi-temporal field observations with regard to the fire behaviour, and depended upon (1) the relative importance of each factor to increase the fire hazard, and (2) the fact that the final hazard map should have a byte-format, with values varying between 0 and 255. The weights used to represent the different hierarchical levels are equal to 50, 25 and 10, where a higher weight refers to a higher fire hazard.

The different classes of the influencing factors are given a score corresponding with the hazard (0: no hazard; 1: moderate hazard; 2: high hazard).

The weight of each factor and the scores of the individual classes are given in Table 13.2.

The fire hazard is calculated using the formula:

$$\text{Hazard} = V + A + O + S + D$$

where

$$V = 50 \times v \quad (v: \text{score of land cover class})$$
$$A = 25 \times a \quad (a: \text{score of altitude class})$$
$$O = 25 \times o \quad (o: \text{score of aspect class})$$
$$S = 10 \times s \quad (s: \text{score of slope class})$$
$$D = 10 \times d \quad (d: \text{score or distance class})$$

The hazard values vary between 0 and 240. Low values indicate a low hazard, pixels with high values refer to highly sensitive zones. Four classes are distinguished:

no hazard	0–75
slight hazard	76–125
moderate hazard	126–175
severe hazard	176–240

Table 13.2 Weights and scores of the different influencing factors and respective classes

Class	Risk	Score	Class	Risk	Score	Class	Risk	Score
Vegetation (weight 50)			*Aspect* (weight 25)			*Slope* (weight 10)		
Water	None	0	Flat areas	None	0	0–2%	None	0
Bare rocks	None	0	East	Moderate	1	2–6%	None	0
Built up areas	None	0	North-east	Moderate	1	6–12%	Moderate	1
Deciduous trees	None	0	North	Moderate	1	12–18%	Moderate	1
Burnt land			North-west	Moderate	1	18–25%	High	2
(thriften)	Moderate	1	West	Moderate	1	25–35%	High	2
Agriculture			South-west	High	2	35–50%	High	2
Stubble	Moderate	1	South	High	2	>50%	None	0
Crops	Moderate	1	South-east	High	2			
Evergreen trees	Moderate	1						
Phrygana	High	2						
Maquis	High	2	*Altitude* (weight 25)			*Distance to road* (weight 10)		
			>1000 m	None	0	>1500 m	None	0
			500–1000 m	Moderate	1	500–1500 m	Moderate	1
			<500 m	High	2	<500 m	High	2

The resulting hazard map is illustrated in Figure 13.2.

The very southern part of Euboia is highly sensitive to burning. More than 37% of the area shows a severe hazard. These areas are covered with typical Mediterranean vegetation (phrygana, maquis) and are mainly found in the southern and the western part of the region. A moderate risk is obtained for the areas with a poor vegetation cover (former burnt land) and in parts of the agricultural land used for the cultivation of cereals. A slight risk is noted for the agricultural land (vines, irrigated crops) which is located on low and flat lands and in areas covered with deciduous trees at higher altitudes.

The combination of the fire hazard map and the fire locality map showed that more than 19% of the area with severe hazard, actually burnt during the period 1985–89 and only 2.2% of the hazard-free area has burnt during the same period.

FIRE HAZARD MODELLING IN EPARCHY OF PYLIAS (SOUTH-WEST PELOPONNESE)

Environmental setting

The hazard for fire frequency and fire spreading is investigated for the eparchy of Pylias (south-west Peloponnese).

Statistical data are available for the period 1978–92, although it should be noted that, at the time of writing, the data for 1992 are not completed, and about six fires are still excluded. During the 15-year period, 102 fires were recorded by the Forestry Department in the eparchy of Pylias, covering an area of 3461.38 ha of forested land and a total area of 5559.31 ha including the loss of agricultural land.

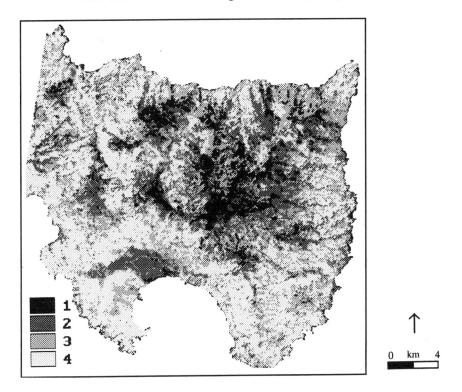

Figure 13.2   Hazard map for environmental degradation caused by fires (South Euboia). 1, no hazard; 2, slight hazard; 3, moderate hazard; 4, severe hazard

Looking at the annual data, it is clear that the most disastrous years were 1988 and 1992 with respectively more than 1200 ha and about 850 ha (uncompleted data) forested land lost by fire, and respectively 11 and 12 fires counted in each year. This corresponds to 110 ha per fire in 1988 and 70 ha per fire in 1992.

Available Information

The available data set for the study region of Pylias consisted of:

(1) Multi-temporal field data on an annual basis for the period 1988–92.
(2) Four topographical maps at a scale of 1:50 000 (Hellenic Army Geographical Service, Athens), indicating the contour lines, hydrographic network, roads and settlements.
(3) Fire statistics for the period 1978–92. This information is made available through the Forestry Department of the Nomos Messinia, (Kalamata, Greece).
    The statistical data are highly detailed and include information about

    —the locality of the wood fires,
    —the date and hour of the start and end of the fire,

—the area (forested land, agricultural land),
—the type of vegetation with density and species,
—the type of fire (soil, low, crown, mixed),
—the average altitude, the slope and the aspect of the area,
—the lithology of the area,
—the cause of the fire,
—the climatic data at the time of the fire (temperature, rainfall, relative humidity, wind speed and wind direction), and
—a general description of the fire seat.

The statistical data are accompanied by a sketch of the burnt area, and a precise location on the 1:50 000 topographical maps.

(4) Meteorological data. A climatic data bank developed under the auspices of the European Union-Less Favoured Areas Collaborative Programme (Messinia project) was at our disposal (Hardy and Moutsoulas, 1991). A climatic model for the Nomos Messinia has been obtained through application of multiple regression using the point climatic data of 24 meteorological stations and taking latitude, longitude and altitude as independent variables and the climatic parameter as the dependent variable. The climatic data bank consisted of information about mean temperature, rainfall and potential evapotranspiration. Additional information about relative humidity is obtained by applying the same method.

(5) A multi-spectral SPOT scene (088-278), dated 12 August 1986. A SPOT-derived digital elevation model, based upon satellite images acquired on five different dates in August 1986, was also available. The original SPOT-DEM was modified because of the exaggeration of the altitude and the exclusion of the islands for which no topographical data were given.

Methodology

A thematic study is performed for the different influencing factors: vegetation, topography (altitude, slope, aspect), accessibility of the area, influence of tourism and climate (annual temperature, annual rainfall, relative humidity and potential evapotranspiration).

Data Input

Vegetation. The study region in the south-west Peloponnese strongly differs from the one in south Euboia regarding the type of vegetation, as well as the degree of homogeneity of the dominant vegetation types. Many gradations can be observed in vegetation density for plant associations with identical species (for example, *Quercus* spp.). As a consequence, the difference between phrygana and maquis is not that clear. Because this would result in a strong overlap between the various classes and consequently lead to a high number of misclassifications, it was decided to calculate the normalized difference vegetation index (NDVI), according to the formula:

$$NDVI = [(IR - R)/(IR + R)] \times 100 + 100$$

The values of the resulting image vary between 0 and 200. The higher the NDVI value, the higher will be the density of photosynthetic active material.

Other Thematic Information.   The topography is investigated using the available, modified SPOT-DEM out of which slope and aspect are calculated.

Other information about the accessibility of the area and the influence of tourism are obtained by digitizing the available information and calculating distances.

Climatic data are incorporated in the GIS by applying multiple regression of existing meteorological point data.

Hazard Mapping

The modelling of fire behaviour will be performed for two different aspects of the wild fires, namely the temporal aspect and the spatial aspect.

The temporal aspect of the wild fires is concerned with the possible frequency of fire occurrence. Because the location of fire seats is available only for a limited number of fires, a representative point for each fire spot is determined which corresponds with the centroid of the fire polygon.

The spatial analysis investigates the spread of the fire.

The statistics obtained by combining the different map layers are represented in combined column–line graphs and scattergrams. An example is shown in Figure 13.3. The ratio between the proportional frequency of fires per thematic class and the proportional frequency of the thematic class is calculated. This ratio can be considered as a measure for fire susceptibility.

Figure 13.3(a) illustrates the column–line graphs. The x-axis gives the thematic class and the proportional frequency is plotted along the y-axis: columns refer to the proportional frequency of the thematic class; lines indicate the proportional occurrence of fire within a specific thematic class.

The scattergram is illustrated in Figure 13.3(b). The proportional frequencies for the thematic class and the occurrence of wild fires are respectively plotted along the x-axis and y-axis of the scattergram. The diagonal drawn on the scattergram refers to a random distribution of fires. In general, this is not the case. Points located below this diagonal are characterized by the fact that they occur less than would be "expected" if they were randomly distributed. These points are represented in Figure 13.3(a) by a line smaller than the corresponding column. The ratio "proportional frequency of fire/ proportional frequency of thematic class" will have a value < 1. The influence of a certain class on fire behaviour is greater when the proportional amount of the fires observed exceeds the proportional frequency of the class. These points are located above the diagonal; the corresponding line exceeds the column and the ratio is greater than 1.

First Results

The ratios between the proportional frequency of fire and the proportional frequency of the thematic class for the different influencing factors are given in Table 13.3.

From the relationship between the thematic maps of the different influencing factors and the fire locality maps (fire seat and fire area), the following comments may be made.

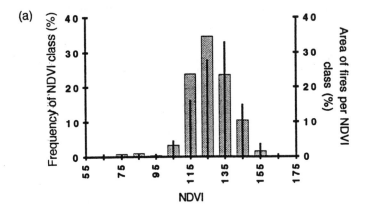

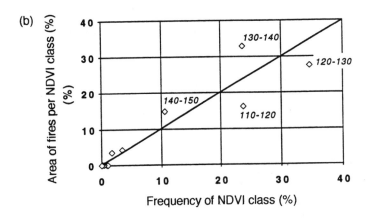

Figure 13.3 Distribution of fire area in function of NDVI. (a) Column–line histogram; (b) scattergram

Vegetation

The NDVI value of 130 forms a distinct limit for fire spreading since the proportional amount of burnt area per vegetation index class exceeds the proportional frequency of the NDVI class when the NDVI is greater than 130. This means that the hazard for fire spreading increases with increasing density of the vegetation cover. The poor vegetation covers have a much lower risk and can better withstand the fire. This can be deduced from Figure 13.3(b) where the ratio "fire area per NDVI/frequency NDVI class" is located below the diagonal, meaning that less area is burnt for NDVI < 130 than is the case when the spreading of the fire is randomly distributed. Conversely, points representing the areas with NDVI > 130 are situated above this line.

Fire seats are equally distributed over the different NDVI classes. As shown in Figure 13.4, the distribution of the ratio for the different classes is located along the diagonal. This means that the beginning of the fire is more or less randomly distributed regarding

Table 13.3 Ratios "proportional frequency of fires/proportional frequency of thematic class" for the different influencing factors

NDVI	Area	Seat	NDVI	Area	Seat	NDVI	Area	Seat
60–70	0.00	0.00	100–110	1.31	1.62	140–150	1.40	1.27
70–80	0.11	0.00	110–120	0.68	0.87	150–160	2.20	0.55
80–90	0.08	0.00	120–130	0.80	1.12	160–170	2.30	0.00
90–100	0.37	0.00	130–140	1.39	0.88			

Altitude (m)	Area	Seat	Altitude (m)	Area	Seat	Altitude (m)	Area	Seat
0–100	0.22	0.62	400–500	1.07	2.36	800–900	11.15	0.00
100–200	1.57	1.19	500–600	2.32	2.97	900–1000	13.33	0.00
200–300	1.31	0.79	600–700	3.71	2.41			
300–400	0.43	0.69	700–800	6.21	1.70			

Slope (%)	Area	Seat	Slope (%)	Area	Seat	Slope (%)	Area	Seat
0–2	0.68	0.29	12–18	0.93	1.14	35–50	1.56	2.03
2–6	0.81	0.35	18–25	1.07	1.25	50–...	2.19	2.37
6–12	0.84	0.68	25–35	1.26	1.82			

Aspect	Area	Seat	Aspect	Area	Seat	Aspect	Area	Seat
N	1.18	0.76	SE	1.06	1.29	W	0.88	1.19
NE	1.38	1.02	S	0.89	0.77	NW	0.89	1.34
E	1.35	1.13	SW	0.66	0.97	Flat	0.74	0.29

Mean temperature (°C)	Area	Seat	Mean temperature (°C)	Area	Seat	Mean temperature (°C)	Area	Seat
13	7.33	0.00	16	0.98	1.86	19	0.20	0.57
14	7.61	1.41	17	0.79	0.67			
15	2.89	2.75	18	1.14	1.01			

Rain (mm)	Area	Seat	Rain (mm)	Area	Seat	Rain (mm)	Area	Seat
700–750	0.37	0.99	850–900	0.32	0.61	1000–1050	5.03	2.27
750–800	0.44	1.45	900–950	0.26	0.81	1050–1100	10.83	0.00
800–850	2.14	0.95	950–1000	1.90	1.49			

Distance to road (m)	Area	Seat	Distance to road (m)	Area	Seat	Distance to road (m)	Area	Seat
0–250	0.53	0.87	1500–1750	2.68	1.46	3000–3250	0.07	0.00
250–500	1.04	1.13	1750–2000	1.67	1.01	3250–3500	0.47	5.00
500–750	1.47	1.23	2000–2250	0.01	0.00	3500–3750	1.03	10.59
750–1000	1.84	0.75	2250–2500	0.00	0.00	3750–4000	1.11	0.00
1000–1250	2.50	1.23	2500–2750	0.00	0.00	4000–4250	0.09	0.00
1250–1500	3.01	0.48	2750–3000	0.02	1.88			

Distance to coast (m)	Area	Seat	Distance to coast (m)	Area	Seat	Distance to coast (m)	Area	Seat
0–1000	0.37	1.47	5000–6000	1.59	0.64	10000–11000	1.79	0.57
1000–2000	1.31	1.92	6000–7000	0.85	0.12	11000–12000	0.00	0.00
2000–3000	1.59	1.31	7000–8000	0.65	1.52	12000–13000	0.22	0.49
3000–4000	1.22	0.69	8000–9000	0.10	0.70	13000–14000	1.16	1.33
4000–5000	1.18	0.64	9000–10000	0.87	0.88	14000–15000	1.17	1.05

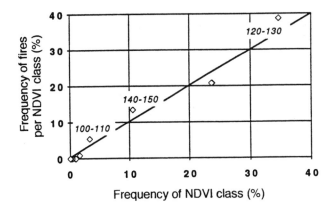

Figure 13.4 Scattergram of NDVI and fire frequency

the density of the vegetation. The class with the highest risk, thus with the highest ratio of "frequency fire per NDVI/frequency NDVI class" (1.62), has NDVI values varying between 100 and 110. This corresponds with zones where the amount of photosynthetic active material is very sparse.

Topography

The spreading of the fire is positively correlated with the altitude. Areas at higher altitudes are more susceptible to fire expansion than the low lying lands. It is mostly the areas above 500 m which are highly sensitive to the spreading of fire (Table 13.3). The ratio of "fire per altitude class/frequency altitude class" varies between 2.32 for the class 500–600 m and 13.33 for the class 900–1000 m. As a comparison, the ratio for the class 0–100 m amounts to 0.22.

Considering the general trend that the temperature decreases and humidity increases with increasing altitude, this fire behaviour is odd. It is expected that the area of fires should be the biggest at lower altitudes, at places with the highest temperature and with the lowest precipitation. The findings reveal that other factors are influencing the fire spreading in a more explicit way, such as the accessibility of the area.

Concerning the slopes, the most sensitive zones for fire spreading are steep to very steep (>18%) (Table 13.3). This can be explained by the fact that the speed by which fire catches is much higher on steep slopes because fuels which grow further uphill are brought into closer contact with the upward moving flames.

Concerning the frequency, fire seats are mostly found in areas with slopes >12%. The ratio of "frequency fire per slope class/frequency slope class" amounts to 2.37 for the slope class >50%, compared to 0.29 (0–2%) and 0.68 (6–12%).

As a result of the statistical analysis, it appears that the spreading of the fire in the eparchy of Pylias is relatively independent of the orientation of the relief (Table 13.3). The ratio of "fire area per slope class/frequency slope class" varies between 0.66 (SW) and 1.38 (NE).

Climate

As stated above, the influence of climate on fire behaviour is less pronounced than, and contradictory to, expectations. From the combination of the different thematic maps and the two fire locality maps it can be concluded that it is mostly areas with a mean annual temperature below 16 °C which are affected by fire (Table 13.3). The ratio of "fire area per temperature class/frequency temperature class" changes between 2.89 (15 °C) and 7.33 (13 °C). The same ratio gives a value of 0.20 for the class of 19 °C.

Fire is most frequently started in areas where the mean annual temperature is lower than 17 °C. These classes are characterized by a "frequency fire/frequency class" ratio going from 1.14 to 2.75.

The influence of the rainfall is less pronounced. Regions with a mean annual rainfall of 800–850 mm and of more than 950 mm are receptive to fire spreading. The highest ratio for fire ignition is found for areas with a mean annual rainfall of 1000–1050 mm.

Accessibility of the Area

The largest areas affected by burning are situated at a distance of more than 500 m from a road. The ratio of "fire area per distance to roads class/frequency distance to roads class" is at a maximum for areas at a distance of 1000–1750 m (Table 13.3). In comparison, the same ratio gives a value of 0.53 for the class 0–500 m. Regarding the relationship with the localization of the fire seats, it can be deduced that the areas with the highest danger are located at remote distance from roads (3250–3750 m), with a ratio of 5.00 to 10.59.

Distance to the Coast

This measure may reflect significantly the influence of tourism: the closer to the coast, the higher will be the possible influence of tourism and the related building activities of the tourist project managers. The best relationship is found for the locality of fire seats. The most sensitive areas to ignition are located at a distance of 0 to 3000 m (Table 13.3). The ratio of "fire area per distance to coast class/frequency distance to coast class" ranges between 1.31 and 1.92.

CONCLUSION

The methodology used for this study, based upon a combination of different techniques (multi-temporal field survey, remote sensing and GIS) is an appropriate tool for the assessment and modelling of fire hazard. The different influencing factors depend upon the region, and their determination requires an in-depth study of the area for which field survey is obligatory. However, it is noted that the availability of highly detailed fire statistics is of great importance to the success of the model.

The results obtained for the eparchy of Pylias indicate areas of future development of the fire hazard model. From the preliminary results presented here, it is clear that other factors which are not yet included should be studied. The high number of wild fires during the month of October invites further investigation of the influence of the proximity to olive orchards. Also other climatological factors, such as the effect of the wind, should be investigated.

ACKNOWLEDGEMENT

This research is a part of the Belgian impulse programme "Global Change", project Environmental Degradation in Past, Present and Future in the Mediterranean (Belgian State Prime Minister's Services for Science Policy).

REFERENCES

Anon. (1987) *Course on Wild Fires and Fire Ecology in Mediterranean Forest Ecosystems*, Chania, Greece, 15–21 January 1987.
Chuvieco, E. and Congalton, R. G. (1988). Mapping and inventory of forest fires from digital processing of TM data. *Geocarto International*, **4**, 41–53.
Chuvieco, E. and Congalton, R. G. (1989). Application of remote sensing and geographic information system to forest fire hazard mapping. *Remote Sensing of Environment*, **29**, 147–159.
Dagorne, A., Dauphiné, A., Escleyne, G., Gueron, L., Baudoin, L. and Lenco, M. (1990). L'utilisation de la télédétection aérospatiale en mode multi-satellites, multi-capteurs et multi-dates pour l'étude de la reprise de la végétation après incendie. L'example du massif de Tanneron (Vars-Alpes-Maritimes). *Photo-interprétation*, **1990–5**, 45–51.
De Vliegher, B. M. (1991). *Studie van de actuele landdegradatie in Zuidelijk Euboia (Griekenland), gesteund op teledetectie en GIS*. Unpublished PhD thesis, Universiteit Gent, Belgium.
Diamantopoulos, J. and Paraskevopoulos, S. (1986). The use of remote sensing techniques in the study of vegetation recovery after fire in Mediterranean countries. A preliminary study. In *Proceedings ISLSCP Conference*, 2–6 November 1985, Rome, Italy, ESA SP-248, pp. 537–538.
Hardy, J. R. and Moutsoulas, M. (1991). Climatic data for local area planning: an example from Messinia, Greece. In Moutsoulas, M. and Kontoes, C. C. (Eds), *Proceedings from Workshop and Seminar on the Messinia Project of the European Collaborative Programme*, 19–20 November 1990, Athens, Greece, pp. 44–83.
Kailidis, D. S. (1992). *Forest Fires in Greece–Italy–France–Spain–Portugal–USA and Canada*. Aristotelian University of Thessaloniki, Dept of Forestry Natural Environment, Laboratory Forest Protection, Thessaloniki, Greece, **1/1992**.
Kailidis, D. S. and Pantelis, D. (1988). *Sizes of Forest–Shrub and Grazing Land Fires and Relationship with Meterological Conditions during the Year and the Day*. Aristotelian University of Thessaloniki, Dept of Forestry Natural Environment, Laboratory Forest Protection, **3/1988**.
Karteris, M. A. and Kritikos, G. (1992). Assessment of forest fire damages in Holy Mount Athos using remote sensing techniques. In Folving, S., Ertner, G. and Svendsen, T. B. (Eds), *European Collaborative Programme Workshop on Remote Sensing for Forestry Applications*, 13–15 November 1992, Copenhagen, Denmark, pp. 197–210.
Lopez Soria, S., Gonzalez Alonso, F., Llop Pomares, R. and Cuevos Gozalo, J. (1988). An evaluation of the utility of NOAA-AVHRR images for monitoring forest fires in Spain. In *Proceedings of the 8th EARSeL Symposium—Alpine and Mediterranean Areas: A Challenge for Remote Sensing*, 17–20 May 1988, Capri, Italy, pp. 246–254.

Matson, M., Stephens, G. and Robinson, J. (1987). Fire detection using data from the NOAA-N satellites. *International Journal of Remote Sensing*, **8**, 961–970.

McKinley, R. A., Chine, E. P. and Werth, L. F. (1985) Operational fire fuels mapping with NOAA-AVHRR data. In *Pecora 10 Proceedings,* 20–22 August 1985, Fort Collins Colorado, USA, pp. 295–304.

Root, R. R., Stitt, S. C. F., Nyquist, M. O., Waggoner, G. S. and Agee, J. K. (1985). Vegetation and fire fuel models mapping of North Cascades National Park. In *Pecora 10 Proceedings*, 20–22 August 1985, Fort Collins, Colorado, USA, pp. 287–294.

Tanaka, S., Kimura, H. and Suga, Y (1983). Preparation of a 1:25 000 Landsat map for assessment of burnt area on Etajima island. *International Journal of Remote Sensing*, **4**, 17–31.

Thirgood, J. V. (1981). *Man and the Mediterranean Forest. A History of Resource Depletion*, Academic Press, London.

Trabaud, L. (1981). Man and fire: impacts on Mediterranean vegetation. In Di Castri, F. and Mooney, H. A. (Eds), *Mediterranean-type Shrublands, Ecosystems of the World, 11*, Elsevier Scientific Publishing, Amsterdam, pp. 479–521.

Werth, L. F., McKinley, R. A. and Chine, E. P. (1985). The use of wildland fire fuel maps produced with NOAA AVHRR scanner data. In *Pecora 10 proceedings*, 20–22 August 1985, Fort Collins, Colorado, USA, pp. 326–331.

14 Sea-Level Rise and Coastal Management

ROBERT J. NICHOLLS* and STEPHEN P. LEATHERMAN
Department of Geography, University of Maryland, USA

ABSTRACT

Projections of an accelerated global sea-level rise in the coming century warrant a longer-term perspective concerning decisions in the coastal zone. However, the future magnitude of sea-level rise causes much confusion. From a management perspective it is the future rate of relative (or local) sea-level rise that must be considered, which includes land subsidence/uplift. High rates of subsidence are occurring in many densely populated, low-lying coastal areas, often due to excessive groundwater withdrawal. This mandates a relative rise in sea level, with or without an accelerated global rise. An important management goal is to avoid such anthropogenically produced subsidence.

Studies of the impacts and possible responses to a 1.0 m rise in sea level for nine developing countries—China, Malaysia, Bangladesh, Egypt, Senegal, Nigeria, Venezuela, Uruguay and Argentina—show about 200 000 km^2 of land that could be lost with an existing population of 94 million people. This assumes existing patterns and levels of coastal development. Protection of most developed areas appears feasible in response to accelerated sea-level rise. However, a global decline of coastal wetlands appears almost certain.

The results support the urgency of the international commitment to implement integrated coastal zone management plans which include adaptation to accelerated sea-level rise. Many of the potential impacts of accelerated sea-level rise can be minimized by appropriate anticipatory adaptation. Effective anticipatory action requires careful identification of vulnerable areas and a long-term institutional viewpoint. Given the uncertainty regarding future rates of sea-level rise, anticipatory adaptation should ideally have a small cost and provide much greater flexibility in the future. Existing examples of anticipatory adaptation to accelerated sea-level rise include sea-wall design in Britain and the Netherlands and the West Kowloon Reclamation in Hong Kong.

INTRODUCTION

The coastal zone is one of the most dynamic environments on the earth's surface. In general, its position has moved significantly landward over the last 18 000 years due to a global rise in sea level of about 100 m. Change continues today: the Intergovernmental Panel on Climate Change (IPCC) concluded that global sea levels

---

Present address: School of Geography and Environmental Management, University of Middlesex, UK.

Geomorphology and Land Management in a Changing Environment. Edited by D. F. M. McGregor and D. A. Thompson.
©1995 John Wiley & Sons Ltd

have risen 0.1 to 0.2 m over the last century (Warrick and Oerlemans, 1990). At the same time, best estimates are that 70% of the world's sandy beaches are eroding (Bird, 1985). While shoreline position is an interplay between wave energy, sediment supply and sea level, it has been argued that sea-level rise is a major causal factor in these recent changes (Vellinga and Leatherman, 1989). Coastal wetlands also appear to be experiencing loss at a global scale (IPCC, 1992). This can be attributed to a combination of direct human reclamation for other more "productive" uses (Nicholls and Leatherman, 1994a) and losses due to sea-level rise (e.g. Stevenson et al., 1986). Rapid changes are expected to continue in the future, as a possible acceleration in global sea-level rise is one of the more crucial impacts of anthropologically induced global warming (Wigley and Raper, 1992).

The present trend of sea-level rise and its possible acceleration focuses attention on existing and planned land use within the coastal zone. Coastal populations are burgeoning worldwide, and significant human development in the coastal zone is occurring at a global scale. Already half of the world's rapidly growing population is thought to live within 60 km of the coast, and 13 of the world's 20 biggest cities are situated in coastal settings. This population is expected to more than double in the coming century.

Much existing and planned development does not even consider existing coastal hazards, let alone the possibility of accelerated sea-level rise. A metaphor describing this important problem is "The Coastal Zone: A Collision Course!" (Figure 14.1). Other coastal aspects of climate and global change are also of concern, such as more frequent, stronger and more widespread hurricanes (Emmanuel, 1988).

This chapter discusses the implications of sea-level rises for coastal management in the light of new vulnerability assessments of a number of developing countries.

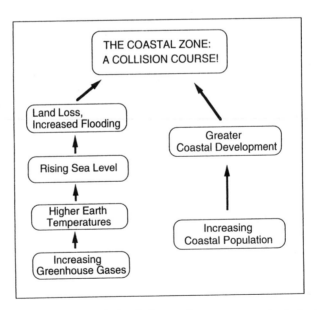

Figure 14.1 While coastal population is increasing at unprecedented rates worldwide, the ocean is rising, and this rise is predicted to accelerate due to greenhouse-induced warming. Without appropriate management actions, these two trends place the coastal zone on a "collision course"!

These studies support the urgency of international calls for implementation of integrated coastal zone management plans which include adaptation to accelerated sea-level rise.

SEA-LEVEL CHANGES

Global and Relative Sea-Level Rise

There is often confusion between global sea-level rise and relative (or local) sea-level rise. However, from a management perspective it is vital to understand the distinction. An increase (or decrease) in the volume of the oceans will cause a *global* rise (or fall) in sea level. A rise or fall of the land surface causes a *local* fall or rise of sea level, relative to the land. Observations at the shoreline measure relative sea-level change: the sum of the global sea-level change and the local land uplift/subsidence. Given that land uplift/subsidence varies from place to place, then relative sea-level changes similarly vary from place to place.

Therefore, while global sea level is presently rising, tide gauges around the world are measuring varying rates of sea-level rise, and in a few cases, sea-level fall (e.g. Juneau, Alaska). From a planning perspective, it is the future of relative sea-level rise that needs to be considered: a 1 m rise in sea level due to a global rise or local subsidence will have exactly the same physical impacts at the local scale (Figure 14.2). Therefore, global scenarios of sea-level rise must always be transformed into relative sea-level rise scenarios.

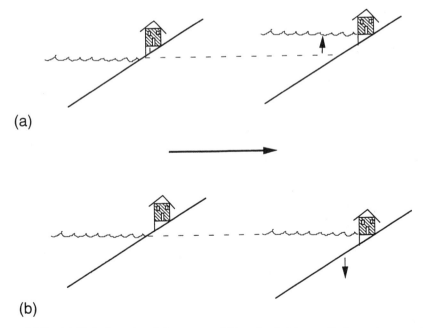

Figure 14.2   (a) Global sea-level rise versus (b) local subsidence. Both produce a relative rise in sea level, making any coastal land/infrastructure more vulnerable to a range of impacts

Developing reliable relative sea-level rise scenarios can be difficult, as high quality data on local uplift/subsidence is often unavailable (Nicholls and Leatherman, 1994b). Programmes to improve global tide gauge coverage such as the Global Sea Level Observing System (GLOSS) and new high-precision technology such as global positioning systems (GPS) and absolute gravity measurements will provide improved data in the coming decade (e.g. Parker, 1991).

Present and Future Global Sea-Level Rise

Best estimates of global sea-level rise are 1.8 ± 0.1 mm/year over the last century (Douglas, 1991). This global rise in sea level represents thermal expansion of the upper layers of the ocean and the melting of land-based ice, particularly the small mountain and high latitude glaciers (Revelle, 1990; Warrick and Oerlemans, 1990).

In the coming century, global sea-level rise is predicted to accelerate due to global warming. As part of the IPCC process, a wide-ranging consensus was developed concerning future rates of sea-level rise (Warrick and Oerlemans, 1990). However, considerable uncertainty remains, and this is expressed by using a range of scenarios, including a best estimate. The IPCC 1992 update, implies scenarios of sea-level rise (from 1990 to 2100) between 15 cm (no acceleration) and 90 cm, with a best estimate of 48 cm (Wigley and Raper, 1992). Even if greenhouse gas concentrations are stabilized early in the next century, the best estimate remains an acceleration in sea-level rise (Warrick and Oerlemans, 1990).

Subsidence and Relative Sea-Level Rise

Land subsidence or uplift occurs for a variety of natural reasons: long-term tectonics and neotectonics; post-glacial isostatic rebound from the last Ice Age (Tushingham and Peltier, 1991); and compaction of geologically young sediments (e.g. Penland and Ramsey, 1990). In addition, subsidence due to anthropogenic actions such as the withdrawal of groundwater and other fluids can be significant. Further, there is often an association with high rates of groundwater withdrawal and high coastal population (Baeteman, 1994). Many of the world's largest coastal cities have experienced significant subsidence, increasing their vulnerability to inundation and flooding: for instance, New Orleans, USA; Venice, Italy; Tokyo, Japan; and Taipei, Taiwan.

In Shanghai, China, pumping of shallow groundwater from 1921 to 1965 caused subsidence locally in excess of 2 m with short-term rates of subsidence up to 29 cm/year (Wang et al., 1994)! Since the 1960s, improved extraction techniques and associated mitigation strategies have greatly reduced subsidence to about 3 mm/year. The net subsidence is highest in the most developed downtown area and has necessitated significant additional protection to stop flooding during typhoons, since some areas might be flooded by regular high tides without dykes and flood walls. Another related problem is flooding during major rainfall events due to impeded gravity drainage.

Deltaic areas are particularly prone to subsidence (Milliman et al., 1989). They usually subside naturally as they are composed of thick sequences of young consolidating sediments. The deposition of new sediments generally makes up the deficit and maintains the land surface relative to the local sea level. However, the removal of sediment sources by upstream dams (e.g. the Nile delta: Stanley and Warne, 1993) or flood levees (e.g. the Mississippi delta: Day *et al.*, 1993) has upset this natural dynamic equilibrium in many deltas and caused high rates of relative sea-level rise.

Areas reclaimed from the sea may also be vulnerable to subsidence. In Hong Kong, some densely developed land reclamations are subsiding at up to 5 mm/year (Yim, 1994). This causes a significant, but highly localized relative rise in sea level.

Thus, many coastal areas will experience a significant rise in relative sea level, regardless of global changes. In these areas, a global rise in sea level simply exacerbates the problem of subsidence. Therefore, identification of coastal areas that are vulnerable to subsidence is an important first step in coastal management.

POTENTIAL IMPACTS OF ACCELERATED SEA-LEVEL RISE

There are five major physical impacts of sea-level rise: (1) erosion; (2) inundation; (3) salinization; (4) increased flooding and storm damage; and (5) rising water tables (Nicholls *et al.*, 1994). Sea-level rise does not act in isolation and these impacts can be offset or reinforced by other factors such as sediment availability, or changing freshwater runoff. It is also important to recognize that the coastal zone will evolve due to processes other than sea-level rise. Therefore, when examining potential impacts of sea-level rise for planning purposes, it is important to consider all coastal processes (e.g. Stive *et al.*, 1990).

New results on the vulnerability of selected countries from around the world to accelerated sea-level rise have recently been completed (Nicholls and Leatherman, 1994b). The primary focus of the studies were reconnaissance-level estimates of potential land loss (erosion and inundation) and associated impacts. The countries considered here are China, Bangladesh, India, Egypt, which were studied using existing map data; and Senegal, Nigeria, Venezuela, Uruguay and Argentina, which were studied with aerial videotape-assisted vulnerability analysis (or AVVA). After briefly outlining the AVVA methodology, some selected results are outlined to illustrate possible impacts of sea-level rise.

AVVA Methodology

The studies examined the potential impacts of a range of scenarios of global sea-level rise by the year 2100: 0.2 m (no acceleration), 0.5 m and 1.0 m (Nicholls and Leatherman, 1994a). Impacts for the 1.0 m scenario are used as a benchmark for comparison, following existing convention (IPCC, 1990, 1992).

The basic data comprise: (1) a contemporary aerial video record of the coastline, collected at low elevation flying over the ocean; (2) ground-truth information such as occasional coastal cross-sections, land and structure values, etc.; and (3) existing information such as maps and census data. The video record provides the following inventory of information on the coast: (a) an index of terrain and relief changes; (b) coastal environments; (c) land use; (d) infrastructure; and (e) population indicators.

While each study differs depending on local circumstances, the video record allows integration of the other data sources for the vulnerability analysis.

The primary focus of the studies was land loss due to erosion and inundation, including loss of coastal wetlands. Erosion was modelled using the Bruun Rule, while inundation was modelled using simple drowning (Nicholls et al., 1994). If possible, the dynamic response of wetlands to sea-level rise was considered. After identifying coastal areas vulnerable to loss, their existing use, capital value in terms of structures and land, and population was estimated. Then the magnitude of impacts and response costs for a range of response options was examined (Nicholls et al., 1994). Only two responses are considered here: (1) *No Protection*, i.e. existing protection is ignored; and (2) *Important Areas Protection*, i.e. strategic and medium to highly developed coastal areas such as cities, tourist beaches, factories and harbours are protected or upgraded. For tourist areas, beach nourishment is the assumed response, while elsewhere, the construction of sea-walls is assumed.

Limitations

Three important limitations of these studies are:

(1) only the present pattern and level of coastal development are considered, so the results represent minimum impacts;
(2) only the impacts of sea-level rise were modelled, in keeping with the national scale of the assessments;
(3) extreme events are not considered.

Results

Land, Capital Value and Population

For existing patterns and levels of coastal development, the impacts of a 1 m rise in sea level could be significant (Table 14.1). Almost 200 000 km^2 of land could be flooded more frequently or totally lost, with an existing population of 94 million, based on results from nine countries. China, Egypt and Bangladesh appear particularly vulnerable, due largely to the potential for inundation of large, low-lying and densely-populated deltaic areas. Assuming "No Protection", substantial assets could be lost: in absolute terms for the 1.0 m scenario, US$18 billion in Nigeria and US$5 billion in Argentina (Table 14.2). In relative terms, the threatened assets appear to be largest in Nigeria (>50% of 1990 GDP). However, these cost inventories are variously incomplete; for instance, the loss of harbours, utilities and transport infrastructure is not included. This reinforces the message that significant capital losses could occur due to accelerated sea-level rise.

The relationship of value loss versus sea-level rise scenarios strongly reflects the pattern of coastal development. Uruguay has a lower normalized value loss for the 0.2 m and 0.5 m scenarios than Senegal (Figure 14.3), because relatively few structures are built within 250 m of the Uruguayan coast. This buffer zone originally developed as Uruguayans often built a coastal boulevard near the coast. In the late 1970s, a

Table 14.1 Land loss and population displaced for a 1.0 m rise in global sea level. These results assume *No Protection*, and the existing pattern and level of development. Ranges reflect uncertainties. Results for China include increased flooding and storm damage

Country	Land loss (km²)	(%)	Population (millions)	(%)
China	125 000	1.3	72	6.5
Egypt	4200/5250	12–15[a]	6.0	10.7
Bangladesh	25 000	17.5	13.0	11.0
Malaysia	7000	2.1	n.a.	n.a.
Senegal	6042/6073	3.1	0.1/0.2	1.4/2.3
Nigeria	18 398/18 803	2.0	3.2	3.6
Venezuela	5686/5730	0.6	0.06	0.3
Uruguay	96	<0.1	0.01	0.4
Argentina	>3430/3492	>0.1	n.a.	n.a.
TOTAL	194 852/196 498		>94.4/94.5	

n.a. = not available.
[a]Of arable land in Egypt.

Table 14.2 Land and structural value loss (millions of US dollars) versus sea-level rise scenario, assuming *No Protection*. The 1.0 m scenario is given as a percentage of 1990 GDP (The World Bank, 1992). Estimates exclude loss of ports and harbors, utilities and transport infrastructure. Ranges indicate uncertainties

Rise (m)	0.2	0.5	1.0	(%GDP)
Argentina	1251/1340	2621/2846	5151/5585	(5.5/6.0)
Uruguay	21	183	1818	(22.1)
Venezuela	111	224	349	(0.7)
Senegala	142/228	345/464	494/707	(8.5/12.1)
Nigeria	3552	9003	18 134	(52.2)

law was enacted to preserve a 250 m coastal strip for public utilization and access to the coast (Volonte and Nicholls, 1994). While it is not for erosion mitigation purposes, it also creates a uniform building setback which reduces the value of structures vulnerable to any reasonable rise of sea level, especially for smaller scenarios. However, the coastal boulevards and roads often situated in the undeveloped zone would be impacted or destroyed by the 0.2 m and 0.5 m scenarios. The implications of such impacts were not evaluated by Volonte and Nicholls (1994).

In Senegal, small rises in sea level cause disproportionately large losses (Figure 14.3). This is mainly due to tourist infrastructure (Figure 14.4) which is often located close to the ocean in otherwise undeveloped locations (Dennis *et al.*, 1994). Therefore, the important and growing international tourist industry in Senegal appears vulnerable even to present rates of sea-level rise.

Response Costs

Surprisingly small lengths of open-coast shoreline require Important Areas Protection: 73 km to 200 km (or 2.6% to 22.1%), depending on the country (Table 14.3).

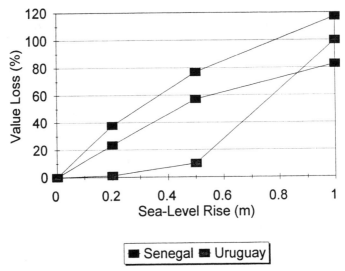

Figure 14.3 Value loss (representing primarily structures) versus sea-level rise scenario for Senegal (low and high estimates) and Uruguay (single estimate). The estimate of value loss assumes *No Protection* and is normalized to the 1.0 m scenario

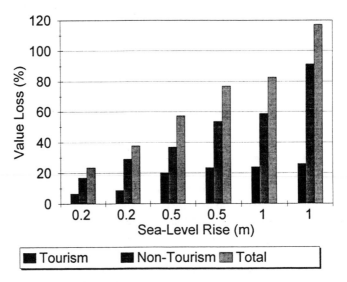

Figure 14.4 Value loss for (i) tourism-related structures, (ii) non-tourism structures, and (iii) all structures in Senegal (low (left) and high (right) estimates) versus sea-level rise scenarios of 0.2, 0.5 and 1.0 m. The estimate of value loss assumes *No Protection* and is normalized to the 1.0 m scenario

However, the estimated costs appear to be significant and can be largely attributed to beach nourishment of tourist beaches and harbour upgrade, although there are exceptions. A relative cost can be developed using existing (1990) gross investment (in simple terms, the money available within the economy for investment). To simplify

Table 14.3 Estimated impacts given *Important Areas Protection* and a 1.0 m rise in seal level: length of open coastline protected, including per cent; protection costs, including per cent existing investment;[a] and land loss, value loss, and people displaced as a percentage of land loss, value loss and people displaced, assuming *No Protection* (see Tables 14.1 and 14.2). Ranges indicate uncertainties

Country	Length protected (km)	Length protected (%)	Cost of protection US dollars (millions)	Cost of protection Investment (%)	Land loss (%)	Value loss (%)	People displaced (%)
Senegal	73	14.6	255/845	0.7/2.2	>99.8	0.0	0.0[b]
Nigeria	160	18.8	558/688	0.2/0.3	>99.0	6.6	33.3
Venezuela	200	7.0	999/1517	0.5/0.7	99.8	7.2/18.0	n.a.
Uruguay	150	22.1	—/2993[c]	—/6.1	76.9	0.7	0.0
Argentina	132	2.6	580/1298	0.1/0.3	>99.3	2.3/2.4	n.a.

n.a. = Not available.
[a]Uses 1990 Gross Investment (World Bank, 1992) and assumes costs are uniformly distributed over 50 years (2051 to 2100).
[b]Some population may be displaced in the Senegal delta.
[c]No low estimate for protection costs.

the analysis, it was assumed that the response costs would be uniformly spread over 50 years (2051 to 2100). Uruguay and Senegal face much higher relative costs than Nigeria, Venezuela and Argentina (Table 14.3). While we do not know the future gross investment of these countries, these results suggest that the relative burden of response costs to sea-level rise may be quite different at a national level.

In terms of value loss and people displaced, Important Areas Protection significantly reduces the impacts compared to No Protection (Table 14.3). However, over one million people could still be displaced in Nigeria, based only on existing population. In contrast, land loss is hardly reduced compared to No Protection. This reflects that "Important Areas" only occupy a relatively small area and much of the land loss represents coastal wetlands.

Coastal Wetlands

Coastal wetlands respond to slow rates of sea-level rise by vertical accretion due to sediment/biomass inputs (Nicholls *et al.*, 1994). Thus, they can maintain or even expand the area which they occupy. However, above some threshold rate of sea-level rise, which is site-specific, the sediment/biomass inputs become insufficient to keep pace with the rising water level and inundation ensues.

Loss of wetlands at a global scale appears almost certain under the scenario of accelerated sea-level rise. It was estimated that about 37 000 km^2 of wetlands, including mangroves, could be lost due to a 1.0 m rise in sea level in six countries, including (almost) total loss in three countries (Table 14.4). However, the threshold response of these systems to sea-level rise was not considered, or based on studies in other locations (Nicholls *et al.*, 1994). Therefore, these results probably overstate losses and reduced areas of wetlands may persist. Losses can be further minimized if natural processes of inland migration are allowed. However, except in a few unusual areas, this is unlikely to replace the areas lost, as the land available for conversion to new coastal wetlands is smaller than the vast areas vulnerable to inundation.

Another important issue is human destruction of coastal wetlands (Nicholls and Leatherman, 1994a). At a global scale, many of the existing coastal wetlands are likely to be destroyed by human activities long before they are inundated by sea-level rise. China represents the endpoint of this process as almost all the coastal wetlands in

Table 14.4 Estimated loss of coastal wetlands for the 1.0 m scenario (rounded to two significant figures). These results exclude wetland migration

Country	Wetland loss (km^2)	Wetland loss (% of existing wetland)
Senegal	6000	100
Argentinaa	1100	51
Uruguay	23	100
Venezuela	5600	50
Nigeria	18 000	77
Bangladesh	5800	100
TOTAL	37 000	

the four major river plains have already been reclaimed for other "more productive" uses (Han *et al.*, 1994a). Even accreting mudflats are reclaimed as soon as practical. It is important to note that the new land use, such as rice paddy and aquaculture, remains vulnerable to sea-level rise, unless the reclaimed area is raised substantially.

PLANNING FOR SEA-LEVEL RISE

Many of the potential impacts of accelerated sea-level rise can be minimized by appropriate planning and action. In addition to an unplanned "do-nothing" approach, there are three, conceptually distinct, planned responses to sea-level rise (IPCC, 1990, 1992):

(1) *planned retreat*—allowing land loss to occur progressively with minimal loss of associated infrastructure;
(2) *accommodate*—changing the way the land is used as water levels rise, e.g. raising buildings on piles above the new flood levels;
(3) *protect*—building dykes, levees, beach nourishment, etc.

Reactive versus Anticipatory Adaptation

Considering these four possible responses raises the important question: "How can we *best* adapt to and plan for sea-level rise (and other changes in the coastal zone)?" Historically, doing nothing, accommodating the rise in sea level or protecting against it have been the major responses to a change in the coastal zone. This reflects a tendency for a reactive approach to change. Extreme events, such as severe storms, have often shaped human response to slower changes, such as sea-level rise. Around the North Sea, much of the present flood protection was only constructed after the disastrous 1953 storm. The vulnerability of these areas to flooding was poorly understood and had been progressively increasing due to sea-level rise for a century or more (Gilbert and Horner, 1984). However, it took a disaster of major proportions and the loss of thousands of lives around the North Sea to promote action. A similar event-driven response to future sea-level rise should be avoided. The progressively increasing risk of disaster can be contained at an acceptable level by anticipatory action such as raising dykes or land use planning. Thus, risk analysis will probably be an important tool for planning in the coastal zone.

The vulnerability studies indicate that significant areas of the world's coastline remain relatively undeveloped (97% in Argentina; 78% in Uruguay—Table 14.3). This represents a great opportunity for a comprehensive anticipatory approach to hazard management and planning, assuming we act before these areas are developed. Sea-level rise, and climate change in general, should not be considered in isolation from other coastal problems. Such planning is best implemented within the context of integrated coastal zone management plans as recommended by IPCC (1990, 1992). It is hoped that an unplanned, do-nothing approach ceases, except in totally undeveloped areas.

Selection of Approaches

The best planning approach will depend on local geomorphological and socio-economic factors. In developed areas, this includes the existing level and pattern of development. As discussed earlier, Uruguay and Senegal have different patterns of vulnerability to sea-level rise and this will probably influence planning and response decisions in these countries.

More generally, there is an immediate need for a better understanding of the best application of the range of possible responses, including hybrid approaches. Many engineering approaches are relatively easy to implement given the financial resources. However, more substantial problems are encountered in land use and socio-economic planning. It is necessary to question what administrative mechanisms will be sufficiently robust to deal with both sea-level rise and climate change? This requires extension of existing research beyond simple vulnerability analysis to true dynamic analysis of response planning to sea-level rise at decadal time-scales. This will necessitate multi-disciplinary studies embracing the physical and social sciences. Assessment of possible planning policies should also recognize societal factors. A policy which works effectively in one society may not be effective in a society with different traditions.

The benefits of planned retreat are long term (decades to centuries). Therefore, this policy needs to be evaluated in the coming decade if it is to be implemented and provide benefits in any useful planning time frame. The long lead times of large-scale coastal engineering projects must also be considered (Nicholls and Leatherman, 1994a).

Maximizing future flexibility should be an important consideration. Future rates of sea-level rise, and hence coastal change, are uncertain and policies which manage the coastal zone should reflect this uncertainty. Again risk analysis will probably be an important tool to evaluate options. As an absolute minimum, present rates of coastal change should be considered in all decisions. This will require mapping of existing hazards, if such programmes do not already exist (cf. National Research Council, 1990).

Existing Anticipatory Actions

Many anticipatory actions can be viewed as sensible insurance policies—a small outlay today to provide greater flexibility in the future. This is most important for long time frame decisions where the costs of a reactive response could be substantial. Examples existed prior to concern about an acceleration in sea-level rise. For instance, the design of the Thames Barrier which protects London, UK, from flooding allowed for existing rates of relative sea-level rise to the year 2030 (Turner *et al.*, 1990). There is a small but growing number of examples of similar allowances for accelerated sea-level rise.

(1) The Massachusetts Water Resources Authority included an additional 0.46 m of height in the Deer Island sewage treatment plant. This is a factor of safety to maintain gravity-based flows under higher sea levels without the additional costs of pumping (Smith and Mueller-Vollmer, 1993).

(2) In eastern Britain and the Netherlands *new* sea-wall constructions are 0.25 m and 0.66 m, respectively, above previous design standards. The difference in additional height reflects a 50-year, versus a 100-year design life, respectively.

(3) In Hong Kong, the West Kowloon reclamation is being built 0.8 m above earlier design levels (Yim, 1994). This raises total costs by less than 1% and future reclamations are expected to be similarly raised.

Selection of an appropriate sea-level rise scenario for design purposes depends on a number of factors, including the time frame, cost, and implications if the scenario is exceeded. Based on Wigley and Raper (1992), the best and high estimates of the global rise in sea level are about 20 cm and 40 cm by 2050, and 50 cm and 90 cm by 2100, respectively.

Identification and Action in Vulnerable Areas

Certain coastal areas and environments are more vulnerable to sea-level rise for a variety of physical and socio-economic reasons. These areas should be identified and appropriate action implemented. Many coastal cities are vulnerable to subsidence due to groundwater withdrawal. In China, Shanghai has brought its subsidence under control (Wang *et al.*, 1994), while around Tianjin, demand for water is intense and growing, and significant coastal subsidence continues (Han *et al.*, 1994b). In general, these subsidence problems could be anticipated and hence avoided by application of appropriate hydrogeological modelling, within a long-term management framework (Baeteman, 1994).

Deltas and small islands are particularly vulnerable to sea-level rise and other aspects of global change (IPCC, 1992). In addition, the physical processes that shape these environments, including the human influences, are often complex and poorly understood. Therefore, it is important that basic research on this vulnerability begins in a timely manner in parallel with the implementation of coastal zone management guidelines. Present and likely future rates of subsidence in many deltas, such as in Bangladesh (Huq *et al.*, 1994), are poorly defined and should be the subject of prompt research.

Coastal wetlands are also vulnerable. Their survival will be assisted by policies which allow inland migration as sea level rises. The application of new techniques to help preserve existing coastal wetlands under rising sea levels should also be investigated. Lastly, the local, regional and global consequences of rapid loss of coastal wetlands should be assessed in terms of impacts on marine fishery resources, biodiversity and any other issues.

The Institutional Viewpoint

Sea-level rise is beyond the time frame of most traditional institutional perspectives. Therefore, planning for sea-level rise requires the development of a long-term institutional viewpoint.

In the US, both local and federal efforts are encouraging a longer perspective appropriate to sea-level rise (e.g. Craig, 1993). For instance, the Coastal Zone

Management Act is mandating inclusion of existing rates of relative sea-level rise, and conceptual planning for an acceleration in sea-level rise, within the design of any sponsored project. Similarly in Australia, six out of seven of the states and territories address accelerated sea-level rise in their coastal flooding and erosion policies (Caton and Eliot, 1993).

The Netherlands have developed a long-term coastal management policy, including legislation (Koster and Hillen, 1993). No dryland loss is to be permitted and the existing shoreline position will be maintained with beach nourishment. However, significant loss of wetlands and tidal flats is still expected given accelerated sea-level rise.

Internationally, the Coastal Zone Management Sub-Group of the International Panel on Climate Change is active in promoting adaptation to accelerated sea-level rise (IPCC, 1990, 1992). They have developed guidelines for vulnerability analysis (The Common Methodology) and are prompting the widespread application of integrated coastal zone management.

CONCLUSIONS

Considering the present and projected trends of sea-level rise and the rapid population growth in the coastal zone, it appears likely that many of the coastal landscapes around the world will change significantly in the coming decades. This chapter has shown that accelerated sea-level rise could cause serious impacts at a global scale. At the same time, there is a great opportunity to respond to this problem in a positive manner and minimize future vulnerability to coastal hazards, reduce their associated economic costs and help maintain important coastal ecosystems.

Climate change, including sea-level rise, cannot be considered in isolation. Integrated coastal zone management provides a framework to consider and balance all existing and potential coastal issues and problems, including climate change. While there is uncertainty about future sea levels, the direction of change appears certain and planning in the coastal zone should be based upon a global rise in sea level. The best estimate is for a 0.5 m rise in sea level by 2100. In addition, local subsidence or uplift must be considered to develop relative sea-level scenarios.

Coastal zone management should aim to establish a long-term institutional framework to develop and progressively improve flexible policies towards the impacts of global change, including sea-level rise. This includes the related issues of risk and timing. In particular, when and where are the range of possible response mechanisms best applied, given the uncertain magnitude of future change? The development of objective procedures to answer these questions is urgently required.

ACKNOWLEDGEMENTS

This chapter presents research completed under funding from the US Environmental Protection Agency (Project Officer Mr Jim Titus) and the W. Alton Jones Foundation. Dr Ian Eliot, University of Western Australia and Ms Lynda Downs commented on an earlier draft of this manuscript.

REFERENCES

Baeteman, C. (1994). Subsidence in coastal lowlands due to groundwater withdrawal: The geological approach. *Journal of Coastal Research*, (Special Issue no. 12), in press.

Bird, E. C. F. (1985). *Coastal Changes—A global review*, John Wiley, Chichester.

Caton, B. and Eliot, I. (1993). Coastal hazard policy development and the Australia Federal System. In McLean, R. F. and Mimura, N. (Eds), *Vulnerability, Assessment to Sea-Level Rise and Coastal Zone Management*, Proceedings of the IPCC Eastern Hemisphere Workshop, Tsukuba, Japan, 3–6 August 1993 Conference Secretariat, Tokyo, pp. 417–427.

Craig, D. (1993). *Preliminary Assessment of Sea Level Rise in Olympia, Washington: Technical and Policy Implications*, Policy and Program Development Division, Olympia Public Works Department, Olympia.

Day, J. W., Conner, W. H., Costanza, R., Kemp, G. P. and Mendelssohn, I. A. (1993). Impacts of sea level rise on coastal systems with special emphasis on the Mississippi River deltaic plain. In Warrick, R. A., Barrow, E. M. and Wigley, T. M. L. (Eds), *Climate and Sea Level Change: Observations, Projections and Implications*, Cambridge University Press, Cambridge, pp. 276–296.

Dennis, K. C., Niang, I. and Nicholls, R. J. (1994). Sea-level rise in Senegal: Potential impacts and consequences. *Journal of Coastal Research*, **14** (Special Issue), 243–261.

Douglas, B. C. (1991). Global sea-level rise. *Journal of Geophysical Research*, **96** (C4), 6981–6992.

Emmanuel, K. A. (1988). The dependence of hurricane intensity on climate. *Nature*, **326**, 483–485.

Gilbert, S. and Horner, R. W. (1984). *The Thames Barrier*, Thomas Telford, London.

Han, M., Hou, J. and Wu, L. (1994a). Potential impacts of sea-level rise on China's coastal environment and cities: A national assessment. *Journal of Coastal Research*, **14** (Special Issue), 79–95.

Han, M., Hou, J., Wu, L., Liu, C., Zhao, G. and Zhang, Z. (1994b). Sea-level rise and the North China Coastal Plain: A preliminary analysis. *Journal of Coastal Research*, **14** (Special Issue), 132–150.

Huq, S., Ali, S. I. and Rahman, A. A. (1994). Sea-level rise and Bangladesh: A preliminary analysis. *Journal of Coastal Research*, **14** (Special Issue), 44–53.

Intergovernmental Panel on Climate Change (1990). *Strategies for Adaptation to Sea-Level Rise*, Rijkswaterstaat, The Hague.

Intergovernmental Panel on Climate Change (1992). *Global Climate Change and the Rising Challenge of the Sea*, Rijkswaterstaat, The Hague.

Koster, M. J. and Hillen, R. (1993). Combat erosion by law: Coastal defence policy for the Netherlands. In Bruun, P. (Ed.) *The Hilton Head Island South Carolina U.S.A. International Coastal Symposium*, Vol. 2, Hilton Head, South Carolina, pp. 583–594.

Milliman, J. D., Broadus, J. M. and Gable, F. (1989). Environmental and economic implications of rising sea level and subsiding deltas: the Nile and Bengal examples. *Ambio*, **18**, 340–345.

National Research Council (1990). *Managing Coastal Erosion*, National Academy Press, Washington, DC.

Nicholls, R. J. and Leatherman, S. P. (1994a). Sea-level Rise. In Strzepek, K. and Smith, J. B. (Eds), *As Climate Changes: Potential Impacts and Implications*, Cambridge University Press, Cambridge, in press.

Nicholls, R. J. and Leatherman, S. P. (Eds) (1994b). The potential impacts of accelerated sea-level rise on developing countries. *Journal of Coastal Research*, **14** (Special Issue).

Nicholls, R. J., Leatherman, S. P., Dennis, K. C. and Volonte, C. R. (1994). Impacts and responses to sea-level rise: Qualitative and quantitative assessments. *Journal of Coastal Research*, (Special Issue no. 14), 26–43.

Parker, B. B. (1991). Sea level as an indicator of climate and global change. *Marine Technology Society (MTS) Journal*, **25** (4), 13–24.

Penland, S. and Ramsey, K. E. (1990). Relative sea-level rise in Louisiana and the Gulf of Mexico: 1908–1988. *Journal of Coastal Research*, **6**, 323–342.

Revelle, R. R. (Ed.) (1990). *Sea-Level Change*, National Academy Press, Washington, DC.

Smith, J. B. and Mueller-Vollmer, J. (1993). *Setting Priorities for Adapting to Climate Change*. Prepared for Office of Technology Assessment, Oceans and Environment Program, Contract Number 13-5935.0 by RCG/Hagler, Bailly, Arlington VA.

Stanley, D. J. and Warne, A. G. (1993). Nile delta: Recent geological evolution and human impact. *Science*, 260, 628–634.

Stevenson, J. C., Ward, L. G. and Kearney, M. S. (1986). Vertical accretion in marshes with varying rates of sea level rise. In Wolfe, D. A. (Ed.), *Estuarine Variability*, Academic Press, New York, pp. 241–258.

Stive, M. J. F., Roelvink, J. A. and DeVriend, H. J. (1990). Large-scale coastal evolution concept. In *22nd International Conference on Coastal Engineering*, American Society of Civil Engineers, Delft, The Netherlands, pp. 1962–1974.

Turner, R. K., Kelly, P. M. and Kay, R. C. (1990). *Cities at Risk*, BNA International, London.

Tushingham, A. M. and Peltier, W. R. (1991). ICE 3-G: A new global model of late Pleistocene deglaciation based upon geophysical predictions of post glacial relative sea level change. *Journal of Geophysical Research*, 96, 4497–4523.

Vellinga, P. and Leatherman, S. P. (1989). Sea-level rise, consequences and policies. *Climatic Change*, 15, 175–189.

Volonte, C. R. and Nicholls, R. J. (1994). Sea-level rise in Uruguay: Potential impacts and consequences. *Journal of Coastal Research*, (Special Issue no. 14), 262–284.

Wang, B., Shenliang, C., Keqi, Z. and Jian, S. (1994). Potential impacts of sea-level rise on the Shanghai area. *Journal of Coastal Research* (Special Issue no. 14), 151–166.

Warrick, R. A. and Oerlemans, H. (1990). Sea-level rise. In Houghton, J. T., Jenkins, G. J. and Ephramus, J. J. (Eds), *Climate Change: The IPCC Scientific Assessment*, Cambridge University Press, Cambridge, pp. 257–281.

Wigley, T. M. L. and Raper, S. C. B. (1992). Implications for climate and sea level of revised IPCC emissions scenarios. *Nature*, 357, 293–300.

World Bank (1992). *World Development Report 1992. Development and the Environment*, Oxford University Press, New York.

Yim, W. W.-S. (1994). Implications of sea-level rise on Victoria Harbour, Hong Kong. *Journal of Coastal Research*, 14 (Special Issue), 167–189.

Part 5

GEOMORPHOLOGY IN PRACTICE: MODELLING AND MANAGEMENT

15 River Channel Adjustment Sensitivity to Drainage Basin Characteristics: Implications for Channel Management Planning in South-East England

PETER W. DOWNS

Department of Geography, University of Nottingham, UK

ABSTRACT

Integrated river basin management potentially forms the most fundamental means of land management and should embrace the sensitivity of hydrogeomorphological systems to adjustment. Understanding of sensitivity can form the predictive basis for assessing how natural change and the effects of direct human influence such as land use changes and channel management practices will alter river channels. The results of an exploratory empirical analysis are used to assess the relative sensitivity of river channel adjustments to drainage basin controls and human influences in the Thames catchment. An indication of sensitivity is given by logistic regression equations of the form $y = f(a_1 x_1, a_2 x_2, \ldots a_n x_n)$ where y represents categories of river channel adjustment, $x_1 \ldots x_n$ are dummy variables representing potentially influential drainage basin characteristics, and $a_1 \ldots a_n$ express the relative sensitivity of each adjustment to the chosen influences. Evidence for river channel adjustment was collected by field survey utilizing a structured checklist of observations which suggested that, in the Lambourn, Ravenbourne, Roding and Sor basins, ten logically-derived forms of adjustments could be defined and that 63% of the channels show some form of adjustment. Drainage basin characteristics were gathered primarily from map sources into class groups of Rock Type, Gradient, Land Use and Channel Management which represent the range of natural and human influences on the channels. The equations, which include an assessment of upstream and downstream influences, facilitate the calculation of a probability of occurrence of each channel adjustment. Comparison of these probabilities can indicate the most likely location of influences on individual channel adjustments and thus provide guidance for, and an input to, channel management procedures.

GEOMORPHOLOGY AND INTEGRATED RIVER BASIN MANAGEMENT

Integrated river basin management represents the most comprehensive form of terrestrial water resource control and manipulation (see definitions in Biswas, 1990a; Cunningham, 1986; Falkenmark, 1983; Mitchell, 1990; Saha, 1981). The corresponding

Geomorphology and Land Management in a Changing Environment. Edited by D. F. M. McGregor and D. A. Thompson.
©1995 John Wiley & Sons Ltd

land management strategies should encompass a wide range of policies designed to ensure a sustainable approach, and should therefore involve a commensurately broad spectrum of contributing disciplines. The success of these policies not only requires suitable political will (Wengert, 1981) and institutional organization and co-operation (Crabb, 1988; Mitchell and Pigram, 1989), but also demands adequate scientific knowledge in order to implement procedures appropriate to the desired management objectives. Biswas (1990b) suggests that we may not possess either the knowledge or the procedures at present. As management objectives, and thus land uses, will evolve continuously according to societal changes (Parker and Penning-Rowsell, 1980) and technological capabilities (Wengert, 1981) then the physical environment should be expected to respond to these human influences as well as to fluctuations in natural controls. Therefore, in relation to river channels, attempts must be made to quantify the probable geomorphological response to a suite of natural or anthropogenic "forcing" elements.

Many previous integrated river basin management strategies have not adequately appreciated the geomorphological integrity of the fluvial system (Downs *et al.*, 1991) and are thus unlikely to utilize geomorphological approaches to engineering problems. However, this potential is unlikely to be realized without the development of practical methods by which to distinguish location-specific geomorphological responses to drainage basin characteristics. This chapter explores the provision of such a method to differentiate styles of river channel adjustment. It is based upon studies in fluvial geomorphology which suggest that river channel adjustments can be promoted both by the natural characteristics of the drainage basin and by human influences, and is designed to estimate the empirical *sensitivity* of river channel adjustments (Downs and Gregory, 1993) to these various sources of influence. Figure 15.1 schematically represents the process by which drainage basin characteristics create the conditions for river channel adjustments; the influencing characteristics determine the hydrologic and hydraulic conditions for the river channel, thus affecting the prevailing balance of force and resistance and initiating geomorphic processes

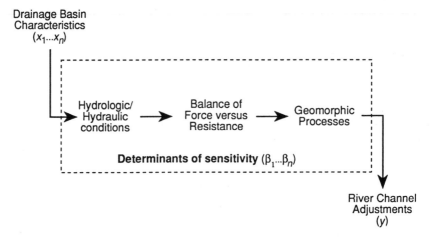

Figure 15.1 Conceptualization of river channel adjustment sensitivity

which cause river channel adjustments. Although process mechanisms have been described to explain the means by which individual characteristics (e.g. river regulation, channelization, urbanization) influence river channel dynamics, no studies exist which assess the relative influence of multiple drainage basin characteristics. As these extremely complex interactions would necessitate a physical modelling capability beyond that which currently exists, this study uses a statistical approach in which, for each drainage basin characteristic, the three internal links in Figure 15.1 are summarized by a single measure. These relative weightings describe the sensitivity of channel adjustments to individual drainage basin characteristics. The method can potentially be used to guide channel management practices by the approach described in this chapter. The analysis also highlights which characteristics appear to have the greatest geomorphological significance; these should be given prominence in future modelling strategies.

An important objective of this preliminary stage was to normalize the units associated with each drainage basin characteristic so that comparable measures of the river channel adjustment sensitivity are obtained. This requirement, and the desire to provide a rapid drainage-basin-scale approach suitable for management utilization, dictated the use of categorical data analysis in the form of logistic regression. This approach allows the probability of each type of adjustment to be calculated at individual locations in the basin, and potentially forms the basis for choosing system-sympathetic channel management options. Limitations and future requirements of the approach are discussed. The study is centred upon catchments within the Thames drainage basin, south-east England and therefore encompasses lowland channel environments which may exhibit only low-intensity river channel dynamics.

DATA COLLECTION

As an initial approach to estimating the interaction indicated in Figure 15.1, a linear relationship was sought to relate different styles of river channel adjustments (y) to potentially influential drainage basin characteristics (x_1 to x_n) according to a relative weighting (β) which expresses the relative sensitivity to adjustment. The requirement of a comparable information base which is consistent at the scale of the drainage basin is a major constraint in determining the types of data collected and the subsequent form of analysis.

The measure chosen for river channel adjustments (y-variables) is primarily dictated by the requirement of consistent coverage. Three common forms of data type are therefore precluded. Monitored rates of change are ideal but do not exist over a drainage basin extent; historical records archived by the governing water institutions will, at best, cover only their "Main River" networks and not full fluvial systems (for example the 1:25 000 Ordnance Survey "blue-line" network); and historical evidence provided from map sources can indicate only lateral, and not vertical, river channel adjustments. The remaining option is to utilize field indicators of adjustment obtained from interpretive evaluation of the channel morphology, its vegetation, and any in-channel or near-channel structures. Evaluation is based upon interpretation of a comprehensive checklist of indicators of channel character and was pioneered by

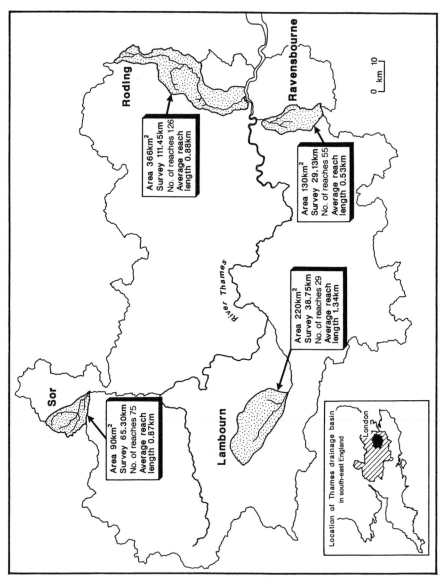

Figure 15.2 Location of the study drainage basins within the Thames catchment, and the extent of field survey

Kellerhals *et al.* (1976) in order to classify river channels and valleys; it has been used subsequently to indicate river channel instability by others such as Lewin *et al.* (1988), Simon *et al.* (1989), Thorne (1992), Gregory (1992) and Gregory *et al.* (1992). The precise set of indicators chosen will depend on research intentions (Mosley, 1987) and the current scheme is primarily designed for the rapid evaluation of river channel dynamics in lowland streams. It was tested for feasibility and for consistency between seasons on the Burstow Stream (Surrey/West Sussex) and for agreement between surveyors on the Monks' Brook (Hampshire). The test of independent surveyors indicated differences in the interpretation and delimitation of channel reaches of approximately 5% (see Gregory *et al.* (1992) for details). Subsequently, four river basins within the Thames catchment (indicated on Figure 15.2) were surveyed in late summer 1990 and were re-assessed in the following winter. In total, 285 reaches were delimited within the four basins, each being homogenous with respect to river channel adjustments. The reaches ranged in length from under 50 m to in excess of 8 km with average basin reach lengths of between 0.53 km (Ravensbourne) and 1.34 km (Lambourn; see Figure 15.2). The reaches were initially categorized into 10 styles of adjustment which were simplified to four major groups (see Table 15.1 for descriptions) for the purpose of statistical analysis. Channel adjustments are therefore categorized as either "depositional" (27% of total survey extent), "laterally migrating" (26%), "enlarging" (10%) or "stable" (37%). The survey, covering approximately 245 km of channels indicated that the amount of active channel (that is, the 63% not "stable") varied from under 17% of the Lambourn to nearly 83% of the Roding. Of these active channels, 63% displayed only minor indications of adjustment as defined by the full scheme (types *d*, *m* and *e* in Downs and Gregory, 1993).

The collection of information about drainage basin characteristics (*x*-variables) is governed by the needs of comparability between variables and for a consistent derivation across the drainage basin extent. The chosen variables will partially depend on the study environment and should summarize a range of potential geomorphological influences succinctly to facilitate statistically valid analysis. As a result, four major groups of variable were chosen and Table 15.1 describes the individual variables within each group. *Rock type* and *gradient* are surrogates for the natural channel resistance to change and available energy for change respectively, while human influences are categorized into *land uses* and *channel management* and use composite variables which incorporate drainage basin characteristics according to their potential ability to promote or discourage different styles of channel adjustment. This potential was adjudged from previous geomorphological studies of river channel adjustments due to individual human activities. Information was obtained from a combination of map evidence and the field survey period and, where a delimited channel reach possessed several variables within a particular group, assignment rules based upon the geomorphological literature were used to assess the strongest influence.

The data collection and classification stages may introduce errors into the analysis. For instance, observational misjudgements made during the field survey or in the subsequent geomorphological interpretation of these observations will result in inaccurate allocation of channel adjustment categories. Furthermore, the procedure

Table 15.1 Descriptions of variables used in this study

Variable group	Variable name	Description
Channel adjustment	*Stable*	No observable indication of adjustment in progress
	Depositional	Channel width and/or depth decreasing
	Laterally migrating	Cross-sectional movement but dimensions preserved
	Enlarging	Channel width and/or depth increasing
Rock type	*Clay*	Alluvium, London Clay, Woolwich/Reading Beds, Lower/Middle/Upper Lias
	Sand/gravel	Floodplain/terrace gravels, clay with flints, Head Boulder clay, Blackheath Beds, Claygate Beds, Marlstone Rock Beds, Oolites
	Chalk	Upper Chalk
Gradient	*Gradient*	Continuous measure, derived from 5 m contours
Land use	*Rural*	Pasture, arable, woodland, rough ground, gardens, construction
	Urban	Urban areas, main roads
Channel management	*Limited*	No measures apparent, two-stage channels, local bank protection, set-back embankments
	Historical	Total, partial or local straightening prior to this century—no more recent measures
	Confined	Culvert, bed and bank lining, continuous or majority bank lining
	Regulated	Weir (downstream end), recent re-sectioning, temporary channel modifications
	Straightened	Total, partial or local straightening, channel-edge embankments

has assumed that the tenfold categorization of channel adjustments has a physical basis and that, in simplifying these 10 categories into four to enable statistical analysis, similar dynamics are not introduced into these "mutually exclusive" groupings. In relation to the drainage basin characteristics (*x*-variables), the classification of characteristics into the variables described in Table 15.1 depends largely on the representativeness of case studies in the geomorphological literature. The procedure also requires the most "influential" characteristic to be correctly assigned in cases when a delimited reach possesses more than one variable from within the rock type, land use or channel management groups as any cross-classification will reduce the integrity of the dummy variables.

ANALYSIS

One reason for incorporating geomorphology into river channel management is that studies have indicated that individual drainage basin characteristics (notably human influences) are capable of promoting changes upstream and downstream of their location in the channel network. Therefore, analysis should attempt to assess this capability. However, quantifying the linear extent of such influences is hindered by the complex nature of local channel conditions which can, for example, preclude spatially contiguous channel adjustments (Petts, 1979). The distance over which statistical associations are sought is therefore arbitrary and in this experiment is deemed to involve three channel reaches upstream, and three channel reaches downstream of the target reach. The average reach length over the four drainage basins is 0.9 km thus statistical associations are sought over an average distance of 2.7 km. A reach multiple is preferred to a distance measure because, if the delimited reaches are physically homogeneous and thus logically attributable to the same set of causal influences, then longer reaches will exist where few formative influences prevail while shorter reaches will result from a rapid succession of influential characteristics. Figure 15.3 illustrates the format of the resulting analysis: separate regression equations are generated between channel adjustments and drainage basin characteristics in seven positions relative to any one reach (i.e. within the reach, and each of the three reaches upstream and the three reaches downstream), except towards the extreme headwaters and mouth of individual basins. A consequence of performing upstream and downstream associations is that where channel bifurcations exist, rules of precedence were necessary to dictate the channel along which influences should be sought.

The collated data are all categorical in type with the exception of the channel gradient which is multiplied by a factor of two to provide an approximate comparability. Incorporating these data into ordinary least-squares (OLS) linear regression would violate several Gaussian random distribution assumptions, not least those of providing meaningful values of the response variable, y, when y is categorical, and of violating the condition of constant error variance or homoscedasticity (see Wrigley, 1985). One possibility is to convert the channel adjustment categories into a series of dichotomous variables (which are either *present* or *absent*) and to calculate logistic regression equations based upon maximum likelihood parameter estimates. The resulting equations allow y to be expressed as a cumulative probability function; this probability, $P_{1/i}$, will vary between 0 and 1 as the x-variables vary between $+\infty$ and $-\infty$ as:

$$P_{1/i} = \frac{e^{(\beta_1 + \beta_2 X_{i2} + \beta_3 X_{i3} \ldots \beta_n X_{in})}}{1 + e^{(\beta_1 + \beta_2 X_{i2} + \beta_3 X_{i3} \ldots \beta_n X_{in})}} \tag{15.1}$$

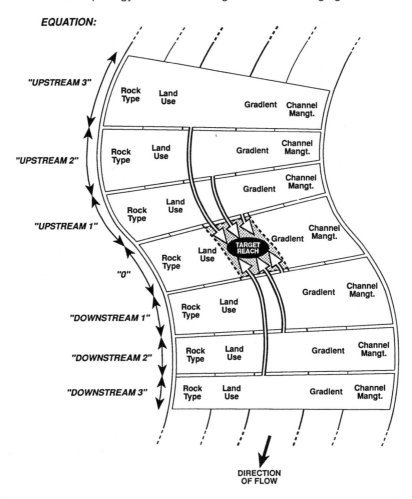

Figure 15.3 Representation of analysis in present study. Associations are sought separately between each of the delimited reaches and their adjacent drainage basin characteristics ("0"), and the characteristics of the three neighbouring reaches both upstream and downstream. Therefore seven equations are generated for each channel adjustment category. (Channel Mangt. = Channel Management)

The categorical *x*-variables are incorporated into the regression as "dummy" variables (nominal variables which are *present* (1) or *absent* (0)) and where each major group drainage basin characteristic requires *n*-1 dummies to avoid perfect linear dependence (Wrigley, 1985). The format of the equation for this study is therefore:

$$y = \beta_1 + \beta_2 Sand/Gravel + \beta_3 Chalk + \beta_4 Gradient + \beta_5 Urban$$
$$+ \beta_6 Historical + \beta_7 Confined + \beta_8 Regulated + \beta_9 Straightened \quad (15.2)$$

As one variable within each category of *x*-variables is not given a parameter estimate, the intercept (β_1) defines a default channel environment indicating the combined statistical influence of the three non-parameterized dummy variables, namely a *sand/gravel* channel with only *limited* channel management and *rural* land uses (see Table 15.1 for descriptions of these variables). Incorporating, singly or in combination, any of the named variables (β_2–β_9) produces a change in the estimate of *y* which is relative to this default situation. The GLIM statistical package (Numerical Algorithms Group, 1987) was used to generate separate logistic regression equations for each category of channel adjustment and for each of the seven positions relative to each reach (see Figure 15.3) thus producing 28 equations. Chi-square analysis was used to eliminate from analysis any of the significantly interrelated categorical *x*-variables. Individual variables were introduced into the equations only when they proved to be individually significant to the 95% level in a test analogous to, but not strictly comparable (Wrigley, 1985) to, generating a *t*-statistic from the ratio of the parameter estimate to its standard error in ordinary least-squares regression (that is, the result is significant at the 95% level where $t \geqslant 1.96$). Improvements in the overall performance of the equations were assessed by testing the reduction in the scaled deviance (the unexplained variation) brought about by the inclusion of additional parameters into the equation. A summary of the statistically significant variables according to these tests is given in Figure 15.4; this is depicted in the style of Figure 15.3 whereby statistical associations with the target reach are generated independently for each step upstream or downstream. Figure 15.4 thus characterizes the most common environmental setting of each of the four channel adjustment categories.

POTENTIAL APPLICATION

The results obtained have two potential applications. One is geomorphological and involves interpreting the statistically significant drainage basin characteristics from this study against previous case studies of channel adjustment to see whether, for this multiple, basin-wide situation, they confirm or conflict with previous results. A second application involves translating the derived equations into indicators of reach-specific management implications. Achieving this second purpose involves applying the parsimonious solution for each of the 28 equations to the 285 delimited reaches and obtaining the probability of response according to equation (15.1). For each channel reach, the equation providing the highest probability indicates the drainage basin characteristics which, theoretically, have the most likely association with that reach within the constraints of current experimental conditions. Where these predictions match the *observed* channel adjustment, one, or a number of characteristics incorporated by the highest probability equation are suggested to be strongly associated with the adjustment. If the association appears to have a geomorphologically rational basis, then the relationship could be interpreted as indicative of cause and effect and therefore channel management practices ought to accommodate the highlighted characteristics in current or future management strategies. By grouping similar associations which suggest similar "causes", a limited range of management planning models might be constructed.

Following the procedure above results in 48.4% (138) of the predictions matching the observed channel adjustment category, and this figure can be considered as an

256

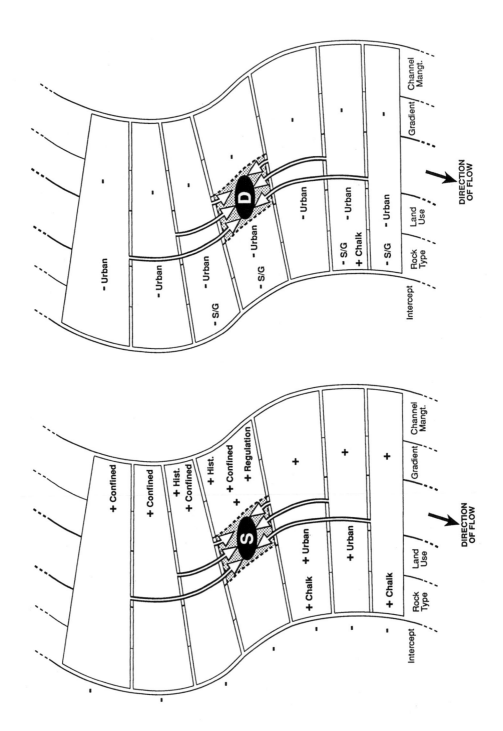

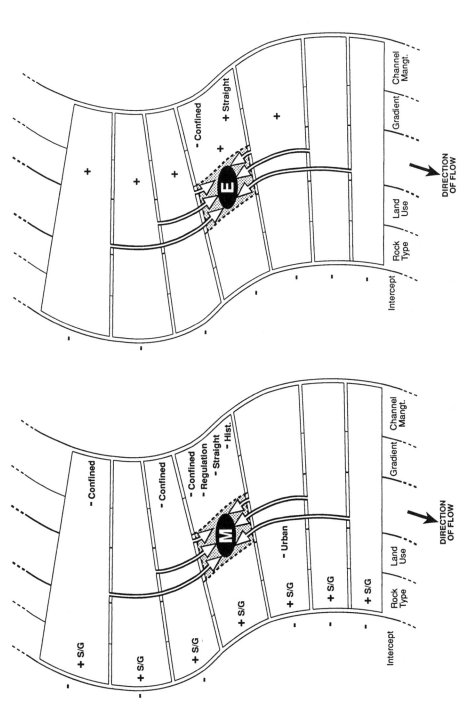

Figure 15.4 The statistically significant (95% confidence interval) variables for each of the four channel adjustment categories. The associations are given as positive (+) or negative (−) and include the intercept (β_1). In relation to the nominal variables in Table 1, S/G = *Sand/Gravel*; Straight = *Straightened*; Hist. = *Historical* (straightening prior to this century)

overall goodness-of-fit of the data. In 65 cases, the most highly associated probability originates from an equation either upstream or downstream of the target reach, thus implying that the source of the (potential) influence may be remote from its "effect". The overall result improves on the probable random success rate of 25% (arising from four channel adjustment categories) but is obviously not a sufficient basis for orchestrating channel management decisions. Some of the incorrect predictions must result from the data collection and classification errors outlined previously but, in addition, errors caused by physical circumstances not currently accommodated by this empirical approach are likely to be of consequence. A brief discussion of four of these problems follows; the final issue can be used in establishing the cause of incorrect predictions of river channel adjustment and forms the basis of an approach which may be developed in relation to channel management planning.

The first problem is that, in choosing an approach which can accommodate a comprehensive variety of drainage basin characteristics, the resulting equations are likely to be insensitive to local characteristics which may determine the precise nature of the channel adjustment. This appears to be confirmed by the fact that the Ravensbourne, which is the basin with the most consistent channel conditions, possesses the highest number of correct predictions (71% correct), while the Roding, the basin with the most varied channel conditions, is the least successfully predicted (40.5% correct). A second potential source of error arises because some channel reaches may not yet have reacted to individual drainage basin characteristics, and so morphological adjustments of a particular style should be expected in the future. However, as a majority of the incorporated drainage basin characteristics are established in nature this is probably of minor concern; it would be of far greater relevance in basins in which land uses and channel management practices are currently changing. A third issue is that no account is taken of any relationship between the river channel adjustments in consecutive reaches. The problem of spatial autocorrelation is common in geomorphological and hydrological applications of statistics (e.g. Anderson and Richards, 1981) and the results of the current exploratory analysis are being used in order to omit insignificant variables from future analysis; this will permit the inclusion of a spatial-lag function to assess the links between adjacent channel adjustments.

The fourth potential source of error arises where the equation providing the highest probability is from upstream or downstream of the target reach, and it occurs because associations between drainage basin characteristics and the target channel adjustment are generated independently for each equation. Therefore, although there may be a reasonable theoretical linkage between drainage basin characteristics possessed by the source reach and river channel adjustments in the target reach, the drainage basin characteristics possessed by the target reach, or any reaches between the source and the target, may act to interfere with this association. A diagrammatic representation of this potential is provided in Figure 15.5 whereby the highest statistical association is derived from three reaches upstream of the target reach. Table 15.2(a) exemplifies the use of this circumstance in relation to channel management planning for cases where the highest obtained probability is for a *stable* channel associated with an upstream source; as the significant variables in each upstream equation are very similar

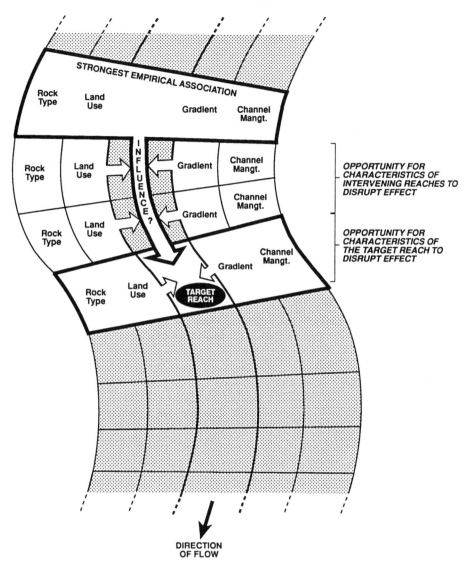

Figure 15.5 Possibilities for "interference" in the current analysis. The example, where the strongest association is with the characteristics possessed by the channel three reaches upstream, illustrates possibilities of interference from both the *intervening* reaches and the *target* reach

(see Figure 15.4, "stable") their results are amalgamated. Table 15.2(a) thus highlights, from the four studied basins, the most frequently occurring drainage basin characteristics possessed by the reach providing the *source* of association, and those of the *target* reach (the characteristics of *intervening* reaches are not incorporated in this table), in cases of correct and incorrect predictions. It is suggested that where the predicted channel adjustment matches observations, then a comparison of the most common drainage basin characteristics from the source reaches (which will relate closely to the significant variables of the relevant equation) with those of the target reaches will provide a geomorphologically reasonable basis for the observed adjustment (see Table 15.2(a)). Consequently, channel management planning could incorporate specific "causes" (associations) from known locations. Conversely, where a predicted channel adjustment does not match the observation, then some combination of the characteristics within the source and target reach should, in comparison with the correct prediction, provide a physical explanation for the observed adjustment. Possible explanations from the current study are

Table 15.2 A demonstration of the potential application of the approach in channel management planning: the example, for *stable* channels, utilizes the results obtained when the highest probabilities are generated from upstream reaches. The "common" characteristics of the source or affected reaches are those which occur in 50% or greater of the examples

(a) The most common drainage basin characteristics possessed by the source and affected reaches.

For "stable" channel predictions	Common characteristics		
	Source of association	Presumed influence	Target reach
			Observed condition: Stable — 14 reaches
Rock type	not Chalk		not Chalk
Gradient	*Low/medium*	→	*Low/medium*
Land use	*Urban*		Urban
Channel management	*Confined*		not Confined/Limited
			Observed condition: Depositional — 11 reaches
Rock type	*Clay*		*Clay*
Gradient	mixed	→	*Medium*
Land use	*Urban*		Urban
Channel management	*Confined*		*Straightened*
			Observed condition: Migrating — 9 reaches
Rock type	*Clay*		*Clay*
Gradient	*Low*	→	*Low*
Land use	*Urban*		Urban
Channel management	*Confined*		not Confined/Regulated
			Observed condition: Enlarging — 11 reaches
Rock type	*Clay*		*Clay*
Gradient	*High*	→	mixed
Land use	*Urban*		Urban
Channel management	*Confined*		*Straightened*

(b) Use of these common characteristics to explain the correct and incorrect predictions, and some possible management implications

For "Stable" channel predictions	Hypothesized explanation for observed condition, based on common characteristics in Table 2(a)
Correct predictions: Observed condition: Stable	As channel adjustment might be expected to arise from differences in the characteristics possessed by the source and target reach, then the channel management measures in the target reach must offset any potential for erosion caused, potentially, by the high velocity flows exiting the confined reaches. The transportation of sediments carried through the confined reach, rather than their deposition in the target reach, may be ensured by the high runoff from the urban area in the target reach.
Incorrect predictions: Observed condition: Depositional	Deposition of fine material appears to relate to the change from a confined to a straightened river channel in an area in which gradients are not high enough to compensate for this change. Quite probably, the straightened channels are re-sectioned into a trapezoidal form which is wider in cross-section than the lined reach upstream, and thus possess a lower stream power which leads to deposition.
Observed condition: Migrating	The distinctive features of *stable* predictions in *migrating* reaches appears to be the occurrence of low gradients and the lack of channel management practices which restrict the free dissipation of energy. The low gradients in the target reach may also indicate reaches in which some channel sinuosity remains, thus focusing the energy available for erosion at the apex of existing meander bends.
Observed condition: Enlarging	The erosional capabilities of the high gradient source reaches will have been curtailed by their confinement. Upon exiting the confined reach, the excess energies are expended eroding the downstream section.
Management implication—potential means of achieving the predicted *stable* condition	
Depositional	Reduce channel width, or restore sinuosity to ensure high velocity filament through channel.
Migrating	Use restrictive channel management measures if necessary or, preferably, leave to develop.
Enlarging	Reduce the gradient in the upstream reach.

provided in Table 15.2(b) which also suggests how management of the incorrectly predicted cases might provide conditions which promote the predicted adjustment category.

CONCLUSION

The preceding discussion has summarized a location-specific procedure for providing information for channel management using easily derived characteristics of the drainage basin and geomorphological reconnaissance surveys to overcome data deficiencies in relation to river channel adjustments. The approach is reasonably successful, with the equation set correctly predicting 48.4% of the observed adjustments, and with the potential for both the correct and the incorrect predictions to be used in channel management planning. However, the greatest value of the current analysis is to highlight the structures present in the data set (Haining, 1990) and thus to guide future analyses. For instance, the current classification of x-variables is based on geomorphological studies of channel change; reiterative exploratory analysis may reveal a more efficacious classification and, in this respect, procedural automation to reduce analysis time is particularly desirable. River channel morphology data might also be included to improve precision. In addition, incorporating the drainage basin characteristics and river channel adjustments of the target and intervening reaches into the statistical model is necessary to overcome problems of spatial autocorrelation, but the consequences in terms of degrees of freedom and thus of data sample size require this stage to follow attempts to identify and eliminate other, consistently insignificant, variables.

The potential of this approach is that land use or channel management plans may be designed whilst anticipating the likely consequences for the river channel of the proposed environmental changes, or in order to induce particular channel adjustments. Alternatively, the approach could be used to identify probable causes of river channel adjustments where protection is necessary in relation to Sites of Special Scientific Interest or Regionally Important Geomorphological Sites. The approach is also analogous to that foreseen for the environmental sciences by Newson (1992:393) whereby policy guidance in environmental management can be achieved, but the search for broad-based and holistic understanding will always carry some risk of uncertainty; the probabilistic nature of these equations provides an opportunity to quantify this uncertainty.

ACKNOWLEDGEMENTS

This work was initiated during the tenure of NERC studentship GT4/88/AAPS/43, CASE with the National Rivers Authority Thames Region. The support and guidance of Ken Gregory and Andrew Brookes is greatly appreciated. The constructive comments of two anonymous referees have markedly improved this chapter. Any views expressed are those of the author and not of the NRA.

REFERENCES

Anderson, M. G. and Richards, K. S. (1981). Hydrology. In Wrigley, N. and Bennett, R. J. (Eds), *Quantitative Geography: A British View*, Routledge & Kegan Paul, London, pp. 273–283.
Biswas, A. K. (1990a). Watershed management. In Thanh, N. C. and Biswas, A. K. (Eds), *Environmentally-Sound Water Management*, Oxford University Press, Delhi, pp. 155–175.
Biswas, A. K. (1990b). Watershed management. *Water Resources Development*, 6, 240–249.
Crabb, P. (1988). Managing the Murray-Darling basin. *Australian Geographer*, 19, 64–88.
Cunningham, G. M. (1986). Total catchment management—resource management for the future. *Journal of Soil Conservation, NSW*, 42, 4–6.

Downs, P. W. and Gregory, K. J. (1993). The sensitivity of river channels in the landscape system. In Thomas, D. S. G. and Allison, R. J. (Eds), *Landscape Sensitivity*, Wiley, Chichester, pp. 15–30.

Downs, P. W., Gregory, K. J. and Brookes, A. (1991). How integrated is river basin management? *Environmental Management*, **15**, 299–309.

Falkenmark, M. (1983). The multiple roles of water in the human environment. *Ambio*, **12**, 111.

Gregory, K. J. (1992). Vegetation and river channel process interactions. In Boon, P. J., Calow, P. and Petts, G. E. (Eds), *River Conservation and Management*, Wiley, Chichester, pp. 255–269.

Gregory, K. J., Davis, R. J. and Downs, P. W. (1992). Identification of river channel change due to urbanisation. *Applied Geography*, **12**, 299–318.

Haining, R. (1990). *Spatial Data Analysis in the Social and Environmental Sciences*, Cambridge University Press, Cambridge.

Kellerhals, R., Church, M. and Bray, D. I. (1976). Classification and analysis of river processes. *Journal of the Hydraulics Division. Proceedings of the American Society of Civil Engineers*, **102**, 813–829.

Lewin, J., Macklin, M. G. and Newson, M. D. (1988). Regime and environmental change: irreconcilable concepts? In White, W. R. (Ed.), *International Conference on River Regime*, Wallingford, Hydraulics Research Ltd, pp. 431–445.

Mitchell, B. (1990). Integrated water management. In Mitchell, B. (Ed.), *Integrated Water Management: International Experiences and Perspectives*, Belhaven Press, London and New York, pp. 1–21.

Mitchell, B. and Pigram, J. J. (1989). Integrated resource management and the Hunter Valley Conservation Trust, NSW, Australia. *Applied Geography*, **9**, 196–211.

Mosley, M. P. (1987). The classification and characterisation of rivers. In Richards, K. S. (Ed.), *River Channels: Environment and Process*, Blackwell, Oxford, pp. 295–320.

Newson, M. D. (1992). River conservation and catchment management: a UK perspective. In Boon, P. J., Calow, P. and Petts, G. E. (Eds), *River Conservation and Management*, Wiley, Chichester, pp. 385–396.

Numerical Algorithms Group (1987). *The Generalised Linear Interactive Modelling System*, Manual for release 3.77, Royal Statistical Society, Oxford.

Parker, D. J. and Penning-Rowsell, E. C. (1980). *Water Planning in Britain*, George Allen & Unwin, London.

Petts, G. E. (1979). Complex response of river channel morphology subsequent to reservoir construction. *Progress in Physical Geography*, **3**, 329–362.

Saha, S. K. (1981). River basin planning as a field of study: design of a course structure for practitioners. In Saha, S. K. and Barrow, C. J. (Eds), *River Basin Planning: Theory and Practice*, J. Wiley & Sons, Chichester, pp. 9–40.

Simon, A., Outlaw, G. S. and Thomas, R. (1989). Evaluation, modeling, and mapping of potential bridge scour, West Tennessee. In *Proceedings of the National Bridge Scour Symposium*, Federal Highway Administration Report, FHWA-RD-90-035, pp. 112–129.

Thorne, C. R. (1992). *Field Assessment Techniques for Bank Erosion Modeling*, Final Report to the US Army European Research Office, Contract R&D 6560-EN-09, University of Nottingham, Department of Geography.

Wengert, N. (1981). A critical review of the river basin as a focus for resources planning, development and management. In North, R. M., Dworsky, L. B. and Allee, D. J. (Eds), *Unified River Basin Management*, Minneapolis, American Water Resources Association, pp. 9–27.

Wrigley, N. W. (1985). *Categorical Data Analysis for Geographers and Earth Scientists*, Longman, London and New York.

16 The Use of Synthetic Weather for Soil Erosion Modelling

DAVID FAVIS-MORTLOCK

Environmental Change Unit, University of Oxford, UK

ABSTRACT

Modelling is a frequently used approach to the quantitative assessment of certain geomorphological impacts of climate change, for example the estimation of rates of soil erosion by water on UK agricultural land. Stochastically-generated sequences of synthetic weather data are widely used as input to simulation models such as EPIC (the Erosion-Productivity Impact Calculator). Such sequences may be constructed with any desired distributional characteristics, while retaining the internal correlations of real data.

   The present study compares predicted erosion rates using both measured and generated weather. Results indicate that generated weather sequences are deficient in large rainfall events. Since a small number of large rainfall events often produce virtually all erosion in a given season, failure of the weather generator to model accurately these extreme events will considerably influence predicted erosion rates, which may be underpredicted by as much as 40%.

SYNTHETIC WEATHER AND CLIMATE IMPACT STUDIES

Introduction

Soil erosion and land degradation form a threat of increasing severity to agricultural productivity worldwide, yet much basic work remains to be done in quantifying their effects (e.g. De Ploey *et al.*, 1991). Still less is known about how greenhouse-gas-induced climate change might affect regional soil quality. Although UK arable land has been much studied, we are only now beginning to be aware of the implications of climate change for British soils and agriculture (e.g. Armstrong and Castle, 1989; Parry, 1989; Parry *et al.*, 1989; Boardman *et al.*, 1990; Bullock, 1991; Favis-Mortlock *et al.*, 1991; Parry *et al.*, 1991; Rounsevell and Loveland, 1992; Boardman and Favis-Mortlock, 1993a; Hulme *et al.*, 1993; Rounsevell, 1993; Brignall and Rounsevell, 1994; Favis-Mortlock and Boardman, in press).

   There is a clear need to develop methodologies which may be used to study the impacts of climate change upon regional soil quality. This study investigates the viability of a possible tool, the use of stochastically-generated synthetic weather

Geomorphology and Land Management in a Changing Environment. Edited by D. F. M. McGregor and D. A. Thompson.
©1995 John Wiley & Sons Ltd

sequences, for estimating erosion rates under a changed climate, using the UK South Downs as an example.

Weather Data Input for Impact Studies

A modelling approach is frequently adopted in climate change impact studies (Carter *et al.*, 1992). However, General Circulation Models (GCMs) are not yet capable of providing reliable projections of regional climate parameters. Estimates of future regional rainfall are particularly problematic (Katz, 1988a; Simmons and Bengtsson, 1988; Hulme *et al.*, 1990; Legates and Wilmott, 1992; Hulme *et al.*, 1993). The direct use of GCM-produced weather data for impact studies is therefore not a currently realistic option.

Sequences of synthetic weather data possessing similar statistical properties to runs of real present-day data (Nicks *et al.*, 1990) are useful in modelling studies where measured data are unavailable in sufficiently long runs (Williams *et al.*, 1990). The statistical parameters which are used to generate such sequences are drawn from observed data. However, modification of these parameters will produce sequences with statistical properties differing from those of current weather but maintaining the time dependence, internal correlation and seasonal characteristics of observed data (Richardson and Nicks, 1990). Additionally, synthetic weather sequences are free from long-term trend, which may not be true of measured data although subsequent superimposition of a trend for a transient impact study is straightforward (Favis-Mortlock and Boardman, in press). Also any number of different (but statistically similar) realizations of the same sequence can be easily produced.

If the statistical parameters are modified to represent the characteristics of regional weather expected under a greenhouse-gas-changed climate, the use of such sequences as model input would appear to offer distinct advantages as a tool for regional climate change impact studies.

Generating Synthetic Weather Sequences

Synthetic weather sequences are created by a weather generator. Currently these models are invariably stochastic, in contrast with the deterministic nature of GCMs (Gregory *et al.*, 1993). The first weather generators were constructed in the 1950s (Racsko *et al.*, 1991); and subsequent workers have included Gabriel and Neumann (1962), Fitzpatrick and Krishnan (1967), Nicks (1974, 1975), Katz (1977), Larsen and Pense (1981) and Richardson (1981). A weather generator was incorporated in the EPIC (Erosion/Productivity Impact Calculator) (Williams *et al.*, 1984; Sharpley and Williams, 1990) and SWRRB (Simulator for Water Resources in Rural Basins) (Arnold *et al.*, 1989) erosion models. WXGEN (Weather Generator), a standalone version, will also produce weather sequences for the GLEAMS (Groundwater Loading Effects of Agricultural Management Systems) (Davis *et al.*, 1990) erosion model and the Ceres (e.g. Jones and Kiniry, 1986) suite of crop models. The CLIGEN (CLImate GENerator model) weather generator model is a development (Nicks and Lane, 1989) for use with the WEPP (Water Erosion Prediction Project) erosion model (Lane and Nearing, 1989; Laflen *et al.*, 1991); it will also produce weather sequences suitable for the

CREAMS (Chemicals, Runoff and Erosion from Agricultural Management Systems) (Knisel, 1980) erosion model. The precipitation components of the EPIC and WEPP weather generator models are both first-order two-state Markov chain types (Nicks and Lane, 1989; Richardson and Nicks, 1990). There are two conceptual subcomponents: an event (or occurrence) submodel and an amount submodel. On each day of the simulation, the event submodel controls whether the day is wet or dry (a wet day is defined as one with at least 0.2 mm of rainfall) (Richardson and Nicks, 1990). On any day of the simulation a probability for the occurrence of rainfall is chosen randomly. This probability is then compared with a threshold value (the "rainfall state probability"); if it exceeds the threshold then rainfall occurs. The threshold probability depends both on whether rainfall occurred on the previous day (although this is of course unknown for the first day of the simulation), and on the month. Because the occurrence of rainfall on this previous day is dependent in its turn on the occurrence of rainfall on the day preceding that, and so on, patterns of wet or dry spells extending over several days ("Markov chains") are built up. Only two states—wet or dry—are stipulated, and the submodel considers only one previous day's state in determining the threshold probability. It is therefore considered to be a first-order, two-state model.

The quantity of precipitation on wet days is determined by the amount submodel. That in the EPIC and WEPP weather generators assumes a skewed distribution (or "skewed normal" in Nicks and Lane (1989) and Richardson and Nicks (1990)) of rainfall amounts, with the parameters of the distribution changing each month (Nicks and Lane, 1989; Richardson and Nicks, 1990). Precipitation is assumed to be all in the form of snow if the average temperature for that day is below 0 °C (Nicks and Lane, 1989). Table 16.1 shows the rainfall parameters required by the EPIC weather generator (the WEPP version requires additional values in order to estimate storm durations).

Sequences of other meteorological quantities such as daily maximum and minimum temperature, solar radiation and wind speed and direction may also be synthesized by the EPIC and WEPP weather generators (Richardson, 1981; Richardson and Nicks, 1990): values for these depend in part on whether the day is wet or dry (Richardson and Nicks, 1990). However, this study focuses only on generated precipitation sequences. Formal mathematical descriptions of the EPIC and WEPP weather generators are given by Richardson (1981), Nicks (1985), Richardson and Nicks (1990) and Nicks and Lane (1989).

Nicks et al. (1990) evaluated the performance of the EPIC weather generator for 20-year sequences of precipitation, solar radiation, and maximum and minimum

Table 16.1   Statistical parameters used to generate synthetic rainfall

---

For each month:
   Average total rainfall
   Standard deviation of daily rainfall
   Skew coefficient of daily rainfall
   Probability of a wet day following a dry day
   Probability of a wet day following a wet day

---

temperature at 134 sites in the United States. They concluded that the model was adequate for use with EPIC, since mean values of the generated rainfall sequences differed significantly from the observed mean for only three months or less, for less than 10% of the sites. Standard deviations of observed and generated sequences were also compared but results were not fully presented. Other statistical parameters for the rainfall sequences (such as extreme values) were not rigorously tested (Nicks *et al.*, 1990). The WEPP weather generator was similarly validated (Nicks, 1985). A sensitivity analysis of EPIC (Favis-Mortlock and Smith, 1990) found that, of all rainfall-related input parameters, only the rainfall state probabilities were moderately sensitive input items.

Previous Studies using Synthetic Weather

The EPIC model has frequently been used with synthetic weather input, the most notable study (although not concerned with climate change) being the analysis for the 1985 US Resources Conservation Act. This used simulation results to assess the long-term impact of soil conservation practices and erosion on US agricultural production (Putman *et al.*, 1988). Climate impact studies include those with a short-term focus such as that of Benson (1989) which simulated the effects of the severe US drought of 1988, and studies concerned with the longer-term effects of CO_2-induced climate change such as those of Robertson *et al.* (1987, 1990), Easterling *et al.* (1992a,b), McKenney *et al.* (1992) and Rosenberg *et al.* (1992) for the US. Boardman *et al.* (1990), Favis-Mortlock *et al.* (1991), Boardman and Favis-Mortlock (1993a) and Favis-Mortlock and Boardman (in press) have used EPIC with synthetic climate input to estimate erosion rates under a changed climate for the UK South Downs. Changes in mean annual soil loss for a South Downs site predicted by EPIC (Boardman and Favis-Mortlock, 1993a) are given in Figure 16.1.

Rainfall Events and South Downs Erosion

Boardman (1990, 1993) monitored soil erosion on arable land for a 36 km² area of the UK South Downs over the period 1982–92. He observed that for the South Downs, although sheet wash erosion may occur under quite small rainfall events, it is the less frequent large rainfalls which initiate rilling and therefore carry out most of the erosion. Rill erosion on the South Downs was found to be initiated by rainfall of 30 mm or more in two days or less for a typical winter cereal field (Boardman, 1990, 1993).

Rainfall events likely to initiate erosion in this area therefore lie well in the upper tail of the frequency distribution of daily rainfall. For example, for the Southover meteorological station in the east of the South Downs monitored area, only 1.1% of wet days in a 41-year sequence had daily rainfall of more than 30 mm. For Ditchling Road (just to the west of the monitored area) the number was even smaller, at 0.6% of all wet days in a 14-year sequence. However, such events are relatively more common in the "erosion season" when cover on winter cereal fields is sparse enough to permit erosion. Around 4.4% of wet days at Southover in the erosion seasons during 1982–91 had two-day rainfall totals of more than 30 mm, and hence were capable of initiating erosion (Boardman, 1993; Boardman and Favis-Mortlock, 1993b).

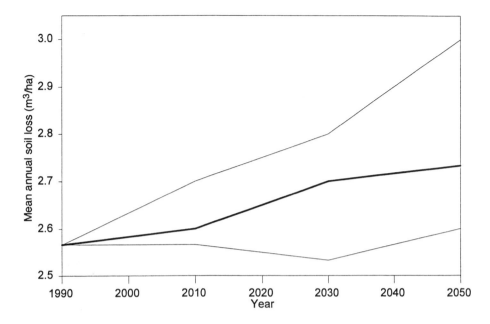

Figure 16.1   Projected erosion rates at the Woodingdean site. The bold line is the result from simulations using the best-guess scenario of Hulme *et al.* (1993); other lines are results from their higher and lower scenarios. Climate scenarios used differ slightly from those in Boardman and Favis-Mortlock (1993a)

Boardman's field observation of a threshold for erosion initiation was further quantified in the form of a Rainfall Index (RI) (Boardman, 1990). Infrequent large rainfall events in a sequence of observed rainfall are allocated a score (Table 16.2), which is then totalled for the period September to February inclusive (outside this period crop cover on the South Downs is generally too dense to permit erosion). The total score is the Rainfall Index. The RI gives a good log-linear correlation with measured erosion in the monitored area for the erosion risk period of that year (Boardman, 1990; Boardman and Favis-Mortlock, 1993b). It would therefore seem reasonable to expect that the equivalent infrequent, high-magnitude events in a synthetic sequence of rainfall should similarly generate the bulk of the simulated erosion.

However, validation of the EPIC/WEPP weather generator models (Nicks, 1985; Nicks *et al.*, 1990) has concentrated on the model's ability to reproduce mean values

Table 16.2   Definition of the Rainfall Index

Rainfall event	Index value
30 mm in 2 days	1
30 mm in 1 day	2
60 mm in 2 days	3
60 mm in 1 day	4

(and, to a lesser extent, numbers of wet days per month) rather than its ability to reproduce extreme values. Data for measured and simulated monthly maximum daily rainfall for one station only are presented in Nicks *et al.* (1990): values differ markedly for some months. Other workers have noted deficiencies in the distributions produced by similar first-order Markov chain models: Wilks (1989) and Gregory *et al.* (1993) found the variability of monthly or annual totals to be too small; while Racsko *et al.* (1991) found that runs of wet and dry weather were not well represented. However, none of these studies examined the weather generator's ability to model the low frequency tail of the distribution, which is of particular importance for erosion. A method was therefore devised to do this.

Evaluation of the Weather Generator

Experimental Method

Two sequences of observed daily rainfall were obtained from the previously mentioned rain gauges in or just outside the monitored area. The length of sequence for Southover was 41 years (1950 to 1990 inclusive) and for Ditchling Road 14 years (1975 to 1988 inclusive). These sequences were processed to give the statistical parameters required by the weather generator incorporated in the 3629 version of EPIC (Williams *et al.*, 1990).

An EPIC data set for a site at Woodingdean in the study area (approximately 7 km from Southover and 4 km from Ditchling Road) was then prepared. This has an area of 0.68 ha, a slope length of 135 m and a mean slope angle of approximately 8°; the soil is a silty, moderately stony, rendzina of the Andover series (Jarvis *et al.*, 1984) over Chalk. Further details of the site are given in Favis-Mortlock *et al.* (1991). Mean annual rainfall in the study area is between 750 and 1000 mm with an autumn peak; mean annual temperature is 9.8 °C, with a January mean of 3.9 °C and a July mean of 16.3 °C (Potts and Browne, 1983). Continuous winter wheat (the dominant crop in the area) was simulated, using typical South Downs agricultural practices (Favis-Mortlock *et al.*, 1991).

Using this data set, a 41-year EPIC simulation was run using the Southover observed rainfall. Five further simulations of the same length were then carried out, using rainfall generated from the previously derived Southover statistical parameters. For each of the five runs a different initial seed was used for the random number generator, thus giving five different (but statistically similar) realizations. The rainfall generated during each run was saved for further analysis. Six further runs, one with real rainfall, five with synthetic, were made using the same data set but this time with the Ditchling Road rainfall data; simulations this time were for 14 years.

The five generated rainfall sequences for each rain gauge were then compared with the real rainfall sequences from which they were derived. Additionally, erosion rates calculated by EPIC were compared for the real and generated rainfall sequences.

Results

Values for monthly rainfall for the observed and synthesized rainfall were compared using a paired samples t-test (Table 16.3): these were not significantly different at

Table 16.3 Real and synthesized monthly total rainfall for Ditchling Road and Southover

	Ditchling Road total rainfall[a]		Southover total rainfall[b]	
	Real	Synthesized[c]	Real	Synthesized[c]
Jan.	85.6	101.46	91.5	107.52
Feb.	47.3	56.88	63.2	69.80
Mar.	78.8	73.42	65.5	62.04
Apr.	48.9	50.84	50.7	51.10
May	56.3	55.42	48.6	49.10
June	52.7	49.80	57.8	56.28
July	53.5	43.88	55.5	51.58
Aug.	60.6	52.46	69.3	68.46
Sept.	69.6	65.36	78.7	74.98
Oct.	107.7	86.92	91.4	82.50
Nov.	83.1	89.28	102.3	107.84
Dec.	88.8	93.38	94.9	96.68
Total	832.9	819.00	869.4	877.88
Synthesized/real (%)	98.3		100.9	
Differences using t-test (two-tailed)	not significant at 5% level		not significant at 5% level	

[a]All values 14 year means.
[b]All values 41 year means.
[c]Mean of five runs.

the 5% level for either rain gauge. However, the monthly standard deviations of daily rainfall (not shown) did differ significantly at the 10% level.

Even a cursory comparison of the frequency distributions for Southover observed rainfall (Figure 16.2, upper) and one instance of the synthesized rainfall (Figure 16.2, lower) indicates a clear difference in shape. The difference, however, lies at the low-magnitude, high-frequency end of the distribution: insufficient dry days are indicated in the generated sequence with a corresponding excess of days with 2 to 3 mm of rainfall. Even if wet days only are graphed (Figure 16.3) it is not easy to see whether the other end of the distribution—the large, rare rainfall events—is adequately modelled. While a conventional statistical approach could have been adopted for further analysis (e.g. Katz, 1988b), use of the Rainfall Index was considered preferable since the RI is designed specifically to highlight the presence or absence of the low-frequency, high-magnitude events which are responsible for the bulk of South Downs erosion. Accordingly, an RI value was calculated for both real and synthesized rainfall sequences (Table 16.4).

Synthesized rainfall sequences produce a considerably lower RI value than the real rainfall from which they are derived. This indicates a deficiency in large rainfall events in generated rainfall, which would suggest that lower erosion rates will be calculated if synthesized rainfall is used: comparison of EPIC's mean annual soil loss rates using real and generated rainfall (Table 16.5) confirms this.

(a)

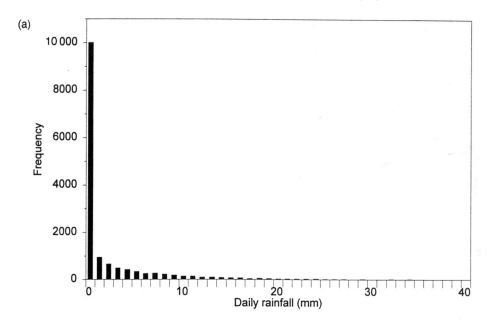

(b)

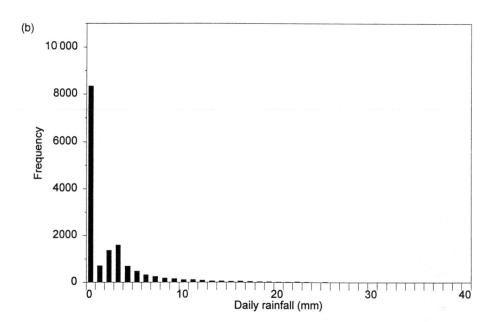

Figure 16.2   Frequency distributions of 41 years of daily rainfall amounts for Southover.
(a) Observed rainfall ($N = 14\,975$); (b) synthesized ($N = 14\,965$)

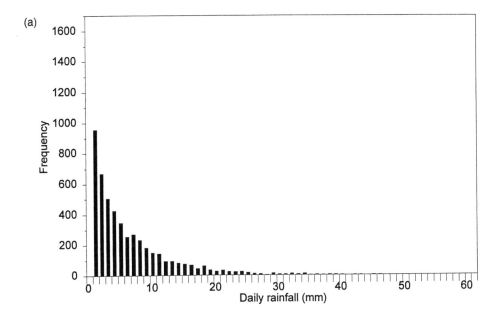

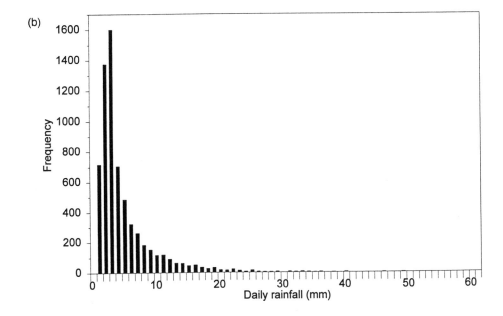

Figure 16.3 Frequency distributions of 41 years of daily rainfall amounts for Southover, wet days only. (a) Observed rainfall ($N = 4958$); (b) synthesized ($N = 6610$)

Table 16.4   Rainfall Index values for real and synthesized rainfall for Ditchling Road and Southover

	Sequence no.	Ditchling Road[a]	Southover[b]
Synthesized rainfall	0	2.08	3.65
	1	3.15	3.75
	2	2.92	3.55
	3	1.77	3.40
	4	2.23	3.60
	Mean	2.43	3.59
Real rainfall		4.08	5.15
Synthesized/real (%)		59.6	69.7

[a]All values from 14 year sequences.
[b]All values from 41 year sequences.

Table 16.5   Measured and simulated erosion rates (m³/ha/year) at Woodingdean site D

	Realization number	Weather data set	
		Ditchling Road[a]	Southover[b]
Simulated using:	0	2.29	2.83
	1	2.36	2.93
	2	2.29	2.85
	3	2.43	2.93
	4	2.43	2.90
	Mean	2.36	2.89
Simulated using real rainfall		3.93	4.24
Measured for 1985–86 only		3.37	
Measured: mean for 1982–88 (whole field)		2.82	
Simulated using synthesized/simulated using real (%)		60.1	68.2

[a]All values 14 year means.
[b]All values 41 year means.

Attempts at Compensation

How does this under-representation of infrequent large daily rainfall events, and the consequent underprediction in erosion rates, affect earlier results, such as those of Figure 16.1? Two methods, both of which proved unsatisfactory, were explored in an attempt to compensate for this deficiency. The first (Correction A) was simply to assume that since predicted present-day erosion rates using synthetic rainfall were only 60% of rates using real rainfall, the same ratio would apply under a changed climate (Figure 16.4, Correction A). There is no obvious reason why this should be true. If such a correction is made then predicted erosion rates (including those for the present) increase to very high levels.

The second method (Correction B) is less crude, but is still somewhat arbitrary. A present-day synthetic weather sequence was modified by applying a weighting function so that the resulting sequence possessed approximately the same RI as an equivalent sequence of measured weather, while changing as few as possible of the

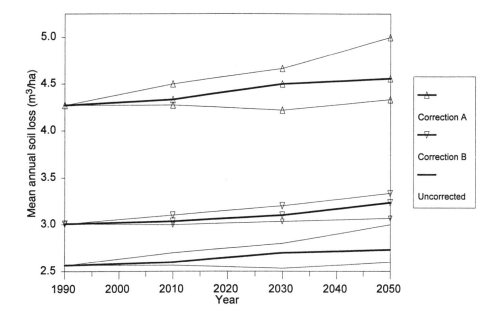

Figure 16.4 Projected erosion rates at the Woodingdean site using "corrected" synthesized rainfall (see text for explanation). In each case the bold line is the result from the best-guess scenario, the other lines are from the higher and lower scenarios

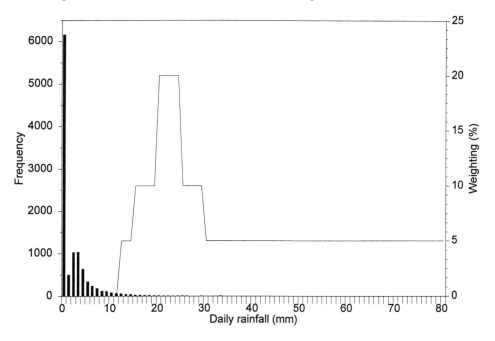

Figure 16.5 "Corrected" synthetic rainfall for Ditchling Road (30 years, $N = 10\ 950$) and the weighting used for correction B (see text for explanation)

other aspects of the distribution such as the mean and maximum. The stepped weighting indicated was used to increment daily rainfall amounts for Ditchling Road as shown in Figure 16.5. The shape of the weighting function was the result of experimentation.

When this was done, the RI for the synthetic sequence was increased from 3.0 to 4.03, yet only 3.4% of daily rainfall records were changed. Mean monthly rainfall increased by only 2.6%. However, the monthly means of the corrected and uncorrected rainfall then differed significantly at the 10% level. This weighting was then applied to the synthetic weather sequences for the changed climate scenarios, giving the results shown as Correction B in Figure 16.4.

DISCUSSION

Implications

The EPIC weather generator underpredicts large daily rainfall events for the rainfall sequences used in this study. Thus for situations where large rainfall amounts rather than high rainfall intensities are responsible for the bulk of erosion (such as the South Downs in winter), EPIC simulations using synthetic weather will underpredict erosion. Additionally, since the CLIGEN weather generator is based upon the EPIC version, it is likely that it too will similarly underpredict large events, with implications for studies undertaken using WEPP. However, this result may not apply in situations where rainfall intensity is the dominant factor controlling erosion (although it is still likely to be true that infrequent events—but high intensity ones in this case—produce most of the erosion).

How representative, then, are the South Downs in this respect? A survey of proposed rainfall-erosion thresholds for Britain is given in Boardman (1993). Early UK work on erosion (e.g. Evans and Morgan, 1974) suggested thresholds based on rainfall intensity; however, later workers (e.g. Evans, 1980; Speirs and Frost, 1985; Boardman, 1990) prefer amount-based thresholds. For example, in a one-year study of erosion on 73 arable fields of several soil types in England and Wales, Chambers *et al.* (1992) suggested that erosion was initiated by rainfall events of 15 mm or more in a 24-hour period. Outside the UK, Bollinne (1985) found that rainfall intensity correlated poorly with observed soil loss in a Belgian study, and suggested that intensity-based measures are "less suitable for an oceanic temperate climate than for other climates with intense rainstorms". In a Dutch study, Kwaad (1991) found rainfall amount to be the major controlling characteristic during winter when soils were saturated, with rainfall intensity being of greater importance during summer.

The greater importance of rainfall amount noted in these studies may be explained by consideration of the processes involved. Rill erosion predominates on the saturated (and commonly crusted) soils of the South Downs in winter (Boardman, 1990, 1993). Similarly most western European soil loss results from rill erosion (Evans, 1990; Govers, 1991; Auzet *et al.*, 1993) which is produced by runoff. Low-intensity rainfall events may produce runoff either by means of saturation overland flow upon wet soils (e.g. Kwaad, 1991; Abrahams *et al.*, 1992) or Hortonian overland flow on crusted soils (e.g. Boiffin, 1985; Boiffin *et al.*, 1988; Le Bissonnais and Singer, 1992).

The rainfall/erosion relationships of the South Downs thus appear to be broadly representative of western Europe, and possibly of oceanic temperate climates in general. Therefore, other things being equal, generated rainfall sequences are likely to underpredict erosion in all such situations. However, there is an urgent need to carry out further similar evaluations of synthetic weather sequences for other locations.

Deficiencies of the EPIC Weather Generator

The deficiencies in the EPIC weather generator highlighted by this study result from poor performance by both the event submodel and the distributional submodel.

The EPIC weather generator event submodel is a first-order, two-state type. Other workers have developed multi-state models, where the threshold probabilities for the occurrence of rainfall depend additionally on the amount of rainfall on the previous day. Higher-order models, where the occurrence of rainfall on days earlier than the previous are considered, have also been produced (Gregory et al., 1992; Stern et al., 1982; Woolhiser, 1992; Gregory et al., 1993). However, the greater simplicity of first-order, two-state models—particularly with regard to parameterization—has resulted in their wider use for decision-making purposes (Hutchinson, 1987; Gregory et al., 1992; Woolhiser, 1992). Increasing the order or number of states does not necessarily improve such models significantly (Gregory et al., 1992). The distribution of runs of wet and dry spells in observed data are very sensitive to the period of observation and may show wide variations between adjacent stations: thus there is little point in developing a complex model to precisely fit observed patterns (Woolhiser, 1992).

The distributional submodel appears to offer more opportunities for improvement without sacrificing simplicity. However, although other workers have found that distributions such as the exponential or gamma (or some variant) provide a better fit with observed rainfall distributions (Stern et al., 1982; Hutchinson, 1987), Woolhiser (1992) considers it unlikely that any single distribution shape will fit well at all locations. More research is needed here.

Synthetic Weather as a Tool for Erosion Impact Studies

Are stochastic weather generators a useful tool for impact studies of soil erosion responses to climate change? This study evaluated only one weather generator, although this is by far the most commonly used in erosion modelling. Despite the problem noted here, the EPIC weather generator represents the only practical current source of daily weather data with prescribed distributional characteristics for such studies (cf. Cavadias, 1992).

One "workaround" solution is to aim for relative results only. Barfield et al. (1991) suggest that current erosion models may only reliably be used to produce relative, rather than absolute, answers. The same may well apply to weather generator models. If both present-day (baseline) and changed-climate sequences are synthesized, then both will be similarly deficient in large rainfall events. However, this situation will only exist for the equilibrium condition, for example where there has been only a simple shift in the distributional mean. This would not be true if future rainfall variability was changed. Thus erosion rates calculated from such sequences are likely to be similarly underpredicted in both cases.

Certainly, this study-re-emphasizes the tentative nature of current climate change impact studies. As well as the large uncertainties in input data, the available tools are also less than adequate in many respects.

Further Work

Further work aims to evaluate other weather generators, such as that of Racsko *et al.* (1991), preferably using weather sequences from several locations. Additionally, the study should be extended to examine simulated maximum and minimum temperature sequences: failure to correctly model extreme temperature minimums, for example, would have clear implications for crop modellers.

However, a priority must be the development of improved weather generators which are capable of producing sequences of synthetic weather data with distributional characteristics more closely comparable with observed sequences, particularly with respect to extreme values.

ACKNOWLEDGEMENTS

I am grateful to the British Geomorphological Research Group for assistance with travel to K. U. Leuven for discussion with Mark Nearing (USDA WEPP development team); to Arlin Nicks (USDA) for assistance with CLIGEN; to the EPIC development team; to Jonathan Gregory (Meteorological Office) for access to unpublished material; and to John Boardman, Neville Brown and other colleagues at the Environmental Change Unit, Oxford, for critical discussion.

REFERENCES

Abrahams, A. D., Parsons, A. J. and Hirsch, P. J. (1992). Field and laboratory studies of resistance to interrill overland flow on semi-arid hillslopes, southern Arizona. In Parsons, A. J. and Abrahams, A. D. (Eds), *Overland Flow*, UCL Press, London, pp. 1–23.

Armstrong, A. C. and Castle, D. A. (1989). Climate change and field drainage. *The Agricultural Engineer*, **44**, 126–127.

Arnold, J. G., Williams, J. R., Nicks, A. D. and Sammons, N. B. (1989). *SWRRB (A Basin Scale Simulation Model for Soil and Water Resources Management) User's Manual*, Texas A&M University Press.

Auzet, A. V., Boiffin, J., Papy, F., Ludwig, B. and Maucorps, J. (1993). Rill erosion as a function of the characteristics of cultivated catchments in the north of France. *Catena*, **20**, 41–62.

Barfield, B. J., Hann, C. T. and Storm, D. E. (1991). Why model? In Beasley, D. B., Knisel, W. G. and Rice, A. P. (Eds), *Proceedings of the CREAMS/GLEAMS Symposium*, Agricultural Engineering Dept, University of Georgia, Athens, Georgia, USA, pp. 3–8.

Benson, V. W. (1989). EPIC: a planning tool for soil and water conservation programs. In *Proceedings of 1989 Summer Computer Simulation Conference*, Society for Computer Simulation, San Diego, California, pp. 718–721.

Boardman, J. (1990). Soil erosion on the South Downs: a review. In Boardman, J., Foster, I. D. L. and Dearing, J. A. (Eds), *Soil Erosion on Agricultural Land,* Wiley, Chichester, pp. 87–105

Boardman, J. (1993). The sensitivity of Downland arable land to erosion by water. In Thomas, D. S. G. and Allison, R. J. (Eds), *Landscape Sensitivity*, Wiley, Chichester, pp. 211–228.

Boardman, J. and Favis-Mortlock, D. T. (1993a). Climate change and soil erosion in Britain. *Geographical Journal*, **159**, 179–183.

Boardman, J. and Favis-Mortlock, D. T. (1993b). Simple methods of characterizing erosive rainfall with reference to the South Downs, southern England. In Wicherek, S. (Ed.), *Farmland Erosion in Temperate Plains, Environments and Hills,* Elsevier Science, Amsterdam, pp. 17–29.

Boardman, J., Evans, R., Favis-Mortlock, D. T. and Harris, T. M. (1990). Climate change and soil erosion on agricultural land in England and Wales. *Land Degradation and Rehabilitation*, **2**, 95–106.

Boiffin, J. (1985). Stages and time-dependency of soil crusting in situ. In Callebaut, F., Gabriels, D. and De Boodt, M. (Eds), *Proceedings of the Symposium on Assessment of Soil Surface Sealing and Crusting*, Flanders Research Centre for Soil Erosion and Soil Conservation, pp. 91–98.

Boiffin, J., Papy, F. and Monnier, G. (1988). Some reflections on the prospect of modelling the influence of cropping systems on soil erosion. In Morgan, R. P. C. and Rickson, R. J. (Eds), *Agriculture: Erosion Assessment and Modelling*, Commission of the European Communities Publication EUR 10860, Brussels, pp. 215–234.

Bollinne, A. (1985). Adjusting the Universal Soil Loss Equation for use in western Europe. In El-Swaify, S. A., Moldenhauer, W. C. and Lo, A. (Eds), *Soil Erosion and Conservation*, Soil Conservation Society of America, Ankeny, Ohio, pp. 206–213.

Brignall, A. P. and Rounsevell, M. D. A. (1994). *The Effects of Future Climate Change on Crop Potential and Soil Tillage Opportunities in England and Wales*, Environmental Change Unit/Soil Survey and Land Research Centre, Research Report No. 4, Oxford.

Bullock, P. (1991). Soils. In United Kingdom Climate Change Impacts Review Group (Ed.), *The Potential Effects of Climate Change in the United Kingdom*, HMSO, London, pp. 15–25.

Carter, T. R., Parry, M. L., Nishioka, S. and Harasawa, H. (1992). *Preliminary Guidelines for Assessing Impacts of Climate Change*, Environmental Change Unit/Center for Global Environmental Research, Oxford.

Cavadias, G. S. (1992). *A Survey of Current Approaches to Modelling of Hydrological Time-Series with respect to Climate Variability and Change*, World Meteorological Association Publication WCASP-23, Geneva.

Chambers, B. J., Davies, D. B. and Holmes, S. (1992). Monitoring of water erosion on arable farms in England and Wales, 1989–90. *Soil Use and Management*, **8**, 163–170.

Davis, F. M., Leonard, R. A. and Knisel, W. G. (1990). *GLEAMS User Manual*, US Department of Agriculture, Agricultural Research Service Southeast Watershed Research Laboratory, Tifton, Georgia, USA.

De Ploey, J., Imeson, A. and Oldeman, L. R. (1991). Soil erosion, soil degradation and climatic change. In Brouwer, F. M., Thomas, A. J. and Chadwick, M. J. (Eds), *Land Use Changes in Europe*, Kluwer, Dordrecht, pp. 275–292.

Easterling, W. E., McKenney, M. S., Rosenberg, N. J. and Lemon, K. M. (1992a). Simulations of crop response to climate change: effects with present technology and no adjustments (the 'dumb farmer' scenario). *Agricultural and Forest Meteorology*, **59**, 53–73.

Easterling, W. E., Rosenberg, N. J., Lemon, K. M. and McKenney, M. S. (1992b). Simulations of crop responses to climate change: effects with present technology and currently available adjustments (the 'smart farmer' scenario). *Agricultural and Forest Meteorology*, **59**, 75–102.

Evans, R. (1980). Characteristics of water-eroded fields in lowland England. In De Boodt, M. and Gabriels, D. (Eds), *Assessment of Erosion*, Wiley, Chichester, pp. 77–87.

Evans, R. (1990). Water erosion in British farmers' fields—some causes, impacts, predictions. *Progress in Physical Geography*, **14**, 199–219.

Evans, R. and Morgan, R. P. C. (1974). Water erosion of arable land. *Area*, **6**, 221–225.

Favis-Mortlock, D. T. and Boardman, J. (in press). Nonlinear responses of soil erosion to climate change: a modelling study on the UK South Downs. *Catena*.

Favis-Mortlock, D. T. and Smith, R. F. (1990). A Sensitivity analysis of EPIC. In Sharpley, A. N. and Williams, J. R. (Eds), *EPIC (Erosion/Productivity Impact Calculator). 1. Model Documentation*, USDA-ARS Technical Bulletin 1768, pp. 178–190.

Favis-Mortlock, D. T., Evans, R., Boardman, J. and Harris, T. M. (1991). Climate change, winter wheat yield and soil erosion on the English South Downs. *Agricultural Systems*, **37**, 415–433.

Fitzpatrick, E. A. and Krishnan, A. (1967). A first order Markov model for assessing rainfall discontinuity in central Australia. *Archives for Meteorology, Geophysics and Bioclimatology*, **B15**, 242–259.

Gabriel, K. R. and Neumann, J. (1962). A Markov chain model for daily rainfall occurrence at Tel Aviv. *Quarterly Journal of The Royal Meteorological Society*, **88**, 90–95.

Govers, G. (1991). Rill erosion on arable land in central Belgium: rates, controls and predictability. *Catena*, **18**, 133–155.

Gregory, J. M., Wigley, T. M. L. and Jones, P. D. (1992). Determining and interpreting the order of a two-state Markov chain: applications to models of daily precipitation. *Water Resources Research*, **28**, 1443–1446.

Gregory, J. M., Wigley, T. M. L. and Jones, P. D. (1993). Application of Markov models to area-average daily precipitation series and interannual variability in seasonal totals. *Climate Dynamics*, **8**, 299–310.

Hulme, M., Wigley, T. M. J. and Jones, P. D. (1990). Limitations of regional climate scenarios for impact analysis. In Boer, M. M. and De Groot, R. (Eds), *Landscape-Ecological Impact of Climatic Change*, IOS Press, Amsterdam, pp. 111–129.

Hulme, M., Hossell, J. E. and Parry, M. L. (1993). Future climate change and land use in the UK. *Geographical Journal*, **159**, 131–147.

Hutchinson, M. H. (1987). Methods of generation of weather sequences. In Bunting, A. H. (Ed.), *Agricultural Environments*, CAB International, Wallingford, pp. 149–157.

Jarvis, M. G., Allen, R. H., Fordham, S. J., Hazelden, J., Moffat, A. J. and Sturdy, R. G. (1984). *Soils and their Use in South-East England*, Soil Survey of England and Wales Bulletin 15, Harpenden.

Jones, C. A. and Kiniry, J. R. (Eds) (1986). *Ceres-Maize: a Simulation Model of Maize Growth and Development*, Texas A&M University Press, College Station, Texas.

Katz, R. W. (1977). Precipitation as a chain-dependant process. *Journal of Applied Meteorology*, **16**, 671–676.

Katz, R. W. (1988a). Statistics of climate change: implications for scenario development. In Glantz, M. H. (Ed.), *Societal Responses to Regional Climatic Change*, Westview Press, Boulder, Colorado, pp. 95–112.

Katz, R. W. (1988b). Statistics and decision making for extreme meteorological events. In Antal, E. and Glantz, M. H. (Eds), *Identifying and Coping with Extreme Meteorological Events*, Hungarian Meteorological Service, Budapest, pp. 15–32.

Knisel, W. G. (Ed.) (1980). *CREAMS—a Field Scale Model for Chemicals, Runoff and Erosion from Agricultural Management Systems*, US Department of Agriculture Research Report No. 26.

Kwaad, F. J. P. M. (1991). Summer and winter regimes of runoff generation and soil erosion on cultivated loess soils (the Netherlands). *Earth Surface Processes and Landforms*, **16**, 653–662.

Laflen, J. M., Lane, L. J. and Foster, G. R. (1991). WEPP—a new generation of erosion prediction technology. *Journal of Soil and Water Conservation*, **46**, 34–38.

Lane, L. J. and Nearing, M. A. (Eds) (1989). *USDA—Water Erosion Prediction Project: Hillslope Model*, USDA-ARS National Soil Erosion Research Laboratory Report No. 2, West Lafayette, Indiana.

Larsen, G. A. and Pense, R. B. (1981). *Stochastic Simulation of Daily Climate Data*, US Department of Agriculture Statistical Reporting Service Research Division.

Le Bissonnais, Y. and Singer, M. J. (1992). Crusting, runoff and erosion response to soil water content and successive rainfalls. *Soil Science Society of America Journal*, **56**, 1898–1903.

Legates, D. R. and Wilmott, C. J. (1992). A comparison of GCM-simulated and observed mean January and July precipitation. *Palaeogeography, Palaeoclimatology, Palaeoecology (Global and Planetary Change Section)*, **97**, 345–363.

McKenney, M. S., Easterling, W. E. and Rosenberg, N. J. (1992). Simulation of crop productivity and responses to climate change in the year 2030: the role of future technologies, adjustments and adaptations. *Agricultural and Forest Meteorology*, **59**, 103–127.

Nicks, A. D. (1974). Stochastic generation of the occurrence, pattern and location of maximum amount of daily rainfall. In *Proceedings of Symposium on Statistical Hydrology*, United States Department of Agriculture Miscellaneous Publication 1275, pp. 154–171.

Nicks, A. D. (1975). *Stochastic generation of hydrologic model inputs*. Unpublished PhD thesis, University of Oklahoma.

Nicks, A. D. (1985). Generation of climate data. In *Proceedings of the Natural Resources Modeling Symposium*, US Department of Agriculture, Agricultural Research Service Publication ARS-30, pp. 297–300.

Nicks, A. D. and Lane, L. J. (1989). Weather generator, In Lane, L. J. and Nearing, M. A. (Eds), *USDA—Water Erosion Prediction Project: Hillslope Profile Model*, USDA-ARS National Soil Erosion Research Laboratory Report No. 2, West Lafayette, Indiana, pp. 2.1–2.19.

Nicks, A. D., Richardson, C. W. and Williams, J. R. (1990). Evaluation of the EPIC model weather generator. In Sharpley, A. N. and Williams, J. R. (Eds), *EPIC—Erosion/Productivity Impact Calculator. 1. Model Documentation*, US Department of Agriculture Technical Bulletin 1768, pp. 105–124.

Parry, M. L. (1989). Potential impacts of climatic change in the UK. *Agricultural Engineer*, Winter 1989, 124–125.

Parry, M. L., Carter, T. R. and Porter, J. H. (1989). The greenhouse effect and the future of UK agriculture. *Journal of the Royal Agricultural Society of England*, **150**, 120–131.

Parry, M. L., Hossell, J. E. and Wright, L. J. (1991). Land use in the United Kingdom. In Whitby, M. C. (Ed.), *Land Use Change: the Causes and Consequences*, HMSO, London, pp. 7–14.

Potts, A. S. and Browne, T. E. (1983). The climate of Sussex. In Geographical Editorial Committee (Ed.), *Sussex: Environment, Landscape and Society*, Alan Sutton, Gloucester, pp. 88–108.

Putman, J., Williams, J. R. and Sawyer, D. (1988). Using the erosion–productivity impact calculator (EPIC) model to estimate the impact of soil erosion for the 1985 RCA appraisal. *Journal of Soil and Water Conservation*, **43**, 321–326.

Racsko, P., Szeidl, L. and Semenov, M. (1991). A serial approach to local stochastic weather models. *Ecological Modelling*, **57**, 27–41.

Richardson, C. W. (1981). Stochastic simulation of daily precipitation, temperature, and solar radiation. *Water Resources Research*, **17**, 182–190.

Richardson, C. W. and Nicks, A. D. (1990). Weather generator description. In Sharpley, A. N. and Williams, J. R. (Eds), *EPIC—Erosion/Productivity Impact Calculator. 1. Model Documentation*, US Department of Agriculture Technical Bulletin 1768, pp. 93–104.

Robertson, T., Benson, V. W., Williams, J. R., Kiniry, J. R. and Jones, C. A. (1987). Impacts of climate change on yields and erosion for selected crops in the southern United States. In Meo, M. (Ed.), *Proceedings of the Symposium on Climate Change in the Southern United States*, Science and Public Policy Program, University of Oklahoma, pp. 73–88.

Robertson, T., Rosenzweig, C., Benson, V. W. and Williams, J. R. (1990). Projected impacts of carbon dioxide and climate change in the Great Plains. In Unger, P. W., Jordan, W. R., Sneed, T. V. and Jensen, R. W. (Eds), *Challenges in Dryland Agriculture—A Global Perspective*, Texas Agricultural Experiment Station, College Station, Texas, pp. 675–677.

Rosenberg, N. J., McKenney, M. S., Easterling, W. S. and Lemon, K. M. (1992). Validation of EPIC model simulations of crop responses to current climate and CO_2 conditions: comparisons with census, expert judgement and experimental plot data. *Agricultural and Forest Meteorology*, **59**, 35–51.

Rounsevell, M. D. A. (1993). A review of soil workability models and their limitations in temperate regions. *Soil Use and Management*, **9**, 15–21.

Rounsevell, M. D. A. and Loveland, P. J. (1992). An overview of hydrologically-controlled soil responses to climate change in temperature regions. *SEESOIL*, **8**, 69–78.

Sharpley, A. N. and Williams, J. R. (Eds) (1990). *EPIC—Erosion/Productivity Impact Calculator: 1. Model Documentation*, US Department of Agriculture Technical Bulletin 1768.

Simmons, A. J. and Bengtsson, L. (1988). Atmospheric general circulation models: their design and use for climate studies. In Schlesinger, M. E. (Ed.), *Physically-Based Modelling and Simulation of Climate and Climate Change—Part I*, Kluwer, Dordrecht, pp. 23–76.

Speirs, R. B. and Frost, C. A. (1985). The increasing incidence of accelerated soil water erosion on arable land in the east of Scotland. *Research and Development in Agriculture*, **2**, 161–167.

Stern, R. D., Dennett, M. D. and Dale, I. C. (1982). Analysing daily rainfall measurements to give agronomically useful results. II. A modelling approach. *Experimental Agriculture*, **18**, 237–253.

Wilks, D. S. (1989). Conditioning stochastic daily precipitation models on total monthly precipitation. *Water Resources Research*, **25**, 1429–1439.

Williams, J. R., Jones, C. A. and Dyke, P. T. (1984). A modeling approach to determining the relationship between erosion and soil productivity. *Transactions of the American Society of Agricultural Engineers*, **27**, 129–144.

Williams, J. R., Dyke, P. T., Fuchs, W. W., Benson, V. W., Rice, O. W. and Taylor, E. D. (Eds) (1990). *EPIC—Erosion/Productivity Impact Calculator: 2. User manual*, US Department of Agriculture Technical Bulletin 1768.

Woolhiser, D. A. (1992). Modeling daily precipitation—progress and problems. In Walden, A. T. and Guttorp, P. (Eds), *Statistics in the Environmental and Earth Sciences: New Developments*, Wiley, New York, pp. 71–89.

17 Post-fire Land Use and Management and Runoff Responses to Rainstorms in Northern Portugal

R. P. D. WALSH, D. J. BOAKES
Department of Geography, University of Wales Swansea, UK

C. de O. A. COELHO, A. J. D. FERREIRA
Departamento de Ambiente e Ordenamento, Universidade de Aveiro, Portugal

R. A. SHAKESBY and A. D. THOMAS
Department of Geography, University of Wales Swansea, UK

ABSTRACT

This chapter examines medium-term (2–6 years after forest fire) temporal changes in runoff responses to rainstorms for runoff plots and catchments of contrasting pre- and post-fire forest cover and land management in the Águeda Basin, northern Portugal, following a major forest fire in 1986. Runoff responses in unburned *Eucalyptus globulus* and *Pinus pinaster* forest are used as "standards" against which to assess temporal changes in runoff response of regenerating vegetation on burned land. The three principal post-fire land managements investigated are: (1) "natural" regeneration of pine forest; (2) regeneration of eucalyptus from burned stumps; and (3) deep-ploughing and planting of eucalyptus seedlings (usually on previously pine-forested terrain). Streamflow and rainfall records for four catchments (three burned in 1986, one unburned) and at four 8 m × 2 m bounded runoff/erosion plots are used to assess runoff response changes. On pine regeneration land, runoff responses had already fallen to levels similar to those on unburned land only three years after the 1986 fire; responses remained high, but for different reasons, on eucalyptus stump regrowth and have increased on rip-ploughed/planted eucalyptus management types (where an increase in the quantity of embedded surface stones and inter-stone surface sealing following loss of fines are regarded as the prime causes). On all burned land, runoff responses tend to be higher in storms following long dry periods, when hydrophobicity is enhanced. Implications for soil erosion and the significance of the unusual dryness of the monitoring period as regards the representativeness of the results are also discussed briefly.

INTRODUCTION

The general nature of the impact of wildfires on catchment hydrology and erosion is reasonably well-established (e.g. Krammes, 1960; Campbell *et al.*, 1977; Burgess

---

Geomorphology and Land Management in a Changing Environment. Edited by D. F. M. McGregor and D. A. Thompson.
©1995 John Wiley & Sons Ltd

et al., 1981; Swanson, 1981; White and Wells, 1982; Kutiel and Inbar, 1993; Lavabre *et al.*, 1993). Effects include: (i) increases in total streamflow and the size of flood peaks; (ii) a fall in evapotranspiration loss; (iii) increased overland flow and soil erosion on slopes, associated in part with an increase in the percentage bare area and the development of hydrophobic soils; (iv) increases in sediment transport and peak suspended sediment concentrations; and (v) enhanced dissolved and organic loads as dead vegetal matter and soil nutrients are flushed out of catchment ecosystems. These impacts are generally considered to peak in the first major storms after fire and to decline as vegetation cover becomes re-established and soil recovers. Magnitudes of impact and the rates and extents of recovery towards pre-fire levels vary and both the nature of and factors influencing these variations are much less well understood. Although many factors, such as pre-fire vegetation and soil conditions, fire intensity, post-fire land management and land use, and post-fire weather, clearly play a role, their relative importance and interplay need much further investigation in areas of contrasting climate, topography, lithology and land use history if further progress towards general predictive models of fire impact is to be made.

This chapter examines medium-term impact/recovery curves (2–5 years after a severe forest fire) of overland flow and storm peaks of streams in relation to contrasting post-fire land management in *Eucalyptus globulus* and *Pinus pinaster* forested areas with a wet Atlantic–Mediterranean transitional climate in northern Portugal, where forest fires have become increasingly frequent, extensive and a major factor influencing land use and management over the past decade. The northern Portuguese environment is of particular interest for two reasons. First, inductive reasoning about how impact/recovery curves in the wet (annual rainfall 1200–1900 mm) parts of northern Portugal might differ from drier Mediterranean and semi-arid areas is equivocal. The wetter environment on the one hand might be expected to result in more pronounced hydrological and erosional impacts and delayed recovery because of larger more frequent heavy rainstorms in post-fire months, but on the other hand it might lead to a quicker recovery because of more rapid vegetation regrowth and hence higher evapotranspirational losses, better ground protection from erosion and a quicker recovery of soil permeability. The second point of interest is the contrasting types of post-fire land management followed within the region.

THE STUDY REGION

The study area lies approximately 7–10 km east of Águeda (latitude 40°35′ N, longitude 8°26′ W) in the western foothills of the Caramulo Mountains, north-central Portugal (Figure 17.1). The area is deeply dissected and drainage densities are high (4.0–4.7 km/km²), reflecting the steep terrain, impermeable lithology and intense rainstorms of the area (Walsh *et al.*, 1992). Slopes tend to be convex–rectilinear with little or no basal concavity and maximum slopes are typically about 20° although they are higher in places. The steeper slopes are characterized by shallow stony Humic Cambisols with patches of deeper Dystric Cambisols on the more gently-sloping watersheds and hollows.

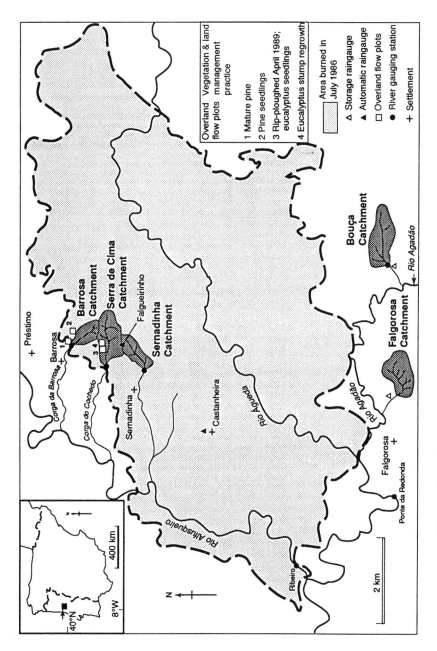

Figure 17.1 Location map of sites and instrumentation in the study region

The climate can be described as Atlantic–Mediterranean, with most of the rainfall resulting from the passage of Atlantic depressions (often in the form of intense storms) mainly during late autumn, winter and spring. The summer dry period is relatively short, usually lasting for the months of July and August. The long-term mean annual rainfall for the study area estimated from records for Campia (15 km to the north-east, mean annual rainfall = 1925 mm) is about 1600 mm. Rainfall measured at the main climatic station (Castanheira) in the research area has been consistently below the long-term mean over the monitoring period (October–September 1988–89, 875 mm; 1989–90, 1242 mm; 1990–91, 1488 mm, 1991–92, 904 mm). The highest daily rainfall recorded at Castanheira was 114 mm on 20–21 December 1989. At Campia, falls exceed 90 mm in most years and an exceptional fall of 165 mm occurred on 14 January 1977.

There have been several major land use changes affecting the study area during this century. Prior to the 1920s, land use was predominantly pastoral and the ground flora was regularly burned to promote new growth for grazing (Rego, 1986). Fears about erosion due to overgrazing led to extensive pine (*Pinus pinaster*) afforestation during the 1920s. Fast-growing *Eucalyptus globulus* was introduced during the 1940s and this has become increasingly favoured on privately-owned land. A major fire of severe intensity (*sensu* Wells *et al.*, 1979) on 13–14 June 1986 destroyed over 60 km^2 of pine (70%) and eucalyptus (30%) forest in the Águeda Basin (Figure 17.1). In the burned area, the three principal post-fire vegetation/land management types, which form the focus of this chapter, were: (1) *eucalyptus stump regrowth*, which consists of regrowth of shoots from the chain-sawn, fire-damaged eucalyptus trunks; (2) *rip-ploughed eucalyptus*, which comprises planted eucalyptus seedlings following downslope rip-ploughing of cleared pine areas; and (3) *pine regrowth*, which is regeneration by self-sown pine seedlings and found mainly on state-owned land. Several fires of lesser extent occurred in 1988, 1989, 1990 and 1991 in the region, but outside the sub-catchments of the Águeda Basin studied in this chapter.

Shoots from the eucalyptus stumps and planted eucalyptus seedlings grow at an extremely fast rate reaching heights of up to 6–8 m after only 3–4 years. By the same time, pine seedlings, which grow at a considerably slower rate, form together with shrubs a lower (1.5–2.0 m) but denser canopy. The "mature" (i.e. ready for cutting as pulpwood in as few as 9 years) eucalyptus forest floor is typically covered in a cover up to 1 m high of broom (*Chamaespartium tridentatum*), tree heather (*Erica aborea*) and gorse (*Ulex europaeus*) with large quantities of eucalyptus leaf and bark litter. Mature (> 25 years old) pine usually has a less dense ground flora which includes the species already mentioned together with bracken (*Pteridium aquilinum*). A litter layer of pine needles up to 10 cm thick covers the soil surface. Encroachment of two non-native, vigorous acacias (*Acacia longifolia* and *A. dealbata*) has occurred on a large scale on state-owned pine forests burned in 1986 and allowed to regenerate with pine seedlings.

RESEARCH METHODOLOGY

Both the aims and approach were constrained by a lack of pre-1986 fire hydrological data and the commencement of the project two years after the fire. This precluded the ideal approach of "before and after" monitoring of burned catchments or plots of contrasting post-fire management and comparisons with unburned "control" areas. The present study restricted itself to an assessment of differences in storm runoff response 2–5 years after fire between burned land of contrasting post-burn land management and land use, and unburned forest at two spatial scales: at the plot scale on slopes using bounded runoff/erosion plots and at the small catchment scale using continuous flow measurement.

Flood Peaks of Streams

River flow measurement stations were established in late 1988 in five small catchments (three burned in June 1986, two unburned) to investigate the effects of post-fire land management changes on runoff. All catchments are underlain entirely by schist and are of broadly similar relief and surface area (Table 17.1) and annual rainfall. There were originally two unburned "control" catchments. Because of the increasing threat of fire, however, one (Falgorosa) was subject to widespread "premature" clear-cutting in 1989–90 and its results are not used here. The second (Bouça), covered by a mixture of "mature" eucalyptus about 12 years old and mature pine more than 25 years old, is used as a "standard" against which changes through time in the storm peak responses of the burned catchments as they "recovered" could be measured. The three burned catchments were of different "dominant" post-burn land management: Sernadinha (stump regrowth eucalyptus), Serra de Cima (rip-ploughed and planted with eucalyptus) and Barrosa ("natural" regrowth of *Pinus pinaster* and *mato* scrub). The topography and changes in land use between 1985 and 1990 for the three burned catchments and the unburned "control" catchment are shown in Figure 17.2.

Ott Type X horizontal water-level recorders (at Bouça, Barrosa and Sernadinha) and a British Rototherm pressure bulb water-level recorder (at Serra de Cima) were installed in in-stream stilling wells at modified natural rated-section sites to provide continuous records of river stage from November 1988 onwards. Stage–discharge rating curves (Figure 17.3) derived from dilution gauging using the relative method (Littlewood, 1986) and at very low flows by volumetric gauging were used to convert stage records to discharges.

For successive water years (September–August) from 1988–89 to 1991–92, all hydrograph peaks in which rainstorms were of comparable magnitude at all four

Table 17.1 Morphometric data for the study catchments

Catchment	Burn status	Basin altitude (metres a.s.l.)			Catchment area (km²)
		max.	min.	mean	
Bouça	Long unburnt	540	170	359.5	0.61
Falgorosa	Long unburnt	400	110	246.3	0.65
Sernadinha	Burnt in 1986	485	295	431.6	0.33
Barrosa	Burnt in 1986	470	245	401.1	0.33
Serra de Cima	Burnt in 1986	475	280	432.0	0.51

288

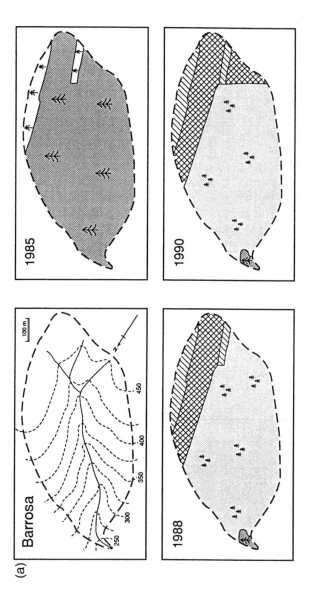

Figure 17.2a

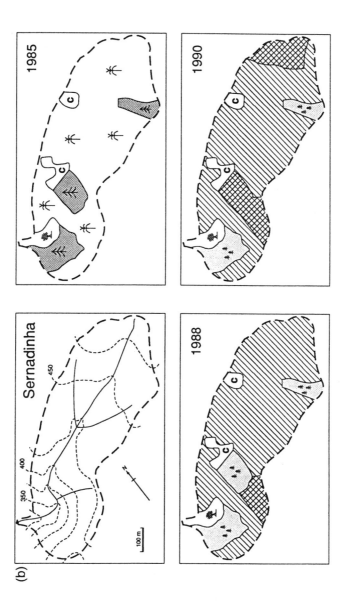

Figure 17.2b *(for caption see p. 291)*

290

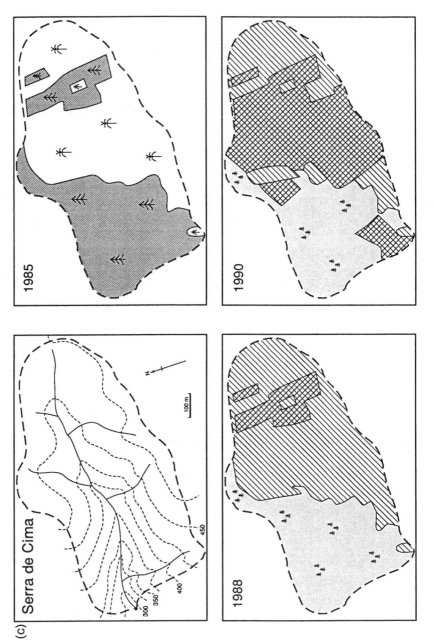

Figure 17.2c

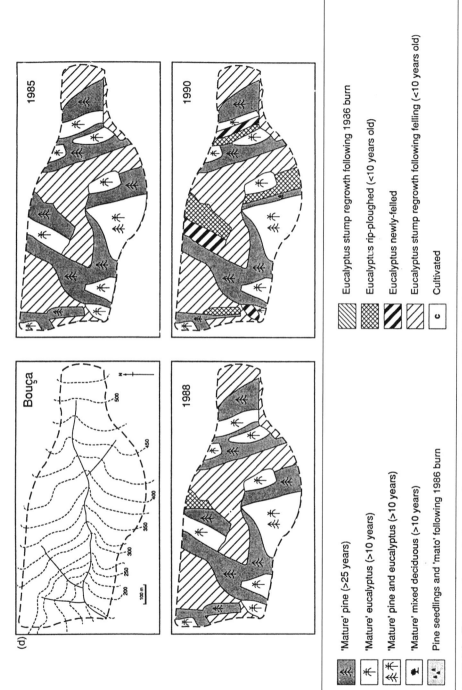

Figure 17.2d Topography and changes in vegetation/land use 1985–90 in the study catchments: a. Barrosa; b. Sernadinha; c. Serra de Cima; d. Bouça

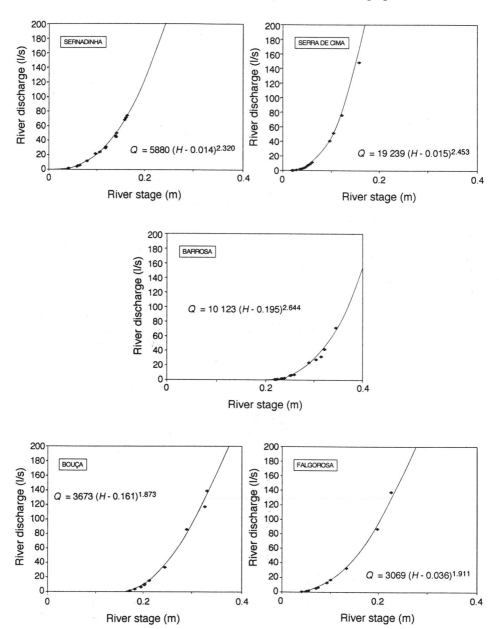

Figure 17.3 Stage–discharge rating curves for the study catchments

catchments were selected for analysis. In order to facilitate direct comparison of storm peak magnitudes between catchments, peakflows were converted to specific peakflows (in $l/km^2/s$ and mm/hr) by dividing by the appropriate catchment areas (Table 17.1). In the absence of post-fire discharge records, sizes of storm peaks at the three burned catchments were expressed as the ratio of the specific peakflow at the unburned Bouça catchment. Changes in this ratio for a burned catchment over the four-year monitoring period would therefore indicate changes in its storm runoff response and to some extent permit assessment of rates of recovery in storm peak responses back to pre-fire levels.

Overland Flow and Soil Loss at Runoff Plots

Overland flow and sediment loss were monitored from October 1989 to August 1992 using 8 m × 2 m runoff/erosion plots sited in mid-slope positions on rectilinear slopes of about 18° (±3°). Results are reported here from four long-term plots, but altogether 10 plots were established in the joint soil erosion project. The four long-term plots were established at an unburned mature (about 30 years old) pine forest site and at three sites burned in the June 1986 fire: on pine regrowth, on eucalyptus stump regrowth, and on land (formerly pine) that was rip-ploughed 22 months after the fire and planted with eucalyptus seedlings. Each plot was instrumented with from one to three 200 l tanks to collect overland flow and with a sediment trap (Shakesby et al., 1991) to monitor soil erosion. Locations of the plots within or close to the Barrosa and Serra de Cima catchments are shown in Figure 17.1. Measurements of overland flow were made at frequent but irregular intervals during the four-year monitoring period and were aggregated to give overland flow amounts for longer periods. Rainfall amounts and intensities recorded at Falgueirinho were converted to rainfalls at the plots using an altitudinal correction procedure described later. Overland flow amounts were then expressed as percentages of plot rainfalls for each of the aggregated periods. A problem, particularly at the Serra de Cima rip-ploughed plot, was overflowing tanks. This was remedied to some extent by increasing the number of tanks in series below the plots. For periods in which overflows were noted, any recorded overland flow value represented a minimum possible amount. A maximum possible overland flow value was calculated by assuming that all rainfall in an overflow period had runoff as overland flow. The true overland flow values for such a cumulated period were thus assumed to lie somewhere between the two values.

Rainfall Measurements

Rainfall gauges were installed in or close to each catchment, with automatic recording gauges (Casella natural siphon type) located at the project base at Castanheira (altitude 200 m) and at the high altitude station of Falgueirinho (460 m) (Figure 17.1). Rainfall at the higher station was consistently 16–17% higher than at Castanheira in each of the four years 1988–89, 1989–90, 1990–91 and 1991–92, allowing a simple equation to be developed relating rainfall to altitude for the area. Using this relationship, rain gauge totals were adjusted to yield altitudinally corrected rainfall estimates for individual catchments (using their mean altitudes) and runoff plots. As the four runoff plots were all located within 1 km of the high altitude Falgueirinho gauge, such a procedure was considered accurate except for a few localized convectional storms in summer.

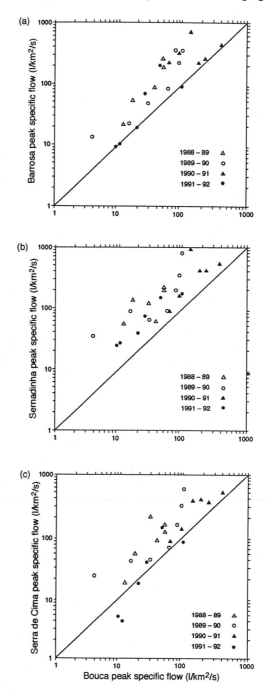

Figure 17.4 Flood peaks (l/km^2/s) of catchments burned in 1986 compared with the unburned Bouça catchment for the hydrological years from 1988–89 to 1991–92. Lines of equivalence are inserted to aid comparisons

RESULTS AND ANALYSIS

Catchment Scale: Storm Peak Magnitudes

Storm peak data (converted to specific peakflows) for 24 storms between November 1988 and September 1992 for the unburned Bouça catchment and for the three catchments burned in 1986 were used in the analysis. Storms in which storm rainfall varied between the catchments were excluded. Figure 17.4 plots storm peaks, categorized by hydrological year, for each of the burned catchments compared with storm peaks at the unburned catchment. Variations between catchments in topography and other factors mean that it cannot be assumed that prior to fire (or after full recovery) specific peakflows should be similar and hence lie close to the equivalence lines of Figure 17.4. However, it is argued that a decline in peakflows with vegetation and soil recovery during the monitoring period should be indicated by a downward shift in the position of storm events relative to the equivalence lines. In all three catchments, such downward shifts can be discerned (Figure 17.4). In order to quantify these shifts, specific peakflows for the burned catchments were expressed as a ratio of the specific peakflow at the unburned catchment, and mean peakflow ratios were calculated for the burned catchments for each of the four hydrological years from 1988–89 to 1991–92 (Table 17.2). Mean ratios for all three post-burn catchments fell substantially over the four years. At Sernadinha (eucalyptus stump regrowth) the mean peakflow ratio fell from 4.32 to 2.42, but peakflows were significantly higher than at the other two catchments throughout the period. Peakflow ratios at the pine regrowth Barrosa and the rip-ploughed eucalyptus Serra de Cima catchments fell from 3.20 to 1.82 and from 3.05 to 1.13 respectively.

Runoff/Erosion Plot Scale: Overland Flow

The pattern of daily rainfall at Falgueirinho for component periods of the erosion plot monitoring period from 6 October 1989 to 26 September 1992 is shown in Figure 17.5. Temporal variations in overland flow expressed as a percentage of plot rainfall are shown in Figure 17.6 for the three plots burned in 1986. Percentage overland flow at the unburned pine plot was not graphed as it was minimal

Table 17.2 Changes in the mean ratios of specific floodpeaks in the post-burn catchments to specific floodpeak in the unburned forested Bouça catchment, 1988–92

Winter wet season	Years after fire	Mean ratio[a] of floodpeaks at post-burn catchment compared with the unburned Bouça catchment		
		Serra de Cima (rip-ploughed eucalyptus)	Sernadinha (stump regrowth eucalyptus)	Barrosa (pine regeneration)
1988–89	2.5	3.05	4.32	3.20
1989–90	3.5	2.99	4.44	2.57
1990–91	4.5	1.68	2.57	2.62
1991–92	5.5	1.13	2.42	1.82

[a]Figures for all years are means of 5–7 storm events.

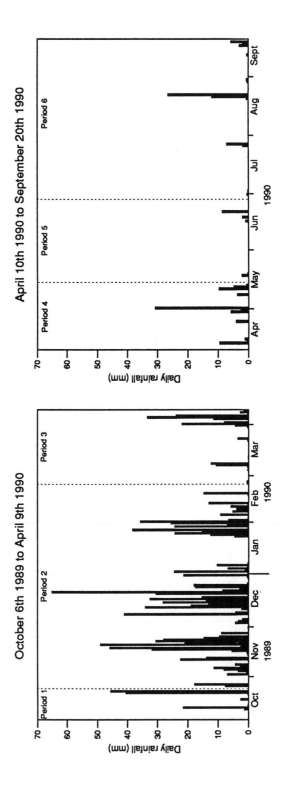

Figure 17.5

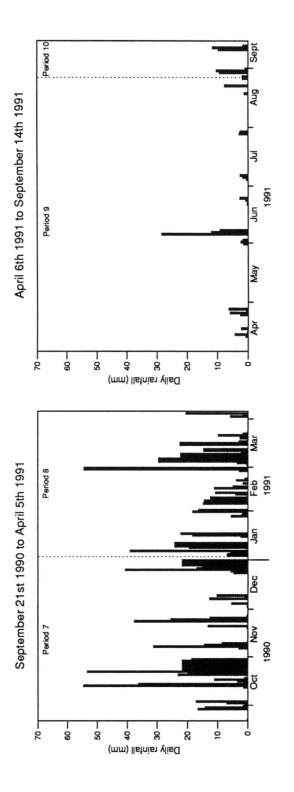

Figure 17.5 *(for caption see p. 298)*

298

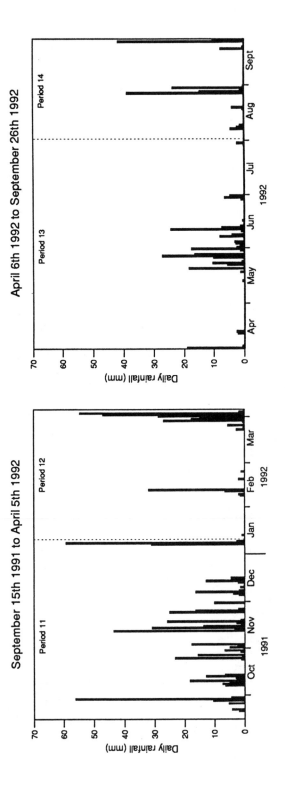

Figure 17.5 Daily rainfall at Falgueirinho during the overland flow measurement periods between October 1989 and September 1992

throughout (0.1% over the three-year monitoring period), with a maximum runoff coefficient of just over 1% occurring in a large storm following very wet antecedent weather in early January 1990 during Period 2.

Overland flow was somewhat higher at the eucalyptus stump regrowth plot than at the pine regrowth plot in all three monitoring years. At both plots, overland flow amounts declined with increasing time since the 1986 fire, but the differential appears to be widening. Thus percentage overland flows in Periods 3–6 in 1989–90 (periods in which there were no overflows and for which direct comparisons are possible) were little different at the two plots, whereas in 1991–92 overland flow was just 1% of rainfall at the pine regrowth site compared with at least 5% at the eucalyptus regrowth plot.

Temporal patterns at the two plots are interesting. Overland flow responses at the pine regrowth site were highest after long dry periods in summer, with percentages exceeding 10% in Periods 1 (October 1989), 6 (July–September 1990) and 10 (late August–early September 1991). Period 14 (August–September 1992), however, showed a more muted propensity for overland flow (2%) despite a similarly long summer dry period. The eucalyptus stump regrowth plot also exhibited high percentages of overland flow in Periods 1, 6 and 10 (11.8%, 14.0% and 9.4% respectively). However, high percentages were not confined to these periods and the highest overland flow responses (including all the tank overflows) occurred in periods of exceptionally wet weather during parts of Periods 2, 8 and 12.

Overland flow responses at the plot that had been rip-ploughed in April 1989 and planted with eucalyptus seedlings were substantially higher than at the "natural recovery" post-burn sites. Although tank overflows, particularly during the first year of monitoring, reduce the precision of overland flow estimates (demonstrated by the wide disparities between recorded and maximum possible overland flow percentages in Figure 17.6), it is clear that overland flow has tended to increase in importance over the three-year monitoring period. Whereas in 1989–90 the likely true percentage overland flow was 40–50% (somewhere between the recorded 23% and the maximum possible 61%), in 1991–92 61.9% was recorded as overland flow (with a maximum possible figure of 73.1%).

The temporal pattern of overland flow at the rip-ploughed site contrasts with those at the pine regrowth and eucalyptus stump regrowth plots. There is no sign of a seasonal peak in overland flow in events following long summer dry periods. Periods 6 and 10 were thus two of only three periods in which overflows did not occur. Percentage overland flow in Period 6 was only 13.2%. The 57.4% figure for Period 10, though high, was exceeded in the succeeding much wetter winter periods 11 and 12.

Soil Losses at the Plot Scale

The pattern of soil losses at the plot scale are more fully reported elsewhere (Shakesby et al., 1993, 1994). Findings are summarized in Figure 17.7 as their temporal variations differ in several respects from the overland flow patterns and also have some bearing on explanations of the overland flow and storm peak patterns reported above. Soil losses are expressed in two ways: in grams per square metre

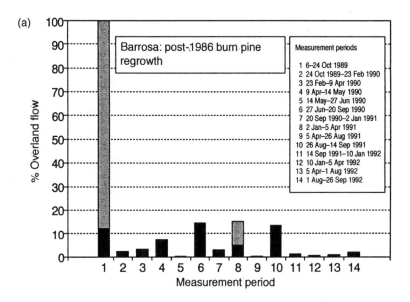

Figure 17.6a

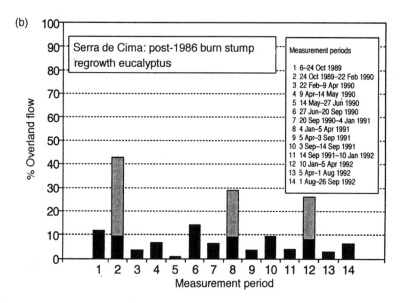

Figure 17.6b

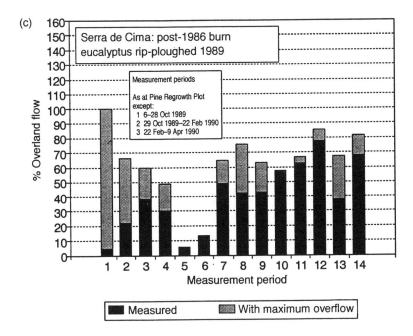

Figure 17.6c Overland flow (as a % of rainfall) at the runoff/erosion plots from October 1989 to September 1992. Where the upper part of a column is lightly shaded, overflows of the collecting tanks occurred on one or more occasions during a measurement period; the black and combined columns are the minimum (i.e. measured) and maximum overland flow amounts that could have occurred (see text)

in each measurement period; and then, arguably more meaningfully, in terms of weight per millimetre of rainfall in each period, which controls for the varying rainfall amounts between each period.

Soil loss rates were at least two orders of magnitude higher at the rip-ploughed site than at the other three sites throughout the monitoring period for which records are available (up to April 1992, nearly six years after the 1986 fire). Rates of erosion at the post-burn pine regrowth and eucalyptus stump regrowth sites were little different from those recorded at the unburned mature pine site, despite the higher overland flow at the burned sites.

At the rip-ploughed site, rates of erosion (per millimetre of rain) were distinctly lower from the second winter after ploughing onwards (Period 7 onwards). There is an indication at all plots that erosion rates per unit of rainfall follow a seasonal pattern of being higher in periods dominated by large storms separated by long dry periods, as in Periods 1, 6 and 9.

INTERPRETATION AND DISCUSSION

Both the overland flow and storm peak results tend to suggest that by 3–6 years after the major fire of 1986, runoff responses fell significantly closer to those of

(a)

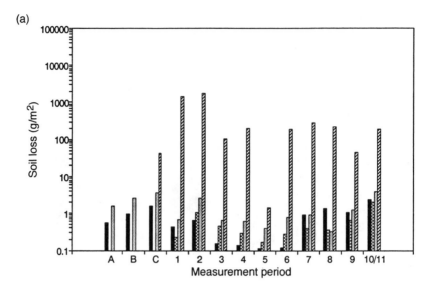

(b)

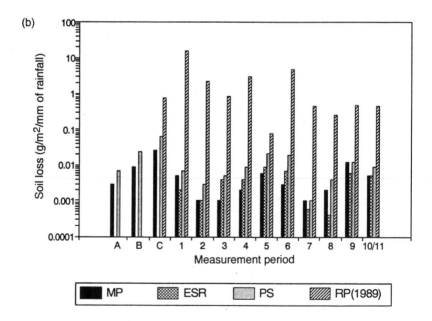

Figure 17.7   Soil erosion at the runoff/erosion plots 1989–92. (a) Amounts of soil erosion (g/m²) in each measurement period. (b) Rates of soil erosion per unit rainfall (g/m²/mm) in each measurement period. Periods 1–11 are as in Figure 17.6; Period A is 2 March–10 May 1989, Period B is 11 May–13 July 1989, Period C is 14 July–5 October 1989. Key to vegetation/land use: MP = mature pine; ESR = eucalyptus stump regrowth post-1986 fire; PS = pine seedling regrowth post-1986 fire; RP(1989) = Post-1986 burn land rip-ploughed in April 1989 and planted with eucalyptus

unburned forest in the pine regeneration areas than on eucalyptus stump regrowth terrain. Thus, mean specific peakflow ratios fell from 3.20 to 1.82 between 1989–90 and 1991–92 for the Barrosa pine regrowth catchment compared with a fall from 4.32 to 2.42 at the eucalyptus stump regrowth catchment over the same period; and percentage overland flow in 1991–92 had fallen to just 1% at the pine regrowth plot compared with over 5% at the eucalyptus stump regrowth site. There are several possible contributory reasons for these differentials:

(a) differences in the speed and nature of undergrowth recovery;
(b) differences in the impact of post-burn timber clearance and the associated land management of pine regrowth and eucalyptus stump regrowth types on soil compaction and erosion;
(c) inherited or residual differences in soil hydrological properties associated with pre-burn pine versus eucalyptus land management;
(d) differences in the impact of burning on the soil of pine compared with eucalyptus regrowth areas;
(e) inherent site differences unrelated to land management.

The first four points require some further explanation.

As regards the nature and speed of vegetation recovery, after 3–6 years the pine regrowth site comprised a dense scrub cover about 1.5–2.0 m high, whereas the faster-growing multiple stems of eucalyptus regrowth have been reduced as part of forest management practice to one or two trunks, with a much taller canopy up to 6–8 m high with some litter but a comparatively sparse ground cover vegetation. It is thought that the more extensive undergrowth in the pine regrowth areas will be more effective in redeveloping a permeable soil by (1) a more extensive near-surface root system, (2) more effective protection against rainsplash, and (3) greater soil fauna activity.

In terms of post-burn management practice and human activity, timber clearance of pine forest land appears to be less disruptive than clearance of burned eucalyptus forest. Also, the pine regrowth areas tend to be left to regenerate once timber clearance has been accomplished, whereas the eucalyptus stump regrowth areas are more intensively "managed". Both differences may contribute to contrasts in soil compaction and proneness to overland flow.

A third factor may be residual from pre-burn land management practices. The eucalyptus stump regrowth site is characterized by downslope-aligned furrows and ridges from ploughing carried out prior to planting the pre-burn eucalyptus forest. These residual furrows may be aiding the concentration of shallow subsurface water and the development of saturation overland flow.

At both the eucalyptus stump regrowth and pine regrowth sites, overland flow responses tend to be enhanced in summer/early autumn events. This is thought to be caused by changes in soil hydrophobicity associated with seasonal and shorter-term changes in soil moisture. Although soil hydrophobicity is most strikingly enhanced by fire (DeBano, 1966; DeBano et al., 1970; Sevink et al., 1989; Imeson et al., 1992) and plays a major role in producing increased overland flow on burned areas, the characteristic can also develop through the build-up of certain hydrocarbons without burning being involved (e.g. Prescott and Piper, 1932; Burch *et al.*, 1989) and can become temporarily enhanced when the soil dries out (Burch *et al.*, 1989). A programme of soil hydrophobicity tests using the standard water drop penetration technique (Adams *et al.*, 1969; Savage, 1974; Wessel, 1988) was carried out on air-dried soil samples from the study area. Results, reported in full elsewhere (Terry and Shakesby, 1993; Shakesby *et al.*, 1993, 1994), demonstrated that dry soil samples from pine regrowth and eucalyptus stump regrowth areas burned in 1986 both showed marked hydrophobicity of the same order as that measured at other sites just two days to three months following fire. The hydrophobic effect, however, tends to disappear as the soil becomes wet in the autumn/winter/spring wet season, as evidenced by the very low overland flow percentages in those periods, particularly in the pine regrowth areas. There is some suggestion in the overland flow results that the seasonal enhancement in hydrophobicity may be greater in the pine regrowth plot, as percentage overland flow there exceeded that at the otherwise more prolific eucalyptus stump regrowth plot in Periods 1 and 10. Such a situation may be logical, as it is arguable that the more extensive ground vegetation at the pine plot may have resulted in greater depletion of near-surface soil moisture via transpiration than would have occurred at the eucalyptus site with its poorer ground vegetation and the increasingly effective protection against soil moisture loss afforded by the eucalyptus litter.

In contrast to the post–1986 burn pine and eucalyptus stump regrowth sites, overland flow percentages at the rip-ploughed eucalyptus plot have tended to increase through time since rip-ploughing took place in April 1989 and by 1991–92 were in excess of 60% of the rainfall. Reasons for the increase in overland flow through time are considered to be: (1) an increase in the number of surface and partially embedded stones (Poesen *et al.*, 1990) as the fine fraction has been selectively detached and transported by rainsplash and overland flow during the very high, albeit declining erosion rates (Figure 17.7) following rip-ploughing; and (2) surface sealing (Poesen, 1992) of the inter-stone areas. The result is that overland flow has increased while erosion (because of armouring) has decreased.

A difficult point to account for, however, is that the largely rip-ploughed Serra de Cima catchment exhibits smaller specific peak flows than the pine regrowth Barrosa and eucalyptus stump regrowth Sernadinha catchment, while at the plot scale its overland flow responses are so high. Possible reasons for this discrepancy are that: (1) much of the 1989 rip-ploughing in Serra de Cima was aligned along rather than across the contour so that some overland flow may have been intercepted and able to infiltrate into the soil before reaching the stream; and (2) rip-ploughing within the catchment was carried out chiefly on low-angled slopes with deeper soils, whereas the plot was on comparatively thin (and hence more easily saturated) soil on a slope of about 20°.

The interpretation of the hydrological and erosional results presented here is rendered more difficult by contemporary environmental changes in the area. First, the period of the project has been considerably drier than the long-term average, and the size and frequency of large rainstorms has also been well below average (Figure 17.8). Second, the appropriate scenario of land use and management in the future is also uncertain and unclear, and the return periods of both fires and cropping of eucalyptus

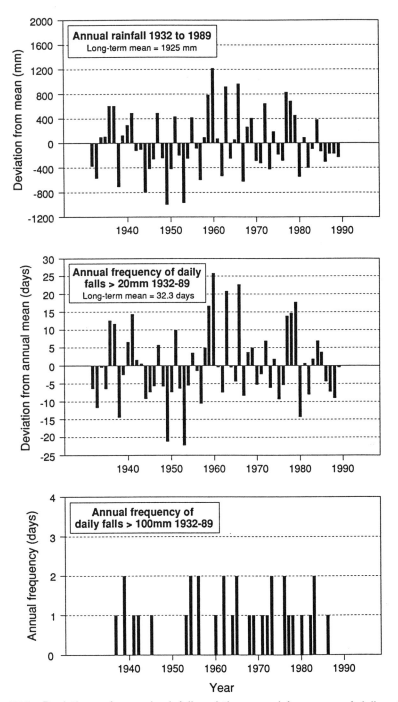

Figure 17.8 Deviations of annual rainfall and the annual frequency of daily rainfalls exceeding 20 mm from the 1932–89 mean and annual frequencies of daily rainfalls exceeding 100 mm at Campia for 1932–89

appear to be contracting. Third, the short- to medium-term context of the soils and their hydrological and erosional character and response to fire is also difficult to assess. The hydrological response of a soil that is already thin, because of the erosion that followed previous fires, is likely to be very different from that of a deep soil that has been long unburned. Thus, because of the wide variation in soil depth, it is difficult to extrapolate into the short- to medium-term our results so far obtained either to catchments as a whole or to other catchments elsewhere. However, the long-term implications of the current trend of disturbance of the soil through fire and post-fire land management seems clear: it will lead to periodic loss of soils, particularly on the deeper soils and steeper slopes, and to reduced timber productivity and enhanced runoff responses during storms.

CONCLUSIONS

There are three principal conclusions from this study. First, different post-fire land use and management practices in the *Pinus pinaster* and *Eucalyptus globulus* forests in the Águeda Basin, north-central Portugal, produce markedly different effects on runoff responses up to six years after fire. At the plot scale, there is a somewhat more rapid decline in the overland flow response of land allowed to regenerate naturally with pine seedlings than with eucalyptus following fire. This is indicated at both the plot and catchment scales. These different rates of decline could be due to differences in undergrowth recovery, land management practice, soil hydrology or soil hydrophobic response. In contrast, land rip-ploughed downslope and planted with eucalyptus seedlings showed an increase in overland flow up to almost three years after ploughing and this has been attributed to a concentration of surface and embedded stones and the development of inter-stone surface sealing resulting from accelerated loss of surface fines by rainsplash and surface wash processes. This pattern could not be discerned at the catchment scale, possibly because ploughing in the catchment was along the contour (rather than downslope) and sited mainly on low-angled slopes.

Secondly, overland flow coefficients are highest during storms following long dry spells on pine seedling and eucalyptus regrowth plots. This is attributed to drought enhancing the marked soil hydrophobicity induced by the passage of fire. Hydrophobicity tends to disappear during prolonged wet weather as the soils become wettened.

Thirdly, the unusually low rainfall during the four years (1988–92) of monitoring, together with variations in soil character and land management treatment to date and uncertainties about treatments in the future, make accurate short- to medium-term prognostication of runoff responses following future fires difficult. However, continuance of the recent trend of contraction of the intervals between disturbance events (fire, cropping or ploughing) seems set to cause a serious increase in both soil losses and runoff responses in the long term.

ACKNOWLEDGEMENTS

We gratefully acknowledge the financial support of a Research Contract (EV4V-0106-C(TT)) from the Commission of the European Communities D. G. XII. We thank Dr Peter Reiniger for his help and encouragement. We thank Sandra Creaner, Luke Keegan, Isabel Ribeiro and Jim Terry for their help in the field. We are also very grateful to the many people in the area who have helped us in so many ways.

REFERENCES

Adams, S., Strain, B. R. and Adams, M. S. (1969). Water-repellent soils and annual plant cover in a desert scrub community of south eastern California. In *Proceedings of the Symposium on Water-Repellent Soils*, University of California, May 1968, pp. 289–295.

Burch, G. I., Moore, I. D. and Burns, J. (1989). Soil hydrophobic effects on infiltration and catchment runoff. *Hydrological Processes*, **3**, 211–222.

Burgess, J. S., Rieger, W. A. and Olive, C. J. (1981). Sediment yield change following logging and fire effects in dry sclerophyll forest in southern New South Wales. In Beschta, R. L., Blinn, T., Grant, G. E., Ice, G. G. and Swanson, F. J. (Eds), *Erosion and Sediment Transport in Pacific Rim Steeplands*, International Association of Hydrological Sciences Publication No. 165, pp. 375–385.

DeBano, L. F. (1966). Formation of non-wettable soils. *USDA Forest Service Research Note* PSW-132, Pacific Southwest Forest and Range Experimental Station, Berkeley, California.

DeBano, L. F., Mann, L. D. and Hamilton, D. A. (1970). Translocation of hydrophobic substances into soil by burning organic litter. *Proceedings of the Soil Science Society of America*, **34**, 130–133.

Campbell, R. E., Baker, M. B., Ffolliott, P. F., Larson, R. F. and Avery, C. C. (1977). Wildfire effects on a ponderosa pine ecosystem: an Arizona case study. *USDA Forest Service Research Paper* RM-191, Rocky Mountain Forest and Range Experimental Station, Fort Collins, Colorado,

Imeson, A. C., Verstraten, J. M., van Mulligen, E. J. and Sevink, J. (1992). The effects of fire and water repellency on infiltration and runoff under Mediterranean type forest. *Catena*, **19**, 345–362.

Krammes, J. S. (1960). Erosion from mountainside slopes after fire in southern California. *USDA Forest Service Research Note* PSW-171, Pacific Southwest Forest and Range Experimental Station, Berkeley, California.

Kutiel, P. and Inbar, M. (1993). Fire impacts on soil nutrients and soil erosion in a Mediterranean pine forest plantation. *Catena*, **20**, 129–139.

Lavabre, J., Torres, D. S. and Cernesson, F. (1993). Changes in the hydrological response of a small Mediterranean basin a year after a wildfire. *Journal of Hydrology*, **142**, 273–299.

Littlewood, I. G. (1986). *The dynamics of acid runoff from moorland and conifer afforested catchments draining into Llyn Brianne, Wales*. Unpublished PhD thesis, University of Wales.

Poesen, J. W. A. (1992). Mechanism of overland-flow generation and sediment production on loamy and sandy soils with and without rock fragments. In Parsons, A. J. and Abrahams, A. D. (Eds), *Overland Flow Hydraulics and Erosion Mechanics* UCL Press, London, pp. 275–305.

Poesen, J., Ingelmo-Sanchez, F. and Mücher, H. (1990). The hydrological response of soil surfaces to rainfall as affected by cover and position of rock fragments in the top layer. *Earth Surface Processes and Landforms*, **15**, 653–671.

Prescott, J. A. and Piper, C. S. (1932). The soils of the South Australian Mallee. *Transactions of the Royal Society of South Australia*, **56**, 118.

Rego, F. (1986). *Effects of prescribed fire on vegetation and soil properties in Pinus pinaster forest of northern Portugal*. Unpublished PhD thesis, University of Idaho.

Savage, S. M. (1974). Mechanism of fire-induced water repellency in soil. *Proceedings of the Soil Science Society of America*, **38**, 652–657.

Sevink, J., Imeson, A. C. and Verstraten, J. (1989). Humus form development and hillside runoff and the effects of fire and management under Mediterranean forest in NE-Spain. *Catena*, **16**, 461–475.

Shakesby, R. A., Walsh, R. P. D. and Coelho, C. O. A. (1991). New developments in techniques for measuring soil erosion in burned and unburned forest catchments, Portugal. *Zeitschrift für Geomorphologie Supplement-Band*, **83**, 161–174.

Shakesby, R. A., Coelho, C. de O. A., Ferreira, A. D., Terry, J. P. and Walsh, R. P. D. (1993). Wildfire impacts on soil erosion and hydrology in wet Mediterranean forest, Portugal. *International Journal of Wildland Fire*, **3**, 95–110.

Shakesby, R. A., Coelho, C. de O. A., Ferreira, A. D., Terry, J. P. and Walsh, R. P. D. (1994). Fire, post-burn land management practice and soil erosion response curves in eucalyptus and pine forests, north-central Portugal. In Sala, M. and Rubio, J. L. (Eds), *Soil Erosion and Degradation as a Consequence of Fires*, Geoforma, Logroño, Spain, pp. 111–132.

Swanson, F. J. (1981). Fire and geomorphic processes. In Mooney, H. A., Bonnicksen, T. M., Christensen, N. L., Lotan, J. E. and Reiners, W. A. (Eds), *Fire Regime and Ecosystem Properties*. USDA Forest Service General Technical Report WO-26, Washington, DC, US Government Printing Office, pp. 401–420.

Terry, J. P. and Shakesby, R. A. (1993). Soil hydrophobicity effects on rainsplash: simulated rainfall and photographic evidence. *Earth Surface Processes and Landforms*, **18**, 519–525.

Walsh, R. P. D., Coelho, C. de O. A., Shakesby, R. A. and Terry, J. P. (1992). Effects of land use management practices and fire on soil erosion and water quality in the Águeda river basin, Portugal, *GeoÖkoplus*, **3**, 15–36.

Wells, C. G., Campbell, R. E., DeBano, L. F., Lewis, C. E., Fredriksen, R. L., Franklin, E. C., Froelich, R. C. and Dunn, P. C. (1979). Effects of fire on soil: a state-of-knowledge review. *US Department of Agriculture, Forest Service, General Technical Report* WO-7.

Wessel, A. T. (1988). On using the effective contact angle and the waterdrop penetration time for the classification of water repellency in dune soils. *Earth Surface Processes and Landforms*, **13**, 555–561.

White, W. D. and Wells, S. G. (1982). Forest-fire devegetation and drainage basin adjustments in mountainous terrain. In Rhodes, D. D. and Williams, G. P. (Eds), *Adjustments of the Fluvial System*, Proceedings of the 10th Geomorphology Symposium, Binghamton, Allen & Unwin, Boston, pp. 199–223.

18 Geomorphology and Rainforest Logging Practices

IAN DOUGLAS
Department of Geography, University of Manchester, UK

TONY GREER
Department of Geography, National University of Singapore, Singapore

WAIDI SINUN
Department of Geography, University of Manchester, UK

STEPHEN ANDERTON
Department of Civil Engineering, University of Newcastle upon Tyne, UK

KAWI BIDIN
Department of Geography, University of Manchester, UK

MIKE SPILSBURY
Fountain Forestry, Banbury, UK

JADDA SUHAIMI and AZMAN BIN SULAIMAN
Department of Geography, University of Manchester, UK

ABSTRACT

Careful comparison of commercially selectively logged and natural mature lowland Dipterocarp forest catchments and plot studies in natural forest and on abandoned logging tracks in Ulu Segama, Sabah show that logging practices which create skid trails downslope lead to the proportion of rainfall which becomes overland flow changing from 5% in natural forest to 55% on compacted trail surfaces. Abandoned tracks have sediment yields approaching $24000 \text{ t km}^2 \text{ y}^{-1}$ immediately after logging. As vegetation grows back these yields decline to around $1500 \text{ t km}^2 \text{ y}^{-1}$ after 12 months. Overland flow length, gradient and surface roughness all affect erosion rates on skid tracks. Unsupervised construction of earth barriers across the trails by bulldozer drivers on abandonment reduces sediment yield, experiments indicating a drop from $1900 \text{ t km}^2 \text{ y}^{-1}$ to $105 \text{ t km}^2 \text{ y}^{-1}$ with barrier construction. Stream head hollows regulate streamflow and changes to them should be avoided. Hillslope and channel morphology have to be brought together to develop better forest management. Beneath the ephemeral head streams in zero-order basins, water tables respond to all rain events, even when quantities are too small to cause a change in streamflow. Delimiting the areas around stream heads which should be protected involves careful investigation of hydrological and geomorphological processes.

Geomorphology and Land Management in a Changing Environment. Edited by D. F. M. McGregor and D. A. Thompson.

INTRODUCTION

In the humid tropics, any disturbance of the forest cover that exposes the ground surface to high intensity rains leads to acceleration of erosion. In natural forest, occasional tree-fall or landsliding creates new sediment sources by exposing soil and regolith materials to splash erosion and providing opportunities for overland flow to develop. Land clearance of any dimensions tends to have more drastic impacts than most natural disturbances, especially when complete exposure of the soil occurs for long periods. Normal selective logging operations do not usually expose a high proportion of the total ground surface, even though they may damage as much as 70% of the canopy. However, to remove logs a hierarchy of log drag paths (snig tracks), temporary access roads, log landing areas, trucking yards and trunk log haulage routes is required. Each of these surfaces becomes compacted, provides a potential surface runoff pathway and acts as a sediment source. The cost of constructing and maintaining roads is a major part of the total cost of a selective logging operation. Yet all these log movement routes provide the main source of changes in water and sediment discharge in tropical rainforest catchments undergoing logging. This chapter on tropical forest logging and geomorphology therefore concentrates on the process and sediment volume changes created by the hierarchy of forest roads.

The role of forest access roads in creating sedimentation problems was recognized early in the history of forest hydrology experiments:

> In the spirit of the times [he] used natural materials and labour intensive methods to stabilise them. Cut grass or weeds were laid on slopes and held in place with stakes cut from local materials. This mulch broke the eroding force of raindrops, halted the sloughing due to frost action and encourages growth of planted material or naturally seeded vegetation.
>
> (C. R. Hursh (1935) quoted in Swift, 1988:313)

Despite these early indications of the need to prevent erosion, roads remain a major sediment source in selectively logged tropical rainforests. This chapter examines the precise magnitude of such erosion in lowland forest in Sabah, Malaysia, and seeks to ascertain why the excellent guidelines produced by several temperate forest management agencies (e.g. Rothwell, 1978), and often adapted for tropical rainforest conditions, are not practised by most tropical logging operators.

GUIDELINES FOR TEMPERATE AND TROPICAL FOREST ROAD DESIGN AND MAINTENANCE

The control of runoff along forest access roads and skid trails is the key to minimizing the severe erosion that occurs in many areas of timber extraction (Megahan and Kidd, 1972). Obstacles to concentrated flow along roads are required. Vegetative methods, including the spreading of plant material as a mulch, are highly favoured (Swift, 1988). However, in the tropics, soil-retaining structures may be needed to provide quick, short-term relief from erosion until plants become established (Harcharik and Kunkle,

1978). In Indonesia, for example, planted vegetation was not much help in controlling erosion on areas suffering severe sheet and gully erosion unless gully plugs were constructed to prevent enlargement of existing gullies (Van Dillewijn, 1976). Thus on logging tracks, the alternative of earth mounds or barriers is attractive as a technique which can be adopted by bulldozer drivers. These water bars are effectively a 3% reverse slope dip of 6 m length which obstructs the water flowing down the road and diverts it laterally into the forest vegetation on either side of the road. The plants and litter debris impede the flow of water and trap the sediments entrained with it. In temperate areas, the average spacing between such dips would be 60 m (Swift, 1988).

Such concepts are widely incorporated into the excellent guides for temperate forest management, such as those of the US Department of Agriculture, Forest Service Transportation Engineering Handbook (1960 and 1982) and the FAO *Watershed Field Manual—Road Design and Construction for Sensitive Watersheds*. Careful attention to road design and maintenance reduces the risk of erosion and mass movements (Gresswell *et al.*, 1979). For tropical forests, guidelines, such as those for *Selective Logging of Rainforest Areas in North Queensland State Forests and Timber Reserves* and *Harvesting Specifications, Forestry Department, Peninsular Malaysia* (Pearce and Hamilton, 1986), provide excellent advice. All these proposals have the objective of achieving minimal environmental damage during commercial logging through changing the way personnel use equipment and treat the ground in the forest.

REALITY OF EROSION CONTROL DURING FOREST OPERATIONS IN THE TROPICS

In reality, even where forest guidelines exist on paper in the developing countries of the humid tropics, precautions against erosion are seldom carried out, due largely to the rapid rate at which roads are constructed and logs are extracted and to the general absence of forest officers in the field. Often the logging operator is completely unaware of any guidelines and has little incentive to implement any of them independently.

Recent years have seen a growing awareness at high levels in many countries exporting timber of the precautions needed to reduce siltation problems and in some areas simple, non-time consuming, non-technical, yet economically viable, measures are being implemented by field crews to reduce soil loss from skid trails. In Sabah, water bars, low earth barriers, are bulldozed across snig tracks at intervals, to intercept overland flow and trap sediment. Elsewhere, broken branches and foliage are spread across abandoned tracks to provide some protection against raindrop splash and eventually some mulch to encourage recolonization of the tracks by vegetation. Another alternative is to break up the surface of the track to provide resistance to runoff and encourage infiltration. Not all the measures are effective. Water bars work well for about six months but then begin to be degraded by splash erosion and eventually are breached. However, they do prevent some of the peak sediment supply and by the time they are breached, vegetation had begun to grow across much of the abandoned track. Nevertheless, the rate of adoption of such techniques is slow. Applications of geomorphic principles can contribute to making them more effective and thus increase the likelihood of their being widely adopted.

METHODOLOGY

In 1987 an experiment was established to examine the effects of natural and anthropogenic disturbance on tropical rainforest hydrology and geomorphic processes at the Danum Valley Field Studies Centre, Ulu Segama, Sabah, Malaysia (Douglas *et al.*, 1990). The Danum Valley Field Studies Centre lies in north-eastern Borneo, in the rugged country of short, but steep, slopes of the geologically heterogeneous melange unit of Kuamat Formation, whose siltstones, sandstones, cherts, spillites and tuffs contain many easily eroded lithologies. At 4°N of the equator, in north-eastern Borneo, the area experiences only the edge effects of the seasonal monsoons, with a main wet season during the north-east monsoon from November to March and a lesser somewhat wetter period in the south-west monsoon during June and July. In the period 1986–93, monthly rainfalls totals ranged from 28 mm in April 1992 to 674.9 mm in January 1986. A "drought" of only 277 mm rainfall in four months occurred in January to April 1992. The maximum 24-hour rainfall recorded in 1986–93 was 177.2 mm, with rainfalls of over 100 mm per day occurring five times in those eight years.

Three small catchments were instrumented (Figure 18.1), one of which was later logged, enabling the effects of normal commercial forestry operations to be assessed. Float-switch-activated automatic water samplers collected samples at 7.5-minute intervals during the rising and falling stages of storm runoff events. The logging activity in the affected catchment took place in three stages over an eleven-month period in 1988–89. By 1991 data were available to analyse the initial impact of these activities.

The logging in the 0.54 km² Steyshen Baru (Baru) catchment (C in Figure 18.1) was by tractor yarding and high-lead lines. Tractor yarding involved dragging logs up snig tracks by tracked caterpillar tractors, while high lead logging involves setting up a jib on a spur of high point and dragging logs upslope by cable, so that only the end of the log touches the ground. While tractor yarding creates wide snig tracks, high lead logging disturbs a large area in the immediate vicinity of the jib. The choice of logging method was affected by both the nature of the terrain and, as is often the case, the availability of particular types of equipment in the field. Disturbance first occurred in October 1988 when large earth-moving bulldozers inserted a primary logging track across the headwaters. Although primary tracks are later abandoned after timber has been extracted from the designated parcel forest, they carry pneumatic-tyred vehicles during the logging period and are therefore well constructed and generally follow the contours in the difficult, rugged, undulating terrain.

During the logging procedure, skid trails were extended from the primary track to the cut trees. Two series of experiments were set up to examine runoff and erosion on these trails.

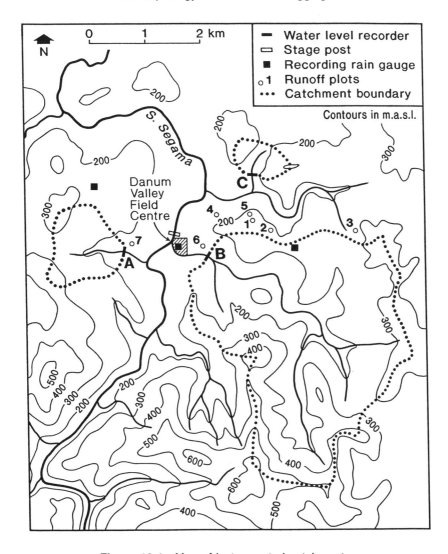

Figure 18.1 Map of instrumented catchments

In the first, short-term, investigation in July 1989, two small 1 m × 5 m bounded runoff plot experiments were set up on recently abandoned skid trails (Plots 1 and 2 on Figure 18.1). One plot allowed uninterrupted runoff downslope, while an adjacent plot examined a skid track which had been blocked at its upper end by a 2 m high earth barrier bulldozed up in a simple unsupervised operation. This plot therefore samples reduced runoff conditions. Two further plots were established on a one-year-old skid trail (Plot 3 on Figure 18.1) and in adjacent primary forest (Plot 4).

The second, longer-term experiment had a single 1 m × 5 m plot on an abandoned trail (Plot 5) and plots under primary forest on different slopes (Plots 6 and 7) (Sinun *et al.*, 1992). Small erosion plots may be criticized as yielding data that cannot be extrapolated to larger areas (Thornes, 1980), but they provide a means of comparing runoff management treatments of small areas.

THE DANUM STUDY: IMPACTS OF DISTURBANCE BY LOGGING OPERATIONS

Although no further earth-moving occurred in the Baru catchment for three months after road construction, immediate hydrographic changes affecting runoff became apparent. The primary access track for tyred vehicles was oriented in such a way that it captured some storm runoff that would have drained to an adjacent catchment and redirected it into the Baru. This artificial addition to the ephemeral headwater channel network increased storm runoff and contributed to the reduction in lag time and increase of the hydrograph peak. Base-flow at this time was largely unaltered as the road merely re-routed surface runoff and collected rain falling directly onto its surface. During storm runoff events, this diversion effectively increased the contributing area supplying the Baru gauge by up to 9%.

Once the primary access road ceased to be used by logging traffic, runoff began to erode gullies on its downslope side. Later, as the hollow log culverts, used to allow small streams to pass under the road, decayed, larger gullies began to incise across the road. These gullies continued to enlarge actively while much of the remainder of the areas from which the plant cover was removed during logging became revegetated. The gullies provide continuous paths for concentrated runoff to stream channels thereby increasing drainage density, and thus creating higher, earlier storm runoff peak discharges.

Sediment sources have thus become spatially reduced in area, and largely confined to the active walls and heads of incising gully systems. This reduction in sources is the last phase of a series of changes in stream suspended sediment discharge which closely followed stages in logging activity (Douglas *et al.*, 1992) (Figure 18.2). When compared with the neighbouring undisturbed W8S5 catchment (Catchment A) (Figures 18.1 and 18.3) the yield from Baru increased from a 1:1 ratio to 18:1 following peak disturbance and 5:3 two years after logging had ceased. By 1992 sediment yield had been further reduced, but short peaks of high sediment discharge from the Baru still occur during major storms (see the major storms of May 1990 and November 1991 in Figure 18.2). Gullies along roads and skid trails were still active in 1992, and channels were still eroding their banks at locations affected by road crossing and dumping of organic debris. On the slopes, areas where organic debris had impounded sediment were being dissected by rills as the plant matter decayed, and were continuing to supply sediment for downstream transport.

Although the runoff plots could not be established until vehicle movements on the skid tracks had ended, the protected plot quickly began to show a difference in adjustment. After a few weeks, vegetation growth on the protected plot was much more luxuriant than on that subject to runoff from upslope. After two years, the protected plot was densely vegetated, whereas that subject to uninterrupted runoff had only a sparse cover. Bounded plots act as self-contained units (Mykura, 1985). The unprotected plot became subject to severe gullying, whereas that protected by the

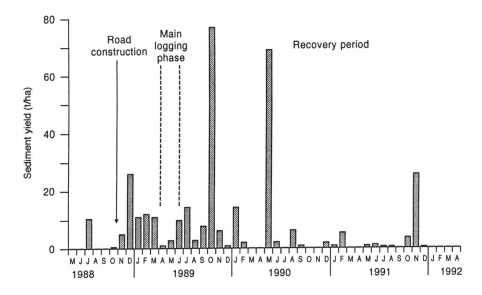

Figure 18.2 Stages of logging activity and changes in suspended sediment discharge, Steyshen Baru

soil barrier was quickly colonized by grasses and herbaceous material. In the unprotected plot, disturbed, loose soil was quickly evacuated, but such losses declined rapidly in the protected plot as vegetation grew. On the unprotected track, soil losses continued to rise for the first few months after road use ceased (Sinun, 1991). Compaction of the soil surface on tracks greatly reduces infiltration, with 52% of the incident rainfall running off the surface of the bounded plot on the abandoned track, compared to only 3% in nearby primary forest (Sinun, 1991).

In July 1989, the unprotected skid trail plot had a sediment yield of 190.5 t/ha, compared to 10.5 t/ha from the trail with the earth barrier. By July 1990 the unprotected plot was covered with vegetation and yielded only 10.5 t/ha. Yields in any one time period reflect the prevailing hydrometeorological events as well as the progress of post-logging recovery. In the stream catchments in July 1989, the logged Baru had a yield of 15.5 t/ha, while the undisturbed W8S5 only exported 2.96 t/ha (Figure 18.3). In July 1990 the Baru yield had dropped to 0.25 t/ha and that of W8S5 to 0.16 t/ha. Recovery of the logged stream system lags behind that of individual plots because the movement of sediment is episodic with much temporary storage behind obstacles on slopes and in stream channels. Major storms in the Baru continue to flush sediment out of these stores and to create storm peak sediment concentrations of well over 100 mg/l. The largest such flushing event was on 30 May 1990 when 5.67 t/ha were evacuated in a single day, accounting for 55% of the total sediment yield for the year.

The four plots show variable, but positive, correlation between increased runoff and increased sediment yield (Figure 18.4). The one-year abandoned track yielded

316

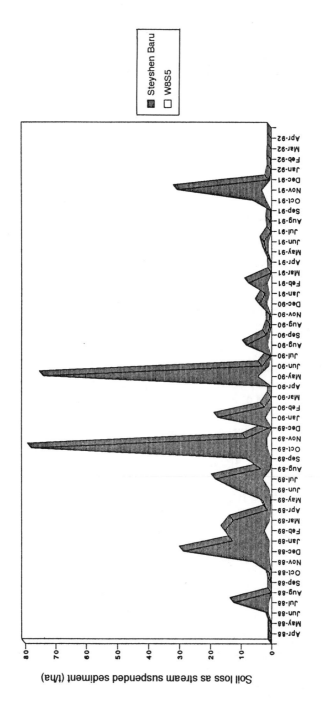

Figure 18.3 Comparison of sediment yields from Steyshen Baru and W8S5

317

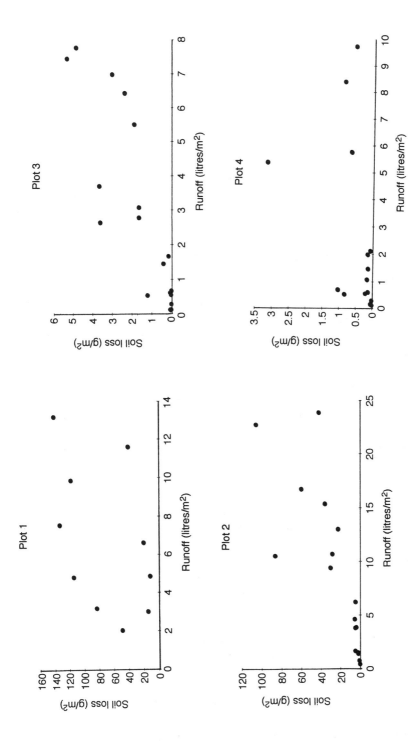

Figure 18.4 Plot of soil loss against runoff for erosion plots 1 to 4. Plots 1 and 2 were recently abandoned snig tracks; plot 3 was a track which had been abandoned for over one year and plot 4 was in undisturbed forest

0.53 t/ha, little more than the 0.38 t/ha from the adjacent primary forest plot. Differences between the plots were far greater in terms of soil loss than in runoff with individual storm losses of up to 150 g/m^2 on Plot 1. Rainsplash plays a major part in the erosion process, and even on these bare areas, sediment yield is supply limited. Reduction of the rainsplash effect thus leads to a decrease in soil loss (Anderton, 1990).

DISCUSSION

Logging road construction may lead to increases or decreases in effective catchment contributing areas which would have to be considered in any hydrograph analysis in relation to land use or geology.

When using runoff plots, the stage at which the plot is established is critical, as the act of making the plot itself creates disturbance. In the case of the track with a barrier, establishment of the plot immediately after construction of the soil barrier would lead to measurement of the combined effects of barrier and vegetation regrowth, not just vegetation recovery alone.

Establishment of vegetation can be rapid in the tropical rainforest environment, providing soil surface conditions are suitable. Compaction and subsequent continued runoff and erosion inhibit vegetation growth. However, where conditions are suitable, once grasses are established, other herbaceous growth quickly follows. The rate at which this occurs is highly site-dependent, steeper areas often having a sparser vegetation cover than more gently sloping localities. Reduction of runoff as soon as possible after use of tracks and skid trails ceases is the key to encouraging rapid vegetation recolonization. Earth barriers to impede runoff should be constructed as quickly as possible. They will be more effective in reducing erosion in the early months after logging than any tree planting, such as that of *Acacia mangium* which used to be practised in Sabah.

Traffic density will affect compaction. In these experiments skid trails may have been used to remove only a few logs, while major trails close to access roads may have had up to 50 tractor movements over them. Actual logging operations and site are thus most important elements in the analysis of the impact of disturbance (Rice and Datzmann, 1981).

The inhibition of surface runoff is the key to reduction of erosion and sedimentation during logging operations in tropical rainforests. When commercial logging activities are unsupervised, poor road design and badly sited skid trails lead to large amounts of erosion and the accumulation of sediments behind obstacles on slopes and in stream channels. These stores of sediment are then evacuated further downstream in subsequent major storms, the effects persisting for at least four years after initial disturbance. Under favourable conditions, skid trails recover quickly and after one year yield little more sediment than adjacent primary forest areas. However, that recovery depends on vegetation regrowth. Construction of barriers to surface runoff greatly reduces removal of sediment and positively assists recolonization of bare areas by plants. Conservation measures should therefore be implemented as soon as possible after disturbance. Barriers to block runoff should be constructed at the top of all skid trails, and preferably at intervals down them, by the tractor operator immediately after the last log is hauled out of the area.

CONCLUSIONS

The means of managing tropical forest lands wisely do exist. Soil can be conserved. Treatments that encourage water to take paths akin to those in the natural forest are required. Infiltration has to be encouraged and surface runoff avoided. Protection against rainsplash erosion is needed. Much can be done in the design of logging systems and the location of access tracks and skid trails, particularly by avoiding stream crossings and long runs down steep slopes. However, even when such steep gradients are needed, the implementation of inexpensive, simple erosion control techniques, such as barriers to block surface runoff, immediately after log extraction ends will reduce much of the persistent erosion that cumulatively aggravates sedimentation downstream. Such techniques are well documented (Pearce and Hamilton, 1986) and given appropriate supervision, should be effective. As Bruijnzeel (1990:184) observed:

> . . . the adverse environmental conditions so often observed following "deforestation" in the humid tropics are not so much the result of "deforestation" per se but rather of poor land use practices after clearing the forest. *This is precisely where our hope for the future lies.*

Even though the selective logging of the lowland rain forests of south-east Asia has removed mature trees over the majority of the continental and island areas, new logging techniques aimed at minimizing impacts on the soil are being introduced. However, the institutional frameworks within which forestry is managed mean that these new approaches often lack an adequate geomorphological or soil conservation input. Often experiments have had inadequate sampling of storm runoff so that sediment yields are underestimated and thus the real magnitude of the erosion problem is not apparent. Hydrology has a small place in the training and work of foresters; geomorphology is less understood. Successful erosion mitigation involves encouraging understanding of earth surface processes, not only by professional foresters, but by those who actually operate machinery and extract the timber. Fortunately, where such on-site field training has been attempted, the response by individual operatives has been good. Particularly encouraging responses have been obtained from operatives in a reduced impact logging programme begun by Innoprise Sdn. Bhd. at Danum Valley in 1993.

ACKNOWLEDGEMENTS

Research at the Danum Valley Field Studies Centre was begun under Natural Environment Research Council Grant GR3/6360 and further supported by the Royal Society. This chapter is based on material collected while the authors were participants in the Royal Society's South-east Asian Rainforest Research Programme (Programme Publication No. A/108). The assistance of the field centre staff and the support of Yayasan Sabah (the Sabah Foundation) is gratefully acknowledged.

REFERENCES

Anderton, S. (1990). *Logging and soil erosion: an examination of the effects of logging on soil erosion in the rain forests on Ulu Segama, eastern Sabah*. Unpublished BSc dissertation, University of Manchester.

Bruijnzeel, L. A. (1990). *Hydrology of Moist Tropical Forests and Effects of Conversion: A State of Knowledge Review*, UNESCO, Paris.

Douglas, I., Greer, T., Wong, W. M., Spencer, T. and Sinun, W. (1990). The impact of commercial logging on a small rainforest catchment in Ulu Segama, Sabah, Malaysia. *International Association of Hydrological Sciences Publication*, **192**, 165–173.

Douglas, I., Spencer, T., Greer, T., Bidin, K., Sinun, W. and Wong, W. M. (1992). The impact of selective commercial logging on stream hydrology, chemistry and sediment loads in the Ulu Segama Rain Forest, Sabah. *Philosophical Transactions of the Royal Society of London B*, **335**, 397–406.

Greswell, S., Heller, D. and Swanston, D. N. (1979). *Mass Movement Response to Forest Management in the Central Oregon Coast Ranges*, US Department of Agriculture, Forest Service, Pacific Northwest Forest and Range Experiment Station, Resource Bulletin, PNW-84.

Harcharik, D. A. and Kunkle, S. H. (1978). Forest plantation for rehabilitating eroded lands. *FAO Conservation Guide*, **4**, 83–101.

Hursh, C. R. (1935). *Control of Exposed Soil on Road Banks*, US Department of Agriculture, Forest Service, Appalachian Forest Experiment Station Technical Note **12**.

Megahan, W. F. and Kidd, W. J. (1972). Effects of logging and logging roads on erosion and sediment deposition from steep terrain. *Forestry*, **70**, 136–141.

Mykura, H. (1985). Research note: design and operation of a simple erosion plot. *Ilmu Alam*, **14**, 105–113.

Pearce, A. J. and Hamilton, A. S. (1986). Water and soil conservation guidelines for land use planning. *Seminar Workshop on Watershed Land Use Planning*, 5–16 May 1985, Queensland, Australia. East-West Centre, Honolulu.

Rice, R. M. and Datzmann, P. A. (1981). Erosion associated with cable and tractor logging in north-western California. *International Association of Hydrological Sciences Publication*, **132**, 362–374.

Rothwell, R. L. (1978). Watershed management guidelines for logging and road construction in Alberta. *Information Report Nov-X-28*. North Forest Research Centre, Canadian Forest Service, Edmonton, Alberta.

Sinun, W. (1991). *Hillslope hydrology, hydrogeomorphology and hydrochemistry of an equatorial lowland rainforest, Danum Valley, Sabah, Malaysia*. Unpublished MSc thesis, University of Manchester.

Sinun, W., Wong, W. M., Douglas, I. and Spencer, T. (1992). Throughfall, stemflow, overland flow and throughflow in the Ulu Segama Rain Forest, Sabah. *Philosophical Transactions of Royal Society of London B*, **335**, 389–395.

Swift, L. W. Jr. (1988). Forest access roads: design, maintenance and soil loss. In Swank, T. and Crossley, D. A. Jr. (Eds), *Forest Hydrology and Ecology at Coweeta*, Springer, New York, pp. 313–324.

Thornes, J. B. (1980). Erosion processes of running water and their spatial and temporal controls: a theoretical viewpoint. In Kirkby, M. J. and Morgan, R. P. C. (Eds), *Soil Erosion*, Wiley, Chichester, pp. 129–182.

Van Dillewijn, F. J. (1976). *Forestry*, Draft terminal report prepared for the Government of Indonesia, INS/72/006, FAO, Rome.

Index